AFRICAN ECONOMIES AND THE PERMANENT CRISIS, 197

This book explains why sub-Saharan Africa remains mired in a devastating economic crisis despite two decades of efforts to renew economic growth. It focuses on the manner with which political authority is exercised in the region, the dynamics of interaction with international forces, and the effect of past efforts at economics reform.

By comprehensively examining contemporary African political economy, this study shows that there has been little societal opposition to reform in Africa and that the dominant obstacles to reform lie not in interest-group pressures on the state, as others have argued, but within the state itself; that donor-supported structural adjustment programs strengthen the status quo rather than promote reform; that aid does not advance the interests of international capital but is a substitute for foreign private capital; and that the legacies of past reform failures continue to influence the dynamics of present efforts of reform.

Nicolas van de Walle is a Professor of Political Science at Michigan State University. He received his Ph.D. from Princeton University in 1990. In recent years, he has conducted field research in Botswana, Cameroon, Niger, Senegal, Uganda, and Zambia. He has served as a consultant to UNDP, UNIDO, USAID, the Global Coalition for Africa, and the World Bank. He has received research grants and awards from the National Science Foundation, the Rockefeller Brothers' Fund, the John D. and Catherine T. MacArthur Foundation, the Carnegie Corporation of New York, and the Ford Foundation. He is the co-author of *Democratic Experiments in Africa: Regime Transitions in Comparative Perspectives* (1997), *Improving Aid to Africa* (1996), and *Of Time and Power: Leadership Duration in the Modern World* (1991). He is the co-editor of *Agenda for Africa's Economic Renewal* (1996) and *Foreign Aid in Africa: Learning from Country Experiences* (1997).

POLITICAL ECONOMY OF INSTITUTIONS AND DECISIONS

Series Editors

Randall Calvert, Washington University, St. Louis
Thrainn Eggertsson, Max Planck Institute, Germany, and University of Iceland

Founding Editors

James E. Alt, Harvard University
Douglass C. North, Washington University, St. Louis

Other Books in the Series

Alesina and Howard Rosenthal, *Partisan Politics, Divided
Government and the Economy*
Lee J. Alston, Thrainn Eggertsson and Douglass C. North, eds.,
Empirical Studies in Institutional Change
Lee J. Alston and Joseph P. Ferrie, *Southern Paternalism and the Rise of the
American Welfare State: Economics, Politics, and Institutions, 1865–1965*
James E. Alt and Kenneth Shepsle, eds., *Perspectives on Positive
Political Economy*
Jeffrey S. Banks and Eric A. Hanushek, eds., *Modern Political
Economy: Old Topics, New Directions*
Yoram Barzel, *Economic Analysis of Property Rights*, 2nd edition
Robert Bates, *Beyond the Miracle of the Market: The Political
Economy of Agrarian Development in Kenya*
Peter Cowhey and Mathew McCubbins, eds., *Structure and Policy in
Japan and the United States*
Gary W. Cox, *The Efficient Secret: The Cabinet and the Development
of Political Parties in Victorian England*
Gary W. Cox, *Making Votes Count: Strategic Coordination in the
World's Electoral System*
Jean Ensminger, *Making a Market: The Institutional
Transformation of an African Society*
David Epstein and Sharyn O'Halloran, *Delegating Powers: A
Transaction Cost Politics Approach to Policy Making under
Separate Powers*
Kathryn Firmin-Sellers, *The Transformation of Property Rights in the Gold
Coast: An Empirical Analysis Applying Rational Choice Theory*
Clark C. Gibson, *Politics and Poachers: The Political Economy of
Wildlife Policy in Africa*
Ron Harris, *The Legal Framework of Business
Organization: England 1720–1844*

Continued on page following index

Pour Michèle

AFRICAN ECONOMIES AND THE POLITICS OF PERMANENT CRISIS, 1979–1999

NICOLAS VAN DE WALLE

Michigan State University

CAMBRIDGE
UNIVERSITY PRESS

CAMBRIDGE UNIVERSITY PRESS
Cambridge, New York, Melbourne, Madrid, Cape Town, Singapore, São Paulo, Delhi

Cambridge University Press
32 Avenue of the Americas, New York, NY 10013-2473, USA

www.cambridge.org
Information on this title: www.cambridge.org/9780521008365

First published 2001
8th printing 2008

Printed in the United States of America

A catalog record for this publication is available from the British Library.

Library of Congress Cataloging in Publication Data

Van de Walle, Nicolas, 1957–
African economies and the politics of permanent crisis, 1979–1999 / Nicolas van
de Walle.
    p. cm. – (Political economy of institutions and decisions)
Includes bibliographical references and index.
ISBN 0-521-80364-0 – ISBN 0-521-00836-0 (pb.)
1. Africa – Economic conditions – 1960–. 2. Africa – Economic policy.
3. Africa – Politics and government. I. Title. II. Series.
HC800.V357   2001
338.96 – dc22   2001025171

ISBN 978-0-521-80364-9 hardback
ISBN 978-0-521-00836-5 paperback

Contents

Contents

Tables

Acknowledgments

This book has been improved by the assistance of many people. I first started to think about these issues as a graduate student at Princeton, where Henry Bienen and John Waterbury shaped my thinking about the politics of economic reform in fundamental ways. My department at Michigan State University has provided useful release time during which most of the writing has taken place. Mike Bratton has been a perfect colleague, providing not only constant intellectual support and guidance, but also a steady supply of great music. Two years spent at the Overseas Development Council as the Davidson Sommers Fellow in 1994–1996 helped clarify the role of aid in Africa's political economy. I thank ODC's president, John Sewell, for his always generous support.

The empirical materials in this book are based on fieldwork in sub-Saharan Africa during the last decade. Hundreds of public officials, journalists, and academics in a dozen countries spent long hours putting up with my questions. It is impossible to repay them fully for the insights they shared with me or for their graciousness. Many will not want to be named. My fieldwork was also assisted by a number of friends and colleagues. Samba Ka taught me much of the little I know of Senegalese politics. Recent visits to Dakar have benefited from the assistance of Michelle Kuenzi and Ibrahima Gaye. I spent a wonderful couple of weeks in Niger in 1998 thanks in large part to the hospitality of John Davis and Jen Burt. Several long conversations with Tidjani Alou were particularly insightful. In Zambia, Dominic Mulaisho and Dennis Chiwele were particularly helpful. In Cameroon, finally, Joe Ntangsi was a gracious guide on more than one occasion.

Writing is a solitary experience, but many friends have made writing this book a less lonely one: For their extraordinary willingness to listen, argue, and share their own views these last few years, I particularly wish to thank Deborah Bräutigam, David Gordon, Devesh Kapur, Peter Lewis, and Howard Stein. Pierre Englebert, John Heilbrunn, Atul Kohli, Alice Sindzingre, and Crawford Young read the entire manuscript with great care and provided many helpful comments. Two anonymous readers for Cambridge University Press also provided incisive reviews. A large number of people have commented on drafts of individual sections of the manuscript at different stages: I wish to thank Joan Atherton, Robert Bates, Linda Beck, Tom Callaghy, Gyimah Boadi, Catherine Gwin, Steph Haggard, Tim Johnston, Jon Kraus, Carol Lancaster, Kimberly Ludwig, Célestin Monga, Benno Ndulu, Joan Nelson, Lise Rakner, Vij Ramachandran, Richard Snyder, Sam Wangwe, Ernie Wilson, and Dwayne Woods. Their input has immeasurably improved the final product, and any remaining flaws are my responsibility alone.

My greatest debt is to my wife, Michèle. I could never have finished this book without her judicious mixture of unconditional support and occasional incredulity concerning my work habits. This book is dedicated to her with love.

Introduction

Senegal received its first structural adjustment loan from the World Bank in 1979, the first such loan extended to Africa.[1] The economy appeared overheated, with a burgeoning balance of payments crisis and a fiscal deficit exceeding 12.5 percent of gross domestic product (GDP). Agricultural production was stagnant and had been weakened by recurrent drought. The country's small industrial sector seemed incapable of competing with imports, barely surviving thanks to protection and subsidies. Overall, Senegal's GDP had grown by 2.1 percent annually between 1960 and 1980, even though its population was growing 2.8 percent a year over the same period. A year later, the government signed a three-year enhanced structured adjustment facility (ESAF) loan with the International Monetary Fund (IMF). At the time, the *IMF Survey* blamed the crisis largely on drought and announced confidently that the loan would quickly restore macroeconomic balance.[2]

Since then, the country has been undergoing "adjustment."[3] The country's international debt burden in 1980 totaled $1.47 billion,

1. Throughout I use Africa and sub-Saharan Africa interchangeably to refer to the forty-eight countries below the Sahara Desert, including the Republic of South Africa and Eritrea.
2. *IMF Survey*, April 9, 1979, p. 111.
3. Senegal's two decades of adjustment have been well documented. See Gilles Duruflé, *l'Ajustement structurel en Afrique* (Paris: Karthala, 1988); Gilles Duruflé, *Le Sénégal peut-il sortir de la crise?* (Paris: Karthala, 1994); Mustapha Rouis, "Senegal: Stabilization, Partial Adjustment and Stagnation," in Ishrat Husain and Rashid Faruqee (eds.), *Adjustment in Africa: Lessons from Country Case Studies* (Washington, DC: World Bank, 1994), pp. 286–351; and Samba Ka and Nicolas van de Walle, "The Political Economy of Structural Adjustment in Senegal, 1980–1991," in Stephan Haggard and Steven B. Webb (eds.), *Voting for Reform: Economic Adjustment in New Democracies* (New York: Oxford University Press, 1994), pp. 290–359.

representing a dangerous but still manageable 49 percent of GDP, but the government did not hesitate to borrow from the international financial institutions (IFIs) and France to face the crisis. In the 1980s, it received fifteen different stabilization and adjustment loans from the Bank and Fund, several of which were canceled for noncompliance with conditions.[4] In addition, it would receive some $350 million a year in bilateral assistance, and 2 billion French francs' worth of debt forgiveness by the French government in 1989. Yet, after the June 1991 Paris Club meetings that rescheduled its debts for the eighth time since 1981, Senegal's total international debt stood at some $3.5 billion, equivalent to 63 percent of its GDP and 225 percent of its exports that year.

Adjustment programs continued in the 1990s. The Fund provided ESAF and stand-by loans in 1994. The Bank followed with agricultural sector and private sector adjustment loans in 1995 and a transport sector loan in 1997. France extended further debt forgiveness in 1994, following the devaluation of the Communauté Financière d'Afrique (CFA) franc in January. Overall, the country received an average of $473 million a year in aid between 1990 and 1995, some 14 percent of GDP.

Actual progress on economic policy reform has been desultory throughout these two decades of official adjustment. On the economic stabilization front, progress in the mid-1980s was followed by slow reversal and then a disastrous spell in 1991–3, which resulted in fiscal deficits creeping back to 6 percent of GDP by 1994. Structural reform also proved problematic. Long stalled, privatization lurched forward in the 1990s with 55 of 188 parastatal enterprises being privatized.[5] On the other hand, the substantial trade reform achieved between 1986 and 1988 was largely reversed by the government in the 1990s. Civil service employment actually increased between 1990 and 1995, despite the government's repeated commitment to a civil service reform program that was to require substantial retrenchment.[6]

---

4. Including from the IMF six stand-by arrangements, one structural adjustment facility, one enhanced structural adjustment facility, and one extended fund facility; and from the Bank, four structural adjustment loans and two sectoral adjustment loans.
5. See Table 1 in Paul Bennell, "Privatization in Sub-Saharan Africa: Progress and Prospects during the 1990s," *World Development* 25 (1997): 1785–803.
6. From 65,600 to 67,000 civil servants, according to the IMF. See Ian Lienert and Jitendra Modi, "A Decade of Civil Service Reform in Sub-Saharan Africa," IMF Working Paper WP/97/179 (Washington, DC: International Monetary Fund, Fiscal Affairs Department, December 1997), p. 43.

In the late 1990s, the situation in Senegal appeared more promising. The long overdue devaluation of the CFA franc in January 1994 reinvigorated the economy, with GDP growth rates of 4.8 and 5.1 percent in 1995 and 1996, respectively. The fiscal deficit was down to 1.9 percent in 1996. Once again today, the IMF is arguing that Senegal has finally overcome its economic crisis and is poised for a breakthrough. In 1996 it predicted that Senegal would sustain growth rates of 4.5 percent for the next five years, more than double its growth rates over the last forty years.[7] Perhaps, but many less sanguine observers suggest that most of the obstacles to economic development in Senegal remain; they argue that policy reform programs have not altered the deep-seated problems that undermine investment and growth, from the state's limited capacity and endemic corruption, to the grave deterioration of public infrastructure.[8] Moreover, two decades of policy reform efforts have saddled Senegal with an increasingly onerous debt burden. Various debt forgiveness schemes and biannual rescheduling exercises have not prevented the overall debt burden from reaching 79 percent of GDP in 1995. Meanwhile, the quality of life of the average Senegalese has probably declined over the last twenty years. Her expectation of life has improved, from a woeful 40.6 years in 1970 to a still dismal 52.3 years, just slightly above the African average, but a quarter of a century less than she would live if she had been born in a country that was part of the Organization for Economic Cooperation and Development (OECD).[9] The World Bank estimates that more than half the population lives on less than one dollar a day.[10]

Is Senegal a typical African case? At the dawn of the twenty-first century, most of sub-Saharan Africa remains mired in economic crisis despite two decades of donor-sponsored reform efforts. A handful of countries like Botswana and Mauritius are prospering, but most economies in the region still have not overcome the fiscal and balance of payments deficits that have undermined economic stability since the first oil crisis in the mid-1970s. The severity of these deficits has waxed and waned over the years, but they have never been overcome.

7. *IMF Survey*, January 8, 1996, p. 14.
8. For instance, the blunt assessment in Elliot Berg et al., "Sustaining Private Sector Development in Senegal: Strategic Considerations," (Bethesda, MD: DAI, June 1997).
9. United Nations Development Program, *The Human Development Report, 1999* (New York: Oxford University Press, 1999), Table 8, p. 171.
10. World Bank, *World Development Indicators* (Washington, DC: World Bank, 1998), p. 66.

Meanwhile, many if not most Africans are poorer today than they were twenty years ago.

An improvement in economic indicators throughout Africa in the mid-1990s led some observers to argue that the region had finally solved its economic conundrums and could now expect sustained economic growth.[11] Conditions appeared to be favorable: several civil wars had ended and a wave of democratization had brought to power a number of new leaders who appeared resolved to address economic ills. Between 1994 and 1997, per capita growth averaged 1.2 percent a year, the fastest rate in a generation. Growth was also spread across an unusually large number of states, with all but four economies in the region recording positive growth rates in 1996. International investors were said to be taking another look at the region. When President Clinton visited the region in the spring of 1998, he spoke of the beginning of an "African renaissance," in which Africa, thanks to economic and political reform, would now enjoy sustained economic growth and political stability.[12] Inevitably, talk of a renaissance faded soon after Clinton's trip. A sharp slowdown of the world economy followed the East Asian financial crisis that began in July 1997, and a number of African countries suffered sharp terms-of-trade shocks in the following year.[13] Deadly civil wars were reactivated in the Horn of Africa or in Angola, while new conflicts emerged in Central Africa. Investors closed their wallets, and by 1998, growth appeared to be slowing down again, although some countries continued to enjoy economic expansion (including Senegal). While the IMF remained relatively optimistic, forecasting 1.3 percent GDP per capita growth for the region in 1998, the World Bank was more gloomy, predicting –0.5 percent growth in 1998 and only 0.4 percent in 1999.

The growth spurt may turn out to be a harbinger of things to come, but there have been several previous short bursts of growth in the past

11. See, for instance, the optimistic assessment of the IMF in Stanley Fischer et al., *Africa: Is This the Turning Point?* IMF Papers on Policy Analysis and Assessment (Washington, DC: International Monetary Fund, May 1998); for an optimistic Washington perspective, see David Gordon and Howard Wolpe, "The Other Africa: An End to Afro-Pessimism," *World Policy Journal* 15 (1998): 49–59; and the more measured assessment by Deborah Bräutigam in her essay, "Economic Takeoff in Africa," *Current History*, 97 (1998): 204–8.
12. "Clinton's Dream for Africa: Many Snags to Overcome," *New York Times*, April 3, 1998, p. 8.
13. Elliott Harris, "Impact of the Asian Crisis on Sub-Saharan Africa," *Finance and Development* 36 (1999): 14–17.

that then only sputtered out. The bottom line at the beginning of the twenty-first century is that the African region continues to be outperformed by all other regions, and that efforts to redress this poor performance during the last twenty years have not been successful. Other regions of the developing world have demonstrated a much greater ability to manage their economic affairs over the course of the last twenty years, ever since the various shocks to the world economy in the early 1970s ended the Bretton Woods system of fixed exchange rates and introduced a new volatility in the world economy. As demonstrated in Table A.1, African growth has continued to lag behind other regions of the developing world in the 1990s, with the exception of the Middle East and North Africa category of countries, which are highly dependent on oil resources and suffered from their declining value during this period. Africa's relative performance is even more preoccupying if population growth is taken into account, as Africa's population growth is the fastest in the world. The data suggest that African countries have to exceed East Asian growth rates by a full percentage point just to keep up with them in per capita terms.

Africa's poor economic performance has resulted in its progressive marginalization from the world economy. As shown in Table A.2, Africa's share of global economic activity is small and declining; though

Table A.1. *Annual Rates of GDP Growth by Region, 1980–1999*

Region	1980–90	1990–96	1997	1998	1999*	Annual Population Growth 1965–96
Sub-Saharan Africa	1.7	2.0	3.5	2.4	3.2	2.7
East Asia	7.7	10.2	7.1	1.3	4.8	1.8
South Asia	5.7	5.6	5.0	4.6	4.9	2.2
Latin America and the Caribbean	1.8	3.2	5.1	2.5	0.6	2.1
Middle East and North Africa	0.4	2.6	3.1	2.0	2.8	2.7
All Low, Middle Income	3.1	2.9	4.8	2.0	2.7	1.9

* Provisional estimates.

Source: Adapted from World Bank, *World Development Indicators, 1998* (Washington, DC: World Bank, 1998), Table 4.1 and Table 1.4; and World Bank *Global Economic Prospects and the Developing Countries, 1998/99* (Washington, DC: World Bank, 1998), p. 28.

Table A.2. *Africa's Share of*
Global Economic Activity, 1980–1996 (as a
percentage of world total)

	1980	1996
Population	8.6	10.3
GDP	2.5	1.1
Value added, Manufacturing	1.4	0.9
Merchandise Exports	3.8	1.3
Foreign Direct Investment	0.3	0.6

Source: Calculated from World Bank, *World Development Indicators, 1998* (Washington, DC: World Bank, 1998), Tables 4.2, 4.3, 4.4, and 6.8. Additional data from the World Bank, *African Development Indicators* (Washington, DC: World Bank, 1997), Table 5.1.

it accounts for 10 percent of the world's population, its economies account for 1.1 percnet of world GDP. On the other hand, the region includes fifteen of the world's twenty poorest countries. Africa's continuing problems have resulted in a sharp increase in international debt, which rose from $84 billion in 1980 to $227 billion in 1996. Even in the so-called success story of Ghana, total external debt increased from $1.4 to $4.2 billion in this period, and the country remains poorer today in per capita terms than it was in the mid-1970s, after more than a decade of reform implementation and sustained growth.

This book explains the failure of African economies to renew with sustained economic growth over the last twenty years. Why has Africa lagged behind every other region of the developing world? Why have the donor-supported structural adjustment programs not succeeded in improving growth rates and poverty alleviation? What has been the political impact of such a long economic crisis? This book tries to answer these questions by offering a political explanation for the persistence of Africa's economic crisis and the failure of reform to bring about renewed growth. I seek to shed light on some of the distinct institutional features of the crisis, by analyzing the political implications of its seeming permanence on the African landscape for so long.

THE STRUCTURAL ADJUSTMENT DEBATE

The persistence of Africa's economic crisis is puzzling given the international efforts to promote economic renewal in the region. For the last

6

decade, almost all African states have been engaged in some kind of economic reform program with funding from the West. With the assistance of the international financial institutions (IFIs), in particular the World Bank and the IMF, they have attempted to implement stabilization and structural adjustment programs that seek, respectively, to return to macroeconomic equilibrium in the short term and promote more rapid sustainable economic growth in the long term. The donors have encouraged African states to undertake these reforms with substantial financial support. Between 1980 and 1989, for example, some thirty-six sub-Saharan African countries contracted for 241 different loans with the Bank and the Fund on behalf of stabilization and adjustment operations.[14] Eleven of these countries received ten or more loans during these ten years. At the end of 1998, the IMF still had operational loans in twenty-six African countries.[15] In the 1990s, the Bank progressively moved away from broad adjustment programs, preferring instead to focus its conditionality on individual sectors. But these sectoral adjustment programs retain much of the same logic in terms of leveraging policy reform with resources. In addition to the multilateral donors, bilateral donors have provided substantial support for structural adjustment programs as well, although they typically do not distinguish adjustment from other forms of lending, so that it is hard to determine their importance relative to other forms of aid. Somewhere between a third and half of the aid going to Africa in the 1990s explicitly sought to bring about policy reform.

It has long been fashionable in certain circles to advocate a "Marshall Plan" for Africa to spur economic growth, but in fact Africa's dismal performance has come in the context of a substantial flow of aid resources to the region. The donors responded to the onset of the debt crisis in Africa with a sustained increase in aid, which grew by an astounding annual average of over 5 percent in real terms between 1970 and 1995. As a result, Africa received 24 percent of total official development assistance (ODA) in 1980 but some 37 percent in 1993. At their peak, the Marshall Plan resources accounted for some 2.5 percent of the

14. A useful summary is provided in Eva Jesperson, "External Shocks, Adjustment Policies and Economic and Social Performance," in Giovanni Andrea Cornia, Rolph van der Hoeven, and Thandika Mkandawire (eds.), *Africa's Recovery in the 1990s: From Stagnation and Adjustment to Human Development* (New York: St. Martin's Press, 1993), pp. 9–52.
15. Including three stand-by loans, one extended fund facility, and twenty-two enhanced structural adjustment facility loans. See *IMF Survey*, December 14, 1998, p. 398.

GDP of countries like France and Germany.[16] By 1996, excluding South Africa and Nigeria, the average African country received the equivalent of 12.3 percent of its GDP in ODA, an international transfer that is unprecedented in historical terms.

Why have these policy reform efforts not succeeded? Why has reform proved so much more elusive in Africa than in other regions? Throughout the last twenty years, economists have argued about the causes of and the solutions to the African crisis. When the crisis first emerged, mainstream economists and the staffs of the World Bank and IMF largely blamed what they viewed as the wrongheaded economic policies of African governments for the crisis. In particular, they blamed excessive government expenditures, overvalued exchange rates, various domestic price distortions, high levels of public ownership, and protectionistic trade policies. They therefore prescribed policy reform: the IMF's stabilization programs included measures to cut the fiscal deficit, devalue what was typically an overvalued currency, and contract the money supply. The World Bank promoted structural adjustment programs that pursued price liberalization and deregulation, trade reform, and the divestiture or liquidation of state-owned enterprises in order to improve economic incentives and promote higher investment rates.[17]

Many critics disagreed with the IFI diagnostic. African governments defended their policies and argued that it was international economic

---

16. Stephen O'Connell and Charles Soludo, "Aid Intensity in Africa," paper presented to the AERC/ODC conference, "Managing the Transition from Aid Dependence in Sub-Saharan Africa," Nairobi, May 21–22, 1998.
17. The literature assessing the impact of economic reform in Africa continues to grow. Recent representative contributions include the World Bank, *Adjustment in Africa: Reforms, Results and the Road Ahead* (Washington, D.C.: World Bank, 1994); William Easterly and Ross Levine, "Africa's Growth Tragedy: Policies and Ethnic Divisions," *Quarterly Journal of Economics* 112 (1997): 1203–50; Giovanni Andrea Cornia and Gerald K. Helleiner (eds.), *From Adjustment to Development in Africa* (New York: St. Martin's Press, 1994); Jean-Claude Berthelemy, *Whither African Economies?* (Paris: OECD, 1995); Rolph Van der Hoeven and Fred Van de Kraaij (eds.), *Structural Adjustment and Beyond in Sub-Saharan Africa* (London: James Currey, 1994); Howard White, "Review Article: Adjustment in Africa," *Development and Change* 27 (1996): 785–815; Benno Ndulu and Nicolas van de Walle (eds.), *Agenda for Africa's Economic Renewal* (Washington, DC: Overseas Development Council, 1996), pp. 81–108; Thomas Callaghy and John Ravenhill (eds.), *Hemmed In: Responses to Africa's Economic Decline* (New York: Columbia University Press, 1994); David E. Sahn, Paul A. Dorosh, and Stephen D. Younger, *Structural Adjustment Reconsidered: Economic Policy and Poverty in Africa* (New York: Cambridge University Press, 1997); and Paul Collier and Jan Willem Gunning, "Explaining African Economic Performance," *Journal of Economic Literature* 37 (1999): 64–111.

volatility – in particular the wild commodity price swings of the 1970s – that was the real cause of the crisis.[18] In the academic community, the old structuralist arguments about IMF stabilization programs in Latin America in the 1960s resurfaced regarding Africa.[19] Structuralists emphasized that the low-income countries of Africa were undermined by various market imperfections, bottlenecks, and rigidities, and that as a result, IFI prescriptions were inappropriate. For instance, they questioned the wisdom of exchange rate devaluations and trade liberalization, given what they argued to be the structurally inelastic supply of exports and demand for imports. Other critics did not necessarily disagree with the IFI approach but argued that adjustment programs that were being implemented imposed harsh and unnecessary costs on the poor and disadvantaged.[20]

Over time, there has been increasing convergence among economists regarding the African crisis. The IFIs have paid at least lip service to their critics' views, while structuralists have come to agree that basic macroeconomic stability was a prerequisite of growth.[21] This convergence remains imperfect, but it is undeniable. There is less disagreement than before regarding what a good policy environment looks like, and even less disagreement that very few African states have managed to come close to sustaining such an environment these last two decades. As a result, debates about structural adjustment have come to focus less on what constitutes good policy and more on the process and organization

18. This was notably the official stance of the Organization of African Unity (OAU), as expressed in its 1981 Lagos Plan of Action. See OAU, *Lagos Plan of Action for Economic Development of Africa, 1980–2000* (Addis Ababa: Organization of African Unity, 1981). For this early intellectual history, see John Ravenhill, "Adjustment with Growth: A Fragile Consensus," *The Journal of Modern African Studies* 26 (1988): 179–210; and Devesh Kapur, "The Weakness of Strength: The Challenge of Sub-Saharan Africa," in Devesh Kapur, John P. Lewis, and Richard Webb (eds.), *The World Bank: Its First Half Century* (Washington, DC: Brookings Institution Press, 1997), pp. 683–804.

19. See Miles Kahler, "Orthodoxy and Its Alternatives: Explaining Approaches to Stabilization and Adjustment," in Joan Nelson (ed.), *Economic Crisis and Policy Choice: The Politics of Economic Adjustment in the Third World* (Princeton, NJ: Princeton University Press, 1990), pp. 33–62; Tony Killick (ed.) *The Quest for Economic Stabilization: The IMF and the Third World* (New York: St. Martin's Press, 1984) summarizes the earlier debate surrounding stabilization in Latin America.

20. For instance, Cornia et al., *Africa's Recovery in the 1990s*.

21. See Dani Rodrik, "Understanding Economic Policy Reform," *Journal of Economic Literature* 34 (1996): 9–41. Rodrik acknowledges that this consensus does not extend much beyond the world of professional economists. See Chapter 3 for a more complete discussion.

of getting those good policies. In particular, debates often focus on the role played by the World Bank and the IMF, and the manner in which these agencies operate in Africa, rather than about actual policy differences. It is, for example, agreed that a low inflation environment is desirable, or that African governments need to bring their fiscal deficits down, but the speed with which this is done, the precise mix of policies to achieve these objectives, is contested. In other words, debates have come to focus on adjustment programs rather than on adjustment.

A number of recent economic studies have sought to shed light on the African situation by engaging in cross-national statistical analyses that seek to explain economic growth.[22] Typically, some measure of the growth of national income over the last several decades is regressed on an array of country characteristics. On balance, this growth literature tends to strengthen the mainstream claims, although it does provide support for some of the structuralist claims. Much of the differential between growth in the rest of the world and in Africa can be explained by a fairly traditional list of policy variables. Thus, various proxies for the economic policy environment appear significant, notably the degree of openness to trade, the level of inflation, or the size of the fiscal deficit. In addition, the quality of the physical capital and existing levels of human capital appear to matter, factors that are influenced by policy in the long term and where African governments appear particularly deficient. But in many of these studies, a dummy variable for Africa is highly significant, suggesting that specifically African characteristics, not captured by any explanatory variable in the equation, account for much of Africa's slower economic growth. In recent years, the literature has sought to incorporate other explanatory variables to eliminate the dummy. Some of the candidates provide some comfort to the structuralist position in the sense that they are factors not easily manipulable by government policy in the short term, such as whether the country is landlocked, whether it is situated in the tropics, or what its initial level of income is. But this literature also points to the importance of political

22. These studies include William Easterly and Ross Levine, "Africa's Growth Tragedy"; Jeffrey D. Sachs and Andrew M. Warner, "Sources of Slow Growth in African Economies," *Journal of African Economies* 6 (1997): 335–76; Jonathan Temple, "Initial Conditions, Social Capital and Growth in Africa," *Journal of African Economies* 7 (1998): 309–47; Pierre Englebert, "Solving the Mystery of the Africa Dummy," *World Development* (in press); and Paulo Mauro, "Corruption and Growth," in *Quarterly Journal of Economics* 110 (1995): 681–712. See the excellent review in Paul Collier and Jan Willem Gunning, "Explaining African Economic Performance."

factors in explaining Africa's poor economic performance: variables such as the level of corruption, the extent of ethnic fragmentation, the level of political violence, or the quality of government services help explain the growth differential between Africa and other regions.[23]

The IFIs and their critics have sought vindication for their views in the actual record of policy reform since the early 1980s.[24] Almost all observers agree that economic reform has been less successful in Africa than elsewhere in the developing world, but they differ on the reasons for this performance gap. A number of Bank studies since the late 1980s have claimed that the countries that pursue its policy reform prescriptions have achieved better economic records than those that have not.[25] A handful of country experiences have been advanced as success stories: the Bank has pointed to Ghana, for example, where the donor-sponsored economic recovery program launched in 1983 included several devaluations of the cedi, increases in government revenues and cuts in expenditures, and an ambitious privatization program. Since the late 1980s, Ghana has enjoyed healthier public finances and the fruits of several years of sustained economic growth, based on the resurgence of traditional exports such as cocoa and gold.[26]

The critics questioned the validity of these Bank studies and sponsored their own, which typically showed little or no differences in performance between reformers and nonreformers. They called into question either the extent of the success of adjustment in the so-called success stories, or their replicability elsewhere.[27] Mosley, Subasat, and Weeks criticized the Bank's studies on methodological grounds and advanced alternative

23. See Englebert, "Solving the Mystery," in particular.
24. Howard White provides a balanced assessment of these debates, with a complete reference list, in his essay "Adjustment in Africa," See also Thandika Mkandawire and Charles C. Soludo, *Our Continent, Our Future: African Perspectives on Structural Adjustment* (Trenton, NJ: Africa World Press, 1999). Two other useful if now more dated discussions of this debate are Richard Sandbrook, *The Politics of Africa's Economic Recovery* (Cambridge, UK: Cambridge University Press, 1992); and John Ravenhill, "A Fragile Consensus."
25. The World Bank, *Sub-Saharan Africa: From Crisis to Sustainable Growth. A Long Term Perspective Study* (Washington, DC: World Bank, 1989); and World Bank, *Adjustment in Africa: Reforms, Results and the Road Ahead* (Washington, DC: World Bank, 1994).
26. On Ghana, see Robert P. Armstrong, *Ghana Country Assistance Review: A Study in Development Effectiveness* (Washington: World Bank, 1996); Jeffrey Herbst, *The Politics of Reform in Ghana, 1982–1991* (Berkeley: University of California Press, 1992); and Donald Rothchild (ed.), *Ghana: The Political Economy of Recovery* (Boulder, CO: Lynne Rienner, 1991).
27. White, "Adjustment in Africa."

tests to suggest that IFI adjustment policies did not result in improved economic performance.[28] Other critics argued that structural adjustment programs sacrificed long-term growth in its efforts to promote short-term stabilization.[29]

These economic debates have been important in political terms. They have often put the IFIs on the defensive and helped shift part of the responsibility for the crisis from African governments to the Washington institutions. The inconclusiveness of the debate provided African governments with some diplomatic leverage in the various international fora that discussed aid: if the policies they were forced to adopt were inappropriate, then recipient governments should not be held responsible for their poor economic record or the debt they were quickly accumulating. In the 1990s, the notion that "adjustment has failed" has come to be a conventional wisdom. As a result, there has been public pressure in the West for increased resource flows to Africa, debt relief, and a softening of donor conditionality. Under Jim Wolfensohn, the World Bank has come to emphasize lending to address social ills and the environment, a shift which has at least in part been motivated by the need to deflect criticism of structural adjustment.

On the other hand, these economic debates have largely been unhelpful in analytical terms, shedding little light on either the specifically African dimensions of the crisis or the keys to its resolution. First, as I will show in Chapter 2, adjustment programs have rarely been fully implemented, so it is problematic to blame or credit them for Africa's economic performance. Yet, debates about structural adjustment have rarely problematized this partial rate of implementation. The critics of IFI reform have preferred to exaggerate the rate of implementation in order to blame adjustment programs for most of Africa's ills, from rising poverty[30] to the decline of the state.[31] For their part, the IFI community

28. Paul Mosley, Turan Subasat, and John Weeks, "Assessing Adjustment in Africa," *World Development* 23 (1995): 1459–73.
29. For example, Frances Stewart, "Are Short-Term Policies Consistent with Long-Term Development Needs in Africa?" in Giovanni Andrea Cornia and Gerald K. Helleiner, *From Adjustment to Development in Africa* (New York: St. Martin's Press, 1994), pp. 98–128.
30. A good example is Frances Stewart, *Adjustment and Poverty: Options and Choices* (London: Routledge, 1995). See Howard White, "Adjustment in Africa," pp. 800–3, for other examples of this tendency.
31. For instance, Liisa Laakso and Adebayo Olukoshi, "The Crisis of the Post Colonial Nation-State Project in Africa," in Liisa Laakso and Adebayo Olukoshi (eds.), *Challenges to the Nation-State in Africa* (Uppsala, Sweden: Nordiska Afrikainstitutet, 1996), especially, pp. 16–23.

has been happy to point to partial implementation as an explanation for less than stellar economic performance, but has remained remarkably incurious about any patterns in the implementation record and their implications. In fact, there are clear patterns in the way in which structural adjustment programs have been managed by African governments, and it will be clear by the end of this book that restoring economic stability and growth has often taken a back seat in government motivations to preserving political power and protecting rent-seeking opportunities. Indeed, the reform process has increasingly been manipulated for political advantage.

Second, debates about Africa's crisis have been largely atemporal, in the sense that they have not viewed reform as an evolving process, in which past events or decisions have an impact on the present, which in turn will condition the realm of the possible in the future. Perhaps the most striking feature of public policy debates about adjustment is their inattention to the impact of *path dependency* on policy outcomes.[32] First, perceptions about the process of economic reform – what can be accomplished, what are the costs of failure, how will the donors respond to nonimplementation – is clearly conditioned by past experiences. In addition, the protracted nature of the crisis imposes its own path dependencies: failing to maintain infrastructure or to pay the civil service for six months has different economic and political consequences than failing to do so regularly for twenty years. The analysis in the following chapters explicitly restores this temporal dimension. It argues that much of the behavior of both individuals and organizations in Africa reflects learning from past actions and adaptation to changes in the environment.

Third, these debates have remained remarkably economistic, failing to take into account either political or managerial issues. Structuralist critics of the Bank have consistently exaggerated both the capacity of African governments to undertake an alternative package of policies and the political motivation to do so. Thus, Mosley, Subasat, and Weeks simply assume that African states already possess the implementation capacity to undertake the targeted public investment and credit policies that lie at the heart of the heterodox strategy they propose to replace current structural adjustment programs.[33] Often-repeated

---

32. The concept of path dependency was nonetheless first developed by growth economists. See Paul David, "Understanding the Economics of QWERTY: The Necessity of History," in William N. Parker (ed.), *Economic History and the Modern Economist* (Oxford: Blackwell, 1986), pp. 30–49.
33. "Assessing Adjustment in Africa," pp. 1467–9.

references to the applicability of East Asian experiences of state-led development assume against all the available evidence that African state structures possess a similar level of implementation capacity and political discipline.[34]

Since 1989, Bank reports have belatedly recognized that the African crisis is one of "governance," but the Bank has largely failed to integrate this insight into its own lending. In the standard adjustment package promoted by all the donors, governance-type issues are relegated to an eventual "second phase" of reform, after stabilization has been achieved. State reform has overwhelmingly focused on civil service retrenchment and privatization rather than on areas that could positively impact governance, such as transparency, accountability, or judicial reform. As I show in some detail in Chapter 5, structural adjustment loans have had a negative impact on central state capacity and have actually reinforced neopatrimonial tendencies in the region.

A common donor explanation for poor implementation of reform has been the absence of "government commitment" to and, more recently, "government ownership" of reform,[35] but this turns out to be little more than a not very helpful truism, since commitment and ownership usually are defined in circular fashion as the ability and willingness of the government to undertake reform. Where do commitment and ownership come from and under what circumstances? These are questions left unexamined. At most, donor analyses suggest that its technocratic allies in African government are prevented from undertaking reform by vaguely defined "vested interests."

In fact, this book will show that political institutions hold the explanatory key to the African crisis and that there will not be successful economic reform without a prior reform of the region's politics. The inattention to politics by both the IFIs and their critics is a particularly glaring omission because Africa underwent rapid political change during this period, at least in part because of the economic crisis. During this twenty-year period, democratization and political liberalization trans-

---

34. This is notably the case in Mkandawire and Soludo, *Our Continent, Our Future.* Two useful correctives are Deborah Bräutigam, "What Can Africa Learn from Taiwan," *Journal of Modern African Studies* 32 (1994): 111–36; and David Lindauer and Michael Roemer (eds.), *Asia and Africa: Legacies and Opportunities in Development* (San Francisco: ICS Press, 1994).

35. J. H. Johnson and S. S. Wasty, "Borrower Ownership of Adjustment Programs and the Political Economy of Reform," World Bank Discussion Paper no. 199 (Washington, DC: World Bank, 1993).

formed African politics, with the introduction of multiple parties, regular elections, a free press, and an explosion of civic associations.[36] To what extent were these developments related to the failure of economic reform, either as cause or as effect? It is certainly easy to come up with conjectures: perhaps, one is tempted to hypothesize, the economic crisis weakened the state so much it could not contain the participatory explosion we have witnessed. Perhaps democratization makes reform easier because of the greater accountability imposed on state elites; perhaps on the other hand, it makes it harder because of the additional constituency pressures on decision makers. The debate on structural adjustment has been almost entirely silent on these issues.

Given these circumstances, political science should clearly be able to shed light on Africa's economic failures in novel and interesting ways. Yet, with the exception of a handful of country case studies, there have been exceedingly few theoretically informed studies of the politics of economic reform in the region.[37] Much contemporary political economy on the region is furthermore not helpful regarding the role played by the international donors. Political scientists have typically either ignored the donors entirely or blamed them indiscriminantly for the region's ills, but there have been few attempts to integrate them fully into a plausible approach to the contemporary political economy. That is one of the ambitions of the present study.

OUTLINE OF THE ARGUMENT

This book examines why Africa's economic crisis has persisted for two decades, and why efforts to put in place and sustain more effective economic policies and developmental public institutions have proven so much more difficult in Africa than elsewhere. My explanation focuses on political and institutional factors: I examine how the crisis has evolved over the last twenty years, and what are the implications of the long-term persistence of crisis over such an extended period. The next chapter examines the existing literature on economic reform. It has continued to

36. Michael Bratton and Nicolas van de Walle, *Democratic Experiments in Africa: Regime Transitions in Comparative Perspective* (New York: Cambridge University Press, 1997).
37. A critical survey of this literature is provided by Peter Lewis, "Economic Reform and Political Transition in Africa: The Quest for a Policy of Development," *World Politics* 49 (1996): 92–129.

have a societal focus in which the primary obstacles to reform are identified as interest groups and the pressures they bring to bear on decision makers. I argue that this may be an accurate description of reform in political systems in which nonstate organizations are powerful and mobilizational, but that it does not fit the African cases. Observers of African political economy have tended to conflate autonomy and capacity when they have argued that the economic difficulties of African states have been due to low levels of autonomy. Chapter 1 argues, to the contrary, that African states combine high levels of autonomy with extremely low capacity, in a context in which nonstate actors are poorly organized and weak. African regimes have been remarkably stable, with much less frequent leader turnover than in other regions, despite the appearance of instability because of their limited institutionalization and low state capacity.

Chapter 2 focuses on the record of partial implementation of policy reform between 1979 and 1999. Patterns in implementation are revealing of decision makers' preferences and biases. A careful analysis of these patterns reveals that regimes have sought to protect the interests of a narrow stratum of state elites during the reform process and have regularly been willing to inflict austerity on the population, suggesting a good deal of autonomy. Indeed, the trend in the 1990s has been for African states to withdraw from basic developmental activities and focus the expenditures entirely on government consumption. I thus suggest we need a new, state-centered, framework to understand Africa's permanent crisis.

Chapter 3 provides the framework. Policy outcomes are shown as resulting from the interaction between the clientelistic needs of neopatrimonial states, the extremely low capacity of these state structures, and the dominant economic ideas among policy elites in the 1960s and 1970s. The political institutions established following decolonization were weak and endowed with little legitimacy. Chapter 3 explains that state elites quickly came to rely on patronage and the distribution of economic rents in order to ensure political stability. African political systems became *neopatrimonial*, combining an external facade of modern rational-legal administration with an internal patrimonial logic of dyadic exchange, prebendalism, and the private appropriation of public resources by state elites. Neopatrimonial systems tend to favor consumption over investment, they produce unsustainable economic policies, and they systematically underinvest in institutional capacity, which threatens power holders. Neopatrimonialism combined in Africa with a weak civil society and few participatory traditions, a colonial legacy most of the first generation of rulers found useful to maintain.

Chapter 4 then shows how these dynamics have conditioned the state's response to the emergence of crisis in the 1970s. It shows that political leaders initially sought to evade the reforms being pushed on them by the donors because they feared any kind of reform that would dilute their command of state resources. As the crisis has progressed, leaders have sought increasingly to instrumentalize the reform process to derive political benefits from it. They have learned to protect their own interests, even as they implement just enough reform to maintain donor support. This is admittedly a difficult strategy to carry out, and we see two modal patterns emerge over time. In some countries, leaders lack the discipline and political skill to maintain the neopatrimonial order; over time, rent-seeking tendencies spin out of control and state capacity so deteriorates that law and order break down. The result is state decay and even a descent to warlordism. In a second pattern, top leaders use the reform process to recentralize power and readjust patrimonial practices to the lower level of resources available. The reform process may not result in renewed growth, but these states exhibit remarkable political stability.

Chapter 5 examines the role of aid. Following independence, foreign aid helped sustain neopatrimonial regimes by providing the resources and technical capacity for development the state was not able to generate on its own. Aid resources, provided to the state but in the form of distinct projects, could easily be coopted in a patrimonial context, with project benefits being distributed along clientelistic lines. The 1960s and 1970s were the golden years of this postcolonial system, in which the international community buttressed weak and highly vulnerable African states, which would probably not have survived without the legitimacy conferred by the international community of states, as well as economic and military aid.

Many critics of structural adjustment argue that it undermines political stability. On the contrary, Chapter 5 shows that donor support for policy adjustment served to sustain and extend the postcolonial order when a series of exogenous shocks and disastrous public management undermined most African economies during the 1970s. A greatly expanded flow of resources was provided to African states, with conditions states found easy to evade and for which they were generally not held accountable. The increased donor resources lessened the need to undertake adjustment policies, which state elites had few incentives to undertake anyway. The direct consequence was rapidly increasing international debt and a growing reliance on aid, but as long as the flow of resources to the region was in constant increase, the situation was sustainable and state elites had little incentive to promote real reform.

This has changed in the 1990s for several reasons. First, over a decade of structural adjustment has had a deeply corrosive effect on state capacity, which has not only failed to increase during the last twenty years, but has probably declined in a majority of countries in the region. Second, aid flows to the region have been declining since 1993, so that the system is becoming less forgiving to African governments than it was in the past. Third, state weakness and a growing antistate bias in the West has progressively awakened civil society in Africa and created the conditions for greater participation in public life. The democratization wave that hit Africa after 1989 was bound to have some impact on the logic of the system, and this is reviewed in Chapter 6. By comparing the performance of African economies before and after regime changes in the early 1990s, I show that democratization has had little impact on economic decision making, because the new democratic regimes remain governed by neopatrimonial logic. Nonetheless, Chapter 6 speculates that the political and civic freedoms that have been won by African populations in most countries of the region will in the long run increase the accountability of African governments and improve economic governance.

A concluding chapter examines the stability of the present impasse and speculates about the factors that might in time bring about positive change. It then summarizes the argument and places it in a comparative perspective.

Two caveats are in order regarding the approach adopted throughout this text. First, this book is not meant to be a study in public policy. It is about political economy. I do not undertake a comprehensive diagnosis of Africa's economic problems, which have already been well documented elsewhere. No specific policy prescriptions are presented. My policy preferences may become obvious to the perceptive reader, but this book is not about recommending policies to African governments or to donors. I take as axiomatic that better economic performance is associated with macroeconomic stability, including sustainable monetary and fiscal policies; and that increasing the rate of growth necessitates increases in investment, improved infrastructure, and higher levels of human capital.[38] I believe that if African governments were to adopt and sustain policies more or less compatible with this consensus, their economies would flourish within a couple of years. But this book is more about the failure of African governments to implement any such policies through more than two decades of official commitment to policy reform than it is a critique or defense of a specific set of policies.

There is much variation in performance across African countries, so it is tempting to focus the analysis on explaining intra-African variation. A second caveat, however, is that this book focuses on the similarities across African states and the features that distinguish them from non-African political economies. I argue that there is a distinctive politics of reform in sub-Saharan Africa. Admittedly, the model fits best the region's low-income countries. It has less traction for South Africa, a more industrialized economy and institutionalized political system, and which will not feature much in the following pages. I do believe that many of the features are not entirely unique to Africa, but are present in low-income, primarily rural political systems in other regions as well. In fact, I suspect that my criticism of the literature is not completely invalid for other, more industrialized regions of the world as well, but demonstrating this is not my concern in these pages.

This book is sensitive to key differences within Africa and does discuss exceptions to regional patterns because they are usually very instructive. Botswana and Mauritius have escaped the ills I describe for the region. Some countries, most notably Ghana and Uganda, are often argued to have made at least a partial recovery in the 1990s and it will be important to establish what sets them apart. Nonetheless, the regional patterns, that can be observed are too striking to ignore. My main objective is to identify and explain these patterns, which have kept Africa for several decades mired in a seemingly permanent crisis.

38. I have identified this set of desirable policies in an essay co-authored with Benno Ndulu, "Africa's Economic Renewal: From Consensus to Strategy," in Benno Ndulu and Nicolas van de Walle (eds.), *Agenda for Africa's Economic Renewal* (Washington, DC: Overseas Development Council, 1996), pp. 3–32.

I

Approaches to Africa's Permanent Crisis

Since the onset of Africa's economic crisis over twenty years ago, political scientists have sought to explain the inability and or unwillingness
of governments in the region to undertake thorough policy reform. This
chapter reviews the most valuable insights from this literature, before
staking out a modified approach, which will then be considerably
expanded in subsequent chapters. Most analyses of why Africa has not
been able to renew with economic growth in the last twenty years place
the blame squarely on the inability of governments to overcome societal
opposition to the policy reform imposed on them by the international
financial institutions (IFIs). The policy reform literature usually views
societal power as being asserted through organized interest groups, but
disagrees on the extent to which state agents can act to achieve real policy
change. Much of the academic literature on African political economy
also views African governments as prisoners of their societies through
their reliance on clientelist practices to ensure political stability.

Both of these literatures contain valuable insights, but they underestimate the autonomy of African governments from societal forces. Most
states in the region combine weak capacities and discipline with a fair
amount of autonomy to make economic policy decisions, largely because
of the weakness of organized pressure groups that would hold the state
more accountable. Instead, I argue in this book that the main obstacles
to sustained economic reform are to be found within the state itself and
the political institutions that link state and society. Indeed, the partial
and uneven implementation of reform, which will be presented in
Chapter 2, is less of a puzzle if we focus on the interests of top state
agents. Over the last twenty years, African state elites have sought to
adapt to changing circumstances without losing their hold on the state.
That they have been able to do so is in no small part thanks to the more

*adaptation
to globalization*

than $200 billion in foreign economic aid the region has received from donors since the early 1980s. The dependency and neo-Marxist literatures have always viewed donor resources as complementary to private capital. They have argued that aid is designed to better integrate Africa into global trading and financial networks, dominated by Western capital. More mainstream observers have viewed aid as a force for positive change in the region, which would help African countries adapt to changing global circumstances and fashion market-friendly policies to restore economic growth. On the contrary, I argue, public aid has been used as a substitute for private capital and has provided support to African governments to survive the economic crisis while minimizing policy change.

A decade ago, Kahler pointed out that the orthodox economic reform promoted by the IFIs in effect was asking states to pursue policies that undermined them in myriad ways. He labeled this the *orthodox paradox*.[1] But there is no paradox, since African rulers have wholeheartedly resisted implementing the adjustment reforms that would have undermined them, and have instead sought to delay, shape, and redesign reform policies in such a way as to make them less threatening and, in some cases at least, even profitable.

The combination of state prevarication and substantial donor resources has given the African crisis its specific flavor over the years. A key feature of the African crisis is its length. For two decades, these countries have been "stabilizing," never quite able to overcome the economic imbalances that compel them to seek the help of the donors, even if periodically a temporary respite leads observers to predict the end of the crisis. The situation of permanent crisis has important implications for politics in these countries: over time, there has been political adjustment to austerity and economic decline, again with state elites seeking to protect their hold on power, even if it means making economic recovery less likely.

This chapter is divided into three sections after this introduction. The next section reviews the literature on the political economy of reform. I start by focusing on the pure interest group model, in which organized groups out in society are seen to block reforms and the state is little more than a passive register of societal preferences. The chapter then

1. Miles Kahler, "Orthodoxy and Its Alternatives: Explaining Approaches to Stabilization and Adjustment," in Joan Nelson (ed.), *Economic Crisis and Policy Choice: The Politics of Economic Adjustment in the Third World* (Princeton, NJ: Princeton University Press, 1990), pp. 33–62.

examines the "reform mongering" literature, in which states have limited autonomy to out-maneuver the interest groups that still constitute the main opposition to reform. The limitations of the interest group approach are patent for political systems with extremely weak societal organizations and a dominant, albeit ailing, central state. Section three turns to the task of outlining the alternative approach to the politics of reform, which will be developed in later chapters. Reform is shaped by the interaction between three factors within the state itself and the contemporary international aid regime. The neopatrimonial nature of political authority has coincided with the ideological predispositions of policy elites and the state's low capacity to result in a state with a proclivity for ineffectual intervention in the economy and repeated fiscal crises. The current system of international aid has reinforced these tendencies. Section four summarizes the consequences of these factors for the implementation of reform, particularly as they have evolved over a relatively long period of time. I focus on the "partial reform syndrome" in which the absence of sustained reform for two decades creates a unique political economy, with distinctive winners and losers. In most but not all cases, relatively autonomous state elites have manipulated the implementation of reform to advance their own interests, relying on partial reform to create new sources of rent seeking and corruption.

THE POLITICAL ECONOMY OF REFORM

The political economy of policy reform is based on the key insight that policy changes have distributional implications: reform is pursued because broad gains are postulated in the long run, but in the short run, the changes generate winners and losers. First, because reforms are usually sought to respond to an unsustainable macroeconomic disequilibrium, policy reform typically entails some "expenditure reduction" policies in order to decrease the level of aggregate demand that brought about the crisis. Contractionary measures such as decreases in government expenditure or cuts in the money supply bring about recession and hardships on the general population.[2] Second, policy reform includes

2. On the distinction between expenditure reduction and switching, see Stephen J. Turnovski, *Macroeconomic Analysis and Stabilization Policy* (Cambridge, UK: Cambridge University Press, 1977). By definition, expenditure reduction is contractionary. The degree to which IFI stabilization and adjustment packages have in fact been recessionary has been a matter of some debate among economists for two decades; see Paul Krugman and Lance Taylor, "Contractionary Effects of Devaluation," *Journal of Development Economics* 14 (1978): 445–56; and Sebastian

"expenditure switching" policies, such as currency devaluation or trade liberalization, which redistribute income within the economy in order to improve incentives and foster more rapid growth. In the African context, reform has, first, sought to shift resources so as to favor exports; second, it has sought to shift expenditure from consumption to investment. Expenditure switching measures are viewed as especially problematic in political terms because the groups that bear the brunt of the negative effects will usually be the powerful constituencies that had been the main beneficiaries of prereform state intervention in the economy. Moreover, while the gains from reform are diffuse and spread out across a wide proportion of the population and over time in the form of lower inflation and higher economic growth, the costs of reform are concentrated. Thus, the losers of reform are more likely to solve collective action problems and organize to fight against reform than are the winners, though the latter far outnumber the former. These stylized facts of the politics of reform are widely accepted and have long constituted the background for the literature on policy reform.

Urban Bias and Interest Group Models

The most prevalent approach to the politics of economic reform has postulated that the failure to change the mix of macro and micro policies that have brought about an unsustainable macroeconomic imbalance can be explained as the result of the pressure of key constituencies on the government. In particular, that these policies had been designed to placate the well-organized urban interest groups that dominated national politics was a widely held and influential view in academic and policy circles at the outset of the debt crisis in the 1982.[3] A coalition of urban

Edwards, "Are Devaluations Contractionary?" *Review of Economics and Statistics* 68 (1986): 501–8. On the methodological pitfalls involved in determining the precise welfare effects of structural adjustment, see Jean Paul Azam, "The Uncertain Distributional Impact of Structural Adjustment in Sub-Saharan Africa," in Rolph Van der Hoeven and Fred Van Der Kraaij (eds.), *Structural Adjustment and Beyond in Sub-Saharan Africa* (London: James Currey, 1994), pp. 100–13.

3. Following the classic statements in Robert H. Bates, *Markets and States in Tropical Africa: The Political Basis of Agricultural Policies* (Berkeley: University of California Press, 1981); and Michael Lipton, *Why Poor People Stay Poor: Urban Bias in World Development* (London: Temple Smith, 1977). Also extremely influential was Mancur Olson, *The Rise and Decline of Nations* (New Haven, CT: Yale University Press, 1982). See the illuminating discussion in Paul Mosley, Jane Harrigan, and John Toye, *Aid and Power: The World Bank and Policy Based Lending in the 1980s* (London: Routledge, 1991), pp. 9–21.

interests, with strong vested interests in the current policy mix, was successfully preventing reform. Such groups were quickly identified: firms and workers in the import substituting industrial (ISI) sector resist trade liberalization and devaluation, the civil service opposes privatization and government budget cuts, urban consumers contest the end of food subsidies, and big farmers resist the end of subsidies on agricultural inputs. Opposition from these mostly urban groups was the key obstacle to stabilization and policy reform.

This first wave of theorizing about the politics of structural adjustment in the Third World contained some keen insights about the nature of economic crisis and the difficulty of bringing about reform. It offered a coherent explanation as to why governments would prefer to continue policies that were clearly irrational from an economic perspective. As Robert Bates brilliantly demonstrated, in an African context, that economic irrationality was more than compensated for by political rationality, and these policies could be explained as the result of state leaders' seeking to maximize political stability rather than economic growth.[4] Governments could not be expected to undertake economic reforms that would undermine the balance of social forces that maintained them in power. The economic reforms demanded of governments after the oil crisis would surely prove destabilizing. Julius Nyerere is thus alleged to have said that he opposed an agreement with the international monetary fund (IMF) in 1985 because the price of such an agreement "would be riots in the streets of Dar es Salaam."[5] Much anecdotal evidence was adduced to confirm that in fact, economic reform amounted to political suicide for governments. In countries as varied as Morocco and Tunisia in 1984, Egypt in 1979, Zambia in 1986, and Venezuela in 1990, observers noted, government attempts to eliminate subsidies on consumption goods such as bread or gasoline had been met with massive urban unrest.[6] In Sudan, in 1984, it even led to the overthrow of the Niemiri regime. In an often cited statistic, in 1971, Cooper had noted that for the Third World as a whole, in the year following a devaluation, the responsible finance minister had a three times higher

4. Bates, *Markets and States.*
5. Quoted in Aili Mari Tripp, *Changing the Rules: The Politics of Liberalization and the Urban Informal Economy in Tanzania* (Berkeley: University of California Press, 1997), pp. 79–80. The sincerity of these fears may be questioned, but they had the intended effect with the donors. Note that when an agreement was finally reached in 1986 there were no such riots.
6. See, for example, John Walton and David Seddon, *Free Markets and Food Riots: The Politics of Global Adjustment* (London: Blackwell, 1994).

risk of being replaced and the government twice the risk of falling from power.[7]

There are nonetheless several difficulties with theories that attribute great power to urban interest groups in economic policy making in the developing world. First, the empirical record simply does not support the claim that such groups block adjustment with organized activism. The scholars who have looked systematically at the relationship between political stability and critical policy changes such as the removal of consumer subsidies, found that the "food riot" anecdotes were misleading; social protest was as likely in countries that did not undergo reform as in those that did, and governments usually got away with such reforms with little organized opposition. Throughout the Third World, stabilization and structural adjustment programs of important dimensions were put into place during the 1980s, with little increase in political instability.[8] Government expenditures and consumer subsidies were cut significantly in many countries during the 1980s, as part of adjustment programs. In Latin America, in particular, the decade witnessed real progress on reform without the occurrence of the widely predicted social explosion.[9] In Mexico, for example, economic reform after 1982 directly attacked the powerful unions ensconced in the public and parapublic sectors and resulted in massive layoffs and a six-year recession before growth resumed in 1989, yet the regime's hold on power was left undiminished.[10] Even where there was little progress on implementing reforms, governments demonstrated the capacity to impose economic hardship on societal groups that were thought to be the backbone of the political status quo.

Second, the interest group approach to reform would predict that policy reform was likeliest in Africa, since societal groups opposed to

7. Richard Cooper, *Currency Devaluations in Developing Countries.* Princeton Essays in International Finance, no. 86 (Princeton, NJ: Princeton University Press, 1971), pp. 28–9.

8. Henry S. Bienen and Mark Gersovitz, "Consumer Subsidy Cuts, Violence, and Political Stability," *Comparative Politics* 19 (1986): 25–44; and D. R. Sidell, *The IMF and Third World Instability* (London: Macmillan, 1987).

9. An assessment of the extent of economic reform achieved in Latin America during the 1980s is provided by John Williamson, *Latin American Adjustment: How Much Has Happened?* (Washington, DC: Institute for International Economics, 1990).

10. Robert F. Kaufman et al., "Mexico: Radical Reform in a Dominant Party System," in Stephan Haggard and Steven B. Webb (eds.), *Voting for Reform: Economic Adjustment in New Democracies* (New York: Oxford University Press, 1994), pp. 360–410.

reform are weaker and less well organized than their counterparts in Latin America or Eastern Europe. In fact, exactly the opposite proved true, and there was less progress on economic reform than elsewhere in the developing world. Despite this empirical record, much research on economic reform has continued to assume the determinant influence of interest groups in shaping economic policy making in the Third World.[11] Even when researchers find little evidence of interest group pressures against reform, they are loath to recognize that it may translate as the essential weakness of such groups. Thus, a major cross-national study of policy reform directed by Robert Bates and Anne Krueger was based on the premise that interest group actions would determine the success and failures of policy reform. A main finding of the project's case studies, however, was that "the intervention of interest groups fails to account for the initiation, or lack of initiation, of policy reform."[12] Their explanation of this finding, nonetheless, is not to deny the power of interest groups over policy decisions, but rather to argue that the uncertain climate of reform leaves these groups unable to calculate the economic interests of their members. This seems implausible. While uncertainty may affect individual actions, interest group organizations do not need to know with certainty the impact of specific policies as long as they believe that their constituencies' purchasing power is dropping; when it is dropping as substantially as it has in the African context, they will intervene on behalf of their constituencies for specific benefits. In Africa, moreover, there is plenty of evidence of lobbying, strikes, work stoppages, and other forms of interest group participation.[13] These actions are ineffective, however, in persuading governments to change course.

11. For example, Jeffrey Frieden, "Classes, Sectors, and Foreign Debt in Latin America," *Comparative Politics* 21 (1988): 1–20; or Pranab Bardhan, *The Political Economy of Development in India* (London: Blackwell, 1984). Bates himself has moved away from such a society-centric view, notably in his *Beyond the Miracle of the Market: Agricultural Politics in Kenya* (Cambridge, UK: Cambridge University Press, 1989). On the other hand, the approach remains a favorite among economists; see the comments in the recent review essay by Paul Collier and Jan Willem Gunning, "Explaining African Economic Performance," *Journal of Economic Literature* 37 (1999): 64–111, pp. 105–6.
12. Robert H. Bates and Anne Krueger, "Generalization from the Case Studies," in Robert H. Bates and Anne Krueger, *Political and Economic Interactions in Economic Policy Reform* (Oxford, UK: Basil Blackwell, 1993), pp. 444–72, p. 45.
13. John A. Wiseman, "Urban Riots in West Africa, 1977–1985," *Journal of Modern African Studies* 24 (1986): 509–18.

Perhaps the real problem is that scholars who have attributed great influence to interest groups tend to conflate interests and interest groups, assuming that the mere existence of economic interests in a segment of the population will guarantee their effective representation in the political system. Yet that representation is far from automatic, and even when interest group organizations do exist, their ability to act forcefully on behalf of their members varies enormously.[14] Interest group analyses tend to take organization for granted, implying that the level of resources, capabilities, and leadership available to an interest group do not determine its effectiveness or lack thereof. The political influence of interest groups is also mediated by the institutional characteristics of economic decision making and state-society linkages. Yet, Lipton's classic work on urban bias has virtually nothing to say about the internal characteristics of interest groups, beyond the size of their memberships, and it does not describe how they actually have an impact on policy. It is equally striking that Bates's classic work is almost entirely silent on the organizational characteristics of his urban bias coalition in African nations.[15]

More recent political economy work also conflates economic interests and interest group power. Sophisticated models have been developed in which the course of policy reform is determined by the interaction between broad social categories: for instance, Perotti pits the "poor" against "the middle classes" and "the capitalists" to explain the course of policy reform.[16] Similarly, a project on the political feasibility of structural adjustment in Africa by the OECD Development Center modeled the opposition of "civil servants" and other "urban groups" to reforms without any reference to the organizations that would represent them.[17] In these models, economic power translates automatically into political power and organization is irrelevant. Neither the internal organization of groups nor the nature of institutional links to the state

14. A recent paper that makes a similar point in a very different setting is Steven Vogel, "When Interests Are Not Preferences: The Cautionary Tale of Japanese Consumers," *Comparative Politics* 31 (1999): 187–207.
15. This point and others are made about the urban bias hypothesis in Ashutosh Varshney (ed.), *Beyond Urban Bias* (London: Frank Cass, 1993).
16. Cited as an unpublished paper in Dani Rodrik, "Understanding Economic Policy Reform," *Journal of Economic Literature* 34 (1996): 9–42; cited on p. 24.
17. This project is summarized in Christian Morrisson et al., "Adjustment Programs and Politico-Economic Interactions in Developing Countries: Lessons from an Empirical Analysis of Africa in the 1980s," in Giovanni Andrea Cornia and Gerald K. Helleiner (eds.), *From Adjustment to Development in Africa* (New York: St. Martin's Press, 1994), pp. 174–91.

matter. The state cannot have its own policy preferences but has to adopt those of the social category that controls it, and there cannot be state autonomy.

The analysis of interest groups and the politics of economic reform was strongly influenced by events in the developed countries following the first oil crisis. The political understanding of the economic crisis in the Third World was stimulated by the literature then emerging on the politics of stagflation in the Western social democracies, with their powerful trade unions, big state bureaucracies, and vulnerable coalition governments. The very term *structural adjustment* entered the public policy lexicon in reference to the adjustment that industrialized countries had to undergo after 1973 in response to the dramatic increase in the price of energy.[18] Particularly influential was the work of Olson and others in this period purporting to demonstrate that the rise of entrenched economic interest groups, in particular trade unions, doomed industrialized states to economic stagnation.[19]

This analytical framework was adapted to the developing countries by Latin Americanists, for whom it resonated in the countries they studied, with their highly mobilized labor organizations defending entrenched positions in the public and import substitution industrialization sectors, and governments that had responded with unsustainable inflationary spending and monetary policies. Latin American "populism" appeared readily explainable in terms of these same interest group models, though they were soon adapted to fit local circumstances and the Latin Americanists' own analytical frameworks.[20]

Yet, even a cursory comparison between Africa and the industrialized West reveals how woefully organized societal interests are in the former compared to the latter. Long repressed or coopted by government, unions, business associations, and other groups are smaller, more

18. The intellectual history of structural adjustment is recounted in Mosley et al., *Aid and Power*, pp. 27–38.
19. Olson, *The Rise and Decline of Nations*. See also Leon N. Lindberg and Charles Maier, *The Politics of Inflation and Economic Stagnation* (Washington, DC: The Brookings Institution, 1985); Suzanne Berger (ed.), *Organizing Interests in Western Europe* (New York: Cambridge University Press, 1981); John H. Goldthorpe (ed.), *Order and Conflict in Contemporary Capitalism* (Oxford, UK: Clarendon Press, 1984); and Peter Katzenstein (ed.), *Between Power and Plenty* (Madison: University of Wisconsin Press, 1978).
20. See, for instance, Robert Kaufman and Barbara Stallings, "The Political Economy of Latin American Populism," in Rudiger Dornbusch and Sebastian Edwards (eds.), *The Macroeconomics of Populism in Latin America* (Chicago: University of Chicago Press, 1991), pp. 15–43.

poorly organized, and underfunded compared to their Western counter-parts.[21] Even most of the societies in Latin America can claim more pow-erful interest groups than those typically prevailing in Africa. The size and structure of economies there serve to weaken interest groups. Given very low population densities, there is no historical tradition of strong private landed interests outside southern Africa. The weakness of the private sector and the recent development and small size of the indus-trial sector, as well as the preponderance of the civil service within formal sector employment, weaken labor organizations. Senegal, for example, has one of the oldest industrial sectors in west Africa, with a textile industry going back to the 1940s, yet total union membership probably never exceeded 40,000 during the 1980s, out of a formal sector labor force of between 160,000 and 190,000 and a potential labor force of perhaps five million men and women.[22] Ghana has perhaps the largest and traditionally the best-organized labor movement with some 467,000 members in the national Trade Union Congress (TUC), or 13 percent of the labor force. Yet, in Ghana, as in Senegal, the 1980s witnessed a decrease in membership and political influence, as governments clamped down or coopted union leaders, and rank and file workers grew dis-couraged by sharply declining real incomes.[23] Across the continent, it is difficult to argue with Berg and Butler's assessment right after indepen-dence that the striking characteristic of African trade unions was "their limited political impact."[24]

This inadequate attention to the organizational capabilities and resources of interest groups may be explained in part by the fact that a reasonable level of organization can usually be assumed in the industri-alized nations, with their long traditions of corporatist and pluralist interest representation. In addition, paradoxically, organization is prob-ably less important in the electoral democracies of the West, where often

21. Joan Nelson, "Organized Labor, Politics, and Market Flexibility in Developing Countries," *World Bank Research Observer* 6 (1991): 37–56.
22. See Geoffrey Bergen, *Unions in Senegal*, Ph.D. thesis, Department of Political Science, University of California at Los Angeles (Ann Arbor: UMI Dissertation Series, 1991), p. 1.
23. On Ghana, see Herbst, *The Politics of Reform in Ghana*, pp. 64–8.
24. Elliott Berg and Jeffrey Butler, "Trade Unions," in James S. Coleman and Carl G. Rosberg (eds.), *Political Parties and National Integration in Tropical Africa* (Berkeley: University of California Press 1964), pp. 340–81, p. 340. For a some-what more sanguine appraisal, see Richard Sandbrook and Robin Cohen, *The Development of the African Working Class: Studies in Class Formation and Action* (London: Longman, 1975).

only a minimal degree of mobilization is enough for an interest group to unseat an elected official, given their lobbying power and ability to rely on the press. In nonelectoral regimes, on the other hand, preferences cannot be expressed through the ballot, and interest groups are less likely to have influence unless they can mobilize their members for strikes, demonstrations, and other shows of strength. Furthermore, political repression and the absence of civic and political rights in authoritarian systems attenuate the ability of societal interests to organize effectively against government policies. African governments have typically outlawed, emasculated, or coopted economic interest groups such as unions, business associations, and farmer associations.[25]

There are of course exceptions to this generalization of interest group weakness in Africa. Perhaps the most important can be found in the ex-settler colonies of Kenya and especially Namibia and Zimbabwe, where organizations founded by European farmers in the early part of the century have gained real influence over decision making thanks to levels of organization and resources unmatched by the few interest groups in the region. An incisive literature has emerged on the ability of the commercial farmers' association in Zimbabwe to influence agricultural policy making there.[26] But these exceptions are clearly related to the particular nature of colonialism in these countries.

Elsewhere, among the groups that should form the backbone of the urban bias coalition, cases of well-run organizations putting effective pressure on the government can be found. A literature documents the influence of business groups in Nigeria, for instance, that lobbied effectively for trade protection in the 1980s.[27] Unfortunately, the business interests of these groups coincide so completely with rent-seeking inter-

25. See Richard Sandbrook, *The Politics of Africa's Economic Recovery* (Cambridge: Cambridge University Press, 1993), pp. 106–13.
26. Jeffrey Herbst, *State Politics in Zimbabwe* (Berkeley: University of California Press, 1990); Tor Skalnes, *The Politics of Economic Reform in Zimbabwe* (New York: St. Martin's Press, 1995); and Michael Bratton, "The Comrades and the Countryside: The Politics of Agricultural Policy in Zimbabwe," *World Politics* 39, no. 2 (1987): 174–202.
27. See Jeffrey Herbst and Adebayo Olukoshi, "Nigeria: Economic and Political Reforms at Cross Purposes," in Stephan Haggard and Steven B. Webb (eds.), *Voting for Reform: Economic Adjustment in New Democracies* (New York: Oxford University Press, 1994), pp. 453–502, especially pp. 482–7; see also Adebayo Olukoshi (ed.), *The Politics of Structural Adjustment in Nigeria* (Portsmouth, NH: Heinemann, 1993); and Peter Lewis, "Economic Statism, Private Capital and the Dilemmas of Accumulation in Nigeria," *World Development* 22 (1994): 437–51.

ests within the state that also benefited from the protection that it is hard to know how much credit to give them for the policy outcome. Nigeria's manufacturing sector is also the biggest and one of the oldest in Africa. In other countries, such as Senegal, weak manufacturing sectors were not able to protect their positions.[28] Labor groups in Zambia and Nigeria, perhaps the two most powerful in the region, have at times contested policies forcefully.[29] Similarly, there are accounts of effective lobbying by student and teacher organizations.[30] These groups clearly gained power in the 1990s, in part thanks to the opening up of African politics. But their power still appears ephemeral, with temporary episodes of prominence that are not sustained because of weak organization and the continuing power of the state to coopt or manipulate the groups. Indeed, the literature that typically means to put these interest groups at the center of national politics ends up confirming their limited institutional capacity and their limited organizational and financial resources, as well as the absence of institutionalized mechanisms through which they can influence policy. The resort to wildcat strikes and violent protests obviously has the power to scare decision makers, particularly when these events take place in the capital, but the use of these tactics is really, in the final analysis, testimony to the groups' lack of power.

28. Catherine Boone, *Merchant Capital and the Roots of State Power in Senegal, 1930–1985* (Cambridge, UK: Cambridge University Press, 1992); see also John R. Heilbrunn, "Commerce, Politics and Business Associations in Benin and Togo," *Comparative Politics* 29 (1997): 473–93; and Jon Kraus, "Capital, Power and Business Associations in the African Political Economy," in Jon Kraus (ed.), *Capital and Power in African Countries* (unpublished book manuscript, Department of Political Science, SUNY – Fredonia, Fredonia, NY, 1999).

29. On Nigeria, see Yusuf Bangura and Bjorn Beckman, "African Workers and Structural Adjustment: A Nigerian Case Study," in Adebayo Olukoshi (ed.), *The Politics of Structural Adjustment in Nigeria* (Portsmouth NH: Heinemann, 1993), pp. 97–111; and Bjorn Beckman, "The Politics of Labor and Adjustment: The Experience of the Nigeria Labor Congress," in Thandika Mkandawire and Adebayo Olukoshi (eds.), *Between Liberalization and Oppression: The Politics of Structural Adjustment in Africa* (Dakar: CODESRIA, 1995), pp. 281–323; on Zambia, see Tina West, "Politics of Implementation of Structural Adjustment in Zambia, 1985–1987," in *Politics of Economic Reform in Sub-Saharan Africa* (Washington, DC: USAID, 1992) pp. 33–96; and Per Nordlund, *Organizing the Political Agora: Domination and Democratization in Zambia and Zimbabwe* (Ph.D. dissertation, Uppsala University, Sweden, 1996).

30. For instance, Dwayne Woods, "The Politicization of Teachers' Associations in the Côte d'Ivoire," *African Studies Review* 39 (1996): 113–30; Christopher Wise, "Chronicle of a Student Strike in Africa: The Case of Burkina Faso," in *African Studies Review* 41 (1998):19–36.

Formal organizations that openly engage the state in policy debates must be distinguished from the various forms of social groups that have proliferated since the colonial era and which include informal credit associations, women market groups, ethnic associations, and secret societies and church groups. A number of Africanists have theorized that these informal networks are flourishing and play a significant role in both individual and group strategies of social promotion and welfare.[31] In an analysis that could be generalized to much of Africa, Tripp has convincingly shown that informal networks in Tanzania have thwarted the state in certain areas of social and economic policy. Thousands of traders have ignored state attempts to regulate and limit informal trading in Dar es Salaam, forcing the government to admit to effective liberalization of the sector.[32] Some observers have taken such evidence to suggest that these informal networks are able to undermine the state's hegemonic ambitions, and constitute a "revenge of civil society on the state."[33] There can be little doubt that societies take advantage of the gap between the African state's policy ambitions and its capacity to carry them out. Economic agents will be particularly likely to seek relief from state laws and regulation when they can gain a livelihood from so doing. But these informal groups are amorphous and unable to mobilize members on behalf of specific policies in a sustained fashion. We remark on their existence and symbolic significance precisely because the kinds of organized groups that weigh on the policy process in richer countries are so striking by their absence in the region.

There are other reasons for the weakness of interest group organizations in low-income countries. Economic structure results in a tendency for households and individuals to have multiple economic interests. Because of the recent nature of urbanization, many urban households in Africa retain links with their village of origin, may continue to cultivate land there, and help promote extensive urban-rural trade. Members of

31. Among a growing literature, albeit from different theoretical perspectives, see Janet MacGaffey, *Entrepreneurs and Parasites: The Struggle for Indigenous Capitalism in Zaire* (Cambridge, UK: Cambridge University Press, 1987); Jean François Bayart, Achille Mbembe, and Comi Toulabor, *La politique par le bas en Afrique* (Paris: Karthala, 1991); Aili Mari Tripp, *Changing the Rules: The Politics of Liberalization and the Urban Informal Economy in Tanzania* (Berkeley: University of California Press, 1997).
32. Ibid.
33. The phrase is from Jean François Bayart, "La revanche des sociétés Africaines," in *Politique Africaine* 11 (1983): 95–127. See also Naomi Chazan, "The New Politics of Participation in Tropical Africa," *Comparative Politics* 14 (1982): 169–82.

the same household may hold quite different economic interests. Further, households have diversified their portfolios across different sectors in recent years as a response to economic uncertainty.[34] The more diversified they are, the less individuals within these households will be committed to specific policy regimes and willing to join interest groups on their behalf. They invest fewer resources in interest group organizations because they are uncertain about the exact impact of reform on their own economic welfare. In turn, the weakness of interest groups increases the likelihood that people will pursue individual rather than collective strategies to deal with economic uncertainty and hardship. As every economist knows, the favorite such strategy is portfolio diversification. As Tripp reports relative to Tanzania, "there was virtually no visible opposition to the austerity measures that accompanied structural adjustment . . . [because] more than 90 percent of household income was coming from informal businesses" that most households had developed in response to the crisis.[35]

The final and more general weakness of interest group arguments is that they are essentially static. They can arguably explain why economic reform fails to take place and why ineffectual economic policies are maintained, but not why, when, and especially how reform actually does take place.[36] Identifying policy regimes as stable equilibrium points based on social *rapports de force* begs the question of how policy changes actually come about. Observers may be dissatisfied with the pace and extent of policy reform, notably in Africa, but they cannot deny that some real policy changes have taken place, or that established governments throughout history do successfully undertake wholesale policy changes: for example, China in the post-Mao era, Korea in the early 1960s, Mexico in the 1980s. By themselves, interest group theories are not helpful in understanding episodes of rapid policy

---

34. See Sarah Berry, *No Condition Is Permanent: The Social Dynamics of Agrarian Change in Sub-Saharan Africa* (Madison: University of Wisconsin Press, 1993); and Alice Sindzingre, "Crédibilité des etats et nouvelles insécurités: l'economie politique des réformes en Afrique," paper presented to the eighth Congress of the EADI, Vienna, September 11–14, 1996.

35. Aili Mari Tripp, *Changing the Rules*, p. 5. Tripp suggests that the most opposition was in response to governmental attempts to clamp down on such informal activities.

36. Merilee Grindle makes a similar argument in her essay, "The New Political Economy: Positive Economies and Negative Politics," in Gerald M. Meier (ed.), *Politics and Policy Making in Developing Countries: Perspectives on the New Political Economy* (San Francisco: ICS Press, 1991), pp. 41–68.

change.[37] Even in Africa, as I will argue in Chapter 2, there has been significant policy reform. An acceptable theory of reform needs to explain why it does sometimes take place, and why, more interestingly, implementation tends to be so uneven, proceeding quickly in certain areas and not at all in others.

Reform Mongering Approaches

The ability of some governments to challenge societal interests and accomplish unpopular reforms has spawned a second wave of policy reform literature focusing on states and state actors themselves. Joan Nelson, Stephan Haggard and Robert Kaufman, and John Waterbury have focused on the many strategies, deceptions, and resources that state elites could employ to defuse opposition to policy reforms and enlist the support necessary to sustain themselves in power.[38] I will call this loose body of research "reform mongering" approaches, to use Albert Hirschman's phrase to describe such efforts by Latin American governments several decades ago.[39] These scholars have also argued that interest groups pose the main obstacle to reform, but they claim that the state is far from merely the "agency for aggregating private demands" that Bates had posited,[40] and instead seeks ways to act on its own policy preferences. The key issue for these scholars has been the manner in which

37. Olson, *Rise and Decline of Nations*, for example, essentially argues that major political discontinuities are necessary for economic growth to occur since the longer political stability obtains, the more powerful interest groups will become. This allows him to explain the post–World War II "miracles" in Japan and Germany, although not why Japan has continued its rapid growth rate.

38. Joan Nelson, "The Political Economy of Stabilization: Commitment, Capacity, and Public Response," *World Development* 12 (1984): 983–1006; and John Waterbury, "The Political Management of Economic Adjustment and Reform," in Joan Nelson (ed.), *Fragile Coalitions: The Politics of Economic Adjustment* (Washington, DC: Overseas Development Council, 1989), pp. 39–56. This literature is admirably summarized in Stephan Haggard and Robert Kaufman, "Institutions and Economic Adjustment," in Stephan Haggard and Robert Kaufman (eds.), *The Politics of Economic Adjustment* (Princeton, NJ: Princeton University Press, 1992), pp. 3–40.

39. Albert O. Hirschman, *Journeys toward Progress* (New York: Greenwood Press, 1968).

40. Robert H. Bates, *Essays on the Political Economy of Rural Africa* (Cambridge, UK: Cambridge University Press, 1983), p. 121. Bates's own work has since then adopted a much more pro-active and autonomous view of state agents and their interests. See, for example, Robert H. Bates, *Beyond the Miracle of the Market: Agricultural Politics in Kenya* (Cambridge, UK: Cambridge University Press, 1988).

state elites manage social forces during the process, once they are committed to a course of reform.

The focus on state institutions and actors that began to emerge by the mid-1980s reflected the changing concerns of political science. Interest in economic reform in less developed countries was influenced by the move to "bring the state back in," which gained new currency at the time in comparative politics.[41] Scholars in a wide variety of settings emphasized states' ability to shape social reality. Successful reform in less developed countries entailed contemporary variations on the much theorized "revolutions from above" that partly autonomous state elites had engineered in countries like Mexico, Turkey, and Japan against the opposition of entrenched conservative interests.[42] Similarly, the literature on the newly industrializing countries (NICs) of Asia emphasized the role of powerful and well-insulated state technocrats who were able to compress general consumption, direct and shape private investment, and repress labor in order to promote rapid industrialization, all with the blessing and protection of political elites.[43]

This literature did not deny the capacity of vested interest groups to hamper reform efforts, but instead argued that their power had been exaggerated and/or that the ability of the state to overcome them had been underestimated. The old set of economic policies was politically sustained by one social coalition, as Waterbury argued, and the political dilemma for the government was how to maintain a viable coalition of support throughout the adjustment process: "At any point in the reform process, some coalition members stand to lose or gain more than others. The crucial challenge for the political leadership is to avoid injuring the interests of all coalition members simultaneously."[44] To meet this challenge, the government would manage the reform process by manipulating the speed, timing, and sequencing of reform. As it hurt some social

41. Peter Evans, Dietrich Rueschemeyer, and Theda Skocpol, *Bringing the State Back In* (Cambridge, UK: Cambridge University Press, 1985).
42. Nora Hamilton, *The Limits of State Autonomy: Post-Revolutionary Mexico* (Princeton, NJ: Princeton University Press, 1982); and Ellen Trimberger, *Revolution from Above: Military Bureaucrats in Japan, Turkey, Egypt and Peru* (New Brunswick, NJ: Transaction Books, 1978).
43. Stephan Haggard, *Pathways from the Periphery: The Politics of Growth in the Newly Industrializing Countries* (Princeton, NJ: Princeton University Press, 1990); Robert Wade, *Governing the Market: Economic Theory and the Role of Government in East Asian Industrialization* (Princeton, NJ: Princeton University Press, 1991); Alice Amsden, *Asia's Next Giant: South Korea and Late Industrialization* (New York: Oxford University Press, 1989).
44. John Waterbury, "The Political Management of Economic Adjustment," p. 39.

groups, a government would need to appeal to other constituencies to maintain support and remain in power. Partial compensation was the most obvious tactic it could use for this purpose. A government could pair the removal of an expensive consumer subsidy, for example, with the creation of a cheaper and better targeted antipoverty program. It might usher in a devaluation with salary increases to civil servants. In this context, scholars provided a strong rationale for IFI support of economic reform programs, by contending that international finance was useful to leaders committed to reform by supplying them with discretionary resources during the adjustment process with which to pay off opponents of reform and maintain support from critical constituencies. Such a logic brought an additional justification for the World Bank's decision to increasingly accompany structural adjustment loans with "social dimensions of adjustment" (SDA) programs, smaller loans to finance various government welfare and antipoverty programs that seek to cushion the hardships of adjustment.[45]

In addition to compensatory payments, state elites could use a number of other strategies to defuse opposition and maintain support. Governments could utilize the traditional strategies of intimidation and repression on the one hand, and/or persuasion and explanation on the other. Repressing dissent could provide decision makers with short-term freedom of action. For the longer term, governments could undertake public education campaigns to persuade the population of the necessity of reform. Governments could also resort to obfuscation, indirection, and ambiguity to confuse and detract opposition. A good example of obfuscation often mentioned in the literature comes from countries such as Sudan and Egypt where the government chose to reduce the standard size of a loaf of subsidized bread rather than raise its price. A number of interesting African case studies chronicled efforts by states to politically manage the reform process and achieve at least partial reform.[46]

45. This political dimension of the SDA remains mostly unacknowledged by the World Bank, which justifies these measures strictly for their welfare impact on populations affected by adjustment policies. See Peter Gibbon, "The World Bank and African Poverty, 1970–91," *The Journal of Modern African Studies* 30 (1992): 193–220.
46. Jeffrey Herbst, *The Politics of Reform in Ghana, 1982–1991* (Berkeley: University of California Press, 1992); Thomas M. Callaghy, "Lost between State and Market: The Politics of Economic Adjustment in Ghana, Zambia and Nigeria," in Joan Nelson (ed.), *Economic Crisis and Policy Choice*, (Princeton, NJ: Princeton University Press, 1990); Samba Ka and Nicolas van de Walle, "The Political Economy of Structural Adjustment in Senegal, 1980–1991," in Stephan Haggard and Steven B. Webb (eds.), *Voting for Reform: Economic Adjustment in New*

Similarly, this approach led to a renewed interest in the political implications of the design of reform programs. Government elites could after
all manipulate the speed, timing, and sequencing of reform to suit their
political needs: attention now focused on the relative merits of rapid,
radical reform versus slow, incremental reform; of beginning with the
easy reforms versus the difficult ones; of undertaking difficult reforms
before an election versus after one; of phasing the reforms or bundling
them. This literature has so far proven unable to generate viable gener-
alizations or cookbook formulas. First, of course, empirical tests of the
success of these different strategies are difficult because the economic
circumstances in which the program is designed and implemented vary
significantly across cases, and the *counterfactual* – or what would have
happened if governments had tried alternative approaches – is difficult
to establish. In addition, the political justification for a specific strategy
often works at cross purposes with its desirability from an economic
point of view. For example, many economists favor rapid and radical
reform measures, with the argument that only a shock approach can
change the expectations and behavior of economic agents; on the other
hand, most political scientists agree that state leaders prefer incremental
and gradual changes, in which obfuscation and compensation are easier
to achieve, and which allow leaders to adjust implementation progressively as a function of the popular response.[47]

Scholars focusing on the state and economic reform have increasingly
sought to identify the conditions under which state elites are able to
assert their preferences during the reform process. At the heart of the
"state centric" approach to economic reform has been the issue of state
autonomy, defined as the ability of state agents to act according to their
own institutional interests, particularly when these are opposed by nonstate actors. Most observers agree that state autonomy is the sine qua
non of economic reform. What the literature continues to disagree about
is the exact role of state autonomy to the success of reform. For some,
successful reformist governments are those most adept at coalition

Democracies (New York: Oxford University Press, 1994), pp. 290–359; West,
"The Politics of Implementation of Structural Adjustment in Zambia"; and Peter
Lewis, *The Political Economy of Public Enterprise in Nigeria* (Ph.D. dissertation,
Princeton University, 1992).

47. Henry S. Bienen and Mark Gersovitz, "Economic Stabilization, Conditionality
and Political Stability," *International Organization* 39 (1985): 729–54; see pp.
745–7; and Shang-Jin Wei, "Gradualism versus Big Bang: Speed and Sustainability of Reforms," in Federico Sturzenegger and Mariano Tommasi (eds.), *The
Political Economy of Reform* (Cambridge, MA: MIT Press, 1998).

management:[48] skills, strategic foresight, and discretionary resources provide reformist governments with the short-term maneuverability that allows them to undertake unpopular policy changes, even though states have limited long-term autonomy from social forces.

Abstracting from issues of autonomy, this literature often emphasizes the central role played by the technocrat, an apolitical state agent who favors policy reform. Adjustment success relies on the empowerment of effective technocrats, as part of change teams, and their insulation from popular pressures. Waterbury defines a change team as

technocrats with few or no links to the political arena, although their prominence in the realm of macrostrategy may lead to such links. But in their capacity as the brain trust of the political leadership they will be politically isolated and utterly dependent on the head of state. Conversely, for the team to move an agenda will require the visible and consistent support of the head of state.[49]

These analyses spend little time determining the institutional requirements of long-term autonomy, although their arguments do not necessarily deny its possibility. Instead, the change team has been empowered by the political leadership, in an ad hoc manner.

More recently, scholars have focused on two issues to explain successful efforts at policy change. One strain of the literature has emphasized the institutional circumstances that promote state autonomy, by focusing on characteristics of the state itself. Here the critical variable is the degree to which the state apparatus has built up over time traditions of independence, autonomy, and the insulation of technocrats from popular pressures. Scholars have linked successful economic stabilization to the constitutionally based independence of the central bank,[50] traditions of professionalism, and esprit de corps within the civil service.[51] In

48. Waterbury, "The Political Management of Economic Adjustment."
49. John Waterbury, "The Heart of the Matter? Public Enterprise and the Adjustment Process," in Haggard and Kaufman, *The Politics of Economic Adjustment*, pp. 182–210, p. 191.
50. Alex Cukierman et al., "Measuring the Independence of Central Banks and Its Effects on Policy Outcomes," *The World Bank Economic Review* 4 (1992): 353–98; Sylvia Maxfield, *Gatekeepers of Growth: The International Political Economy of Central Banking in Developing Countries* (Princeton, NJ: Princeton University Press, 1997).
51. On Brazil, see Barbara Geddes, "Building State Autonomy in Brazil," *Comparative Politics* 22 (1990): 217–42; on Taiwan, see Robert Wade, *Governing the Market: Economic Theory and the Role of Government in East Asian Industrialization* (Princeton, NJ: Princeton University Press, 1990). On Korea, see Soo Chan Jang, *Driving Engine or Rent-Seeking Super-Cartel? The Business-State Nexus and Economic Transformation in South Korea, 1960–1999* (unpublished Ph.D. dissertation, Michigan State University, 1999).

a theoretical generalization of these arguments, Paul Collier has argued that good economic policies that promote macrostability and economic growth require "agencies of restraint," institutions that increase the resolve of governments to avoid following the sirens of populism.[52]

Note that the emphasis on state autonomy and on the insulation of technocrats leads this literature to a degree of ambivalence regarding the Third Wave of democratization, which swept through Latin America in the 1980s and Eastern Europe and Africa in the 1990s. Most academic specialists of the political economy of reform viewed the political transition as complicating the economic transition. For observers of the left, the neoliberal policy package of adjustment was profoundly antidemocratic, and could only be implemented by authoritarian governments, which repressed political participation.[53] For other observers, democracy was compatible with stabilization and long-term development only if it allowed for extensive delegation of policy making to insulated technocrats who would remain impervious to popular demands.[54] Even if few observers were willing to pose an explicit "cruel choice" between democracy and economic growth, most did believe that this kind of delegation was less likely in Africa following the wave of democratization in the early 1990s, which therefore complicated rather than facilitated economic reform.[55]

In a second strain of the literature, scholars have focused on the productive partnerships between reformist states and proreform societal

52. Paul Collier, "Africa's External; Economic Relations, 1960–1990," in Douglas Rimmer (ed.), *Africa, 30 Years On: The Record and Outlook after Thirty Years of Independence* (London: James Curry, 1991), pp. 155–68; and "Learning from Failure: The International Financial Agencies as Agencies of Restraint in Africa," in Andreas Schedler, Larry Diamond, and Marc F. Plattner (eds.), *The Self-Restraining State: Power and Accountability in New Democracies* (Boulder, CO: Lynne Rienner, 1998), pp. 313–32.

53. See Claude Ake, *Democracy and Development in Africa* (Washington, DC: The Brookings Institution, 1996); and Peter Gibbon, Yusuf Bangura, and Arve Ofstad (eds.), *Authoritarianism and Democracy and Adjustment* (Uddevalla, Sweden: Nordiska Afrikainstitutet, 1992).

54. See, for example, Tom Callaghy, "Political Passions and Economic Interests: Economic Reform and Political Structure in Africa," in Thomas Callaghy, Thomas Ravenhill, and John Ravenhill (eds.), *Hemmed In: Responses to Africa's Economic Decline* (New York: Columbia University Press, 1993), pp. 463–519.

55. See Henry Bienen and Jeffrey Herbst. "The Relationship between Political and Economic Reform in Africa," *Comparative Politics* 29 (1996): 23–42; and the more general treatment by various contributors in Larry Diamond and Marc F. Plattner (eds.), *Economic Reform and Democracy* (Baltimore: Johns Hopkins University Press, 1995).

allies that can allow developmental policies to move forward. Starting with the initial insight that states need to be sustained by viable social coalitions, a number of case studies show that successful governments are likely to be the ones that nurture close and reciprocal relations with specific groups that favor the right kinds of policies. The original interest group literature seemed to imply that all organized societal groups oppose progrowth policies, but this is far from the case, as a number of recent studies demonstrate. Skalnes argues that commercial farmer groups are proreform in Zimbabwe, for instance, while Schamis has suggested that states in Latin America have forged alliances with business groups that benefit from economic liberalization.[56] In a broader context not focusing specifically on reform, Evans has asserted that the close government-business relations that have existed in East Asia result in states having what he calls "embedded autonomy" – in other words, states that are endowed with a felicitous mixture of the autonomy to promote long-term growth with high levels of accountability to society.[57] Weiss makes a very similar argument, although she prefers to call such arrangements "governed-interdependence,"[58] while Stark and Bruzst make an analogous argument about the cases of successful reform in Eastern Europe.[59]

The Limits of Reform Mongering

Much of this research is helpful to understand Africa's inability to undertake economic reform over the last two decades. Its emphasis on the potential power of voluntaristic state agents is a useful antidote to static interest groups analyses. Nonetheless, several of its underlying assumptions can be questioned. In particular, the relationship between state and society in Africa needs to be examined to better understand the nature and degree of state autonomy in the region.

On State Commitment to Reform. The reform mongering literature often takes government commitment to reform for granted. Decision

56. Skalnes, *The Politics of Economic Reform in Zimbabwe*; Hector Schamis, "Distributional Coalitions and the Politics of Economic Reform in Latin America," *World Politics* 51 (1999): 236–68.
57. Peter B. Evans, *Embedded Autonomy: States and Industrial Transformation* (Princeton, NJ: Princeton University Press, 1995).
58. Linda Weiss, *The Myth of the Powerless State* (Ithaca, NY: Cornell University Press, 1998).
59. David Stark and Laszlo Bruszt, *Postsocialist Pathways* (New York: Cambridge University Press, 1998).

makers, particularly technocrats, are typically viewed as committed to reform, even when societal opposition prevents its implementation. A lack of progress on the program is argued to result from the successful opposition of societal forces on a poorly insulated government. In some cases, this is the correct assessment. But all too often, African governments have undertaken reform programs to which they were not committed in order to please external creditors, with little intention of carrying them out. Or, they have failed to undertake reform despite the absence of popular opposition.

Much of the public policy literature labors under the presumption that top decision makers are or at least should be public welfare maximizers and thus be insensitive to political pressures or sectional interests. Donors' repeated search for technocrats represents the understandable yearning to find this decision maker of textbook lore. To be sure, the time horizon and selflessness of decision makers vary, but few successful decision makers will not be attuned to political calculus. There are technocrats who appear to understand the virtues of reform and play a critical role in policy reform. But even they turn out to be easier to identify after the fact: the technocratic credentials of officials who spearheaded a reform effort are often noted in retrospect. But many ministers of finance have failed to advance policy reform despite impeccable credentials. Moreover, identifying the role played by reformist technocrats only begs the question of why they emerge in some countries but not in others, or why they emerge more often in Latin America or Eastern Europe than in Africa. Either technocrats come with their own power base and are thus not readily distinguishable from other politicians, or they are promoted by a political patron, which brings us back to the original question: what explains the patron's commitment to reform?

Of course, it is difficult to distinguish governments that want reform but are not able to carry it out because of low state capability and/or societal pressure from governments that do not want to undertake reform and so do not, particularly when the latter find it useful to blame their inaction on these same factors. The analytical difficulty is heightened when commitment to reform varies within the government, as well as across reform sectors, when it waxes and wanes over time, or when economic performance does not correlate well with the degree of implementation of reforms. Good weather or positive exogenous shocks to the economy can reward undeserving governments, while other governments can faithfully implement reform programs without an improvement in macroeconomic indicators because of inclement weather, for example, or a costly natural calamity. Still, a more sophisticated understanding of policy commitment is necessary if we are to be able to distinguish the absence of commitment from a lack of capabilities.

The usual starting place of an analysis of commitment is the rational choice argument that political leaders want to remain in power and choose policies they believe will maximize their chances of doing so. Political elites will be willing to upset the status quo and face the uncertainty of economic policy change only when their perception of relative risks is unambiguously weighed in favor of economic reform. Thus, the literature argues that reform is more likely in periods of great economic crisis.[60]

Crisis Politics. It is postulated that government leaders will favor reform when they come to believe that maintaining the status quo spells certain doom. There has to be a perception that the present economic policies are almost certainly not politically sustainable. This thesis would help to explain the tendency of governments to delay too long before beginning the reform process. They persist with monetary policies that self-evidently generate inflation until hyperinflation sets in, or they continue deficit-creating fiscal policies and international borrowing until creditors will not lend additional finance and they face a debt default. An earlier effort would have been less arduous, but until the economic crisis is overwhelming and evidently threatening to political stability, governments prefer the certainties of the status quo. Grindle and Thomas thus suggest that the perception of the existence of a major crisis brings popular acceptance that major reform is necessary and thus legitimates the government's reform efforts.[61]

This study accepts the premise that political leaders are rational and wish to remain in power. It seems difficult to deny that, insofar as they have some discretion in the matter, ceteris paribus, leaders generally choose economic policies they believe are not inimical to their self-interests. Nonetheless, by itself such a premise does not provide very much analytical leverage toward explaining the diversity of policy outcomes to which we see leaders appearing to commit.

60. This thesis is best explored in Merilee S. Grindle and John W. Thomas, *Public Choices and Policy Change: The Political Economy of Reform in Developing Countries* (Baltimore: Johns Hopkins University Press, 1991).
61. Ibid.

In fact, studies have not found a statistical correlation between the success of adjustment and the extent of the macroeconomic imbalance at the program's onset.[62] The perception of a severe crisis clearly motivated political elites in Ghana to favor reform after 1983, for example. That year, per capita GDP was declining by 7.1 percent annually, inflation was running at over 120 percent, there was a severe drought, and Nigeria was in the process of expelling a million Ghanaians back into the country. But there are plenty of counterexamples: African states as varied as Congo/Zaire, Sierra Leone, or Tanzania have experienced economic crises just as dramatic without generating the reformist resolve Rawlings and his associates exhibited in Ghana. Outside of Africa, there are plenty of cases in which rapid economic policy shifts were achieved despite the absence of economic crisis. Typically, economic reform was motivated in part by growing dissatisfaction with sluggish economic growth rather than by fear of an unsustainable macrodisequilibrium.

Several factors seem to account for the lack of correlation between crisis and reform. First, policy elites are constrained by previous policies and the social and political commitments they imply. They may feel compelled by previous engagements to stick to old policies, or they may have devoted so much political capital to old policies that their political survival is tied to those policies. In other words, policy preferences are sticky and cannot be changed at will. This helps explain why new governments are more likely to achieve significant discontinuities in economic policy orientation. They are less bound by prior commitments to specific constituencies, both within the state bureaucracy and within society. Governments that are tied to prior policies may maintain them regardless of the risks involved because they have little real choice.

Second, policy elites operate in a world of uncertainty, in which maximizing their self-interest may not be straightforward or unambiguous. The political implications of specific policy reforms may not be obvious to policy elites. Such a climate of uncertainty makes sudden change less likely: the greater the uncertainty, the more leaders are likely to want to engage in incrementalism and satisficing strategies.[63] Yet, in times of crisis, bold new initiatives and drastic policy changes may be necessary,

62. Vittorio Corbo and Patricio Rojas, "World Bank-Supported Adjustment Programs: Country Performance and Effectiveness," in Vittorio Corbo, Stanley Fischer, and Steven B. Webb (eds.), *Adjustment Lending Revisited: Policies to Restore Growth* (Washington, DC: World Bank, 1992).
63. The reference is of course to the classic work by James March and Herbert Simon, *Organizations* (New York: Wiley, 1958).

both to tackle what are severe imbalances and to alter the expectations of economic agents who require credible signals that the government will sustain the needed policy changes before they will modify their own behavior.[64] Such an argument suggests that, ironically, a sense of crisis induces behavior in policy makers that is exactly the opposite of what the economy requires. In sum, even if the likelihood of elite commitment to reform increases with the size of the economic disequilibrium, the complexities and difficulties of achieving reform also increase proportionately with the size of the economic crisis.

Finally, it may simply be wrong to equate economic crisis with a political crisis. When and why do political elites believe there is a crisis? The size of the economic imbalance may not matter all that much, insofar as economic crises or severe macroeconomic disequilibrium do not necessarily lead to regime instability. In Western parliamentary regimes, governments are held closely accountable for shifts in economic performance, so that slight increases in inflation or unemployment translate quickly into voter disaffection,[65] but there is every reason to believe that this kind of political sensitivity to economic performance is unique to mature participatory democracies. In Africa, the evidence suggests that elites may accommodate themselves well, not only to the vagaries of the business cycle, but even to unmitigated economic disaster. Leaders who are not politically threatened by economic failure may not feel any need to upset the status quo. This is most strikingly apparent in African states like Congo/Zaire, where total economic disaster throughout the 1980s did not seem to undermine the power and privilege of the state elite. Below, I describe the particular situation many African countries found themselves in in the 1990s – a *permanent crisis*, in which a disastrous situation was at the same time remarkably stable, and from which some elites clearly derived benefit. The approach that posits crisis as the main instigator of reform clearly does not fit the African situation well.

On the Autonomy of the African State. Finally, I argue that the literature on economic policy reform has misunderstood the nature of state

---

64. On the role of signaling in periods of economic reform, see Dani Rodrik, "Promises, Promises: Credible Policy Reform via Signalling," in *The Economic Journal* 99 (1989): 756–72; and Paul Collier, "The Failure of Conditionality," in Catherine Gwin and Joan M. Nelson (eds.), *Perspectives on Aid and Development*, Overseas Development Council Policy Essay Number 22. (Baltimore: Johns Hopkins University Press for the ODC, 1997), pp. 51–78, especially, pp. 70–3.
65. See, for instance, Michael S. Lewis-Beck, *Economics and Elections: The Major Western Democracies* (Ann Arbor: University of Michigan Press, 1988).

autonomy in Africa. First, as Evans and others have pointed out, it tends to conflate state autonomy with state capacity.[66] Either the two concepts have been used synonymously and interchangeably, or state capacity has been viewed as a critical component of autonomy during the reform stage. Thus, surveying six adjustment success stories, Nelson identifies a strong executive as the common feature they all shared.[67] These executives were strong either because they were popular – often because they had recently ousted an unpopular leader or won an electoral mandate – or because they benefited from traditions of executive autonomy and established state institutions. Haggard and Kaufman similarly conclude that "the insulation of central decision makers from distributive claims will enhance the state's capacity to launch new (reform) initiatives."[68] These scholars find a correlation between successful reform and the presence of proreform technocrats within the state who are able to get things done. Reform was more likely when top state leaders were able to insulate these "change teams" from day-to-day partisan politics so they could plan and carry out reform.

Clearly, both autonomy and capacity are necessary for successful reform. Autonomy from societal interests opposed to reform is needed for committed decision makers to conceive of and design reform programs. Capacity is then necessary to carry them out and sustain them. Problematically, however, most observers either fail to distinguish autonomy from capacity, or assume that these two state characteristics are highly correlated. Is this assumption warranted? In the developmental states of East Asia, autonomy does in fact appear to go in pair with strength and capacity. There seems to be a synergy between the two: state elites in countries like Korea or Taiwan have used their high degree of insulation from societal pressures to advance economic policies that rely on the state's extractive, planning, and regulatory capacities.[69] The remarkable fact about these states is not only their ability to plan and

---

66. Peter B. Evans, *Embedded Autonomy: States and Industrial Transformation*, especially Chapter 1. See also Michael Bratton, "Peasant-State Relations in Post-Colonial Africa: Patterns of Engagement and Disengagement," in Joel Migdal et al., *State Power and Social Forces* (New York: Cambridge University Press, 1994), pp. 231–54.
67. Nelson, "Conclusions," pp. 328–9, in *Economic Crisis and Policy Choice*.
68. Haggard and Kaufman, "Introduction," In Haggard and Kaufman, *The Politics of Economic Adjustment*, p. 23.
69. See, for example, Wade, *Governing the Market*; and Alice Amsden, *Asia's Next Giant: South Korea and Late Industrialization* (New York: Oxford University Press, 1989).

design long-term development strategies involving complex forms of state intervention, but also their ability then to implement these strategies with skill and discipline, over long periods of time and despite significant distributional consequences. In comparison to the NICs of East Asia, Latin American states or Southeast Asian states such as the Philippines are often portrayed as lacking both capabilities and autonomy.[70] A tradition of popular political participation and populism results in inadequate insulation of policy makers, while the state apparatus is weakened by cronyism and a lack of professionalism. The direct result is argued to be economic policies that unduly favor consumption over investment and of imports over exports.

African states fit into neither of these patterns. First, few would contest that the African state has limited capacities. They are "weak states" in Migdal's sense of structures that are rarely able to project power and achieve stated goals.[71] In succeeding chapters, striking evidence of this lack of capacity will be provided, and I will show that low state capacity is an important obstacle to economic renewal. But does the African state lack autonomy? Certainly, African regimes are remarkably durable, despite economic stagnation and their many manifest weaknesses. It is important not to confuse the durability of individual governments and their leaders with the capacity to govern effectively, but such durability does belie the notion of states constantly threatened with being run over by societal interests. A striking paradox in Africa has been the durability of so many of its regimes with disastrous economic records. Since independence, African leaders have remained in power on average almost twice as long as leaders from Asia or Latin America.[72] During the 1980s, Africa was marked by political instability and several regimes did fall, with coups in Burkina Faso (1980, 1983, and 1987), Burundi (1987), Nigeria (1983, 1986), and Sudan (1984). But in each of these cases, instability was not triggered specifically by government attempts to implement policy reform. Although economic

70. On the Philippines, see Paul Hutchcroft, *Booty Capitalism: The Politics of Banking in the Philippines* (Ithaca, NY: Cornell University Press, 1998); Barbara Geddes similarly discusses these issues in relation to Brazil in her book, *Politician's Dilemma* (Berkeley: University of California Press, 1994).
71. Joel Migdal, *Strong Societies and Weak States: State-Society Relations and State Capabilities in the Third World* (Princeton, NJ: Princeton University Press, 1988).
72. See Henry S. Bienen and Nicolas van de Walle, *Of Time and Power: Leadership Duration in the Modern World* (Palo Alto, CA: Stanford University Press, 1991), pp. 55–6.

conditions probably played a role in sealing the fate of these regimes, the economic crisis was no worse in these countries than in others whose governments were not threatened. Indeed, all four of these regimes had actually enjoyed growth rates above the regional average in the five years before the change of ruler. Typically, noneconomic factors such as personal ambitions, rivalries within the military, and ethnic conflict were more important in destabilizing regimes. Much the same could be said of the wave of democratization that unseated a number of incumbents in the early 1990s: economic performance of the regime simply did not explain its ability to survive in office.[73]

This durability has to be understood in historical terms. One of the legacies of colonial rule was a poorly developed civil society. The typically "hard" colonial state only rarely tolerated expressions of an independent civil society, and then only if it included a significant white settler component.[74] Postindependence governments in most states repressed or coopted most of the little formal associational life that had emerged, although, of course, the strategies, methods, and levels of tolerance exhibited by governments varied quite a bit. Within a decade of independence, most African governments had made sure they did not have to worry about parliaments, opposition parties, a free press, or independent interest groups.[75] As a result, formal political nonstate actors have been very weak in Africa, compared to their influence in other regions of the world. The state's weak capacities prevented it from achieving the kinds of corporatist control over civic associations that other authoritarian states in the Third World were able to achieve, and in many African states an extremely rich and varied parallel associational life developed over time, but African states were able to compel the "departicipation" of the nonstate actors that might have threatened the states' dominance.[76] As a result, the state's weakness in Africa is paralleled by the weakness of civic associations and interest groups. In Bratton's elegant phrase, "In Africa, the state projects upwards from its

73. This is demonstrated through a regression analysis in Bratton and van de Walle, *Democratic Experiments in Africa.*
74. A perceptive account is provided in Crawford Young, *The African Colonial State in Comparative Perspective* (New Haven, CT: Yale University Press, 1994).
75. For an analysis of cross-national differences in this process, see the analysis in Ruth Collier, *Regimes in Tropical Africa* (Berkeley: University of California Press, 1982).
76. The term comes from Nelson Kasfir, *The Shrinking Political Arena* (Berkeley: University of California Press, 1976).

surroundings like a veritable Kilimanjaro, in large part because the open plains of domestic society appear to be thinly populated with alternative institutions. . . . In this lilliputian environment, even a weak state can seem to be strong."[77]

In this sense, Migdal's juxtaposition of "weak states, strong societies" is somewhat deceptive. I agree with his analysis of the ability of subnational identities, informal networks, and parallel markets to subvert state authority in Africa. However, *civil society*, in the Western sense of formal organizations occupying a nonstate public arena, is nonetheless weak as a result of the factors just described. Autonomy in the African context must mean something very different from what it does in, say, Latin America, not to mention in western Europe, where state autonomy is typically defined in relation to organized interest groups representing large numbers of individuals. As I have already argued, in most African states, there are virtually no organized interest groups wielding significant influence on policy. Perhaps, it might be suggested, key social constituencies do not need to be well organized within trade unions to be able to effect policy outcomes. Civil servants, for example, may lack organization, but because they are concentrated in the capital in relatively large numbers and because they are well informed, they may be easily mobilized without organization. Governments in turn fear them because of their ability to shut down government services if they choose. Other than civil servants, however, it is difficult to think of a constituency in Africa that is capable of exerting similar social power in the absence of organization. Even for civil servants, the principle remains that their ability to exert social power is closely linked to their degree of independent organization, which, typically, is found wanting.

The African technocrats who have prepared economic reform programs with the experts of the World Bank and the IMF can be argued to be insulated in the sense discussed above. Typically located inside the presidency or the finance ministry, they report only to the executive and his closest associates. They are accountable to no one else. Not only do they not have to handle public, opposition party, or media demands, in most countries they are not accountable to a parliament, to the single party rank-and-file, or even in some cases to the full government cabinet. In Cameroon, for instance, the cabinet has rarely met in recent years, and then only for ceremonial reasons. In Tanzania, Kiondo reports that

---

77. Michael Bratton, "Beyond the State: Civil Society and Associational Life in Africa," *World Politics* 41 (1989): 407–30, especially pp. 410–11.

the prime minister refused to even answer parliamentary questions about negotiations with the IMF during 1986, arguing that the decision of whether to reach an agreement with that organization was strictly an executive prerogative.[78] This insulation does not apply just to decision making during periods of economic crisis, but is typical of all economic decision making, which is circumscribed to a very small number of officials around the president. In Cameroon, in the 1980s, officials in the ministry of agriculture learned about the government's seasonal fixed prices for cash crops such as coffee and cocoa on the radio, just like the peasants themselves.[79]

The experience in Africa thus suggests that state autonomy does not necessarily imply capacity or strength. Autonomous states are not necessarily strong ones, even if strong states are usually autonomous. State structures can formulate policies and preferences autonomously, without necessarily being able to implement them, given low levels of state capacity. Arguably, it is easier for state agents to enhance their autonomy than their capabilities. The former can be done fairly quickly through repression, intimidation, and payoffs, while the former requires self-discipline, foresight, and the time to build up bureaucratic traditions. States can increase their level of insulation artificially, by repressing the expression of societal interests or by relying on external sources to finance their activities. As I shall argue in coming chapters, most African states have done both. Throughout this book, I investigate more deeply the relationship between state capacity, autonomy, and economic policy making during reform episodes.

TOWARD AN ALTERNATIVE APPROACH TO THE AFRICAN CRISIS

In discounting the effect of societal obstacles to policy reform in Africa, I do not want to throw out the baby with the proverbial bathwater. Although less than their counterparts in other regions, African governments do worry about public opinion, and when thinking about which reforms to implement, they may be more hesitant, at the margin, to

78. Andrew Kiondo, "The Nature of Economic Reforms in Tanzania," in Horace Campbell and Howard Stein (eds.), *Tanzania and the IMF: The Dynamics of Liberalization* (Boulder, CO: Westview Press, 1992), pp. 21–42, especially p. 35.
79. This was related to me by an official in the Ministry of Agriculture during interviews in Yaounde in 1987.

undertake measures that will hurt the purchasing power of constituencies that are organized. Furthermore, African governments also have feared the spontaneous eruptions of groups whose purchasing power may be immediately hurt by very specific policies – the removal of a subsidy or a sharp price rise – particularly when those groups are based in the capital. Relatively weak, low capacity, and unpopular governments fear all challenges to their authority. I do argue, however, that the specific pattern of uneven reform implementation that will be described in Chapter 2 cannot be explained by the interest group model or by its revised version, the reform mongering model.

The central argument of this book is that the patterns of reform and nonreform in Africa during the last twenty years can be explained with reference to the nature of political institutions there, first, and second, their interaction with the international community. Given the relative autonomy of African states vis-à-vis societal forces, the real constraints on policy are to be found within the state itself. Three kinds of factors are emphasized in particular: clientelism, low state capacity, and the ideological preferences of decision makers. These three domestic factors reinforce each other and have conditioned changes to the policy status quo. They are largely responsible for the initial resistance to any kind of reform at the outset of the crisis, and then the mixture of partial reform and manipulated reform that we have observed in the 1990s.

Second, I argue that the aid relationship between the Western donors and most African regimes have exacerbated these domestic obstacles to reform. Neopatrimonial rulers could not have resisted the pressure of international markets for two decades had they not had the assistance of the international community; large amounts of aid to the state, coupled with imperfect conditionality of reform program lending have allowed African governments to get away with partial reform. Similarly, aid has unwittingly undermined capacity for institution building. In sum, the peculiar evolution of the African political economy over the last twenty years has to be understood as the fruit of the marriage of neopatrimonialism and the international development business.

The Exigencies of Neopatrimonialism

During the last twenty years, a distinctive body of academic literature has emerged to analyze African politics and political economy, which

places clientelism at their core.[80] Although not always very precise ana-
lytically and occasionally obtuse about economic matters, the debates in
this literature regarding state-society relations and about the nature of
political authority are useful to further understanding the themes raised
above, notably about state autonomy, and the prospects for governments
in the region to engineer a renewal of economic growth.

My starting point is the argument that political authority in Africa
is based on the giving and granting of favors, in an endless series of
dyadic exchanges that go from the village level to the highest reaches
of the central state. Under this general rubric of clientelism can be placed
a wide variety of practices involving the giving and receiving of favors,
almost invariably based on corruption. Clientelism can be associated
with corruption simply because the former relies on privileged access
to public resources and some kind of conflict of interest. Although
different terminologies have been adopted to characterize political
systems in which clientelism is endemic, the most broadly accepted and
perhaps most useful from a comparative perspective is the Weberian
influenced notion of neopatrimonialism.[81] The term captures the thesis
that most African states are hybrid regimes, in which patrimonial practices coexist with modern bureaucracy. Outwardly the state has all the
trappings of a Weberian rational-legal system, with a clear distinction
between the public and the private realm, with written laws and a constitutional order. However, this official order is constantly subverted by

80. A short list of vital works in this broad tradition as applied to Africa would
include Jean François Bayart, *l'Etat en Afrique* (Paris: Fayard, 1989); Catherine
Boone, *Merchant Capital and the Roots of State Power in Senegal, 1930–1985*
(Cambridge, UK: Cambridge University Press, 1992); Robert Fatton, *Predatory
Rule: State and Civil Society in Africa* (Boulder, CO: Lynne Rienner Press, 1992);
Thomas Callaghy, *The State-Society Struggle: Zaire in Comparative Perspective*
(New York: Columbia University Press, 1984); Patrick Chabal and Jean-Pascal
Daloz, *Africa Works: Disorder as Political Instrument* (Bloomington: Indiana
University Press, 1999); Richard Joseph, *Democracy and Prebendal Politics in
Nigeria: The Rise and Fall of the Second Republic* (Cambridge, UK and New
York: Cambridge University Press, 1987); William Reno, *Corruption and State
Politics in Sierra Leone*; and Richard Sandbrook, *The Politics of Africa's Eco-
nomic Stagnation* (Cambridge, UK: Cambridge University Press, 1985). A review
of this literature and an analysis of the key characteristics of neopatrimonialism
is presented in Chapter 2 of Bratton and van de Walle, *Democratic Experiments*.
81. See Jean François Médard, "The Underdeveloped State in Tropical Africa: Political Clientelism or Neo-Patrimonialism," in Christopher Clapham (ed.), *Private
Patronage and Public Power* (London: Frances Pinter, 1982), pp. 162–92. For
Max Weber's theory of political authority, see *Economy and Society* (New York:
Bedminster Press, 1968).

a patrimonial logic, in which officeholders almost systematically appropriate public resources for their own uses and political authority is largely based on clientelist practices, including patronage, various forms of rent-seeking, and prebendalism. These regimes are highly *presidential*, in the sense that power is centralized around a single individual, with ultimate control over most clientelist networks. The president personally exerts discretionary power over a big share of the state's resources. This is true, not only in the smallest, most backward states of the region, but also in some of the bigger, allegedly more institutionalized states, like Côte d'Ivoire or Nigeria.[82]

Neopatrimonialism is argued to undermine economic policy reform in contemporary Africa in at least two ways. First, because clientelism is based on the extensive use of state resources for political purposes, clientelist regimes almost inevitably produce highly interventionist economic policies. Economic liberalization is viewed as anathema to regimes that rely on the politically mediated distribution of access to state resources. Clientelism is viewed as critical in countries with little sense of nationhood and a tendency toward multiple ethnic and regional divisions, and in which few regimes can count on either a successful economy or electoral mandates for their legitimacy. As Sandbrook has asked, "What will hold these societies together when the rulers have little in the way of patronage to distribute?"[83]

Second, it is argued that neopatrimonialism results in a systematic fiscal crisis. As Callaghy has argued about the Zaire of Mobutu, "finances is the Achilles heel" of these regimes.[84] At the outset of the African crisis, the World Bank and the IMF typically accused African states of being "too big," but that is not really the case: relative to the economies they govern, African states are roughly comparable in size to the states in other middle- and low-income regions.[85] True, patronage needs swelled the ranks of the civil service at a remarkable speed following independence, but salaries were also allowed to decline precipitously in real terms, so that the cost of the civil service was not unusually high. In Tanzania, for example, salaries in the civil service were allowed

82. On the Côte d'Ivoire, see Ives A. Fauré and Jean François Médard, *Etat et bourgeoisie en Côte D'Ivoire* (Paris: Karthala, 1982). On Nigeria, see Joseph, *Democracy and Prebendal Politics*.
83. Richard Sandbrook, "The State and Economic Stagnation in Tropical Africa," in *World Development* 14 (1986): 319–32.
84. Callaghy, *The State-Society Struggle*, p. 194.
85. See, for instance, the World Bank, *The World Development Report, 1997* (New York: Oxford University Press for the World Bank, 1997).

to fall by an incredible 90 percent in real terms during the first two decades of independence, even as the size of the civil service more than tripled over the same period.[86] Instead, the real cause of the endemic fiscal crisis that has plagued most African states following independence has been on the revenue side. Despite extensive state intervention in the economy, cronyism and rent-seeking have siphoned off potential state revenues. Taxes are not collected, exemptions granted, tariffs averted, licenses bribed away, parking fines pocketed. As a result, revenues always lag behind expenditures. It is often said that these regimes have low levels of *extractive capacity*, but the problem is not one of capacity so much as it is of the political logic of a system in which the authority of the state is diverted to enhance private power rather than the public domain. In sum, theorists of clientelism viewed the onset of unmanageable fiscal and balance of payments crises as an entirely logical and predictable outcome of the manner in which politics was conducted south of the Sahara, and they were extremely skeptical about the ability of these political systems to give up these practices.

The literature has usually assumed that this pervasive clientelism reflects a fundamental absence of state autonomy. Clientelism is viewed as weakening the state by overwhelming it with particularistic demands and lessening its ability to act according to its own preferences or to carry out a developmental project in the public good. Typical are Chabal and Daloz, for whom "the state in Africa was never properly institutionalized because it was never significantly emancipated from society." As a result, "there is no discernable scope for the elaboration of a political and administrative sphere, a bureaucracy on the western model, both professionally competent and autonomous from society."[87]

It is true that African states that lack electoral legitimacy have come to rely on these relationships for continued political stability. Yet, the powerlessness of states in the face of these clientelist pressures should not be exaggerated. There are simply too many examples in which policy reform has cut off a specific clientele, with little or no overt protest or rise in instability. First, theorists of neopatrimonialism often confuse the political importance of clientelistic practices with their macroeconomic importance. The fact that these practices represent a critical political

86. Mike Stevens, "Public Expenditure and Civil Service Reform in Tanzania," in David L. Lindauer and Barbara Nunberg (eds.), *Rehabilitating Government: Pay and Employment Reforms in Africa* (Washington, DC: World Bank, 1994), pp. 62–81, especially pp. 66–9.
87. Chabal and Daloz, *Africa Works*, p. 4; p. 40.

factor in a specific country, on which hinges stability, probably does not tell you much about their macroeconomic significance in that country. Certain sectors of the economy can be protected from them. For instance, the central bank and or key economic ministries can be run with great efficiency even as social ministries are allowed to fall prey to extensive patronage. Rent-seeking can be extremely widespread but concern relatively small rents so that no single market or policy sector is completely perverted by clientelism. Thus, there is widespread corruption in Asia, but it appears to be considerably less dysfunctional for development because it does not prevent governments from undertaking key functions enabling investment and growth.

Moreover, by itself, clientelism is not necessarily evidence of the absence of autonomy. Outside of a small political elite – which Callaghy has aptly referred to as a *political aristocracy*[88] and which may not total more than a couple of hundred people in any single nation – the low-level beneficiaries of clientelism do not have much influence over policy. In this book, I argue that the obstacles to reform have always been in these elite arrangements within or very close to the state apparatus rather than in the broader version of clientelism. When push comes to shove, states have much more willingly cut back on the latter than the former. In the same way that they are willing to directly attack the purchasing power of urban populations or of the civil service, they prove willing and able to cut back on, for instance, patronage practices, or small time rent-seeking by low-level officials (e.g., trader licensing and permits). On the other hand, states have found it impossible to decrease the size of government cabinets or of the numbers of generals in the army. They have found it impossible to eliminate high-level complicity in tax evasion, diamond smuggling, drug running, bank fraud, and capital flight.[89]

In Latin America or the West, clientelism has been associated with low levels of state autonomy, and this relationship has been wrongly extended to Africa. Yet, patronage practices in the former coincide with relatively strong labor unions, professional associations, and long-standing corporatist traditions. As a result, the beneficiary of patronage has some job security, even when clientelist networks may have originally secured the position. But when it is not relayed by organizational

88. Thomas Callaghy, *The State-Society Struggle: Zaire in Comparative Perspective* (New York: Columbia University Press, 1984), pp. 184–94.
89. For evidence of such high-level corruption, in addition to the references above, see Jean François Bayart, Stephen Ellis, and Béatrice Hibou, *La criminilisation de l'etat en Afrique* (Paris: Editions Complexe, 1997).

power, as it is not usually in Africa, the client position is much weaker. While not denying the reality of ethnolinguistic or regional solidarities that cut across stratifications of power and wealth, in sum, I argue that they are not ultimately constraining to state elites. Instead, a relatively autonomous state elite, long used to exploiting public resources to paper over its own internal differences, has found it difficult to change those habits. They have also found the reform process easy to manipulate to gain new avenues for enrichment, as will be argued below.

State Capacity

The second domestic factor constraining reform is the low state capacity prevailing in the countries of the region. Almost all observers point to Africa's weak administrative capabilities and the "thinness" of the technocratic element within the state.[90] The top technocrats may be very competent and well trained, but they lead underfinanced state structures with very little data gathering, planning, and policy analysis capabilities. The woeful shortage of trained administrative personnel at independence has continued to undermine effectiveness. As a recent World Bank report on civil service reform admits, "the ineffectiveness of the civil service threatens almost all development efforts as well as basic public administration."[91] As a result of these weaknesses, some African states cannot even claim to fully control the territory over which they declare sovereignty. Tax and tariff collection is weak, laws are unevenly applied, superiors exert little authority on subordinates, and the entire administration is weakened by nondevelopmental concerns such as patronage and rent-seeking.

The literature had always treated state capacity as an independent variable – that is, that the level of state capacity was a more or less fixed, exogenous factor that helped explain the inability of governments to

90. For example, Deborah Bräutigam, "State Capacity and Effective Governance," in Benno Ndulu and Nicolas van de Walle (eds.), *Agenda for Africa's Economic Renewal* (Washington, DC: Overseas Development Council, 1996), pp. 81–108; and Merilee S. Grindle, *Challenging the State: Crisis and Innovation in Latin America and Africa* (New York: Cambridge University Press, 1997).

91. Mamadou Dia, *A Governance Approach to Civil Service Reform in Sub-Saharan Africa*, World Bank Technical Paper, 23 (1993), p. 5. See also African Governors of the World Bank, "Partnership for Capacity Building in Africa: Strategy and Program of Action," report presented to the President of the World Bank Group (Washington, DC, September 28, 1996), which actually argues that capacity has declined since independence.

undertake reform. A large literature bemoaned the low level of capacity in most African states, a problem viewed as a legacy of colonialism and Africa's status as a late developer. Terms like *capacity building* and *institution building* were used to describe the essentially technical problem of helping governments increase the level of skills and professionalism in the civil service and to improve the quality of public administration.[92]

In this study I endogenize state capacity and argue that low levels of capacity can at least in part be explained as the outcome of political dynamics within Africa during this period. At least some state actors have found low capacity quite useful if and when they themselves have not precipitated it. States have certainly underinvested in state capacity because they did not view it as a priority. Indeed, neopatrimonial practices are incompatible with the existence of a highly capable state. In turn, the low capacities of states is an important explanatory factor in the course of reform that I will describe.

Elite Beliefs

A third factor which is too often ignored in the literature to explain the course of economic reform is the ideological predilections of policy elites. Arguments about the role of economic ideas in governments' commitment to adjustment policies must be based on the premise that economic ideas can be at least partly autonomous from material interests. This is implicitly denied by much of the policy reform literature. Many analysts argue that an international consensus has in fact emerged around the IFI economic policy reform package, including among African policy elites.[93]

92. Arturo Israel, *Institutional Development: Incentives to Performance* (Baltimore: Johns Hopkins University Press, 1987). A good review of this early literature is found in Mick Moore, *Institution Building as a Development Assistance Method* (Stockholm: SIDA, 1995). This conventional, "technical" approach remains the one most commonly adopted in the aid business. See the recent collection edited by Merilee S. Grindle, *Getting Good Government: Capacity Building in the Public Sector of Developing Countries* (Cambridge, MA: Harvard Institute for International Development, 1997).

93. John Ravenhill, "Adjustment with Growth: A Fragile Consensus," *The Journal of Modern African Studies* 26 (1988): 179–210; and Thomas Biersteker. "The Triumph of Neoclassical Economics in the Developing World: Policy Convergence and Bases of Governance in the International Economic Order," in James Rosenau and Ernst-Otto Czempiel (eds.), *Governance without Government: Order and Change in World Politics* (New York: Cambridge University Press, 1992), pp. 102–31.

The unwillingness of African states to adopt structural adjustment then is interpreted to reflect their understanding of the political difficulties of implementing those reforms and not their rejection of the intellectual logic behind adjustment policies. The socialist orientation officially chosen by African regimes, their vocal attachment to planning, or their concern for equity issues are viewed, then, as anachronisms from an earlier era, which African policy elites retain largely as a posteriori and disingenuous uses of ideology for political purposes, rather than as the sincere affirmation of deeply held beliefs. It is true that egalitarian and socialist rhetoric in the mouth of a Mobutu or a Moi ring false. It is also probably true that adjustment policies may in many cases be less socially regressive than the policies they replace since few governments could in fact claim a progressive orientation to public expenditures before reform.[94]

But does that imply that economic ideas have not played an autonomous role in the rejection of adjustment policies? Very little attention has been devoted to understanding why the economic ideas embodied in policy reform programs have not found more fertile ground in Africa. Yet, if it is true that African states are more autonomous than usually believed, then the economic ideas of decision makers will matter to policy outcomes and we need to focus on them.

A policy consensus has not emerged in Africa around structural adjustment. Indeed, Chapters 3 and 4 will show that a majority of decision makers across Africa do not believe that "adjustment will work" for a variety of reasons, and that for the most part, adjustment programs have been imposed from the outside on dubious governments. African governments are highly dependent on external public finance and cannot afford to disagree too vocally with donors and their policy prescriptions. They agree to reform programs to gain access to the external cash needed for crisis management; they may actually implement parts of the reform program, but often remain unconvinced by the intellectual logic behind these programs.

This book will provide an explanation for the weakness of commitment to adjustment demonstrated by African policy elites. The attractiveness of structural adjustment policies will be assessed as a function of elite perceptions regarding their economic, administrative, and political viability. On all three criteria, key elements of the new

---

94. David E. Sahn, "Public Expenditures in Sub Saharan Africa during a Period of Economic Reform," *World Development* 20 (1992): 673–93.

adjustment orthodoxy are viewed as noncredible to policy elites in much of Africa.

The International Context

The international context has decisively shaped the evolution of the African crisis. Data in Chapter 2 will show that the onset of Africa's economic crisis was met by a massive increase in foreign aid. During the 1980s, foreign aid progressively became a visible and massive force in the African political economy. In the typical country, some thirty official donors in addition to several dozen international nongovernmental organizations (NGOs) provide several hundred million dollars in assistance a year, through over a thousand distinct projects and several hundred resident foreign experts. Other than the state itself, the aid business is today the biggest single employer in most African economies. Most graduates can thank aid resources in some way for the education they have received. Many now consider working for the aid business as more prestigious to employment in the public sector. Aid has taken over many of the state's key functions: for instance, aid accounts for somewhere between a third to one-half of all education and health expenditures in the region.[95]

Despite this obvious importance, the role of aid in the African political economy remains curiously understudied and largely ignored by the academic literature. References to the tough conditionality imposed by the international donors are legion, but the role of donor finance in shaping patterns of accumulation or individual life choices is rarely problematized and often completely ignored.[96] This book seeks to fully integrate the role of aid and donors into the analysis of African political economy.

Most observers agree that the objective of public capital flows is to reintegrate Africa into the world economy, from which it has become increasingly marginalized. For much of the policy community, donor support of structural adjustment programs will provide the necessary incentives for African governments to undertake the policy reforms needed to attract foreign investment in their economies and to increase

---

95. See my essay "Moins d'Etat, Mieux d'Etat? The Politics of State Retrenchment in West Africa," (unpublished manuscript, Michigan State University, 2000), for a discussion of this growing aid role and its implications.
96. One important recent exception is Peter Uvin, *Aiding Violence* (West Hartford: Kumarian Press, 1998).

African exports to the rest of the world.[97] Moving from an inward to an outward orientation in its economic policies is viewed as a sine qua non of renewed economic growth. Conditioned foreign aid is designed to facilitate what is recognized as a difficult policy shift. Nongovernmental organizations and left wing critics of the international financial institutions agree that Africa must be integrated into the world economy, but they oppose what they view as an attempt to secure African economies in a subaltern position relative to world capitalist forces.[98] They view integration as undermining African economies unless it is limited and carefully regulated.[99] The conditionality attached to donor support of reform programs is viewed as a coercive form of blackmail, with disastrous consequences for African society.

In sum, both sides agree that IFI structural adjustment programs are leading Africa down the path of integration into the world economy. Both sides view aid as a *change agent* in the region. In Chapter 4, I argue that on the contrary, aid resources and in particular the aid given for the purpose of structural adjustment, have served an essentially conservative function in the region, by lessening the incentives African governments have to undertake policy reform. The combination of massive aid increases and uneven or ineffective policy conditionality has ensured the sustainability of policies that otherwise would have been disciplined by market forces. In brief, aid has made policy reform less likely, not more. Similar arguments have been made in recent years by Tony Killick and Paul Collier, among others.[100] But I make a broader argument that links the overall aid relationship to the peculiar combination of political stability and state decay that we observe in the region. Aid has had a powerful effect on state institutions in Africa, simultaneously sustaining them and stripping them of decision-making power. It has undermined the development of state institutional capacity, by externalizing policy

---

97. For example, the World Bank, *Adjustment in Africa*, in particular pp. 61–98.
98. See, for instance, Paul Barratt-Brown, *Africa's Choices* (London: Penguin Books, 1996); and Ankie Hoogvelt, *Globalization and the Postcolonial World* (Baltimore: Johns Hopkins University Press, 1997).
99. Such a view is summarized in Thandike Mkandawire, "Crisis Management and the Making of 'Choiceless Democracies' in Africa," in Richard Joseph (ed.), *State, Conflict and Democracy in Africa* (Boulder, CO: Lynne Rienner Press, 1998), pp. 119–36.
100. Paul Collier, "The Failure of Conditionality," in Catherine Gwin and Joan M. Nelson (eds.), *Perspectives on Aid and Development*, Overseas Development Council Policy Essay Number 22 (Baltimore: Johns Hopkins University Press for the ODC, 1997), pp. 51–78; Tony Killick, *Aid and the Political Economy of Policy Change* (London: Routledge, 1998).

making and arresting the processes of *policy learning* among African policy elites. At the same time, aid has comforted if not reinforced the state's neopatrimonial tendencies by turning the decision-making process into a series of largely uncoordinated projects with tangible and excludable benefits controlled by state agents.

THE PARTIAL REFORM SYNDROME

These three domestic factors – clientelism, low capacity, and elite beliefs – have interacted with the international aid system to drag out the process of reform for several decades. Yet, the early literature on reform tended to view the reform process as a relatively short-term, unified, and concentrated process. Of course, it recognized that any reform process involved dozens of distinct policy changes with often quite different political implications. From the earliest, for instance, it usefully distinguished between stabilization policies, which sought to restore macroeconomic equilibrium but did not aim to alter the long-term trend growth rate, from longer term adjustment policies, which sought institutional changes to increase the economy's growth potential. Nonetheless, it was not really equipped to deal with the persistence of crisis over several decades, in which the reform impulse waxes and wanes, with temporary improvements followed by relapses and progress in some areas combined with worsening in others. Much of the intellectual apparatus of policy reform analysis was ill-designed to understand countries in which there appeared by the mid-1990s to be a permanent crisis, or in the words of one observer, a "tradition of adjustment."[101] In much of Africa, by then, the management of economic crisis had institutionalized itself with, for instance, the establishment of permanent "stabilization ministries" and almost annual and certainly routinized recourse to debt rescheduling exercises that had once been considered exceptional responses to major emergencies. What could be the meaning of terms like *crisis* or *government commitment* in countries that had been officially adjusting for two decades? Moreover, we need to ask, why did some reforms get achieved but not others? How much progress had really been achieved? Was the economic situation not improved despite

---

101. This was the semi-ironic title of a book on economic development in Burkina Faso. See Pierre Zagre, *Les politiques economiques du Burkina Faso: une tradition d'ajustement structurel* (Paris: Karthala, 1994).

the reforms achieved? Or because of them, as some critics of the IFI policy package have argued? Or because the wrong policies were implemented?

The failure to sustain reform over such a long period of time has created a series of unintended effects or of feedback loops that today condition the nature of African political economy and pose distinct problems for the renewal of growth. As will be developed in much greater length in Chapter 5, at least three of these unintended effects can be identified. Together, they make up what can be called the *partial reform syndrome*.[102]

First, a donor role in the adjustment process has come to be accepted and even institutionalized. The sustainability of the macroeconomic situation in most African states was substantially improved by the large increases in public capital flows to the region during the 1980s. The initial, emergency response of the donors to the African economic crisis in the late 1970s and early 1980s had progressively transformed itself into a stable international *regime*, with its norms, institutions, and myths. Though conditionality has been weak at best, external public funding has resulted in a growing role for the donor agencies in day-to-day decision making and the increasing marginalization of central state decision-making bodies to the benefit of ad hoc, donor-funded, parallel institutions. This intrusive donor presence continues because the non-implementation of reform, notably to restore fiscal balance, necessitates annual donor-funded bailouts.

Second and related to this last point, prolonged nonreform has resulted in a striking erosion of state capacity, which now complicates the renewal of growth. Virtually all observers agree that in most African countries, the state's ability to get things done has weakened over the last twenty years. On one level, the persistent economic crisis during this time inevitably led to resource cutbacks for public sector infrastructure, civil service salaries, and recruitment. Sustained rates of high inflation, fiscal deficits, and stagnant economic growth have clearly had a devastating effect on the state. On another level, however, the decline of state capacity cannot be blamed entirely on the economic crisis. In addition, Chapter 4 will show that declining state capacity is not merely an

102. The term was introduced by Joel Hellman, "Winners Take All: The Politics of Partial Reform in Postcommunist Transitions," *World Politics* 50 (1998): 203–34.

accidental by-product of reform failure, but that it is abetted by concrete interests that benefit from the current state decay.

Third, partial reform has produced a specific political economy, with winners and losers, which early observers of reform had not anticipated, but which may make future reform less likely. In general, I will argue that the course of reform has tended to recentralize power to presidents and their closest cronies, even as other forces threatened to move power away from them. By weakening the private sector and devastating state capacity, partial reform has also weakened the rational legal elements within these states to the benefit of neopatrimonial tendencies. In the midst of the economic devastation that is picked up by national accounts statistics, profits can be handsome and fortunes are being made. To be sure, states that undermine their own capacity are sawing off the branch on which they sit. In the region's weakest states, the descent into war-lordism during the 1990s was precipitated by the short-sighted depre-dations of neopatrimonial leaders. But in the short run at least, comforted by donor support and glum about their country's economic future, rent-seeking and other predatory behaviors appear to be viable strategies.

There are many reasons for the partial implementation of reform in Africa during these last twenty years, but the peculiar nature of policy change in the region can often be linked to the interests of state elites as they seek to adapt the course of reform in such a way that clientelist networks are maintained or allowed to be reinvented. Note that, here too, the main beneficiaries of partial reform tend to be top state elites, who are close enough to the policy process to take advantage of the illicit opportunities around the process of policy change. The classic example of this is in privatization, where low-level parastatal employees have been laid off even as their managers and patrons in the adminis-tration have engineered sweetheart deals to benefit from the divestiture. Privatization is usually delayed by factional infighting within the elite as to who will be allowed to access state assets at bottom rates and or protected markets, rather than by a fear of the reaction of parastatal employees.

Standing between their own societies and their donors, top state elites have sought to use the policy reform process to gain maximum auton-omy from both. Even as the course of partial reform is used to recen-tralize public resources and restore greater discipline to clientelist networks, it has also kept the donors at bay. Governments can always point to one area or sector in which some progress is being achieved, even as the previous progress in another area is being eroded. With little knowledge of local politics, remarkably little institutional memory, and a bias toward optimism about the course of reform, donors are easily fooled. The big losers are of course to be found among the vast majority of Africans, whose welfare continues to decline.

2

Patterns in Reform Implementation, 1979–1999

The Zambian government first committed itself to civil service retrenchment in 1979, in response to growing fiscal deficits and donor pressures.[1]
Fairly reliable government statistics from the *Monthly Digest of Statistics* indicate there were 129,600 public employees that year, in addition
to 136,220 parastatal employees. The government's stated commitment
to eliminate up to half of the civil service was praised by the World Bank
and heavily criticized by the ZCTU, the Zambian Trade Union Federa-
tion. A reform package was not put in place until 1986 and it resulted
in minor staff removals, through a lowering of the retirement age. In
May 1988, a cabinet office task force on restructuring the public service
submitted a new action plan calling for a 25 percent reduction in the
civil service. The plan was not implemented, but in August 1990 the government contracted a local consulting firm to develop another ambitious
retrenchment exercise, under the donor-financed Public Service and
Retrenchment Project. Reform efforts continued throughout the 1990s,
though to little effect. In November 1993, the government launched the
Public Service Reform Program, vowing to cut the civil service by 25
percent within three years, again with support from the donors. The
United Nations Development Program (UNDP) financed a team of
experts to oversee a plan for retrenchment, reorganization, and upgrad-

---

1. This account of civil service reform in Zambia is taken from the World Bank,
Public Expenditure Review of Zambia, Report No. 11420-ZA (Washington,
DC: World Bank, December 1, 1992); and Nicolas van de Walle and Dennis
Chiwele, "Democratization and Economic Reform in Zambia," *MSU Working
Papers on Political Reform in Africa*, no. 9, Michigan State University, 1994. I
also thank Malcolm McPherson for an immensely enlightening personal commu-
nication on these issues, but I absolve him of any responsibility for the account
given here.

ing of the civil service. Critics of the government actually blamed civil service retrenchments for the rise in unemployment.[2]

What was the impact of these various reform programs? The truth is that we do not really know. The government stopped reporting credible employment statistics in the early 1980s, and the different numbers that are cited in various donor and government reports are contradictory. The Zambian Central Statistical Office reported 152,400 "central and local government employees" in 1993.[3] IFI reports suggest some 130,000 "central government employees" in the mid-1990s,[4] while a report by the Zambian Prices and Incomes Commission indicated 111,630 "public sector employees" in 1990,[5] and a more recent government report estimates at 164,478 the number of staff in "public administration."[6] There have been well-publicized layoffs in the 1990s, but also evidence of steady new hiring. Various accounts suggest a problem of ghost workers, so that at least some of these totals are fictitious. Sifting through the different numbers suggests a back-of-the-envelope guestimate of 140,000 people on the government payroll in the mid-1990s, and argues against the idea that the reform era has seen a sharp drop in public employment, but the picture is muddled at best.

Many observers of Africa appear to take as fact that structural adjustment resulted in an assault on public employment during the 1980s and 1990s.[7] Indeed, as we shall see, in a small number of countries, there have been significant civil service retrenchments. Yet, Zambia is far from unique in this situation of intense reform activity and costly donor support probably yielding few retrenchments, in the midst of poor statistics and ambiguity about actual numbers. Is civil service reform

2. See Peter Henriot, "Effect of Structural Adjustment Programmes on African Families" (Lusaka, Zambia: Jesuit Center for Theological Reflections, April 1995).
3. Personal communication, Malcolm McPherson.
4. For instance, Ian Lienert and Jitendra Modi, "A Decade of Civil Service Reform in Sub-Saharan Africa," IMF Working Paper WP/97/179 (Washington, DC: International Monetary Fund, Fiscal Affairs Department, December 1997), p. 43.
5. "Report on Development of Incomes of Unionized Formal Sector Workers, 1983–1991" (Lusaka, Zambia: Prices and Income Commission, May, 1992), Table 3.
6. *Economic Report, 1996* (Lusaka, Zambia: Ministry of Finance and Economic Development, January 1997), p. 32.
7. In their review of adjustment in the region, Thandika Mkandawire and Charles Soludo argue that "retrenchment in the civil service has played an important role in swelling the ranks of the poor" throughout Africa. See p. 73 of their otherwise excellent book, *Our Continent, Our Future: African Perspectives on Structural Adjustment* (Trenton, NJ: Africa World Press, 1999).

unusual in this respect? How much policy reform has actually occurred in Africa during the last twenty years? What kinds of policy biases have governments demonstrated during this period of austerity and fiscal crisis? Are there patterns across the region in terms of which policies have been modified and which remain largely as they did twenty years ago? Are the statistics always as deficient as in the case of public sector employment? At the outset of our analysis it is important to examine the empirical record carefully, given the heated rhetoric that has surrounded debates on the topic of structural adjustment and has often obscured more than it has revealed. Twenty years of continuous fiscal crisis was bound to bring about a degree of de facto policy change, so we need to focus on actual government choices and areas in which the state appears to have acted in the context of a discernible political strategy. In fact, although there is variation across the economies of the region, a clear pattern of partial reform does emerge, with much progress in some areas, but little in others. Most strikingly, I show that overall government consumption has actually increased if aid is taken into account, even as the government has used the reform process to significantly pare down its development effort. Thanks in part to substantial donor support to state structures, twenty years of crisis have resulted in a bigger state that does less for its citizens, particularly its poor and rural ones. These patterns are fully compatible with this book's thesis that the origins of economic policy are to be found within the state and not, as usually posited, in societal pressures on decision makers.

This chapter begins the process of presenting evidence on behalf of the hypotheses advanced in the previous chapter. The rest of this chapter is divided into three sections. First, it is necessary to establish clearly the nature of the empirical record regarding policy outcomes in Africa. The next section examines the record of implementation of policy reform during the last twenty years. There has been more progress on stabilization policies than on the more complex institutional reforms of structural adjustment, but much of the progress appears vulnerable to reversal and manipulation by state elites. A third section then turns to a political interpretation of the evolution of public spending. I provide evidence to cast doubt on the argument that state elites have responded to fiscal austerity in ways that show they are beholden to specific societal interests. Instead, governments in the region have managed the reform process to protect the state expenditures that serve elite interests.

REFORM IMPLEMENTATION: HOW MUCH?
HOW SUSTAINABLE?

How much has the policy environment actually changed during the last twenty years? To believe both the IFIs and their critics, policy reform has been comprehensive: the World Bank's latest report on the region, published in mid-2000, suggests that "substantial reforms contributed to the resurgence of growth in the second half of the 1990s."[8] On the other hand, critics such as Mkandawire and Soludo also assert that "African economies have been subjected to dramatic reforms," but they argue that these reforms are to be blamed for the region's "exceptionally poor [economic] performance" during the 1990s.[9]

In fact, I will argue that the policy environment has changed less than is commonly argued. Belying the claims of its own front office, the World Bank has issued evaluation reports that estimated at only 60 percent the implementation rate of the reform measures included in its structural adjustment and sector adjustment loans during the 1980s for all less developed countries.[10] The effective implementation rate is probably lower, since at least some of these conditions involved policies the government would have undertaken in the absence of a Bank loan, while others did not involve substantial difficulties – for example, sector studies. Moreover, the Bank project management staff, from whom these reports draw their findings, have every incentive to exaggerate the degree of implementation. Independent studies reveal a lower level of implementation. The most thorough data about implementation come from Tony Killick. In one study, Killick surveyed 305 IMF programs in less developed countries between 1979 and 1993 and found that 53 percent had not been completed during the loan period.[11] In another study, on World Bank adjustment loans, he found that 75 percent of the

---

8. The World Bank, *Can Africa Claim the 21st Century?* (Washington, DC: World Bank, 2000), p. 28. In a now well-established pattern, the report actually consists of a detailed diagnostic of the region's problems and ends with a renewed call for further policy reform.
9. Mkandawire and Soludo, *Our Continent, Our Future,* p. 81.
10. See World Bank, *Adjustment Lending: An Evaluation of Ten Years of Experience*, Country Economics Department, Policy, Planning, and Research (Washington, DC: World Bank, 1988), Tables 4-3 and 4-4. The implementation rate is even lower for the low-income countries that predominate in sub-Saharan Africa.
11. Tony Killick, *IMF Programmes in Developing Countries: Design and Impact* (London: ODI, 1996). Killick defined a program as uncompleted if the country had failed to implement 20 percent or more of the program's conditions.

disbursements of the second tranche of adjustment loans were delayed more than twelve months, suggesting a widespread problem of noncompliance.[12]

If implementation of policy reform has been less than complete, the obvious question is this: what patterns and biases have characterized the reform process? There is clearly much variation across the forty-eight African economies, but extremely suggestive trends in implementation can be identified from a careful analysis of the different components of most reform programs. I structure the following analysis by making use of the standard distinction between *stabilization policies*, which seek to restore macroeconomic balance in the short to medium term, and *adjustment policies*, which seek to alter the basic economic institutions of the country to foster higher growth in the medium to long term.

Stabilization Policies

The majority of African economies have made substantial progress on implementing basic stabilization policies. These are designed to restore macroeconomic stability in the short term, a goal typically at the core of IMF programs.[13] Significant progress had been made on cutting fiscal deficits, which declined on average from well over 10 percent (excluding grants) at times in the 1970s and 1980s, to 9 percent of GDP in 1992, and to 4.5 percent in 1997.[14] Current account deficits have undergone a similar improvement and were only, on average, 4 percent of GDP in 1997. Exchange rate policies have perhaps undergone the most dramatic improvements. In the countries outside of the Franc Zone, repeated devaluations during the 1980s and movement toward a more flexible exchange rate system has resulted in a definite trend toward more reasonable exchange rates. In the Franc Zone, in which currencies are pegged to the French franc, the devaluation of January 1994 served to bring down what had been typically fairly overvalued exchange rates. Thus, if between 1975 and 1984, eighteen of the region's economies had

12. Tony Killick, *Aid and the Political Economy of Policy Change* (London: Routledge, 1998), p. 30.
13. Tony Killick, *IMF Programmes in Developing Countries*.
14. See Stanley Fischer et al., *Africa: Is This the Turning Point?* IMF Papers on Policy Analysis and Assessment (Washington, DC: International Monetary Fund, May 1998), p. 1. For a broader assessment of fiscal adjustment, see Jayati Datta-Mitra, *Fiscal Management in Adjustment Lending*, a World Bank Operations Evaluation Study (Washington, DC: World Bank, 1997).

parallel exchange rates at least 50 percent higher than the official exchange rate, by 1995–96, such a black market premium existed only in three countries: Guinea-Bissau, Nigeria, and São Tomé and Principe.[15]

These continental averages disguise large intercountry variation, of course, but they do imply a significant amount of progress on macroeconomic policy throughout the region. It is nonetheless important to put this progress in perspective. First, much of the progress has been quite recent, occurring in the 1990s rather than the 1980s, during which there was remarkably little progress on much of the reform front. In a sense, the delay in stabilization is striking given Africa's situation. Faced with extremely high fiscal and balance of payments crises from the late 1970s on, and generally unable to raise significant capital on private markets, African governments had little choice but to borrow from the donors, despite their policy conditions. Without the option of printing money,[16] various pressures would probably have induced equilibration of deficits in time, regardless of government policy and with or without donor pressures to do so. As I will argue in Chapter 5, donor finance and the ability to accumulate debt rapidly has served to delay this inevitable adjustment to fiscal realities.

The slow rate of initial progress is true even of the countries usually perceived today as success stories: the current star pupil of the international financial institutions, Uganda, provides a good example. Lax monetary and fiscal policies through the early 1990s resulted in an inflation rate of over 50 percent in that country as late as 1992. In the same vein, Kenya's fiscal deficit – in 1998 a sterling 2 percent of GDP, according to the World Bank[17] – had been 11.8 percent of GDP as recently as 1993. In French west Africa, the devaluation of the CFA franc in January 1994, followed by several good rainy seasons, were the key events that account for the present apparent successful stabilization. As a result, in most countries, it is too early to tell whether the progress will be sustained.

15. Calculated from World Bank, *African Development Indicators*, 2000 (Washington, DC: World Bank, 2000), p. 51. Unless otherwise indicated, the statistics attributed to the World Bank throughout this chapter are from this volume.
16. It is interesting that with the notable exception of Zaire, African governments on the whole did not resort to the expedient solution of printing money. In the Franc Zone, strict rules apparently served as an effective deterrent. Governments appear to have been dissuaded from doing so by the examples of disastrous hyperinflation elsewhere, notably in Latin America. Perhaps as important has been the influence of extensive and long-standing technical assistance to central banks and finance ministries from the IMF, the French treasury, and other Western donors.
17. *African Development Indicators*, p. 190.

Second, progress on macroeconomic management remains vulnerable to reversals. By their nature, most stabilization measures are the policy reforms that are the easiest to achieve in the short run, but also the hardest to sustain because they are the easiest to undo. This is particularly true for measures that are, in effect, the subject of annual decisions. For instance, balancing the budget this year does not necessarily make it any easier to balance it next year, or less necessary to do so to maintain macrostability. In countries like Ghana, Kenya, or Gabon, past progress on stabilization was abruptly jettisoned in the months before an election by a government eager to hold on to power. Thus, Ghana's budget deficit went from 4.9 percent of GDP in 1991 to 12.7 percent in 1992, an election year in which Rawlings faced the voters for the first time. Coupled with an unexpected decline in oil revenues, Omar Bongo's campaign to retain the presidency in Gabon in 1999 led to a mushrooming of the deficit from 2 percent of GDP to an estimated 30 percent as he stoked public expenditures to ensure political support.[18] Similarly, the positive impact of the devaluation of the CFA franc on Francophone west African economies will inevitably abate; even with inflation rates comfortably in the single digits, these countries typically have higher rates than those prevailing in the West, so that real, effective exchange rates are almost sure to appreciate, slowly but surely, until the countries are faced with another competitiveness crisis.[19]

Third, much of the recent improvement in the basic macroeconomic picture is probably not sustainable without large amounts of external support. Balance of payments and fiscal deficits often remain too large to be sustained without external assistance or regular debt forgiveness and rescheduling. Thus, only nine countries in the region had fiscal deficits of under 3 percent of GDP in both 1997 and 1998, if external grants are not taken into account – a level that can be viewed as a benchmark of prudent fiscal management in countries with limited access to

18. Calculated from the Economist Intelligence Unit's *Country Report: Gabon*, Second Quarter, 1999 (London: Economist Intelligence Unit).
19. A recent assessment of the CFA Zone is provided in Bruno Cabrillac, "La situation macroéconomique des pays Africains de la Zone Franc à la fin de l'année 1998," *Afrique Contemporaine* 189 (1999): 23–9. More generally, on the operation of the zone, see Jean Clement et al., *Aftermath of the CFA Franc Devaluation*, International Monetary Fund Occasional Paper # 138 (1996); and the earlier essay by Nicolas van de Walle, "The Decline of the Franc Zone: Monetary Politics in Francophone Africa," *African Affairs* 90 (1991): 383–405.

international investment and low levels of savings.[20] In a number of countries, progress on controlling government expenditures has been achieved thanks to high levels of donor support, creative accounting and the deferring of core expenditures into the future. There is something profoundly disingenuous about donors and governments claiming progress on fiscal balance when it is taking place in the context of aid flows totaling a tenth of GDP, usually with a pretty high loan component. In several countries, significant debt relief largely explains ostensible improvements in macro-indicators in recent years. But this can only be temporary if the underlying balance of payments and fiscal deficits have not been overturned – unless one is willing to make the unreasonable assumption that the current high aid flow is permanent.

In order to remain in good standing with the donors, moreover, governments commonly resort to various budgetary manipulations. A favorite ploy is to accumulate arrears on civil service wages or other obligations. In 1999, reports from Francophone Africa indicated that Gabon had accumulated seven to eight months of salary arrears since 1995, while these arrears had reached eleven months in Niger, six to eight months in Togo, and up to eighteen months for some civil servants in Congo-Brazzaville.[21] Elsewhere, Guinea-Bissau's salary arrears were six to eight months in early 2000,[22] while Nigeria has routinely run several months of such arrears for its state employees in the last couple of years.[23] Such salary arrears are particularly pronounced in the Franc Zone countries, given strict rules limiting government financing of deficit spending. Because civil service wages are invariably the biggest single item in the budget, including these financial obligations

---

20. *African Development Indicators*, Table 7-2. The countries are Cameroon, Côte d'Ivoire, Equatorial Guinea, Kenya, Mauritania, Senegal, Sudan, Swaziland, and Tanzania. Note that only Mauritania and Swaziland had also enjoyed deficits under 3 percent as recently as 1995.

21. On Gabon, see *Marchés Tropicaux*, April 16, 1999, p. 797; arrears are reported for Niger in "Lassitude Pre-Electorale," in *l'Autre Afrique* 99 (October 12, 1999): 40–1; in Togo, "L'armée sans le sous," in *Lettre du Continent*, October 14, 1999, p. 3; and in Congo Brazzaville, "Brazzaville Mortuary Workers on Strike," Panafrican News Agency, December 31, 1998.

22. "L'élection de Kumba Yala traduit une volonté de changement," Agence France Press, January 22, 2000.

23. See the following stories from Nigerian newspapers, all found on the Internet: "Governor Seeks Advice," *P.M. News*, June 7, 1999; "Nigeria; Minimum Wage: Enugu, Oyo Resolve Wage Crisis," *This Day*, August 3, 2000; and "Nigeria; Why States Are Boiling," *Vanguard Daily*, June 24, 2000.

in the deficit would significantly worsen the fiscal situation. Yet the IFIs typically look the other way to keep adjustment programs officially on track.

Some oil exporters like Cameroon and Congo have similarly sold oil forward several years into the future, despite strict IFI rules against the practice. According to the World Bank's statistics, Congo's fiscal deficit in the 1990s averaged 10.8 percent of GDP between 1990 and 1996, excluding donor support, but the precise meaning of these numbers is unclear when rumors suggest that the government had sold forward five years' worth of national oil production – thought to represent well above 90 percent of total government revenues – in secret agreements with private oil companies.[24] Countries like Tanzania, Uganda, and Zambia have adopted "cash budgets" in the 1990s, whereby expenditures are monitored and strictly controlled throughout the year relative to available revenues, in order to achieve a balanced budget.[25] Cash budgets have been widely praised for the fiscal turnaround in these countries. But in all three countries, the practice has led to the accumulation of arrears, as line ministries pay for goods and services with promissory notes. In Zambia in 1997, the Ministry of Finance itself admitted that arrears accounted for the equivalent of 1.5 percent of GDP.[26] Reports suggested that the transport and communications sector alone totaled debts of over 100 billion kwacha to private contractors in late 1999, while the official capital expenditures budget that year for the sector amounted to only 66.5 billion kwacha![27] Typically, these arrears are not included in fiscal statistics.

24. These sales have been widely reported. See, for instance, "Les, Milliards en l'Air du Congo," in *l'Autre Afrique,* May 19, 1998, 99, which mentions the conservative estimate of 3.5–3.75 billion French francs' worth of sales to oil companies on production through 2004. See also various issues of the Economist Intelligence Unit Country Reports on Congo in the mid-1990s.
25. David Stasavage and Dambisa Moyo, "Are Cash Budgets a Cure for Excess Fiscal Deficits (and at What Cost)?" Center for the Study of African Economies, University of Oxford, Paper WPS/99-11, May 1999; and Bruce Bolnick, "Establishing Fiscal Discipline: The Cash Budget in Zambia," in Merilee S. Grindle (ed.), *Getting Good Government: Capacity Building in the Public Sector of Developing Countries* (Cambridge, MA: Harvard Institute for International Development, 1997), pp. 297–332.
26. Stasavage and Moyo, "Are Cash Budgets a Cure," p. 13. My own interviewing of officials and businessmen in Lusaka in May of 1999 suggests this figure may be a significant underestimate.
27. See "Zambia: Gearing Up for Growth," in *African Review of Business and Technology,* March 17, 2000. One U.S. dollar bought roughly 2,000 kwacha at the time.

Fiscal adjustment has been held back by the stagnation in revenue levels that has characterized the adjustment pattern of most African economies. The impact of policy reform programs on government revenues is the subject of some disagreement. Jawarajah and Branson find that state revenues declined from 18.7 to 17.7 percent of GDP during the course of Bank adjustment programs in their sample of Africa countries.[28] This accords with the findings of several studies that tax revenues and level of foreign aid have had a significant negative correlation.[29] On the other hand, the IMF has usually argued that its own stabilization operations have not resulted in systematic changes in the government's tax effort.[30] No one, on the other hand, has argued that the last two decades have witnessed significant increases in government revenues, despite the IMF's stated intention in virtually all of its adjustment operations to increase them. World Bank data show that African government revenues have stayed around an average of 19 to 20 percent of GDP. As shown in Table 2.1, this average disguises significant variation.

The table identifies seventeen countries in which revenues were less than 15 percent of GDP in 1995–98 and fifteen countries in which revenues averaged more than 25 percent of GDP in that period. The low-extraction countries are typically low-income states without mineral or oil wealth, the presence of which clearly helps explain the performance of the high-extraction countries. Nonetheless, the striking differences in revenue levels for similar countries does suggest that economic structure explains only some of the variation and that institutional differences must be significant as well. Compare, for example, Kenya and Uganda, similar economies with small manufacturing and large commercial agricultural sectors.

The table also compares these countries over time, to see whether revenue collection has improved over the last decade. Interestingly, only two of the low-extraction countries improved their performance during this period. In a much higher number of countries, revenues declined substantially. Clearly, in many countries, the weakness of revenue collection constitutes a real handicap for sustained macroeconomic stabilization,

28. Jayarajah and Branson, *Structural and Sectoral Adjustment*, p. 134.
29. For example, Howard White, "Foreign Aid, Taxes and Public Investment: A Further Comment," in *Journal of Development Economics* 45 (1994): 155–64.
30. For instance, Karim Nashashibi et al., *The Fiscal Dimensions of Adjustment in Low-Income Countries*, IMF Occasional Paper, number 95 (Washington, DC: International Monetary Fund, April 1992); Nashashibi provides data suggesting that government revenues went up in nine African cases and down in nine, relative to a "base year."

Table 2.1. *Extractive Performance of African States, 1985–1988, 1995–1998 (government revenue as a percentage of GDP)*

Low-Revenue Countries			High-Revenue Countries		
	1985–88	1995–98		1985–88	1995–98
Sierra Leone	6.6	7.1	Lesotho	38.4	50.2**
Chad	5.4	7.4**	Seychelles	46.8	44.4*
Sudan	9.0	7.5	Botswana	46.8	40.7*
Central African Republic	9.4	8.0	Eritrea	..	35.5
Niger	10.8	8.1*	Swaziland	..	34.5
Rwanda	10.6	9.1	Angola	33.7	34.3
Madagascar	13.2	9.4*	Namibia	28.1	33.8**
Uganda	6.5	10.3**	Gabon	32.8	28.5*
Guinea	14.1	10.7*	South Africa	24.4	28.5**
Mozambique	10.6	11.3	Djibouti	..	28.2
Guinea-Bissau	13.4	11.5	Zimbabwe	26.8	28.1
Burkina Faso	10.9	12.3	Kenya	22.6	27.6**
Tanzania	14.4	12.9	Mauritania	32.7	27.0*
Togo	26.2	14.6*	Cape Verde	17.1	26.3**
Cameroon	19.3	14.6*	Congo-B	26.9	26.1
Comoros	12.6	14.8			
Burundi	17.4	14.9*			

Notes: High-revenue countries are those in which total government revenues averaged above 25% of GDP (excluding grants) in 1995–98; low-revenue countries are those in which total government revenues averaged below 15% of GDP (excluding grants) in 1995–98.
* Revenues decreased by at least 2% of GDP between 1985–88 and 1995–98.
** Revenues increased by at least 2% of GDP between 1985–88 and 1995–98.
Sources: Calculated from *African Development Indicators*, Table 7.6.

let alone more rapid growth and structural transformation. With such low extraction levels, the burden of adjustment must be disproportionately on the expenditure side.

Structural Adjustment Policies

Structural adjustment policies are policy reforms that may not have a direct incidence on macroeconomic stability in the short run, but are designed to affect the long-term prospects for economic growth. In general, they can be thought of as "stickier" reforms than stabilization policies, with more complex implementation issues but with a lower chance of reversibility once they have been pushed through. The record here is even more ambiguous and uneven across the economies of the region. Certainly, widespread progress has been sustained in certain areas. Almost all countries have undergone extensive price liberalization, with significant progress on the elimination of domestic price controls and the liberalization of bank credit and interest rates.[31] Liberalization measures were almost invariably at the core of the World Bank's conditionality in its first generation adjustment programs. The 1980s witnessed considerable deregulation in the banking sector, which had long been a privileged site for government intervention. Banking services had constituted a public monopoly in well over a third of the countries in the region in the late 1970s; today, no country retains such a monopoly. In the agricultural sector, governments have done away with many of the agricultural marketing boards that enjoyed statutory monopsonies over the commercialization of export crops and often fixed producer prices excessively low.[32] Elimination of these marketing boards or the encouragement of private competition in the commercialization process was designed to improve incentives for farmers.

The record on domestic liberalization is nonetheless ambiguous. Even more than for stabilization, positive trends tend to be recent, with relatively little real progress until the late 1980s and early 1990s. Ghana, for instance, has often been heralded as an early reformer; on inspection,

---

31. A good, if biased summary of the progress achieved up to the early 1990s is provided by the World Bank, *Adjustment in Africa: Reforms, Results and the Road Ahead* (Washington, DC: World Bank, 1994). The country case studies on which much of that assessment is based have been published as Ishrat Husain and Rashid Faruqee (eds.), *Adjustment in Africa: Lessons from Country Case Studies* (Washington, DC: World Bank, 1994). See also David E. Sahn, Paul A. Dorosh, and Stephen D. Younger, *Structural Adjustment Reconsidered: Economic Policy and Poverty in Africa* (New York: Cambridge University Press, 1997); and Carl Jayarajah and William Branson, *Structural and Sectoral Adjustment: The World Bank Experience, 1980–1992*, a World Bank Operations Evaluation Study (Washington, DC: World Bank, 1995).

32. Adjustment in the agricultural sector is reviewed in Jacob Meerman, *Reforming Agriculture: The World Bank Goes to Market*, a World Bank Operations Evaluation Study (Washington, DC: World Bank, 1997); Andrew Shepherd and Stefano Farolfi, *Export Crop Liberalization in Africa: A Review*, FAO Agricultural Services Bulletin, Number 135 (Rome: FAO, 1999); and Pekka Seppälä, "Food Marketing Reconsidered: An Assessment of the Liberalization of Food Marketing in Sub-Saharan Africa," U.N. University, WIDER Research for Action Paper 34 (Helsinki: WIDER, 1997). I thank Chris Delgado for bringing these papers to my attention. See also Peter Gibbon, Kjell J. Havnevik, and Kenneth Hermele, *A Blighted Harvest: The World Bank and African Agriculture in the 1980s* (Trenton, NJ: Africa World Press, 1993).

however, reform implementation has clearly been belated as well as partial.[33] President Rawlings came to office in 1981 and economic reform is said to have started in 1983. Cocoa producer prices were increased almost immediately, quadrupling in real value between 1983 and 1988, but exchange rates were not fully liberalized until 1992–1993, the import licensing system was abolished only in 1989, and the privatization of Ashanti Gold Fields was not completed until 1994.

Furthermore, key elements of the old apparatus of state control have survived in some countries. Often, the policies have changed on paper, but in practice, something resembling the status quo ante continues to prevail.[34] In some cases, the old policies were reinstated under a new name or with some new policy objective. In Kenya, the government restored fixed prices for maize and a tariff on maize imports in 1997. The government justified this return to the prereform status quo by alluding to food security and welfare concerns for small farmers, but one study estimates that the policy overwhelmingly favors big farmers, who dominate the maize market.[35]

In other cases, governments ignore the spirit of their own liberalization efforts by continuing to interfere in officially deregulated markets. The hurdles facing private sector investors in many countries offer an excellent example of this situation. Officially, most governments welcome private investment and have removed all the red tape that previously discouraged it. In practice, as a recent review of these issues put it, it is still the case that "in most African countries, the procedures for

33. Ghana's reform path has been much examined. See Jeffrey Herbst, *The Politics of Reform in Ghana, 1982–1991* (Berkeley: University of California Press, 1992); Eboe Hutchful, "Ghana," in Poul Engberg-Pedersen, Peter Gibbon, Phil Raikes, and Lars Udsholt (eds.), *Limits of Adjustment in Africa: The Effects of Economic Liberalisation 1986–1994* (London: Zed Books, 1995), pp. 141–214; Alice Sindzingre, "Politiques economiques, instabilités et secteur privé," in Comi Toulabor (ed.), *Ressources politiques et légitimité au Ghana* (Paris: Karthala, in press); and Donald Rothchild (ed.), *Ghana: The Political Economy of Recovery* (Boulder, CO: Lynne Rienner, 1991).

34. In her excellent book on the informal sector in Dar es Salaam, Aili Tripp documents cases in which old laws were so consistently evaded by the citizenry that public officials stopped trying to enforce them. In such cases, the actual policy regime is quite ambiguous. See Aili Mari Tripp, *Changing the Rules: The Politics of Liberalization and the Urban Informal Economy in Tanzania* (Berkeley: University of California Press, 1997).

35. T. S. Jayne et al., *Do Farmers Really Benefit from High Food Prices?* Policy Brief, Tegemeo Institute for Agricultural Policy and Development, no.1 (September 2000). The authors estimate (p. 5) that the new policy offers an average subsidy of U.S.$19,200 to an average large farm of 200 acres.

setting up a company and entering into legitimate business are a night-mare."[36] Despite Mozambique's long-standing reform efforts, for example, registering a company still takes six months, and the various payments required in licenses and mandatory notary fees typically approach 10 percent of capital.[37] Elliot Berg has concluded that in Senegal, much deregulation and price liberalization has little impact on private sector investment, which continues to be undermined by "skepticism about the government of Senegal's commitment to liberalization; the lack of transparency in decision making and implementation coupled with a generalized suspicion that the playing field is uneven; and the persistence of administrative delays, weaknesses and harassment."[38] A recent report on Tanzania, often cited as an example of successful investment liberalization, sounds a similar tone:[39] the authors recognize that the country has made "substantial progress on economic reform" (p. 1), but argue that "the government continues to exhibit the laxity and indifference to performance of the socialist era" (p. 20), and note that "virtually every interaction with the government (by private businessmen) seems to require some sort of side payment to assure that necessary licenses, approvals or clearances are processed favorably" (p. 22).

The agricultural sector is also emblematic of this tendency of what one is tempted to call virtual reform. Although policy reform appears to have advanced more in southern and eastern Africa and less in west and central Africa,[40] nonetheless, much has changed throughout the region.

---

36. James J. Emery and Melvin T. Spence, "Administrative Barriers to Investment in Africa: The Red Tape Analysis," unpublished paper Washington, DC: World Bank, June 1999, p. 9.

37. Ibid, p. 18.

38. Elliot Berg et al., *Sustaining Private Sector Development in Senegal: Strategic Considerations* (Bethesda, MD: DAI, June 1997), p. 17. For a slightly different emphasis focusing specifically on the import sector, see Ibrahima Thioub, Momar-Coumba Diop, and Catherine Boone, "Economic Liberalization in Senegal: Shifting Politics in Indigenous Business Interests," in *African Studies Review* 41 (1998): 63–89. They agree with Berg that despite official trade liberalization, infighting between business and "old style politician businessmen" continues to exist over the lucrative imported manufacturing market, but they emphasize the state's declining ability to control rent-seeking networks, in a context of declining administrative capacity and political legitimacy.

39. Michael F. Lofchie and Thomas Callaghy, *Diversity in the Tanzanian Business Community and Its Implications for Growth*, Report to the USAID Mission, Dar es Salaam, Tanzania, Contract #621-0176-C-00-5035-00, December 5, 1995.

40. So concludes an excellent recent review of agricultural adjustment: Hans Binswanger, Robert Townsend, and Tshikala Tshhibaka, "Spurring Agriculture and Rural Development," paper presented at the second research workshop, African Development Bank, Abidjan, July 6–11, 1999, pp. 13–15.

The expensive fertilizer, seed, and pesticide subsidies of the past have often been withdrawn,[41] while the many parastatals that had once promoted a crop or region with extension services, input delivery, and other activities have often been closed or had their activities sharply curtailed. Typically, the agriculture sector reform programs that oversaw these reforms also mandated price liberalization, but here reform implementation has been much more ambiguous. It is important to distinguish export from food crops and east and southern Africa from west and central Africa. Many key export crops have not seen their prices completely liberalized. In some countries, poorly informed farmers remain at the mercy of unscrupulous local officials keen to retain their central role in the marketing chain, or of newly empowered private purchasing agents, often in some degree of collusion with state officials. Thus, in Cameroon's cocoa belt, the adjustment program of the early 1990s resulted in the old price-fixing system being eliminated in favor of an annual "minimal indicative price," which theoretically established a floor below which purely private transactions could not go. In practice, the latter prices were more or less enforced as the fixed price.[42] A World Bank review of the agricultural sector suggests this practice is not limited to Cameroon, but is widespread throughout Africa.[43] Reviewing the experience in six countries, Gibbon et al. find that the prices actually received by farmers probably declined during the 1980s in half of the cases.[44]

The policy environment for export agriculture has improved significantly more in countries like Kenya and Zimbabwe; here farmer organizations with long histories stretching back to before World War II have effectively pressured governments for favorable treatment. In Zimbabwe, however, the policy regime has hardly moved in the direction of *liberalization* as large commercial farmers have fought for and retained significant subsidies.[45] In west Africa, on the other hand, the absence of a

41. Meerman, *Reforming Agriculture*, pp. 74–83, covers the record for all input subsidy programs.
42. Georges Courade and Véronique Alary, "Les planteurs Camerounais ont-ils été réévaluées?" in *Politique Africaine* 54 (1994):74–87, p. 79 and passim. See also in the same issue of *Politique Africaine*, Bruno Losch, "Les agro-exportateurs face à la dévaluation," pp. 88–103.
43. Meerman, *Reforming Agriculture*, pp. 70–1. See also Shepherd and Farolfi, *Export Crop Liberalization in Africa*, pp. 13–19
44. Gibbon et al., *A Blighted Harvest*, pp. 107–9.
45. Tor Skalnes makes this argument convincingly for Zimbabwe. See his book, *The Politics of Economic Reform in Zimbabwe* (New York: St. Martin's Press, 1995). Zimbabwe is also marked by growing rural inequality as all farmers are far from

European settler history has resulted in a much slower and haphazard reform process for export agriculture. For cotton, usually the leading export crop in the Sahel, farm gate prices continue to be fixed by a state marketing board throughout French west Africa.[46] The same is true in Senegal for politically sensitive groundnut prices.[47] Governments usually acceded to donor demands to improve price incentives to farmers, long viewed as significantly too low, but have proved extremely reticent to allow markets to set prices themselves, preferring to maintain their power to fix prices annually.

The picture is similarly uneven for the liberalization of food markets. In west and particularly central Africa, few states were ever able to regulate food marketing completely, as private actors found myriad ways to escape state controls.[48] The 1980s witnessed the abolishment of many of the public agencies that states had once created to monopolize food marketing and keep consumer prices down.[49] Typically, however, the government has retained a central regulatory role if not a monopoly on the marketing of imported foods, such as rice and wheat. In east and southern Africa, on the other hand, reform has been characterized by significant backsliding. Typically, controls on food transport and urban consumer prices have been liberalized, but governments have maintained their attempts to set farm gate prices and have resisted donor calls to get rid of food marketing institutions.[50]

benefiting from the same level of political influence. See also Chapter 5 of the fine but now somewhat dated study by Jeffrey Herbst, *State Politics in Zimbabwe* (Berkeley: University of California Press, 1990); and Michael Bratton, "The Comrades and the Countryside: The Politics of Agricultural Policy in Zimbabwe," *World Politics* 39 (1987): 4–202.

46. Claude Freud, "Politiques des prix et performances des fillières cotonnières en Afrique," *Revue Tiers Monde* 15 (1999): 929–41.
47. Mustapha Rouis, "Senegal: Stabilization, Partial Adjustment and Stagnation," in Ishrat Husain and Rashid Faruqee (eds.), *Adjustment in Africa*, Lessons from Country Case Studies (Washington, DC: World Bank, 1994), pp. 286–351.
48. Vali Jamal and John Weeks, *Africa Misunderstood* (London: MacMillan, 1993).
49. Seppälä, "Food Marketing Reconsidered." See also the dated but still excellent Keith Hart, *The Political Economy of West African Agriculture* (Cambridge, UK: Cambridge University Press, 1982). See also Daniel Maxwell, "The Political Economy of Urban Food Security in Sub-Saharan Africa," *World Development* 27 (1999): 1939–53.
50. See the fine review of these issues in T. S. Jayne et al, " Successes and Challenges of Food Market Reform: Experiences from Kenya, Mozambique, Zambia and Zimbabwe," MSU International Development Working Papers, no. 72 (Michigan State University, 1999). On Kenya, for evidence of government manipulation of cereals market liberalization through 1993, see the interesting case study by Gerrishon K. Ikiara, Mohamud Jama, and Justus O. Amadi, "The Cereals

Trade policy reform has progressed even less far.[51] Reform has long sought to lower and simplify tariffs, eliminate nontariff barriers, make customs procedures more transparent, and lower export taxes. Trade reform has been a staple of all reform programs since the early 1980s, even though tariffs constitute a significant source of revenue for most states in the region. Yet, in a majority of cases, reforms have been left unimplemented, or, when undertaken, are often subsequently reversed. Table 2.2 provides the most recent available data on trade restrictions. Officially, trade protection remains significantly higher than in other regions of the developing world, with tariff rates averaging about 25 percent, roughly four times the non-OECD average.[52] Africa is the only region in the world where the degree of openness has not significantly increased during the last two decades.[53] The actual situation on the ground is much harder to assess, however, given the extremely uneven manner with which trade policy is implemented. In some countries, governments have undone the impact of policy by tolerating high levels of corruption within the customs services or extending exemptions from prevailing rates to favored firms. Lofchie and Callaghy argue that in Tanzania, "corruption in the customs bureaucracy is so extensive that Tan-

Chain in Kenya: Actors, Reforms and Politics," in Peter Gibbon (ed.), *Markets, Civil Society and Democracy in Kenya* (Uppsala, Sweden: Nordiska Afrikainstitutet, 1995), pp. 31–68.
51. The progress of trade policy reform is discussed in John Nash, "Trade Policy Reform Implementation in Sub-Saharan Africa: How Much Heat and How Much Light?" World Bank Working Paper (Washington, DC: World Bank, 1995); F. Ng and A. Yeats, "Open Economies Work Better! Did Africa's Protectionist Policies Cause Its Marginalization in World Trade?" World Bank Policy Research Working Paper, no. 1636. (Washington, DC: World Bank, 1996); and Béatrice Hibou. *l'Afrique est-elle protectioniste?* (Paris: Karthala, 1996). Charles Soludu focuses on a sample of countries with a somewhat better trade reform record in his essay, "Trade Policy Reforms and Supply Responses in Africa" (Geneva: UNCTAD, September 1998). On the political economy dimension of trade policy reform, see Dani Rodrik, "Why Is Trade Reform so Difficult in Africa," *Journal of African Economies* 7, Supplement 1 (1998): 43–69; and Henry Bienen, "The Politics of Trade Liberalization in Africa," *Economic Development and Cultural Change* 38, no. 4 (1990): 713–32.
52. Ng and Yeats, "Open Economies Work Better!"
53. This is the conclusion of Jeffrey Sachs and Andrew Warner, "Economic Reform and the Process of Global Integration," *Brookings Papers on Economic Activity* 1 (1995): 1–119; of the World Bank, *Global Economic Prospects and the Developing Countries, 1996* (Washington, DC: World Bank, 1996); and of Robert Sharer et al., "Trade Liberalization in IMF-Supported Programs," *World Economic and Financial Survey* (Washington, DC: International Monetary Fund, February 1998).

Table 2.2. *Trade Restrictions in Africa*

Country	Unweighted Tariff Rates (%)		Unweighted Nontariff Restrictions (%)	
	1984–87	1991–93	1984–87	1991–93
Côte d'Ivoire	23.3	..	6.6	..
Ethiopia	29.0	29.6	..	22.5
Ghana	29.6	..	48.4	..
Kenya*	39.2	43.7	67.3	37.8
Malawi*	16.7	15.2	96.1	91.3
Mauritius*	34.9	27.6	..	35.2
Nigeria	23.8	32.8	17.0	8.8
Tanzania*	32.1	29.8	62.2	79.7
Zimbabwe*	8.7	10.1	2.5	93.6
All Africa	26.3	25.7	43.7	42.9
Sub-Saharan Africa	26.3	25.3	44.0	47.1
Latin America	26.6	12.3	30.2	8.6
South Asia	61.7	47.5	47.6	20.4
East Asia	17.9	16.7	21.2	3.6
All Countries	27.0	22.1	37.7	23.7

* Data are from 1984–7 and 1988–90. Regional averages are taken from 15 sub-Saharan African states, 11 from Latin America, 5 from South Asia, and 7 from East Asia.

Source: Data are from United Nations Conference on Inade and Development. Cited in World Economic Forum, *The Africa Competitiveness Report* (Geneva: World Economic Forum, 1998), p. 41.

zania is, for all practical purposes, a duty-free zone."[54] In other countries, the trade sector continues to face red tape and excessive interference from government bureaucracy, so that reform may not have changed the effective rate of protection faced by business given various transaction costs that appear to have increased. The uncertainty and randomness of the situation in many countries, even when the effective levels of protection are quite low, are almost certainly a strong deterrent to potential trade growth.

Public enterprise reform offers an interesting contrast; after proceeding at a snail's pace during the 1980s, it has picked up speed in the 1990s.[55] Over time, privatization has become more prominent in the

54. Lofchie and Callaghy, *Diversity in the Tanzanian Business Community*, p. 2.
55. A useful survey is provided in Paul Bennell, "Privatization in Sub-Saharan Africa: Progress and Prospects during the 1990s," *World Development* 25 (1997): 1785–803; see also World Bank, *Bureaucrats in Business: The Economics and*

reform agenda, as various schemes to improve the management of public enterprises invariably failed to stem their thirst for costly subsidies. Nonetheless, during the 1980s, privatization appeared stalled by a combination of political opposition and the technical difficulties of arranging for sales. Governments worried about the implications of large retrenchments. In the more recent past, however, privatization transactions have been completed in a number of countries. According to Bennell, the period of 1980–1987 witnessed some 227 privatization transactions, while 657 transactions occurred between 1988 and 1995, and over 300 in 1994–95 alone.[56] Initial resistance to privatization appears to have been overcome primarily by the growing unwillingness to bear the burden of subsidizing loss-making parastatals combined with the attraction of the revenues to be generated by selling off public assets. Bennell (p. 1790) thus points out that privatization transactions raised almost 2 billion in the region between 1990 and 1995.

In many cases, governments remain unwilling to part with the biggest of their public enterprises. The case of Zambia is particularly revealing. That country has undertaken an ambitious privatization program since 1992, but hesitated throughout the 1990s to privatize the ZCCM, the giant copper mining concern.[57] Successive governments opposed selling the company for ideological and nationalistic reasons, and rationalized that the company was the engine of the national economy. By the late 1990s, however, ZCCM was losing more than $1 million a day, the result of decades of systematic underinvestment and poor management. The government announced its intention to sell in 1996, but now privatization was delayed by investor hesitation in light of the company's financial difficulties, as well as by the accusations of rent-seeking and corruption on the part of senior state managers. President Chiluba had entrusted the sale to a special team rather than the national privatiza-

---

Politics of Government Ownership (Washington, DC: World Bank, 1995); and Elliot Berg, "Privatization in Sub-Saharan Africa: Results, Prospects and New Approaches," in Jo Ann Paulson (ed.), *African Economies in Transition: Volume 2: The Reform Experience* (New York: St. Martin's Press, 1999), pp. 229–89.

56. Bennell, "Privatization in Sub-Saharan Africa," p. 1789.
57. This account of the ZCCM privatization has been compiled from Colin Barraclough, "Trouble in Lusaka," *Institutional Investor (international edition)* 12, no. 23 (1998): 47. I have also relied on the the fine series of articles on the transaction by Theo Bull in *Profit Magazine* throughout 1997 and 1998. The general Zambian context is explored in Lise Rakner, Nicolas van de Walle, and Dominic Mulaisho, "Aid and Reform in Zambia," unpublished report for the World Bank project on aid and reform, Washington, 1999.

tion agency. The head of the team, Francis Kaunda, received a salary of $16,000 a month and was accused of slowing down negotiations purposely to maintain his position. Negotiations were also slowed down when foreign investors learned that company assets were being privately sold to company officials and politicians, and they demanded a precise inventory of company holdings. In particular, some 200 houses owned by ZCCM had apparently been secretly sold off. A deal was almost struck with potential buyer Anglo-American in late 1998 but was allegedly undone by Anglo's refusal to pay the large side payments demanded by the president's office to seal the deal. Agreement was nonetheless reached with Anglo in April 2000; by that point, the company's disastrous finances were weighing heavily on government finances and the donors were conditioning any increases in aid on an agreement.[58]

In other cases, the fear that privatization will benefit certain ethnic groups or foreign business interests has stalled divestiture, or the process has suffered delays following accusations that the transactions appeared to benefit members of the political class, usually by significantly undervaluing assets and selling them to members of this class at fire sale prices.[59] As Lewis comments about the privatization process in Nigeria, much of which was conducted through offerings on the national stock market: "The dispersal of government assets, especially in a tight economy, created numerous opportunities for windfall gains. The weak regulation of securities transactions facilitated the use of insider information for substantial profit . . . private placements and closed bidding provided easy avenues for directing favors to friends and clients."[60] But few governments still retain the pronounced ideological opposition to privatization they openly expressed in the 1970s.[61] No matter how contentious privatization transactions have been, once achieved, they are not challenged. Thus, even with the regime changes brought about by democratization in the early 1990s, there have been no examples of renationalization of privatized firms.

58. ZCCM's belated privatization is chronicled in "Zambia Finalizes Sale of State Copper Mine Group," *The Financial Times*, April 4, 2000, p. 38.
59. This argument is well made by Thandika Mkandawire, "The Political Economy of Privatization in Africa," in Giovanni Andrea Cornia and Gerald K. Helleiner (eds.), *From Adjustment to Development in Africa* (New York: St. Martin's Press, 1994), pp. 192–216.
60. Peter M. Lewis, "Economic Statism, Private Capital and the Dilemmas of Accumulation in Nigeria," *World Development* 22 (1994): 437–51, 446.
61. See Bennell, "Privatization in Sub-Saharan Africa," for a similar argument.

Finally, there has been little progress on civil service reform, which has long been discussed but rarely implemented. The objective of reform is both to cut down on unnecessary staff and to improve the conditions of service for the remaining staff. Virtually every country in the region has undergone some kind of civil service reform program, supported by international finance.[62] The donors have long recognized the need for reform but have hesitated to promote it, given its likely cost, complexity, and perceived political sensitivity. As a result, it has rarely been at the forefront of adjustment programs, relegated instead to a back burner. Governments have been willing to commission studies on the civil service, to institute costly and largely ineffectual donor-funded programs of voluntary retirement or campaigns to get rid of ghost workers, but very few have been willing to lay off sizable proportions of the civil service or to increase salaries to keep up with inflation. For their part, the donors have rarely focused their conditionality on civil service reform progress. Three notable exceptions to these patterns are Uganda, Guinea, and Ghana, where programs resulted in the civil service being cut by 20,000, 30,000, and 60,000 positions, respectively in the late 1980s.[63] Elsewhere, there has been remarkably little progress.

It would have been astonishing if over two decades of fiscal crisis had not served to cut the size of the civil service relative to the population, as it appears to have done; on average, civil servants amount to 1 percent of the population, down from 1.3 percent in 1991, belying the image of

62. See the informative collection of essays in David L. Lindauer and Barbara Nunberg (eds.), *Rehabilitating Government: Pay and Employment Reforms in Africa* (Washington, DC: World Bank, 1994). In her own contribution, Nunberg cites fifty-five World Bank loans with a civil service reform component extended to Africa between 1981 and 1991. See "Experiences with Civil Service Pay and Employment Reform: An Overview," pp. 119–59. See also Bamidele Olowu, "Redesigning African Civil Service Reforms," *Journal of Modern African Studies* 37 (1999): 1–23; and Alice Sindzingre, "Dimensions economiques des réformes de l'etat en Afrique sub-Saharienne," in Comi Toulabor and Dominique Darbon (eds.), *Réforme de l'etat: Reconstruction institutionelle et modes de régulation* (Paris: Karthala, in press).
63. Louis de Merode and Charles Thomas, "Implementing Civil Service Pay and Employment Reform in Africa: The Experiences of Ghana, Gambia and Guinea," in David L. Lindauer and Barbara Nunberg (eds.), *Rehabilitating Government: Pay and Employment Reforms in Africa* (Washington, DC: World Bank, 1994), pp. 60–210. The Ugandan numbers are ambiguous, given the high number of ghost workers and the distinction between general public employment and the civil service. The overall public employment rolls were cut by an amazing 160,000 employees between 1990 and 1996. See Table 9 of Lienert and Modi, "A Decade of Civil Service Reform."

an overdeveloped state.[64] Nonetheless, the best available estimates from the IMF suggest that between 1986 and 1996, the number of civil servants actually increased in eleven of the eighteen countries for which there are complete data. The more ambitious elements of the reform agenda, focusing on increasing civil service professionalization and effectiveness, have progressed even less. The same IMF data indicate that average real salaries increased in only seven countries during this same period, suggesting that in most countries working conditions are not improving.[65]

Neglected Issues

This chapter has so far focused on the agenda of reform defined by the international financial institutions since the late 1970s. It has not said anything about an array of other issues African governments need to address, in all likelihood, for their economies to sustain rapid growth. Issues like judicial sector reform have been mostly neglected by the donors until recently despite obvious deficiencies and the general recognition that improved performance is a prerequisite of growth.[66] In Côte d'Ivoire, for instance, one review of judicial reform efforts by the donors from 1990 to 1996 notes, "Donor involvement was half hearted, even perfunctory. French aid was limited in volume and in scope.... The Bank's commitment seems to have been lukewarm and partial, with intermittent involvement. Judicial component funds were cut for . . . lack of activity. No conditionality was attached until 1996."[67]

The health sector presents similar situations. In spite of any progress in reforming the health sector across the region, access to health services remains far inferior to every other region of the world. An African child in 1995 was 60 percent more likely to have been vaccinated against measles than she would have been in 1980, but she remained more than

---

64. Lienert and Modi, "A Decade of Civil Service Reform," p. 44. The size of the African state and its economic implications were recently analyzed by Arthur A. Goldsmith in his fine essay, "Africa's Overgrown State Reconsidered: Bureaucracy and Economic Growth," *World Politics* 51 (1999): 520–46.
65. Ibid, p. 43.
66. A general survey is presented in Richard E. Messick, "Judicial Reform and Economic Development: A Survey of the Issues," *World Bank Research Observer* 14 (1999): 117–36.
67. Elliot Berg, Patrick Guillaumont, Jacques Pegatienan, and Jacky Amprou, "Aid and Reform in the Côte d'Ivoire," Case Study for the World Bank Project "Aid and Reform in Africa," unpublished paper, Washington, DC, December 1999, p. 60.

a third less likely to have been vaccinated than the average Latin American child![68] Furthermore, two decades of crisis leave most countries tragically unprepared to address the current AIDS/HIV crisis, which threatens to reduce life expectancy in the region from fifty-nine years today to forty-five in 2010, or the various other health epidemics that may be lurking around the corner, from the ebola virus to drug-resistant strains of tuberculosis and malaria.[69]

Perhaps even more seriously, all across Africa, investment budgets have been sacrificed to protect the more politically sensitive recurrent budget from the cuts in expenditure made necessary by the economic crisis and mandated by reform programs, particularly in cases in which revenue generation does prove stagnant. The donors have recognized that reshaping the patterns of public expenditures to favor development is just as important in the long run as cutting the fat out of budgets, but the Bank itself recognizes that its efforts to do so have largely failed.[70] Thus, in the 1990s, gross public investment has declined to an average of less than 6 percent of GDP. The proportion of expenditures devoted to public infrastructure has declined sharply.

Skimping on maintenance and investment is an inevitable feature of macroeconomic stabilization programs and not a cause for alarm in the short run. Over time, however, the prolonged nature of the African crisis is turning what could be justified as a necessary short-term expedient into a critical obstacle to renewed economic growth. The African Development Bank estimated in 1999 that a third of the roads built in the last two decades had eroded due to inadequate maintenance.[71] These accumulated maintenance deficiencies represent significant obligations on future budgets: the World Bank estimated in 1995 that additional outlays of over $1.5 billion a year for a decade were needed simply to restore the existing road network in the region to an appropriate level.[72] Poor roads result in high transport costs, which undermine Africa's competi-

68. Calculated from the World Bank, *World Development Indicators*, p. 94.
69. See the blunt assessment by the National Intelligence Council, *The Global Infectious Disease Threat and Its Implications for the United States* (Washington, DC: National Intelligence Council, January 2000), especially pp. 24–7.
70. The World Bank, *The Impact of Public Expenditure Reviews: An Evaluation*, Report Number 18573, Operations Evaluation Department (Washington, DC: World Bank, November 13, 1998).
71. The African Development Bank, "Infrastructure Development in Africa," in *African Development Report, 1999* (Oxford, UK: Oxford University Press, 1999), p. 131.
72. The World Bank, *A Continent in Transition: Sub-Saharan Africa in the Mid-1990s* (Washington, DC: World Bank, November, 1995), p. 58.

tiveness. In 1998, the Kenyan newspaper, *The Nation*, reported that the country's main commercial highway between Nairobi and Mombasa was so poorly maintained that the 500 kilometer trip took three days for a truck laden with merchandise.[73] Similar levels of maintenance expenditures are likely to be necessary for other government assets, from buildings to public utilities and enterprises.

Without making these essential expenditures, it is difficult to see how many of these economies can sustain growth. There is already much evidence that inadequate public investment has an impact on growth and poverty alleviation. During the 1980s, Africa was the only region of the developing world where agricultural labor productivity actually declined. According to Khan, between 1980 and 1990, it declined by .4 percent a year, while increasing by 2.7 percent in South Asia and 3.9 percent in the Middle East and North Africa.[74] The decline appears to have quickened in the 1990s. There are complex causes for this decline, but the dismal condition of rural infrastructure is surely a primary one. For example, only 4.6 percent of sub-Saharan Africa's (SSA) agricultural land is irrigated, compared to 38.4 percent in Asia.[75] Africa's road network is by far the most poorly developed and the least satisfactorily maintained. Dunstan Spencer has estimated that the humid and subhumid regions of tropical Africa would have to increase the density of their rural road network by a factor of five to reach the level enjoyed by India in 1950.[76]

In turn, declining productivity is one cause of the production stagnation that characterizes the region's agricultural sector. Ali and Thorbecke link all these factors to striking patterns of growing rural poverty in Africa, with 59 percent of the region's rural population living below the poverty line.[77] The region, they conclude, "in comparison with other

---

73. "Despair Road Thwarting Trade," *The Nation* (May 10, 1998): 3.
74. Cited in Ali Abdel Gadir Ali and Erik Thorbecke, "The State of Rural Poverty, Income Distribution and Rural Development in Sub Saharan Africa," paper prepared for a conference of the African Economic Research Consortium on Comparative Development Experiences in Asia and Africa, Johannesburg, November 6, 1997 (revised version, April 1998), p. 10.
75. Ibid, p. 13.
76. Study cited in Christopher Delgado, "Agricultural Transformation: The Key to Broad-Based Growth and Poverty Alleviation in Africa," in Benno Ndulu and Nicolas van de Walle (eds.), *Agenda for Africa's Economic Renewal* (Washington, DC: Overseas Development Council, 1996), p. 167.
77. Ali and Thorbecke, "The State of Rural Poverty," p. 9. Of course, these totals disguise wide variations across the region, from Cote d'Ivoire with a poverty head count ratio of 38 percent to the Central African Republic with an incredible 78 percent.

regions, suffers from greater, more severe and more persistent poverty, more unequal distribution of income, declining food production per capita and agricultural labor productivity; and a continuing population explosion" (p. 11).

These various lacunae almost certainly also explain why the reasonably positive economic climate of the mid-1990s has not produced more than a small increase in investment, which remains too low in most countries.[78] In 1996, the African region received less than 1 percent of global foreign direct investment (FDI), and two-thirds of that went to Nigeria and Angola for oil exploration.[79] The enormous capital flight that has characterized Africa these last twenty years was not reversed despite the apparent improvement of the mid-1990s. One estimate is that 40 percent of the private wealth of Africans is held outside the region.[80] Nigerians alone held an estimated $50 billion outside their country.[81] In surveys, businessmen cite poor governance, uncertain property rights, the dismal condition of the infrastructure, and the cost implications of poor health conditions on labor productivity to explain their reticence to invest in the region.[82] Economic studies suggest that malaria cost the region the equivalent of 1 percent of GDP a year in the mid-1990s, and HIV/AIDS lowers GDP in some countries by .25 percent a year, a testament to the dismal state of the public health system in the region.[83]

There has been a slight increase in investment in a minority of countries like Uganda and Ghana, which have been rewarded for their relatively stable macroeconomic policies in recent years.[84] Both have received

78. Fischer, *Is This the Turning Point?* See also François Bost, "L'Afrique subsaharienne, oubliée par les investisseurs," in *Afrique Contemporaine* 189 (1999): 41–61.
79. See Jeff Sachs, "Foreign Direct Investment in Africa," in *The Africa Competitiveness Report, 1998* (Geneva, Switzerland: World Economic Forum, 1998), p. 37.
80. Paul Collier, Anke Hoeffler, and Catherine Patillo, "Flight Capital as a Portfolio Choice," International Monetary Fund Working Paper WP/99/171 (Washington, DC: International Monetary Fund, December 1999), p. 7.
81. Cited by Lewis Machipisa, "Africa Loses Millions through Capital Flight," on Interpress Service, May 12, 1999, found on a Lexis-Nexis Internet search.
82. See Jeff Sachs, "Foreign Direct Investment in Africa," p. 37.
83. Cited in Vijaya Ramachadran, *Investing in Africa*, Policy Essay no. 25 (Washington, DC: Overseas Development Council, in press).
84. On Uganda, see Robert L. Sharer, Hema R. De Zoysa, and Calvin A. MacDonald, *Uganda: Adjustment with Growth, 1987–1994*; Occasional Paper Number 121 (Washington, DC: International Monetary Fund, March 1995); on Ghana, Robert P. Armstrong, *Ghana Country Assistance Strategy Review: A Study in Development Effectiveness* (Washington, DC: World Bank, 1996).

several hundred million dollars in FDI in recent years.[85] Unfortunately, the perception that the progress on stabilization is not sustainable will tend to be a self-fulfilling prophecy; if private sector agents do not view the reforms as fully credible, they will take a wait-and-see attitude before changing their economic behavior. Even these relatively successful countries have in fact underinvested in basic public goods, such as education and infrastructure. Surveys suggest they suffer from many of the ills, albeit in attenuated form, of their neighbors. A recent survey of barriers to private sector investment gave poor marks to both Ghana and Uganda on such issues as red tape, bureaucratic harassment, and government corruption, for instance.[86]

The conclusion is inescapable that the belated progress on macroeconomic stabilization witnessed in the 1990s will be difficult to sustain, given its shaky foundations and Africa's pressing developmental needs. A small number of countries appear to have begun to put their economies on a solid footing, but in most, improved statistics in the late 1990s will likely proved short-lived.

The uneven implementation of reform policies is summarized in Table 2.3. With the caveat that generalizing across all cases is difficult, the course of reform can be broadly summarized in the following manner. While there has been some undeniable progress on changing economic policies, this is uneven across the region's economies, given to partial implementation and vulnerable to reversals. Basic stabilization reforms have a better implementation record, but they have proven less likely to be sustained. Fiscal adjustment, in particular, has suffered dramatic setbacks after bouts of clear progress. Exchange rate reform has usually been sustained with the greatest consistency. At least outside the Franc Zone, there is a clear pattern of countries moving to more realistic and flexible levels in a way that appears broadly sustainable. These countries have not resorted to the printing presses to finance deficits in the 1990s. But here too, there are no institutional checks to quick reversals.

Structural adjustment reforms have proceeded more slowly, but they appear less vulnerable to reversal. In some areas, reform appears to have taken hold. In particular, privatization, though slow to start, has not been questioned once it has been implemented. There are no examples of renationalization in the region, suggesting that the days of nationalization

85. UNCTAD, *Foreign Direct Investment in Africa: Performance and Potential* (Geneva: United Nations Commission on Trade and Development, July 1999).
86. Emery and Spence, "Administrative Barriers."

Table 2.3. *Policy Reform in Africa: Patterns of Implementation, 1979–1999*

Reform	Degree of Implementation	Probability of Reversals	Comments
I. Stabilization			
a. Fiscal adjustment	mediocre-good	high	Belated progress in mid-1990s Sustainability questionable
b. Exchange rate policy	good-excellent	medium	Early focus of IMF; CFA countries devalue in 1994, maintain fixed rate
c. Monetary policy and external balance	mediocre-good	high	Uneven progress across time; reliance on large aid flow
II. Adjustment			
a. Domestic liberalization	poor-excellent	medium	High variation across cases
– Banking/credit	good-excellent	low	Early focus of adjustment programs
– Investment	mediocre	low	Large gap between de jure and de facto situation
– Export agriculture	mediocre	medium	Prices still set by state, particularly in ex-French states
– Food markets	mediocre-good	medium	Consumer prices liberalized more than producer prices
			Less continuing regulation in west and Central Africa
b. Trade policy	poor-mediocre	high	Little progress and often subverted in practice.
c. Public enterprise reform	poor-mediocre	low	Privatization quickens in 1990s, biggest Public enterprises remain
d. Civil service reform	poor	low	Consistently deferred, high cost and complexity

are over. A broad array of domestic markets have been liberalized, from credit to agricultural inputs. In other areas, there has been virtually no sustained progress. Civil service reform is one such glaring example. Why has there not been more progress on policy reform? How can we explain why certain types of reform have been implemented across the region and not others? Why has the speed of reform varied across policy areas?

THE EVOLUTION OF PUBLIC EXPENDITURES

A more careful look at the evolution of public expenditures holds important clues to help answer the questions posed at the end of the last section. I first look at patterns of public employment and expenditure across major world regions in Tables 2.4 and 2.5. Caution must be used in interpreting these numbers. Cross-national expenditure data are notoriously unreliable as definitions of expenditure types vary across countries, and some governments choose to move expenditures from one category to another for political reasons. For instance, there is much evidence that the category of capital expenditure often includes various recurrent expenditures and subsidies (notably to the parastatal sector), as many developing countries wish to appear to spend less on recurrent expenditures than they actually do.[87] The African subtotals are even more suspect, given missing values for half to two-thirds of the countries in the region, depending on the indicator. It is difficult to be sure how representative of the entire region are the cases for which we have data. In Table 2.5, I recalculated regional averages for only the low-income countries in Africa; at least in the expenditure category of subsidies and current transfers, there was a substantial difference in the estimated regional average between the sets of countries.

Nonetheless, these data can give us a sense of the degree to which state expenditures respond to societal demands. In this respect, the data in Table 2.4 about public sector employment suggest the extent to which, at least in a comparative sense, the African state is not unusually large. To be sure, African state structures grew extremely quickly in the decades following independence and they are unusually large relative to the size

---

87. To cite just one example, the World Bank estimated in the early 1990s that 55 percent of the health sector investment budget in Senegal should really have been designated as recurrent expenditure. See the World Bank, *Senegal: Public Expenditure Review*, Africa Region, Sahel Department (Washington, DC: World Bank, December 31, 1991), p. 20.

Table 2.4. *Government Employment, Early 1990s (as percentage of population)*

	General Government	Administration		Teaching & Health
		Central	Local	
Africa (n = 20)	2.0	0.9	0.3	0.8
Asia (11)	2.6	0.9	0.7	1.0
Eastern Europe & Former USSR (17)	6.9	1.0	0.8	5.1
Latin America & Caribbean (9)	3.0	1.2	0.7	1.1
Middle East & North Africa (8)	3.9	1.4	0.9	1.6
OECD (21)	7.7	1.8	2.5	3.4
Overall	4.7	1.2	1.1	2.4

Note: Coverage is of total civilian public sector; regional averages are unweighted.
Source: Salvatore Schiavo-Campo, Giulio de Tommaso, and Amitabha Mukherjee, *An International Statistical Survey of Government Employment and Wages*, Public Sector Management and Information Technology Team, Technical Department for Europe, Central Asia, Middle East, and North Africa (Washington, DC: World Bank, undated). From World Bank website.

of what is usually a small formal sector. Nonetheless, the growth came from a very low base, so that, as a proportion of their overall populations, they remain significantly smaller than their counterparts in other regions of the developing world.[88] Table 2.4 calls forth the following stylized facts. African states are relatively small; they are primarily based in the capital and involved in central administration. Roughly 40 percent of this employment concerns the educational and health sectors, a proportion that is roughly similar to those of countries in other regions, although again a smaller share of the national population. In addition, the available data indicate that few African states suffered a significant decline in the absolute numbers of public employees in the 1980s and 1990s, though they usually declined relative to the overall population, as the growth in public employment did not keep up with that of the overall population, which grew at 2.5 to 3 percent a year.

There are probably many reasons for these patterns. Nonetheless, this cross-regional comparison suggests a relatively small number of public employees in Africa working for a state that does not provide many

88. Goldsmith, "Africa's Overgrown State Reconsidered: Bureaucracy and Economic Growth."

Table 2.5. *Government Expenditures, Early 1990s (as percent of total expenditures)*

	Goods & Services		Wages & Salaries		Interest Payments		Subsidies & Transfers		Capital Expenditures	
	1980	1995	1980	1995	1980	1995	1980	1995	1980	1995
Sub-Saharan Africa	53	51	29	31	6	13	15	18	25	20
Low-Income Sub-Saharan Africa	54	51	29	31	6	15	15	9	25	22
East Asia & Pacific	..	45	..	27	..	11	..	18	25	28
Latin America & Caribbean	50	36	31	24	6	11	24	26	20	14
Middle East & North Africa	..	55	..	32	..	11	..	13	32	19
South Asia	31	39	..	..	12	24	23	21	17	18
High Income Countries	28	25	13	11	7	9	56	59	7	5

Note: Africa regional totals are unweighted averages of national percentages. Coverage varies by category. Low-income Africa excludes Botswana, Gabon, Mauritius, Namibia, and Republic of South Africa, all middle-income countries in 1997. Wages and Salaries category is included within the Goods and Services category.

Source: Calculated from Table 4.13, World Bank, *World Development Indicators, 1998* (Washington, DC: World Bank, 1998).

services and is largely absent outside the capital. This impression is supported by studies on the *quality* of public expenditures, or the efficiency of expenditures at improving the welfare of the population. For instance, research by Gupta, Honjo, and Verhoeven has concluded that health and education expenditures in Africa consistently underperformed similar expenditures in Latin America and Asia in terms of improving health and education attainments, largely because of the disproportionate amount spent on salaries for state personnel relative to other outlays.[89] Some anecdotal evidence also suggests that staff and expenditures in social sectors may not be oriented toward providing social services. In the early 1990s, more than 10 percent of Senegal's public teaching staff occupied nonteaching jobs in the central ministry offices in Dakar,[90] for example, while in Tanzania, the primary enrollment rate went from 93 to 66 percent between 1980 and 1994–96, even as the number of teachers was increasing from 81,000 to just under 109,000 during this same period.[91] In Mali, a World Bank study[92] noted that the government did not allocate any budgetary resources for primary health care and health education programs in 1997, which were entirely funded by external donors (p. 31). That year, over 80 percent of government health expenditures went to, in order of importance, central administration, logistics, secondary care, and training of staff. Mali is hardly unique: another study notes that donors financed "nearly all capital investments in health in the public sector" throughout Africa during the 1990s.[93]

Table 2.5 offers additional evidence of this phenomenon by providing a comparative look at what governments spend money on. Based on

89. See Sanjeev Gupta, Keito Honjo and Marijn Verhoeven, "The Efficiency of Government Expenditure: Experiences from Africa," IMF Working Paper, Fiscal Affairs Department (Washington, DC: International Monetary Fund, November 1997). Paul Collier and Jan Gunning cite other studies showing that social expenditures in the region consistently underperform public expenditures in other regions, and conclude that this is because "the public sector has been used to create employment rather than to deliver services, and this reduces productivity" (p. 70). See their essay, "Explaining African Economic Performance," *Journal of Economic Literature* 37 (March 1999): 64–111.
90. The World Bank, *Senegal: Public Expenditure Review*, p. 23.
91. The World Bank, *African Development Indicators*, Tables 13–14 and 13–17.
92. The World Bank, *The World Bank and the Health Sector in Mali: An OED Country Sector Review*, Report no. 18112 (Washington, DC: World Bank, June 30, 1998).
93. David H. Peters, Kami Kandola, A. Edward Elemendorf, and Gnanaraj Chellaraj, *Health Expenditures, Services and Outcomes in Africa*, World Bank Health Development Network, Health, Nutrition and Population Series (Washington, DC: World Bank, 1999), p. 14.

a different sample of countries, with different regional aggregates, the data divide overall expenditure into six broad categories. At this broad level of generality, African government expenditures appear to follow allocational patterns roughly similar to those in other developing regions. The one area in which that is not true is for the category of "current transfers and subsidies" in which African governments spend less than other governments, particularly once Africa's four middle-income economies are pulled out of the sample. This category combines transfer payments to individuals (i.e., for pensions and welfare) with subsidies to firms (for example, subsidies for public enterprises). Combined with other data, however, it does offer tentative evidence that African governments spend a smaller percentage of their overall expenditures on improving the welfare of the citizenry than do governments in other regions. Goode, for instance, indicates that in the early 1980s, African governments devoted 3.4 percent of total expenditure to "social security and welfare" compared with 2.6 percent for Asia, 12.7 percent for Latin America, 8.1 percent for middle Eastern states, and 36.1 percent for industrial countries.[94] For his part, Pradhan provides data suggesting expenditures for this same category in Africa to be, on average, half the level in Latin America and a third of the level in South Asia.[95]

This evidence accords pretty well with my argument that most African states are fairly autonomous from social pressures. It suggests a state that is not particularly responsive to societal demands and for which expansion is an end in itself rather than a means to promote economic development and poverty alleviation.

The evolution of public expenditures during the economic crisis of the 1980s and 1990s tends to confirm these patterns. Comparative data across time also suggest that African state structures have weathered the economic crisis better than their Latin American or Asian counterparts. As a proportion of the economy, state expenditures have actually crept upward by one or two percentage points of GDP over the course of the last two decades, according to IMF data for low- and middle-income countries throughout the developing world.[96] In this sense, the evolution

---

94. Richard Goode, *Government Finance in Developing Countries* (Washington, DC: Brookings Institution, 1984), p. 48.
95. Sanjay Pradhan, "Evaluating Public Spending," World Bank Discussion Paper no. 323 (Washington, DC: World Bank, 1996).
96. See, for instance, World Bank, *World Development Indicators, 1998* (Washington, DC: World Bank, 1999), Tables 4-12 and 4-13. In at least some cases, the rise is explained by a decline in GDP during this period.

of public expenditures in Africa does not look unusual. However, when you factor in the role of foreign aid, a different picture emerges. Between the late 1970s and the late 1990s, aid as a share of GDP has grown from an average of under 5 percent of GDP to well above a tenth of GDP across the countries of the region, compared to an average of under 1 percent of GDP for low- and middle-income countries in other regions of the developing world. Since the major proportion of aid takes the form of goods and services provided to states, in effect the size of government expenditures relative to the domestic economy is bigger than national statistics suggest, and has grown, not shrunk, despite two decades of devastating economic crisis.

The evolution of expenditure shares over the last two decades further reinforces the sense that most African states have responded to the crisis by looking out for themselves. As discussed above, government consumption has been protected more assiduously from austerity than was public investment, which collapsed in many countries. This leads to a stylized fact about adjustment in Africa: *a common state response to economic collapse appears to have been to protect its own position and to lessen instead its developmental ambitions.* The patterns of reform in the agricultural sector described in the previous section illustrate this dynamic. The state has withdrawn from the costly and often not very effective developmental apparatus it built up with donor support in the 1970s: extension activities have been curtailed, as has feeder road construction. Most significant, the very costly fertilizer subsidies of the past have been eliminated in most countries. Typically, no pro-active policies for agriculture have replaced the old ones. The state's core services in the countryside have been reduced to virtually none, in many instances, unless there is a donor project in the area. Extension agents continue to receive salaries, but they no longer have a development budget and rely on the local administrative structure (the prefect, or police officer or perhaps a district officer) or NGO for such basic things as transportation.[97] But, on the other hand, as also discussed earlier, the state has often found it useful to retain a role in setting agricultural prices, refusing to accede to donor demands to completely abandon what it continues to view as an element of control over the sector. To call this "neoliberal reform" is to miss the point that the reform moment has been used by

---

97. Such was the case for a Senegalese Ministry of the Interior service for rural development, which I visited some sixty miles south of Dakar in July 1998. The entire development budget for a team of seven officials overseeing an area of several hundred square miles amounted to 50,000 CFA francs a year, roughly $100.

states to withdraw from their rural development responsibilities while retaining their ultimate ability to regulate the sector.

Much the same can be said about the social sectors. Many critics of structural adjustment programs have argued that they impose high social costs as state retrenchment ends up hurting state programs in areas such as health and education. The evidence in Africa for this claim is nonetheless mixed. Sahn and his colleagues have argued that government expenditures for health and education underwent only small cuts in the 1980s and early 1990s.[98] But other studies indicate a deterioration in social services in the region during this period, suggesting a less effective public effort. Thus, school enrollment rates or vaccination services appear to be in decline in a large number of countries.[99]

How can these anomalous findings be reconciled? Data quality may be one factor, and there may simply be significant cross-national differences. Nonetheless, the data are consistent with the interpretation that states have responded to fiscal austerity by cutting investment and developmental activities much more than overall expenditures, increasingly focusing on recurrent consumption (such as salaries and perquisites). The retreat from developmental tasks is particularly striking in Africa's poorest countries, where governmental commitment to development was typically weaker even before the economic crisis and where fiscal austerity is particularly severe.

The evolving state role in Mali's education sector can serve as a telling illustration of these dynamics. In 1995, the World Bank estimated the gross enrollment rate at 32 percent, up only slightly from 26 percent in 1980.[100] Roughly a third of total enrollments were accounted for by private Koranic schools and other private schools, in rapid expansion, suggesting the public sector provided educational services to barely a fifth of the school-age population. According to a 1992 article by Gérard, privately run primary schools increased from 2 in 1985 to 105 in early 1992, so that the public education sector appears to be

98. See Sahn et al., *Structural Adjustment Reconsidered*, p. 102.
99. World Bank, *A Continent in Transition: Sub-Saharan Africa in the Mid 1990s* (Washington, DC: World Bank, 1995), estimates (p. 29) that gross enrollment ratios have declined during the 1980s in twenty of the forty-four countries for which there are data. The decline can be directly linked to civil strife in roughly a third of the cases. Similarly, measles immunization coverage has declined or stagnated in thirteen countries.
100. World Bank, "Fact Sheet, Mali—Education Sector Investment Program (EDSIP)" at the World Bank web cite *www.worldbank.org/pics/pid/ml40650* (1998).

receding.[101] Enrollment rates vary significantly between town and rural areas. Thus, again in 1995, the enrollment rate varied between from 90 percent in Bamako, the capital, to 11 percent in the north region. This low rate of enrollment resulted mostly from an insufficient number of schools and teachers, even though the government has regularly allocated some 20 percent of its national budget to education and has benefited from substantial support from the donors. France has traditionally been a significant source of money and educational policy ideas. In 1995, the World Bank agreed to undertake a $50 million education investment program, the fifth of a series of loans to the sector since 1962. It was never disbursed, however, as the Malian government failed to meet the loan's preconditions. Another similar education loan was being negotiated as this book was being written in 1999.

Although government funding declined slightly during the 1990s, the Malian government and the donors pushed through a series of ambitious reforms, the main objective of which appears to decentralize primary responsibility for education to the local level.[102] Backed by the donors, the government appeared to want to reduce its budgetary commitment but retain a critical regulative role. One initiative consisted of providing partial funding to parent associations to allow them to build schools for private instruction. To qualify for funding, the association had to provide 25 percent of the total cost, a figure Gérard viewed as prohibitively high for most villages.[103] How will the government maintain its regulatory function as it withdraws from direct provision? Though a major architect of this policy, the World Bank itself admitted that Mali's Ministry of Primary Education is poorly equipped to play such a role, as it suffers from "weak capacity for policy analysis and planning, overly centralized decision-making, poor personnel and financial management."[104] Clearly, the numbers of nonteaching personnel will have to be increased considerably if the state is to play this regulatory role effectively, and one is allowed a degree of skepticism about the likely results of such an undertaking, given the past record of donor-inspired institution building in Mali's education sector. In the meantime, public educational expendi-

101. Etienne Gérard, "Entre etat et population: l'ecole et l'education en devenir," *Politique Africaine* 47 (1992): 59–69.
102. Ibid.
103. Ibid, p. 66. Note, however, that a World Bank education specialist familiar with the project suggested this approach had worked reasonably well. Confidential interview, World Bank, November 9, 1999.
104. World Bank, "Fact Sheet," p. 2.

Table 2.6. *The Evolution of Primary School Gross Enrollment Ratios,*
1980–1996

High Enrollment Countries		Low Enrollment Countries	
Botswana	+17.8	Burkina Faso	+21.3
Congo/Zaire	−20.2	Niger	+3.9
Tanzania	−25.7	Mali	+14.6
Mauritius	+13.9	Burundi	+26.2
Cameroon	−9.8	Guinea	+10.8
Swaziland	+16.4	Mauritania	+38.6
Lesotho	+5.9	Djibouti	+1.3
Nigeria	−10.8	Ethiopia	−3.0
Kenya	−29.3		
Togo	−1.3		
Madagascar	−40.1		
Congo, Republic of	−22.5		

Notes: High enrollment defined as a primary school gross enrollment ratio of 90 percent or above in 1980; low enrollment defined as a primary school gross enrollment ratio of 40 percent or below in 1980. The numbers in both columns are found by subtracting the enrollment ratio in 1980 from an average of available ratios for 1994–96. Some countries are missing due to nonavailability of data.

Source: World Bank, *African Development Indicators* (Washington, DC: World Bank, 2000), p. 330.

tures will be buttressed, even as the number of children educated by the state continues to decline.

This evolution is not always quite as stark as in Mali. Two distinct patterns can be discerned in national education statistics. In the poorest African countries like Mali, enrollment rates have continued to creep upward during the period of economic crisis, though less rapidly than during the pre-crisis period, often with substantial assistance from the donors. In the richer countries, on the other hand, in which virtually universal primary education appeared to have been attained before the crisis, enrollment rates have declined over the last twenty years.[105] This evolution is demonstrated quite clearly in Table 2.6.

Of the countries with enrollment rates under 40 percent in 1980, only Ethiopia's enrollment rate went down between 1980 and 1996. In sharp

105. These numbers should be treated with caution as most cross-national data on education are self-reported by governments and subject to wide differences in quality. See Joel Samoff, "The Facade of Precision in Education Data and Statistics: A Troubling Example from Tanzania," *Journal of Modern African Studies* 29 (1991): 669–89.

contrast, eight of the twelve countries with rates over 90 percent in 1980 underwent a decline during this period. In addition, there is some evidence that the quality of public sector educational services appears to be declining, notably in rural areas.[106] In Zambia, with an enrollment ratio of 89 percent in the mid-1990s, perhaps 75 percent of recent school leavers are functionally illiterate, as a result of the low quality of education services. Given declining budgets, "the pupil/textbook ratio in primary schools in 1992 was 8:1 in Mathematics, 5:1 in English and about 20:1 in social studies" and conditions were so insalubrious that many schools close during the rainy season to head off the threat of cholera.[107] In Mozambique, in the mid-1990s, more than half of all teachers had completed only primary school education.[108]

A recurring pattern throughout the region is the combination of a growing donor role in developmental activity and the retreat of the state apparatus from what were once considered central developmental functions. There is considerable variance across countries and across sectors, but the best estimates suggest that somewhere between a third and two-thirds of education and health services now completely bypass the state and are the result of a combination of donor, NGO, and private sector efforts.[109] As Robinson and White note, in many countries, there is a de facto return to the situation during the colonial period when the state's role in social sector provision was peripheral to the effort of the Chris-

106. Ibid. See also Simon Appleton and John MacKinnon, "Enhancing Human Capacities in Africa," in Benno Ndulu and Nicolas van de Walle (eds.), *Agenda for Africa's Economic Renewal* (Washington, DC: Overseas Development Council, 1996), pp. 109–50, especially pp. 110–12. For general evidence of growing rural poverty, see Ali and Thorbecke, "The State of Rural Poverty."

107. See pp. 131–4, World Bank, *Zambia: Prospects for Sustainable and Equitable Growth*, Report no. 11570-ZA (Washington, DC: World Bank, August 23, 1993).

108. Peter Fallon and Luiz Pereira da Silva, "Recognizing Labor Market Constraints: Government-Donor Competition for Manpower in Mozambique," in David L. Lindauer and Barbara Nunberg (eds.), *Rehabilitating Government: Pay and Employment Reforms in Africa* (Washington, DC: World Bank, 1994), p. 87.

109. See Joseph Semboja and Ole Therkildsen (eds.), *Service Provision under Stress in East Africa* (London: James Currey, 1995); Meredeth Turshen, *Privatizing Health Services in Africa* (New Brunswick, NJ: Rutgers University Press, 1999), especially pp. 86–91; and Mark Robinson, "Privatizing the Voluntary Sector: NGOs as Public Service Contractors?" in David Hulme and Michael Edwards (eds.), *NGOs, States and Donors: Too Close for Comfort?* (New York: St. Martin's Press, 1997), pp. 59–78.

tian missions.[110] The current fiscal crisis is leading many governments to forsake the dominant postcolonial ambition to generalize state provision. In Uganda, for example, donors financed 77 percent of health spending in fiscal year 1992/93 while the government's share was 23 percent. In the case of expenditures on hospitals, however, the government's share was 64 percent, suggesting the often noted preference of governments in the region for city-based curative care that benefits the better off.[111] In Tanzania, 58 percent of secondary school enrollments are accounted for by NGO and church organizations, up from 28 percent in 1965. In Zimbabwe, church missions provide more than two-thirds of all hospital beds in rural areas.[112]

Sovereignty Expenditures

The retreat from external obligations is a fairly standard governmental response to economic austerity, one that is far from unique to Africa. More distinctive, however, has been the rest of the political response. Even as African states have withdrawn from development tasks and as salaries for public servants have been allowed to decline precipitously in real terms, the top of the state apparatus often has retained conspicuous consumption patterns. Thus, if the previous paragraphs have suggested that the entire state apparatus has been relatively protected from the ravages of the crisis, it is important to underscore the fact that within the state, there also appear to have been relative winners and losers. In particular, spending patterns suggest a clear shift in spending away from the lower rungs of the civil service to its highest levels and to the political elite at the top of the state. I am speaking in particular of what the French call expenditures "regaliennes," literally translated as regal expenditures, but which can better be defined as expenditures linked to the exercise of state sovereignty. These include defense spending, particularly when it is not related to a direct external threat, as well as

---

110. Mark Robinson and Gordon White, "The Role of Civic Organizations in the Provision of Social Services," United Nations University WIDER Research for Action Paper no. 37 (1997), see pp. 9–13.
111. Emmanuel Ablo and Ritva Reinikka, "Do Budgets Really Matter? Evidence from Public Spending on Education and Health in Uganda," World Bank Policy Research Paper (Washington, DC: World Bank, undated), p. 24.
112. These last two statistics are provided in Robinson and White, "The Role of Civic Organizations," pp. 12–13.

expenditures for international diplomacy, government offices, and other activities that benefit an extremely small stratum of the population. They are all closely tied to the exercise of national sovereignty, be it in symbolic or ceremonial fashion, but they do not have a developmental function and they are not necessarily linked to the exercise of state power, although they do play a role in maintaining political stability.

It is interesting to examine the evolution of these sovereignty expenditures over time, since donors have traditionally shied away from engaging in conditionality over them, despite their very evident impact on the government's ability to finance development. Although the available data are unfortunately very weak, they suggest that these kinds of expenditures have been remarkably unaffected by economic crisis. Defense expenditures are perhaps the most obvious type linked to sovereignty. The best available data are published by the Stockholm International Peace Research Institute (SIPRI). They show that the twenty-one countries in the region for data are available spent an average of 2 percent of GDP on defense, quite a modest amount and probably an underestimate.[113] SIPRI also provides much better coverage of the military indicator perhaps least amenable to manipulation: the number of soldiers in the armed forces: Overall, for the forty countries on which it reports data, the number of soldiers grew by an average of 67 percent between 1985 and 1996.[114] Recognizing the great variety of defense needs across African countries between these two dates, I excluded six countries that were involved in significant military activities during this period (Angola, Burundi, Rwanda, Senegal, Sierra Leone, and Uganda) as well as three countries in which defense needs enormously declined during the period (Ethiopia, Mozambique, South Africa) and recalculated the rate of increase. For the remaining thirty-two countries, the number of soldiers still increased by 28 percent during this period. For every country like Ghana (a 54 percent decline) or Tanzania (down 14 percent) that had decreased the number of soldiers to save money in a context of fiscal crisis, there were states like Gabon (96 percent increase), Zambia (up 33 percent), or Togo (up 94 percent) that had continued to increase the number of soldiers despite no apparent external military threat.

113. SIPRI numbers, cited in the 1999 edition of the United Nations Development Program's *Human Development Report* (New York: Oxford University Press, 1999), pp. 188–91. African governments are widely believed to underreport their defense expenditures, which moreover benefit from sizable foreign assistance, notably through subsidized arms sales.
114. Ibid. UNDP reports index numbers with a base year of 1985.

Another striking if imperfect piece of evidence regarding the continuation of sovereignty expenditures by African governments is offered by the evolving size of government cabinets. I collected data on cabinets at three points of time: April/June 1979, July/August 1988, and August/September 1996. Table 2.7 reports these data, with regional averages for the three dates.[115] Thus, it shows that in 1979, the average cabinet in the region included 19.1 ministers and that this average had climbed to 22.6 by 1996. These averages disguise significant variation, and I have also included data on the biggest and smallest cabinet at each point. Each data point constitutes a snapshot in time. In some cases, the cabinet size recorded underwent big changes soon afterward – because of a military coup, for example; because certain positions were demoted; or because other prestigious governmental bodies (advisory economic and social councils, politburos, a committee for national salvation, etc.) were established or eliminated. The data are nonetheless instructive about general trends.

In most countries, a ministerial appointment is an important position for a member of the political elite, bringing with it patronage opportunities as well as significant perks and status-enhancing privileges. African states have long been notorious for their large cabinets, with ministerial appointments that often have little relevance to policy-making priorities or the size of actual budgets. Large cabinets are rarely a response to economic policy concerns, of course. Typically, they seek to facilitate compromise and cohesion within the political class. Lijphart has shown a strong positive correlation in Western democracies between the number of parties in government and the size of the cabinet.[116] Coalition governments almost invariably have larger cabinets. In Africa, similarly, ethnic diversity appears to have increased cabinet size. A simple correlation between the size of the cabinet in each of the three dates in

115. These totals did not include the head of state even if he or she presided over the cabinet. It did include all positions accorded cabinet or council of ministers rank by the head of state, including deputy ministers and secretaries of state. To minimize problems of comparability, it did not include provincial, prefectoral, or regional ministers, even if they were accorded cabinet status. It also did not include other consultative executive bodies that existed in a number of governments, typically soon after a military coup. Thus, Somalia's five-member politburo is not included in that country's total for 1979; nor is Nigeria's twenty-eight-member Armed Forces Ruling Council in 1988, or Madagascar's twenty-two-member Supreme Revolutionary Council at the same date.

116. Arend Lijphart, *Democracies: Patterns of Majoritarian and Consensus Rule in Twenty-One Countries* (New Haven, CT: Yale University Press, 1984).

Table 2.7. *African Government Cabinet Size, 1979–1996*

	1979	1986	1996
Average Number of Members	19.1	20.9	22.6
– excluding microstates*	20.3	22.0	23.9
Smallest Cabinets*	Ghana (11)	Namibia (8)	Gambia (13)
	Gambia (11)	Gambia (13)	Lesotho (13)
Largest Cabinets	Gabon (35)	Gabon (54)	Cameroon (42)
	Côte d'Ivoire (31)	Cameroon (34)	Sudan (38)

* Micro states include all states with population under one million (Cape Verde, Comoros, Djibouti, Equatorial Guinea, Sao Tome, and Seychelles). Category of Smallest Cabinet also excludes them.

Source: Data from Europa, *Africa South of the Sahara* (London: Europa Publications Limited, 1979, 1986, and 1996); data for 1979 mostly from April 1979 (N = 46); data for 1986 mostly from June 1985 (N = 46); data for 1996 mostly from September 1996 (N = 47). Totals do not include heads of state if they sit in cabinet; does include deputy ministers, secretaries of state, and other subordinate cabinet posts, if they are clearly listed as having cabinet status. The totals do not include provincial governorships or prefects.

Table 2.7 and the country's level of ethnic fragmentation reveals a high positive correlation.[117] It is likely that leaders seek to preserve national unity by including elites from as many salient ethnoregional groups as possible. Large cabinets may thus hold a political function. Certainly, it is difficult to imagine what policy advantages they could advance; large cabinets complicate policy making, posing significant coordination problems within government. Certainly, African cabinets are rarely convened for much more than ceremonial functions.

Cabinets typically have significant expenditure implications and have high opportunity costs in the typically small budgets of African states laboring under fiscal austerity. Côte d'Ivoire, for instance, the third biggest economy in the region after Nigeria and South Africa, had a total national budget in 1996 of U.S.$3.5 billion and a cabinet including thirty-two ministers and four deputy ministers. A more typical state budget in the region is probably under a billion dollars in total expenditures a year, including debt servicing obligations. For the smaller ministries, the recurrent cost obligations of maintaining the minister's office constitute a significant component of the available budget. It might be noted that the fastest growing country in the region, Botswana, had cab-

117. Simple correlation coefficients were estimated between cabinet size in 1979, 1986, and 1996 and a measure of ethnic fragmentation. The correlations were, respectively, .55 (p = .0001), .44 (p = .0003), and .46 (p = .0002).

inets of eleven to fourteen members during this period, while European countries often have cabinets of fewer than two dozen members, though they oversee national budgets considerably larger than the biggest in Africa.

Throughout the region, the cost of maintaining large cabinets has been compounded by fairly rapid turnover of ministerial seats. Ghana, for instance, had eight ministers of finance between 1970 and 1990, twelve ministers of education, and twelve ministers of agriculture.[118] A large number of cabinet reshuffles can be due to political instability and the turnover of heads of state. More often this shifting appears to be symptomatic of the management of the political class by the head of state. Shuffles expand the number of individuals who can benefit from ministerial largesse, allow the president to prevent the emergence of rivals from within the cabinet, and inspire loyalty from ministers who are reminded that their presence in the cabinet depends on presidential goodwill. Whatever the reasons, it is not unusual for ministers to retain certain perquisites and privileges for a couple of months after they have left office, again adding to the fiscal burden of large, unstable cabinets.

The evidence from Table 2.7 suggests that cabinet size has held steady if not actually increased since the beginning of the debt crisis. This evidence is once again instructive regarding the persistence of government consumption privileging the higher levels of the political class with little benefit to the state's developmental functions. Even as the investment budget has withered and key developmental tasks have devolved to donors or been abandoned, the luxury of the big cabinet has been sustained. Indeed, recent events in Kenya demonstrated the degree of attachment to this luxury. There, the cabinet has slowly but surely grown from around twenty members to twenty-seven over the last fifteen years. In mid-1999, Moi responded to pressures from a donor community increasingly impatient with the corruption of the regime by cutting the number of ministries down to fifteen, but he chose to retain all twenty-six of his colleagues within the cabinet, presumably with their full salaries and benefits.[119]

Unfortunately, there are few other systematic data on this kind of government consumption that one can examine to back up the claim that

118. See Nicolas van de Walle and Timothy Johnston, *Improving Aid to Africa* (Baltimore: Johns Hopkins University Press, for the Overseas Development Council, 1996), p. 86.
119. See John Nyaga, "Ridicule and Praise Follow Casualty Free Reshuffle in Kenya," Agence France Presse news release, September 7, 1999.

the crisis has not stopped excessive spending by senior state decision makers. The tendency of cabinets to increase in size is mirrored by an increase in the size of other national bodies. Legislatures, another important site of elite accommodation politics, grew from an average of 89.5 seats across the region following the first postindependence election in the early 1960s, to 140 seats in 1989, and to 149 in 1997.[120] Legislators are probably not as expensive to maintain as ministers, but they too constitute a burden in a small budget. In mid-1999, the Nigerian legislature was embroiled in controversy with the revelation that each of that country's 593 new legislators would be granted a furniture allowance of up to 3.5 million Nigerian naira (roughly U.S.$35,500), an impolitic sum of money in a country in which the average civil servant brought home about $200 a month.[121]

Presidential commissions and advisory councils have tended to proliferate, as have the number of administrative districts, municipalities, and provinces. In Kenya, President Moi created the Presidential Commission on Soil Conservation and the Presidential Commission on Music in the early 1990s, both of which had permanent staffs and secretariats, despite having terms of reference that directly overlapped with, respectively, the Ministry of the Environment and Natural Resources and the Ministry of Culture.[122] But the champion of this kind of multiplication of offices is perhaps Côte d'Ivoire. Its legislature has regularly expanded, from 70 members at independence to 120 in 1970 to 147 in 1980 and 175 in 1985. Over time, the Economic and Social Council has been expanded from 25 members to 120, the number of administrative communes from 34 to 196 (another expansion is planned to 365), and the number of departments from 4 to 49.[123]

---

120. The first two numbers are cited in Bratton and van de Walle, *Democratic Experiments*, p. 71. The numbers for 1997 were calculated by the author from various sources. They concern lower houses of parliament and exclude ex officio members.

121. "Obasanjo's One Hundred Days," *Africa Confidential* (August 27, 1999): 1–3. *The Economist* relates other shenanigans in the Nigerian legislature in "Self Service for Nigerian Senators," *The Economist* (August 12, 2000): 41.

122. See World Bank, *Kenya: Re-Investing in Stabilization and Growth through Public Sector Adjustment* (Washington, DC: World Bank, 1992), p. 43.

123. On the Ivoirian administration and its political functions over time, see Richard Crook, "Patrimonialism, Administrative Effectiveness and Economic Development in Côte d'Ivoire," *African Affairs* 88 (1989): 205–28; Richard Crook and James Manor, *Democracy and Decentralization in South Asia and West Africa: Participation, Accountability and Performance* (New York: Cambridge University Press, 1999); and Tessy Bakary, "Côte d'Ivoire: l'etatisation de l'etat," in

One could multiply the examples of African governments maintaining costly practices for top elites amid austerity budgeting: in one country, the number of generals in the army is in constant progression despite no obvious foreign threat;[124] in another, the government spends huge sums preparing the capital city for an Organization of African Unity summit;[125] and in yet another, the senior civil service maintains an outlandish travel budget.[126] One could also mention in this context, the continuation of the practice of presidential slush funds that are transparently designed to promote political stability. Thus, President Chiluba of Zambia had the legislature approve a presidential fund of 12 billion kwacha in 1998 (approximately 6–8 million), most of which was distributed at his discretion, notably to soccer clubs, church groups, and hospitals.[127] Finally, and in much the same spirit, what should one make of the distribution of honorific medals in Cameroon during a national holiday ceremony in May 1989? As related by Achille Mbembe, slightly over 3,000 eminent citizens were rewarded with gold, silver, and dark-red decorations, at a cost of 30 million CFA francs, or roughly U.S.$110,00.[128] That year, 1989, was a disastrous one for the Cameroon economy, with a 6 percent decline in GDP.

But perhaps the most striking such practices concern the expenses that presidents have continued to lavish on themselves, even as their nation's fiscal crises grew in significance. Presidents all over Africa are notorious for the presidential palaces they have built for themselves, albeit usually

Jean François Médard (ed.), *Etats d'Afrique Noire: Formation, mécanismes et crises* (Paris: Karthala, 1994), pp. 53–91.

124. In Cameroon, President Biya more than doubled the number of generals from seven to fifteen in 1993 in response to the severe internal instability his regime was then facing. See Celestin Monga, "Régime militaire à visage civil," *Jeune Afrique Economie* (March 1993): 118.

125. Togo is thus said to have spent $6–7 million to convene a 1997 meeting of the OAU on resolving the Congo crisis. See "Remettre le Togo en Marche," *Marchés Tropicaux et Méditérranéans* (April 4, 1997): p. 706.

126. In Zambia, the government allegedly approved 27,000 nights abroad by senior Zambian civil servants in 1997. Many of these nights out of the country were paid for by donors, but the same source claimed that the government spent seven billion kwacha that year on international travel, roughly $5 million in that year's very volatile exchange rate (confidential interviews, Ministry of Finance, Lusaka, May 1999). This number may not seem outlandish when it is considered that the Zambian government sent seventeen officials to the May 1999 Consultative Group meetings in Paris.

127. Barraclough, "Trouble in Lusaka."

128. Achille Mbembe, "Provisional Notes on the Postcolony," *Africa* 62 (1992): 2–37, p. 27.

officially with their own personal fortunes. Paul Biya had a personal airport built at his own presidential retreat of Mvomeka'a in the early 1990s, even as his government was disregarding World Bank conditionality and building a new international airport in Yaounde, the capital.[129] When he traveled abroad for official functions in the mid-1990s, Zimbabwean President Mugabe's entourage routinely included more than three dozen officials, assistants, bodyguards, and family members.[130] In 1999 alone, Mugabe reportedly made state visits to sixteen countries in fourteen weeks outside the country. Given an entourage of some forty officials on these trips at an average daily allowance of 10,000 Zimbabwean dollars (40 zim$ = 1 U.S.$), these 1999 trips cost the Zimbabwean taxpayer some U.S.$980,000, not including airfares and incidentals.[131] Not to be outdone, Omar Bongo of Gabon made a visit to Europe and the United States in April–May 1999 with more than seventy people. One objective of the trip was to gain sympathy for Gabon's worsening economy and lobby Western governments for debt relief.[132]

The most egregious excess by an African leader is surely the construction of the Basilica of Our Lady of Peace of Yamoussoukrou by President Houphouët-Boigny in his native village. A replica of Saint Peter's Basilica in Rome, albeit twice as big, containing the equivalent of thirty acres of marble and fully air conditioned, the church is said to have cost several hundred million dollars. Officially, it was built entirely with the president's personal fortune, the ostensible reason for which the donors kept silent about the church's construction in the late 1980s. During this same period, the donors agreed to reschedule Ivoirian foreign debt on an almost annual basis, allowing it to grow quickly, to $12 billion by 1994, the year of Houphouët-Boigny's death. It might be added

---

129. Since his predecessor, Ahmadu Ahidjo, had built an airport in his own home town of Garoua in the late 1970s, Cameroon can now claim four airports able to land wide-bodied jets. The oldest and busiest airport remains the one in the country's economic capital, Douala.
130. As I was able to ascertain first when he came to Michigan State University to receive an honorary degree in 1992, and second at the Summit of the Global Coalition for Africa in Maastricht, the Netherlands, in November 1995. These travel expenses, which have apparently come to be criticized by the press in Zimbabwe, are described, with other examples, in a PANA news release, "Zimbabweans Question Mugabe's Travelling Show," October 19, 1999.
131. Ibid.
132. Economist Intelligence Unit, *Country Report for Gabon*, Third Quarter, 1999 (London: The Economist Intelligence Unit), p. 11.

that between 1980 and 1995, personal income in Côte d'Ivoire fell by 50 percent.[133]

It may be remarked that these scandalous examples are disingenuous and that all governments of the world spend what seem to be large sums on sovereignty expenditures, but that they are unimportant, relative to the size of national budgets and given their political role in maintaining stability. Their political importance will be assessed in later chapters, but here it can be suggested again that in the small economies of Africa, where budgets are also small, sovereignty expenditures do have a very real opportunity cost in terms of development expenditure. Thus, a 1993 World Bank report noted that "every year since 1984, Zambia has spent more on its diplomatic services than on 'land, water and national resource development' (over 2.55 vs. 2.0% [of the budget]). The cost of maintaining Zambian foreign services abroad were more than how much Zambia spent on the provision of primary school services (net of teacher salaries) in the entire country."[134]

CONCLUSION

It is now possible to summarize the patterns of implementation of policy reform over the last twenty years. In broad general terms, there has been more progress on stabilization policies than on the more complex agenda of institutional and structural change. On the one hand, this can be imputed to the technical difficulties of undertaking real lasting change. Much of the stabilization agenda is what are often called "stroke of the pen" reforms, which can involve only a handful of officials in a country's ministry of finance or the central bank for successful implementation. A reform like privatization, however, involves a host of public and private actors, and the technical requirements of components like company valuation almost inevitably take time and are subject to controversy. This is true of most adjustment policies. Even when defining the parameters of policy reform is relatively straightforward, as in much trade reform and many price liberalization policies, implementation of the policy is complex and difficult. Thus, we witness a large and growing gap between the reform that is in the books and the reality on the ground.

On the other hand, differences in implementation should not be imputed solely to technical factors. First, fiscal considerations have also

133. See "Ivory Coast Buries Founding Father," *New York Times*, February 8, 1994, p. 4
134. *Zambian Public Expenditure Review*, p. 55.

played a key role. As the crisis has unfolded, the fiscal implications of policies has become a key factor in the willingness of states to maintain or change them. Thus, the reticence to undertake privatization reform has to a considerable extent been overcome by the lure of revenues from the sale of public enterprises (PEs). Similarly, the withdrawal of fertilizer subsidies in agriculture has been perhaps the most consistent element of reform in the agricultural sector largely because of their budgetary implications. The elimination of food subsidies in east Africa follows the same logic, while much of the rest of the prereform agricultural policy framework has remained in place, because its cost to the treasury is less consequential.

When reforms do not have a net positive fiscal impact, they also appear more vulnerable to delays and reversal. This is true of trade policy reform, for example. It will be noticed that fiscal and rent-seeking interests coincide and interact. Trade policy reform is difficult because states continue to rely on tariffs for revenue, which still amounted, on average, to over 6 percent of GDP in the region in the 1990s.[135] At the same time, uncollected tariff revenues plague many governments and help perpetuate the fiscal crisis. Much the same could be said of PE reform, where privatization sales have been characterized by nontransparent sweetheart deals that have lessened their benefits to states. In these cases, rent-seeking interests compete with revenue exigencies, often delaying reform or creating situations of ambiguity about the effective status of reform, a climate of uncertainty this chapter has noted on a number of occasions. State elites face a clear trade-off here and, as argued in the next chapter, as the crisis has continued and state capacities have declined, fiscal discipline has clearly waned. In any event, the point is that much of the reform process often appears to be less the product of careful strategy on the part of the state and more of a fire sale mentality in which the search for easy budgetary gains outweigh other considerations.

Relatedly, I have argued that political factors have been important constraints on implementation, although not in the manner in which they are usually viewed. Policies that might have been considered politically difficult because they directly affected powerful constituencies have in fact been implemented. We saw that governments have allowed civil servants to lose much of their purchasing power. Marketing boards have been closed with large job retrenchments. Even more striking, we saw

---

135. The International Monetary Fund, *Tax Policy Handbook* (Washington, DC: International Monetary Fund, 1998), Table 3.

that consumer food prices have been almost entirely liberalized, including in east Africa, where the link between controlled maize prices and political stability was long an adage of faith.

Political factors assert themselves in other ways. This chapter has shown that the most plausible interpretation of implementation patterns is the desire of the state to protect itself from fiscal austerity. Of course, governments do not operate in a vacuum, and they worry about the reactions of different groups of citizens to their actions. In some countries, some groups have an evident impact on policy making in certain areas. Farmer organizations in east and southern Africa were identified as having had a significant impact borne of a long legacy of institutional linkages. Governments also fear certain groups more than others. I noted that the accumulation of salary arrears has characterized much of Francophone Africa. Interestingly, the evidence from these countries suggests that arrears invariably are higher for civil servants in the countryside than for those in the cities, and that arrears are lowest for the police and military staff. These divergences of treatment clearly constitute political management of the arrears situation and suggest that governments are aware that there are limits to how far they can push certain groups.

Nonetheless, far more striking is the extent to which governments have worried less about protecting certain societal constituencies than they have in protecting state elites from austerity, generally, and the higher levels of the state elite more specifically. As fiscal pressure has asserted itself, budgets have sacrificed an increasing proportion of the state's developmental activities. First, it skimped on the investment budget, then, increasingly on core social services, as basic health and education services were devolved to the private sector and donors. In much of Africa today, particularly in the poorer countries, the tendency is for the state to do little besides pay for a civil service that is no longer capable of actually promoting development. Admittedly, this trend is further along in the poorer states of west Africa than it is in the richer and more institutionalized states of east and southern Africa, but even in a country like Kenya, we can witness the state withdrawing from service provision.

Governments have sought to accommodate themselves to the fiscal crisis by reducing their developmental obligations, but at the same time, they have wanted to retain control over key markets. Thus, they have resisted donor demands that they give up the prerogative to regulate key prices in the economy, notably in the politically sensitive area of food. They retreat from the provision of education or health services, but continue to want to regulate, license, and tax these sectors with the technical assistance of the donors.

On the other hand, even as developmental ambitions have been curtailed, what I have called sovereignty expenditures have been little affected by the crisis, and the top of the state apparatus continues to benefit from a level of resources that seems impervious to the crisis. Support for the military seems stable, while high-level positions in the cabinet or legislature appear to be continuing their proliferation. Ostentatious expenditures at the very peak of the state also continue to be part of the landscape, amazingly impervious to Africa's economic decline.

3

Decision Making in Postcolonial Africa

The Nigerian government passed decrees in 1972 and 1977 intended to limit and regulate foreign participation in the economy. The general commitment to what came to be called *indigenization* was established in the Second National Development Plan in 1970, and the policy was then implemented through the Nigerian Enterprises Promotion Decrees of 1972 and 1977. They established that certain parts of the Nigerian economy would exclude foreign-owned companies while other parts would tolerate them, as long as Nigerian equity participation was increased to at least 40 percent.[1] Indigenization was motivated by the perception that ten years of independence had not lessened the economic dominance of both Western multinational corporations and of Middle Eastern (mostly Lebanese) family companies. Nigerian businessmen complained they were discriminated against and could not access bank credit to finance their expansion, while state officials, worried that foreign companies were not reinvesting their profits in the economy, wanted to exert greater control over the economy in order to accelerate Nigeria's industrialization.

The impact of the two indigenization decrees is hard to assess. They would affect well over a thousand companies, which were partly or wholly transferred either to private Nigerian business interests or to the public sector. Lebanese businesses were particularly hard hit, although the use of front men, various legal adjustments, and special exemptions helped many survive. Implementation of the decrees proved haphazard,

1. This account is informed in particular by Thomas Biersteker, *Multinationals, the State and Control of the Nigerian Economy* (Princeton, NJ: Princeton University Press, 1987); see also William D. Graf, *The Nigerian State* (London: James Currey, 1988), pp. 53–9, and Tom Forrest, *Politics and Economic Development in Nigeria* (Boulder, CO: Westview Press, 1992), pp. 153–7.

prey to corruption and inefficiency, as "the state lacked the capacity to implement the program as its originators intended."[2] A small class of Lagos-based Nigerian businessmen were the main direct beneficiaries, often thanks to direct links to state decision makers.

The downgrading of foreign property rights in the economy presumably had a dampening effect on foreign investment, but Nigeria's great oil boom started in the mid-1970s, attracting in its wake renewed Western commercial interests as well as the various negative side effects that would leave the country with a massive debt burden within a decade. Biersteker convincingly argues that the two decrees sharply increased economic inequalities in the country, as "less than one-tenth of one percent of the Nigerian public benefitted directly from indigenization."[3] They also spurred the state's involvement in the economy and encouraged the buildup of the parastatal sector, which would eventually fuel the country's descent into debt and corruption.

Nigeria's indigenization campaign was hardly unique. Uganda, Kenya, Zambia, and Zaire all pursued similar policies of nationalization that specifically targeted Middle Eastern or South Asian businesses during the 1970s.[4] In cases like the "Zairianization" episode in Zaire, the policy was a little-disguised grab by the political elite of profitable private companies, and the rhetoric of economic nationalism was perfunctory and superficial. In others, as in Nigeria, legitimate public policy objectives were undermined by low capacity and political clientelism. These campaigns are emblematic of economic policy-making dynamics in postcolonial Africa. The mixture of ideology, rent-seeking, and low state capacity is a common one, repeated across sectors throughout the region and helping to explain the poor performance of African economies.

This chapter begins to explain the patterns in reform implementation observed in the last chapter by focusing on the domestic origins of economic policies in Africa over the last twenty years. In order to understand the response of African governments to the crisis, it is important to understand the context in which economic policy decision making took place when the crisis emerged in the 1980s. As in the example of indigenization in Nigeria, this chapter argues that at the domestic level there are three sets of related obstacles to policy reform within the state

2. Biersteker, *Multinationals*, pp. 296–7.
3. Ibid, p. 144.
4. Leslie L. Rood, "Nationalisation and Indigenisation in Africa," *Journal of Modern African Studies* 14 (1976): 427–47.

apparatus itself: first, a set of political obstacles related to the material interests of senior state elites; second, ideological constraints; and third, the low and declining capacity within the state. My argument is that economic policy decisions in Africa can be understood as resulting from the combination of the state's neopatrimonial tendencies, its low capacities, and its ideological biases, and the negative synergies among these three factors that evolved over time following independence. To say that these factors are related is not merely rhetorical. Instead, a major theme of the chapter is that negative synergies exist between and among these factors. Low capacity reinforces the neopatrimonial tendencies within the state, which in turn maintain a long-standing tendency to underinvest in capacity. The political interests of state elites often dovetail with an ideological proclivity for state intervention in the economy. Understanding how these dynamics evolved in the first two decades of independence will help us understand how African countries responded to the persistent crisis of the 1980s and 1990s.

THE EXIGENCIES OF NEOPATRIMONIALISM

The dynamics and prevalence of neopatrimonialism in Africa has already been well described in the existing literature, and I need not attempt to be comprehensive here.[5] The regimes that emerged following the end of colonialism enjoyed little popular legitimacy and could not rely on a significant constitutional tradition or rich civil society. The political elite to which the departing colonial authorities handed over power could not count on much state capacity to ensure development and political stability, while the economic resources at their disposal were typically meager or difficult to control. Arbitrary borders, colonial divide-and-rule strategies, and the effects of modernization enhanced subnational cultural identities, which put further pressures on the fledgling states.[6] The superficial nationalism that had emerged during an often ephemeral anticolonial struggle could not long sustain governments, particularly once they proved unable to engineer dramatic improvements in the quality of life of the average citizen. The political parties that had spearheaded the

5. See the citations in Chapter 1.
6. Perhaps the best description of these different dynamics at the outset of postcolonial Africa remains the paper by Aristide Zolberg, "The Structure of Political Conflict in the New States of Tropical Africa," *American Political Science Review* 62 (1968): 70–87. See also Ruth Collier, *Regimes in Tropical Africa* (Berkeley: University of California Press, 1982).

brief anticolonial struggle were rarely able to maintain their mobilizational capacity with the return to routine politics.[7]

There were significant exceptions to these general patterns. Not all borders in the region are equally arbitrary, and the sense of national identity was not always weak.[8] Some anticolonial movements managed to build far greater legitimacy than others. Nyerere built the Tanganyika African National Union (TANU) in Tanzania into a relatively effective single party with significant popular support,[9] while the party system that emerged after independence was unusually weak in Chad, a state with virtually no sense of national identity.[10] Clearly, circumstances varied and constraints on leaders were not always equally pressing. Still, the exceptional brevity of the colonial era and the speed with which independence came clearly had an impact on the path of state formation in the region, which distinguishes it from the Asian experience, for example.

To establish political order and sustain their hold on power, the new rulers used the few resources and instruments at their disposal. Political survival dictated certain choices that would have a costly effect on economic growth. As Claude Ake has nicely put it, "The struggle for power was so absorbing that everything else, including development, was marginalized."[11] More specifically, the style of rule that emerged combined the authoritarian legacy of the colonial administration and village traditions of patrimonialism. As a large literature argues persuasively, the emergence of authoritarian states after independence is at least in part a legacy of colonialism.[12] African elites inherited state structures and a style of governance from the colonial era that were illiberal and geared toward

7. Aristide Zolberg, *Creating Political Order: The Party States of West Africa* (Chicago: University of Chicago Press, 1966).

8. Pierre Englebert explores these cross-national differences in his recent book, *State Legitimacy and Development in Africa* (Boulder, CO: Lynne Rienner, 2000).

9. Henry Bienen, *Tanzania: Party Transformation and Economic Development* (Princeton, NJ: Princeton University Press, 1970).

10. On Chad, see Sam C. Nolutshungu, *Limits of Anarchy: Intervention and State Formation in Chad* (Charlottesville: University of Virgina Press, 1996), pp. 27–64.

11. Claude Ake, *Democracy and Development in Africa* (Washington, DC: The Brookings Institution, 1996), p. 7.

12. Crawford Young, *The African Colonial State in Comparative Perspective* (New Haven: Yale University Press, 1994); and Thomas C. Callaghy, "The State and the Development of Capitalism in Africa: Theoretical, Historical and Comparative Reflections," in Donald Rothchild and Naomi Chazan (eds.), *The Precarious Balance: State and Society in Africa* (Boulder, CO: Westview Press, 1988), pp. 67–99.

enforcing law and order rather than the promotion of citizen welfare. Traditions of authoritarian rule, paternalism, and dirigisme were embedded in the institutions the new leaders inherited and largely kept.

In the decades following independence, these structures were reinvented and adapted to suit the needs of individual leaders and local cultural repertoires.[13] Over time, leaders sought to legitimize their nondemocratic rule by multiplying the symbolic references to an imagined traditional African style of rule. Leaders adopted African titles or nicknames: President Mobutu renamed himself Sese Seko Kuku Mgbendo Wazabanga[14] and encouraged the press to call him "the guide." Nyerere liked to be referred to as Mwalimu, the teacher. They adopted political practices that could claim some link to traditional custom. Houphouët-Boigny, for instance, introduced "la palabre," in which he toured the country and staged village "dialogues" where citizens were encouraged to discuss their problems directly with him, a practice designed to emulate a traditional African mode of political participation.[15] President Eyadema of Togo encouraged rumors about his occult powers.[16]

Political leaders manipulated the power of the army or were soon replaced by ambitious officers who could do so; they used access to state resources to gain the support they could not gain at the ballot box and dispensed large amounts of patronage. It is often argued that power was personalized because it was never properly institutionalized. Clearly, the weakness of constitutional institutions and the absence of counterweights to state power in the private sector or civil society favored neopatrimonialism. But, in truth, personal rule defined a series of norms, rules, and standard practices that emerged in lieu of formal political institutions, although the latter usually existed on paper. It thus may not be abusive to talk of informal neopatrimonial institutions, even if the exact mix of repression, patronage, inclusion, and participation varied across countries and individual rulers.[17]

13. This argument is well developed by Jean-François Bayart, *L'etat en Afrique: la politique du ventre* (Paris: Fayard, 1989).
14. Meaning roughly "the all-powerful warrior who by endurance and determination will go from conquest to conquest, leaving fire in his wake."
15. These examples and many others can be found in Robert H. Jackson and Carl G. Rosberg, *Personal Rule in Black Africa: Prince, Autocrat, Prophet, Tyrant* (Berkeley: University of California Press, 1982).
16. Stephen Ellis, "Rumour and Power in Togo," *Africa* 63 (1993): 462–75.
17. I have elaborated this argument with Michael Bratton in Chapter 2 of *Democratic Experiments in Africa* (New York: Cambridge University Press, 1997).

The Characteristics of Neopatrimonial Regimes

Africa's neopatrimonial regimes, the literature agrees, soon exhibited four fairly predictable characteristics, which came to define neopatrimonial rule. It is impossible to understand economic policy outcomes in postcolonial Africa or the failure to carry out policy reforms over the last two decades without referring to these four characteristics.

Clientelism. A first characteristic was the more or less systematic resort to clientelism to gain and maintain political support. The absence or narrowness of a public realm in the Western sense; the strength of clan, ethnicity, and other subnational identities; the predilection for dyadic exchange in primarily rural societies; and the need for mechanisms of "social insurance" in the risky and uncertain environment of low-income societies have all been used in the literature to explain the ubiquitous presence at every level of African life of the exchange of gifts, favors, and services, of patronage and courtier practices.[18]

These practices have often been attributed as well to ethnic and clan politics, in which a position of power was valued for the resources it procured for one's family and kin. Much clientelism and corruption is legitimated by the view that it serves a kind of community purpose rather than individual enrichment. According to one argument, a wide range of corrupt practices is accepted by Africans, not only because stealing from a state widely viewed as illegitimate is believed to be a "victimless crime" but also because it has benefits for a large part of the population. In effect, the argument goes, clientelism helps to redistribute income and assets throughout the economy. Observers like Chabal and Daloz appear to deny that clientelism produces social stratification and reinforces inequalities.[19] They seem to believe that it constitutes a form of economic redistribution that prevents capitalist accumulation, arguing that the communitarian ethos of traditional rural life has survived the transition

18. On the sociology of clientelism in the contemporary African setting from different perspectives, see Peter Ekeh, "Colonialism and the Two Publics in Africa: A Theoretical Statement," *Comparative Studies in Society and History* 17 (1975): 91–112; J. P. Olivier de Sardan, "L'economie morale de la corruption en Afrique," *Politique Africaine* 63 (1996): 97–116; Donal Cruise O'Brien, *Saints and Politicians* (Cambridge, UK: Cambridge University Press, 1975); and Robert Price, *Society and Bureaucracy in Contemporary Ghana* (Berkeley: University of California Press, 1975).
19. Chabal and Daloz, *Africa Works.* See also Olivier de Sardan, "L'economie morale."

to modern state structures and a market economy. Its widespread benefits allegedly help explain why corruption is routinely condemned in general but tolerated and not punished in practice. Leaders, it is argued, engage in these practices out of a deep-seated cultural sense of social obligation that in the end undermines individual accumulation to the benefit of one's community. Clientelism, in this argument, is the expression of social capital.

Clearly, clientelism does reinforce loyalties to kith and kin. Just as clearly, the redistribution that is achieved or at least perceived to be achieved by such practices serves to blunt class consciousness. Even when the exchange is largely symbolic, it links patron and client. As a result, societies with pervasive clientelism are marked by the low salience of social class identities, despite often glaring social inequalities.[20] As Gavin Williams and others have noted, however, "What is striking about many African countries is how little trickles down to the worse off through the patronage network and how much sticks to a few hands at the top."[21] Indeed, it is ultimately more useful to think of the primary function of neopatrimonial politics in most African states as facilitating intra-elite accommodation in young, multiethnic and poorly integrated political systems. In what Rothchild called "hegemonial exchange" and Bayart the "reciprocal assimilation of elites," political stability in Africa has often been constructed by using state resources to forge alliances across different social elites, often in the form of overt power-sharing arrangements.[22] These arrangements facilitated consensus building across region and ethnicity; between the younger, more educated elites emerging from Western universities and the usually older, less educated elites that were often linked to traditional authorities; and between the individuals who emerged to take leadership roles in the different institutions of the states, not only the politicians, but also the military brass and members of the church hierarchy.

Tentative data about patterns of inequality in Africa tend to corroborate the view that clientelist political systems result in extremely

20. See the trenchant discussion of these issues in Christopher Clapham, "Clientelism and the State," in Christopher Clapham (ed.), *Private Patronage and Public Power* (London: Frances Pinter, 1982), pp. 1–36.
21. Gavin Williams, "Primitive Accumulation: The Way to Progress," *Development and Change* 18 (1987): 637–59, p. 639.
22. Bayart, *l'etat en Afrique*; and Donald Rothchild, "State Ethnic Relations in Middle Africa," in Gwendolyn Carter and Patrick O'Meara (eds.), *African Independence: The First 25 Years* (Bloomington: Indiana University Press, 1985), pp. 71–96.

narrow networks of accumulation and are not redistribution mechanisms,[23] but unfortunately, little systematic data exist to back up such claims. Far from preventing accumulation, the neopatrimonial state has allowed a small number of people to reach vast levels of wealth despite a dilapidated economic environment. On the other hand, there is no reason to believe that the overwhelming majority of clients derive significant wealth or empowerment from their relations with state patrons. On the contrary, they are completely or partly dependent on the state for their income and welfare. To ascribe power to clients, such as the young graduate who gets a low-level job in the administration thanks to the intervention of a "big man" from his or her village is to misunderstand the fundamentally asymmetrical nature of clientelist power relations. There is little that clients can do to prevent the patrons from redefining their exchange in a much less generous direction.

Access to State Resources. Second, and more distinctly, it should by now be clear that clientelistic practices were largely based on privileged access to state resources, rationed by state leaders following a strict political logic. Patron-client ties are a feature of all traditional societies; it is the emergence of modern state structures in low-income countries that transforms traditional clientelism to give it its modern face. Control of the state, its resources, and policy levers allowed political elites to dramatically expand clientelistic practices, through patronage, nepotism, and the granting of various exemptions, dispensations, and immunities from laws, taxes, and licenses. In the adaptation of everyday practices at the village level to a political instrument, clientelism moved in the direction of large-scale corruption and fraud. Not all forms of political clientelism are illegal, of course, but all involve the subversion of public norms and objectives for the sake of personal gain.

Although the colonial state had hardly been immune to corruption and clientelistic practices,[24] these were steadily expanded following inde-

23. See, for example, Wayne E. Nafziger, *Inequality in Africa: Political Elites, Proletariat, Peasants and the Poor* (Cambridge, UK: Cambridge University Press, 1988).
24. For instance, Munyae M. Mulinge and Gwen N. Lesetedi, "Interrogating Our Past: Colonialism and Corruption in Sub-Saharan Africa," *African Journal of Political Science* 3 (1998): 15–28; Claude Arditi, "Du prix de la kola au détournement de l'aide internationale: clientelisme et corruption au Tchad, 1900–1998," *Nouveaux Cahiers de l'IUED* (in press); and Robert Tignor, "Political Corruption in Nigeria before Independence," *Journal of Modern African Studies* 31 (1993): 76–117.

pendence. The practices expanded slowly at first: the veneer of rational-legalism of the colonial administration offered some initial resistance to individual abuses, as did the reliance on foreign experts often under contract to the metropole government. African politicians also needed to learn how to wield policy instruments to generate rents. They needed time to figure out what they could get away with. In the Francophone countries, France kept a tight control over economic decision making, at least until the 1972–73 reforms of the two monetary unions of the Franc Zone ceded much administrative power to local officials.[25] In the rest of Africa, the emergence of fiscal deficits and unsustainable monetary policies was more rapid. By April 1970, Liberia and Somalia had already received seven stand-by agreement loans from the IMF to help them address balance of payments and budgetary crises; Burundi had received five such loans; Ghana, Mali, and Rwanda four loans; Sierra Leone and Sudan three; and Congo/Zaire had completed its first IMF supervised devaluation.[26] The granting of multiple stand-by agreements in less than a decade of independence suggests an almost immediate deterioration in management. On the other hand, the IMF had not been called in by any country in the Franc Zone, or by eastern African countries like Kenya and Tanzania.

Clientelist practices not only helped maintain political stability in vulnerable political systems, but they were also attractive to the political class for the selfish reason that they provided a clear path to self-enrichment. As Sklar pointed out many years ago, politics came to be the primary mechanism of class formation in Africa, as material accumulation was closely entwined with political power.[27] The absence of a powerful indigenous private sector that might have sought to enforce its property rights and a greater separation between political power and private accumulation resulted in a business class dominated by rent-seeking. Often foreign and linked to the previous colonial order, antiprivate sector measures were often popular, as suggested by the Nigerian example that opened this chapter.

25. Policy performance deteriorated soon thereafter, though at least in part because of a highly volatile external environment during the 1970s. See Patrick and Sylviane Guillaumont, *Zone Franc et développement Africain* (Paris: Economica, 1984).
26. International Monetary Fund, *Annual Report, 1970* (Washington, DC: International Monetary Fund, 1970), pp. 138–9.
27. Richard Sklar, "The Nature of Class Domination in Africa," *Journal of Modern African Studies* 17 (1979): 531–52.

Over time, the boundaries between the private and public realm were blurred. Not only did political leaders enrich themselves by stealing from the public till, they soon emerged as leading "private" entrepreneurs. Houphouët-Boigny, Mobutu, and Banda were all leading plantation owners, for example: Houphouët was his country's largest single cocoa producer and accounted by himself for a third of Côte d'Ivoire's pineapple production.[28] In Kenya, the Ndegwa Commission of 1970 legitimized this blurring throughout the state administration when it lifted restrictions on civil servants running businesses concurrently with their public service. Data from Côte d'Ivoire by Fauré suggest how systematic the union of political and economic power could be: he traced the business holdings of some 471 individuals in that country occupying the 598 top political positions in the early 1990s and found that 31 percent of them held part ownership in private Ivoirian companies.[29] Moreover, Ivoirian companies with such politician participation were systematically more likely to have had access to state finance and were more likely to be involved in interfirm arrangements including those with foreign capital. Similarly, in the early 1990s, senior civil servants, cabinet ministers, members of parliament, and Zimbabwe African National Union (ZANU) party officials were estimated to own 8 percent of all commercial farm lands in Zimbabwe, much of it acquired as a result of government schemes to resettle white farms.[30]

One inevitable consequence of these dynamics was the emergence over time of corruption sanctioned at the highest levels of the state that systematically lowered government revenues. In a fascinating case study, Emizet reports that in Zaire/Congo, some 45 percent of refined copper exports were smuggled out of the country in the late 1980s, more than 40 percent of coffee exports was being smuggled through Uganda, and an estimated 437 million dollars in diamond exports were also escaping government revenue streams albeit not necessarily the tax and customs duty officials charged with collecting them.[31] Emizet also notes that of

28. See Jean-Louis Gombeaud, Corinne Moutout, and Stephen Smith, *La guerre du cacao* (Paris: Calmann-Levy, 1990), which provides a fascinating account of the Ivoirian president's approach to business.
29. Yves-André Fauré, "Les politiciens dans les entreprises en Côte d'Ivoire: investisseurs ou courtiers?" *Politique Africaine* (1995): 26–40. Note that some politicians occupied more than one position of importance.
30. Carolyn Jenkins, "The Politics of Economic Policy-Making in Zimbabwe," *Journal of Modern African Studies* 35 (1997): 595.
31. Kisangani N. F. Emizet, "Confronting Leaders at the Apex of the State: The Growth of the Unofficial Economy of the Congo," *African Studies Review* 41

425 cars surveyed in Kinshasa in 1992, only three had a tax sticker for vehicle registration on the upper corner of the windshield, suggesting the systematic nature of low-level bribery (p. 117). The precise value of these unrealized government revenues may ultimately not be knowable, but the order of magnitude Emizet reports is probably correct, and his careful fieldwork on a wide variety of goods and services makes clear the systematic complicity of Zairian state agents in illegal economic transactions that did not reduce state revenues. Indeed, he reports that policemen charged a set fee at the roadblocks they manned and shared the bribes with their commanding officers in a chain that went all the way up to the local colonel. Policemen who did not collect the requisite amounts were transferred to less well-remunerated desk jobs.

This is not an isolated example, even if the dynamics in other countries did not always go to the extremes found in Zaire. Throughout the region, state officials used their power to undertake a variety of activities that weakened the economy and robbed the state of its revenues and developmental effectiveness. By the late 1970s, the banking sector throughout Africa had been decimated by the loans it had been forced to make to state elites.[32] Hundreds of public enterprises were being bankrupted by a wide array of manipulations by their managers and governmental overseers. Private businesses were prey to a fickle and inefficient regulatory environment, the chief purpose of which seemed to be to generate bribes.

Lofchie has convincingly argued that rent-seeking concerns have not always motivated the initiation of policies that over time yielded extensive rent-seeking benefits to the political class.[33] True, there are cases in which major economic policies were blatantly designed with rent-seeking interests in mind, perhaps the best example being the Zairianization campaign announced by Mobutu in late 1973;[34] under this policy initiative,

(1998): 99–137. In 1988, just under 94 percent of Belgium's gold imports were from Burundi despite the fact that it lacks gold resources; see p. 107.

32. For numerous Francophone examples, see Olivier Vallée, *Le prix de l'argent CFA: heurs et malheurs de la Zone Franc* (Paris: Karthala, 1989).

33. Michael Lofchie, "The New Political Economy of Africa," in David E. Apter and Carl G. Rosberg (eds.), *Political Development and the New Realism in Sub-Saharan Africa* (Charlottesville: University Press of Virginia, 1994), pp. 145–83, see pp. 157–9.

34. The best account of this sordid episode is probably provided by Crawford Young and Thomas Turner, *The Rise and Decline of the Zairian State* (Madison: University of Wisconsin Press, 1985). See also Thomas M. Callaghy, *The State-Society Struggle: Zaire in Comparative Perspective* (New York: Columbia University Press, 1984).

1,500 to 2,000 of the country's foreign-owned private firms were transferred to national citizens, initially without compensation. In practice, the new owners were invariably leading figures of the regime, notably provincial governors and prefects who often amassed great fortunes out of the process. Mobutu himself wound up with plantations and factories that he would unite into a holding company involving 25,000 employees, mostly in his home province of Equateur. More often, however, and as the example of Nigeria's indigenization campaign described above suggested, nationalization policies or the growth of the parastatal sector was motivated by policy concerns and cannot be reduced to clientelist aspirations. Nonetheless, over time, many economic policies that had proven to be ineffective or downright destructive were maintained because of the benefits they procured for a small number of individuals linked to the pinnacles of the state.

State-led clientelism should not be viewed as lessening state autonomy. A widely expressed view is that the postcolonial state in Africa was entirely captured by societal interests, that it was fundamentally *soft*. To be sure, the inability of African states to defer consumption and promote investment to engineer rapid growth bespeaks softness, as the term was first defined by Myrdal thirty years ago.[35] The absence of a developmental project is not due to extensive kinship or societal pressures on decision makers, however, but to the lack of discipline, vision, and patriotism of a ruling elite that has always viewed its own material enrichment as the primary objective of political power.

How can this elite be identified? While the precise numbers may vary and are obviously not fixed in stone, I am referring specifically to the holders and potential holders of the offices at the apex of the state. Tessy Bakary identifies the main institutions of political power in Côte d'Ivoire as the president's office, the Parti Démocratique de Côte d'Ivoire (PDCI) Political Bureau, the National Assembly, and the Economic and Social Council. The positions of power in these institutions represent 320 positions, and he calculates that only 1,040 individuals held these positions between 1957 and 1980, suggesting the remarkable stability of the political class as well as its narrow nature.[36] Ngayap offers similar if somewhat more expansive numbers for Cameroon since his survey of that

---

35. Gunnar Myrdal, *An Asian Drama: An Inquiry in the Poverty of Nations* (New York: Pantheon Books, 1968), see pp. 895–900.
36. Richard Crook, "Patrimonialism, Administrative Effectiveness and Economic Development in Côte d'Ivoire," *African Affairs* 88 (1989): 205–28, p. 213.

country identifies 950 elite state positions.[37] In other words, the political elite includes several hundred to a thousand individuals and their families in each country. The evidence suggests these individuals do not hold the same position for long, since insecurity of office appears to be a prevalent mechanism for presidential control over the elite, but membership within the elite is relatively stable, as removal from one position usually leads to appointment to another. Nor is power uniformly distributed within this number; levels of influence and material benefits increase sharply as one moves from the lower echelons to the top of the elite.

The Centralization of Power. At the summit is the president. The centralization of power around the president constitutes the third characteristic of these regimes. Not only was the political elite typically an exceptionally narrow one, it was almost entirely based in the capital city. As Wunsch and Olowu have shown, African states after independence were highly centralized in administrative and juridical terms. Virtually all revenues were raised by the central government with local governments having few fiscal prerogatives. Total budgetary resources allocated to local governments were typically minuscule, while only 2 percent of public employees did not work for the central government, a quarter of the levels prevailing in Asia and half those in Latin America.[38]

The centralization of power around the presidency was progressive following independence. In some countries, a first charismatic president pushed the process forward more quickly. President Sekou Touré in Guinea or Eyadema in Togo quickly subverted relatively weak state structures to consolidate their personal hold on power. In others, state institutions were more institutionalized and thus stronger, and the emergence of a powerful president above the reach of the law was slower. In Nigeria, for example, completely personalized rule probably did not emerge until General Abacha's rule in the 1990s.[39]

Over time, throughout the region, power came to be highly centralized around the president. He was literally above the law, controlled in

37. Pierre Flambeau Ngayap, *Cameroun: Qui gouverne? De ahidjo à biya, l'heritage et l'enjeu* (Paris: l'Harmattan, 1983). To Bakary's list, Ngayap adds positions in the military, provincial administration, and diplomatic corps, for instance.

38. James S. Wunsch and Dele Olowu (eds.), "The Failure of the Centralized State," in *The Failure of the Centralized State: Institutions and Self-Governance in Africa* (Boulder, CO: Westview Press, 1990), pp. 1–22, especially pp. 4–5.

39. Personal communication, Peter Lewis, September 2000.

many cases a large proportion of state finance with little accountability, and delegated remarkably little of his authority on important matters. Most important decisions were made directly by the president, often without the assistance of the relevant ministerial staff. The presidency emerged as the dominant arena for decision making, and a state within the state. In Congo/Zaire, Callaghy reports, the presidency controlled between 15 and 20 percent of the national recurrent budget and 30 percent of capital outlays.[40] The office of the president also became a parallel government, with considerably more executive power than the actual ministries. In an interesting essay, Emizet argues that the president's office actually became more institutionalized than the cabinet: whereas Mobutu engaged in at least fifty cabinet reshuffles between 1966 and 1992, he changed his chief of staff only six times.[41] Similarly, in Zambia, toward the end of Kaunda's regime, economic policy making was divided between the Planning Commission, the Ministry of Finance, and the State House, where, Gulhati informs us, "the president had assembled a coterie of influential advisors . . . and frequently made important economic policy decisions without much interaction with the normal civil service machine and without full discussion in Cabinet."[42] Kaunda apparently dominated all personnel decisions, appointing permanent secretaries from outside the civil service without always consulting ministers.[43]

Middle-level managers within the presidency might wield more effective powers than permanent secretaries in the ministries. Even ministers of government often found themselves with little discretion over policy. Cabinet meetings were typically rare and largely ceremonial in nature, with the president giving his directives and offering advice, often less for the benefit of the assembled ministers than for the invited press. When the president was actually interested in economic policy issues, presidential preferences often prevailed over the views of the technocrats in the central bank or ministry of finance. Thus, Gulhati argues that in regimes like the Tanzania of Nyerere or the Malawi of Banda, the president completely dominated the economic policy process, preempting all initiatives by the members of his cabinet, whose role was largely rele-

40. Callaghy, *The State Society Struggle*, p. 179.
41. Emizet, "Confronting Leaders."
42. Gulhati, "Who Makes Economic Policy?" pp. 1151–2.
43. See, for example, Harry Garnett et al., "Managing Policy Formulation and Implementation in Zambia's Democratic Transition," unpublished manuscript, Abt Associates, Washington, DC, January 1996.

gated to one of interpretation of the president's policy choices and of implementation.[44]

Hybrid Regimes. The fourth characteristic of neopatrimonial states is that these informal institutions coexist with the formal trappings of the modern state. I wish to emphasize the hybrid and essentially dual nature of neopatrimonial regimes. Unlike traditional kingdoms, in which the affairs of state are literally treated as an extension of the king's household, in modern African states, personal rule coexists uneasily with a modern bureaucracy and its distinct logic. There are budgets and laws. Prebendal arrangements may dominate in the president's dealings with his top assistants, but officially these individuals derive salaries and are subject to civil service rules. The president's wife or brother may be extremely powerful in the affairs of state, but legal authority rests with the legislature or cabinet.

The public policy community tends to downplay the patrimonial dimensions of these regimes. It views the pervasive clientelism as little more than an odd atavism, which a couple of additional "capacity building" projects promoting greater administrative hygiene and technical expertise will soon entirely do away with. It refuses to accept the idea that clientelism in these states is more than incidental. For example, a striking reality is that most anticorruption strategies being devised in the policy community simply assume that there is a rational-legal logic at the apex of these states that will be available to carry out the strategy;[45] in fact, all too often, leaders at the apex of the state choose to undermine these strategies, which threaten practices they find useful and profitable.

Neopatrimonial tendencies are not traditional African practices undermining the construction of "modern" or "Western" states in the region, another popular misconception in the public policy literature. Rather, the clientelistic and patronage practices witnessed in Africa are products of a process of state formation and modernization and have to be understood historically. Though they harken back to certain longstanding sociological norms and practices, their style, mode, and political function cannot be disassociated from the development of modern bureaucratic states in the region.[46]

44. Gulhati, "Who Makes Economic Policy?"
45. A good example of this tendency is provided by Robert E. Klitgaard, *Controlling Corruption* (Berkeley: University of California Press, 1987).
46. On this point, see the essays in Jean Louis Briquet and Frédéric Sawicki (eds.), *Clientélisme politique dans les sociétés contemporaines* (Paris: PUF, 1998).

On the other hand, many students of neopatrimonialism downplay the rational legal dimension in these states. They argue that formal structures are irrelevant, that all the meaningful decision making takes place within a parallel "shadow state" that is entirely patrimonial.[47] They do not believe that policies or ideologies matter, except as a posteriori justification for state predation. I view both of these views as excessive. Even in the least institutionalized states in the region, there are rational-legal pockets attempting to assert themselves. The intellectual debates about policy are meaningful and cannot be reduced to rent-seeking motivations. On the other side of the spectrum, no state in Africa can claim to have entirely avoided neopatrimonial tendencies at its apex. The two tendencies coexist, overlap, and struggle for control of the state in most countries. The balance of power between the two obviously varies, and it is easy to believe that the prospects for the rational-legal tendencies to win out are better in, say, relatively bureaucratic Côte d'Ivoire than in the decrepit and brutal personal dictatorship that is Equatorial Guinea. The structure of incentives that individuals face within decision-making institutions often determines which will dominate: mechanisms of transparency and accountability, the professionalism of the civil service, the legitimacy of public institutions, and the health of the national economy all probably matter.

The rational-legal order in African countries can be thought of as a public good, on which neopatrimonial interests attempt to free-ride. Thus, rent-seeking and much corruption require that the state set rules that are generally followed, so that the rents created can be abused for personal profit. Excessive free-riding can destroy the public good. Thus, when patrimonial dynamics become excessive, there is a breakdown of order and rent-seeking becomes less profitable. Neopatrimonial regimes thus exhibit an inherent tension between their two constitutive dynamics. State elites are constantly subverting the rational-legal order, but in the end need it to maintain their own positions. It is the ability of leaders to manage this equilibrium that determines the degree of political stability in Africa today. As I show in Chapter 4, the failure to maintain that equilibrium is at the root of the collapse of the central state in countries like Sierra Leone.

In sum, the exact relative power of each tendency varies from country to country, and even within a single political system across time and

47. The shadow state is theorized in Reno, *Corruption and State Politics in Sierra Leone*. An extreme version of this argument has recently been presented in Chabal and Daloz, *Africa Works*.

issues. Nonetheless, an inherent characteristic of these regimes is that both tendencies are present.

STATE CAPACITY

Turning to the evolution of state capacity over time in postcolonial Africa, a central paradox confronts us: at independence, most countries in Africa could count only a handful of native college graduates. The colonial administration was almost entirely in the hands of Europeans, with Africans holding at most clerical posts. The best estimates suggest that there were some 72,500 European civil servants in the parts of continent still under colonial rule in 1960.[48] The Belgian Congo was famously alleged to have had only six African college graduates, while even a rich and fairly urbanized country like Zambia could claim only seventy-six graduates.[49] At Mozambique's independence in 1974, the country had thirty trained doctors for the entire population of 12 million.[50] According to statistics from the United Nations Educational, Scientific, and Cultural Organization (UNESCO), fewer than 7,000 Africans were pursuing college courses within all of sub-Saharan Africa in the late 1950s, on the very eve of independence.[51]

Four decades later, the number of college graduates can be counted in the hundreds of thousands, following a prodigious effort by African individuals and their families, supported by an array of government and donor programs. Bakary and others have pointed to the tremendous returns to personal investments in education in the first years of independence, in which a college degree literally opened the doors to membership in the state elite.[52] Initially, these personal returns were as high

48. Guy Benveniste and William E. Moran, *Handbook of African Economic Development* (New York: Praeger, 1962), p. 61.
49. This often-repeated figure on the number of Zairian graduates is somewhat misleading, given the much larger number of well-educated priests, and the several hundred medical assistants and agricultural extension agents with some postgraduate education. I thank Crawford Young for alerting me to this. On Zambia, see J. Fry, *An Analysis of Employment and Income Distribution in Zambia* (London: Croom Helm, 1979).
50. Margaret Hall and Tom Young, *Confronting Leviathan: Mozambique since independence* (London: Hurst & Co, 1997), p. 57.
51. Benveniste and Moran, *Handbook of African Economic Development*, cited, pp. 76–7.
52. Tessy D. Bakary, "Systèmes educatifs, stratification sociale et construction de l'etat," in Daniel C. Bach and Anthony A. Kirk-Greene (eds.), *Etats et sociétés en Afrique Francophone* (Paris: Economica, 1993), pp. 71–87.

in the social sciences and humanities, where degree-completion rates were much higher, as in the sciences, and a pattern was established early of fewer Africans going into the more demanding fields like engineering and medicine. Pretty quickly, as a result, Africa was generating the wrong mix of graduates, given its most pressing needs.

Tertiary education enrollments grew by an average of 15 percent a year between 1960 and 1980, and in 1989 approximately half a million Africans were enrolled in university, including tens of thousands abroad.[53] It is true that Africa produces considerably fewer university graduates than countries in other developing regions, a gap that is particularly large in the scientific and technical fields,[54] and overall progress disguises some dismal individual cases.[55] Nonetheless, the individual educational level of manpower available to states in Africa increased dramatically in the first three decades of independence. Moreover, the number of Africans with college and postuniversity qualifications continued to increase after the emergence of economic crisis, even as increasingly devastated national education systems stopped making progress on basic literacy.

Yet, and therein lies the paradox, there is much evidence that the capacity of African governments to design, implement, monitor, and evaluate policy actually declined between the early independence era and the 1990s, despite this dramatic change in skills available to governments. Such was certainly the opinion of the African Governors of the World Bank when they presented a report on capacity issues in 1996: "Almost every African country has witnessed a systematic regression of capacity in the last thirty years; the majority had better capacity at independence than they now possess."[56]

53. Cited in Deborah Bräutigam, "State Capacity and Effective Governance," (p. 91) in Benno Ndulu and Nicolas van de Walle (eds.), *Agenda for Africa's Economic Renewal* (Washington, DC: Overseas Development Council, 1996), pp. 81–108.
54. Bräutigam, "State Capacity," points out that Africa averaged 23 students per 100,000 population in scientific or engineering fields at the university level in 1985, compared to 306 students in South America.
55. Thus, in the early 1990s, out of a population of 6.2 million, there were fewer than 2,500 Mozambicans with university-level qualifications, a striking cost of that country's dismal colonial past and violent postcolonial history. See Peter Fallon and Luiz Pereira da Silva, "Recognizing Labor Market Constraints: Government-Donor, Competition for Manpower in Mozambique," in David L. Lindauer and Barbara Nunberg (eds.), *Rehabilitating Government: Pay and Employment Reforms in Africa* (Washington, DC: World Bank, 1994), pp. 82–102.
56. African Governors of the World Bank, *Partnership for Capacity Building in Africa: Strategy and Program of Action, a Report to Mr. James D. Wolfensohn, President of the World Bank Group*, Washington, September 1996, p. 5.

The signs of this progressive loss of state capacity in the region have been much reported.[57] African civil services are characterized by pervasive absenteeism, endemic corruption, politicization, declining legitimacy, and low morale. Low-skill positions tend to be overstaffed, with several officials doing the work of a single individual, while high-skill positions are left unfilled because of the absence of viable candidates at prevailing wages. For instance, a World Bank report on Kenya noted that in 1979, 90 percent of the central administration personnel was constituted of clerk- and secretarial-level staff.[58] Among twenty low-income countries in Africa, half had twenty-five or fewer fully qualified accountants in the entire public sector in 1995, while there were only three qualified accountants in Uganda in 1998.[59] Equipment and technologies at the disposal of personnel are typically inadequate and outdated. Administrative services are plagued by the resignations of a high number of their most experienced managers, who have left for better paying jobs in the private sector, working for donors, or in the increasingly important voluntary sector. Brain drain from the region is a massive problem: one study estimates that some 50,000 to 60,000 middle- and high-level state managers left Africa between 1986 and 1990 alone, while another argues that 100,000

57. The multiple deficiencies of African administrations are well documented and explored from multiple perspectives: in addition to the materials already cited, see, for example, Ladipo Adamolekun (ed.), *Public Administration in Africa: Main Issues and Selected Country Studies* (Boulder, CO: Westview Press, 1999); Gelase Mutahaba, Rweikiza Baguma, and Mohamed Halfani, *Vitalizing African Public Administration for Recovery and Development* (Hartford, CT: Kumarian Press, 1993); David Leonard, "The Political Realities of African Management," *World Development* 15 (1987): 899–910; David L. Lindauer and Barbara Nunberg (eds.), *Rehabilitating Government: Pay and Employment Reforms in Africa* (Washington, DC: World Bank, 1994); David Hirschmann, "Institutional Development in the Era of Economic Policy Reform: Concerns, Contradictions and Illustrations from Malawi," *Public Administration and Development* 13 (1993): 113–28; Mamadou Dia, *Africa's Management in the 1990s and Beyond: Reconciling Indigenous and Transplanted Institutions* (Washington, DC: World Bank, 1996); Arthur Goldsmith, "Africa's Overgrown State Reconsidered: Bureaucracy and Economic Growth," *World Politics* 51 (1999): 520–46; Sadig Rasheed and David Fasholé Luke (eds.), *Development Management in Africa: Towards Dynamism, Empowerment and Entrepreneurship* (Boulder, CO: Westview Press, 1995).
58. The World Bank, *Kenya: Re-Investing in Stabilization and Growth through Public Sector Adjustment* (Washington, DC: World Bank, 1992), p. 49.
59. Cited in Deborah Bräutigam, "Aid Dependence and Governance," Unpublished paper, American University, Washington, DC, March 5, 1999.

trained and qualified Africans chose to work abroad between 1960 and 1987.[60]

As a result, the ability of states to undertake even the most routine tasks has seemed to be in decline throughout this period. Budgeting systems became often barely functional, with the initial budget having little bearing on actual expenditure patterns during the course of the year,[61] while accounting and auditing standards constituted running invitations for various abuses. Statistical services broke down, with even basic national accounts data either unavailable or of increasingly suspect quality. Writing about Nigeria's attempts to devise a home-grown reform effort under Babangida in the mid-1980s, Mosley argues that "inadequacies of data . . . constrain[ed] and very nearly paralyze[d] any attempt at rational policy-making."[62]

The state's ability to deliver basic services also declined steadily. To be sure, this judgment must be nuanced by the recognition that state capacity varies enormously across the states in the region and the different tasks of government. In Côte d'Ivoire, the central state has accumulated considerable capacity and "is a well-financed and effective machine," if one is to believe the accounts provided by Richard Crook.[63] On the other hand, Bierschenk and Olivier de Sardhan have provided a particularly striking account of the Central African Republic, in which the central state has so little capacity it is "very limited as to what it can do when it comes to the institutionalized regulation of the local

60. The first set of numbers is cited in Bräutigam, "State Capacity and Effective Governance," p. 87; the second estimates are from Nadeem Ul Haque and Jahangir Aziz, "The Quality of Governance: 'Second Generation' Civil Service Reform in Africa," IMF Working Paper WP/98/164, November 1998, p. 21.

61. A good recent general survey of budgeting issues in Africa is provided in Alex Sekwat, "Public Budgeting Deficiencies in Sub Saharan Africa: A Review," *Journal of Public Budgeting, Accounting and Financial Management* 9 (1997): 143–61. Stephen Peterson evaluates many of these same issues in the Kenyan context in his essay, "Budgeting in Kenya: Practice and Prescription," *Public Budgeting and Finance* 14 (1994): 55–76.

62. Paul Mosley, "Policy Making without Facts: A Note on the Assessment of Structural Adjustment Policies in Nigeria, 1985–1990," *African Affairs* 91 (1992): 227–240, p. 236.

63. See for instance, "Patrimonialism, Administrative Effectiveness and Economic Development in Côte d'Ivoire"; and "State, Society and Political Institutions in Côte d'Ivoire and Ghana," in James Manor (ed.), *Rethinking Third World Politics* (New York: Longman, 1991), pp. 213–41. See also the Ivoirian materials in Richard Crook and James Manor, *Democracy and Decentralization in South Asia and West Africa: Participation, Accountability and Performance* (New York: Cambridge University Press, 1999).

level in rural areas," and is essentially "absent" from much of the territory.[64] Along with egregious abuses and incompetence, there have also been examples of excellence in the public and parastatal administration in most countries of the region, with dedicated civil servants working effectively under sometimes difficult conditions.[65]

The paradox of a dramatic improvement in individual capacity accompanied by an equally dramatic decline in institutional capacity should alert us to the endogenous nature of the latter. The public policy literature typically ignores the reasons for which capacity improvements have been so halting. Instead, it depicts state capacity levels as exogenously determined, somewhat like a country's level of natural resources,[66] or it makes vague references to the legacy of colonialism and underdevelopment. The message has been that more training programs and foreign experts can get African countries over the hump. Yet, after four decades of independence and tens of billions of dollars in state capacity projects, low state capacity in Africa cannot be viewed as the unfortunate if inevitable by-product of underdevelopment. It should instead be perceived as the direct consequences of the formal policies and informal practices of governments for which a developmental state apparatus is not a high priority.

The first blows against state capacity came early after independence. Patronage exigencies led many governments to allow the excessively fast growth and africanization of their administration.[67] The Nigerian federal and regional civil service grew by 50 percent in the first five years of independence, for instance, while the Senegalese civil service grew from 10,000 to 35,000 in the same period, and the overall Kenyan public sector grew from 188,000 in 1965 to 237,000 in 1978.[68] The rapid

64. Thomas Bierschenk and Jean-Pierre Olivier de Sardan, "Local Powers and Distant State in Rural Central African Republic," *Journal of Modern African Studies* 35 (1997): 441–468, p. 462.

65. See, for example, the fascinating biographies of four senior Kenyan civil servants provided in David Leonard, *African Successes: Four Public Managers of Kenyan Rural Development* (Berkeley: University of California Press, 1991).

66. A good example of this tendency is the World Bank, *World Development Report, 1997* (Washington, DC: World Bank, 1997), which focused on the state and governance issues. Though sometimes compelling on the prescriptive side, the report is entirely silent on the causes of poor state performance.

67. In Tanzania, for instance, nationals went from 12 percent of senior and middle-level civil service posts to 90 percent within a decade of independence. See Goldsmith, "Africa's Overgrown State Reconsidered," pp. 537–8.

68. Cited in David B. Abernathy, "Bureaucratic Growth and Economic Decline in Sub-Saharan Africa," paper presented to the 26th Annual Meeting of the African Studies Association, Boston, Massachusetts, December 7–10, 1983, p. 12.

expansion and exit of experienced colonial administrators undermined the professionalism and esprit de corps of the administration, as well as its basic competence, since so many inexperienced and undertrained staff were thrust into positions of authority.

The actions of African leaders undermined the quality of the civil service in other ways as well. The prospects for effective civil services, it is widely agreed, are enormously enhanced by meritocratic hiring and promotion policies. In Korea, for instance, the practice of competitive civil service exams is a state tradition going back to A.D. 788 and, as late as the early 1990s, there were still more than fifty candidates for every position.[69] In Africa, these principles were directly undermined by governments in the years after independence. Governments guaranteed civil service positions to all college graduates, a policy that remains active in some form or another in many countries to this day. The ex-British colonies usually had followed the British model of all civil service recruitment and promotion being under the authority of an independent civil service commission. In countries like Ghana, Kenya, Tanzania, and Zambia, governments resorted to a constitutional amendment soon after independence to place the commission directly under the authority of the presidency, the first step in the politicization and loss of professionalism of the civil service in those countries.[70]

Much the same can be said of the wage incentives facing civil servants in the region. Adjusting for inflation, civil service salaries collapsed during the 1970s and 1980s. In Anglophone countries, salaries typically lost more than 80 percent of their real value. In the Francophone countries, the situation was somewhat more ambiguous; real salaries officially fared better thanks to the lower levels of inflation within the Franc Zone, but governments often accumulated considerable salary arrears in response to their substantial fiscal deficits, so the effective wage incentives to employees may in some cases have declined as much.[71] Nonwage benefits to civil servants, from housing subsidies to various allowances, apparently increased in importance over time, partly compensating for

69. See Soo Chan Jang, "Driving Engine or Rent-Seeking Super-Cartel? The Business-State Nexus and Economic Transformation in South Korea, 1960–1999" (Ph.D. dissertation, Michigan State University, 1999).
70. Goldsmith, "Africa's Overgrown State Reconsidered," p. 540.
71. On the evolution of civil service wages, see the data provided in D. Robinson, *Civil Service Pay in Africa* (Geneva: International Labor Organization, 1990); Lindauer and Nunberg *Rehabilitating Government*; and Lienert and Modi, "A Decade of Civil Service Reform."

the decline in real wages,[72] but there is little doubt that all but the highest level public sector employees underwent a sharp reduction in their purchasing power in most countries in the region. On the surface, poor wage incentives resulted from inflation and the government's precarious fiscal situation. More profoundly, however, they resulted from conscious policies by state leaders, who abused the civil service as a vehicle for patronage. Low wages were inevitable, given the policy of allowing the civil service to increase rapidly in size, while more or less keeping a lid on the overall wage bill. Studies show a striking correlation in the region between the size of the civil service and wages, with smaller civil services being systematically better remunerated.[73]

Was the excessive growth of the civil service merely due to the inability of weak governments to control patronage demands? It is of course not possible to prove, but it is tempting to speculate that African leaders have often viewed the growing ineffectiveness of the state apparatus with some equanimity, as they understood that low state capacity would lessen the effective constraints on their own behavior. In postcolonial Africa, there has often been a negative synergy between capacity and neopatrimonial tendencies. In other words, low state capacity has facilitated various rent-seeking and corrupt practices. Corruption is easier to sustain when tax inspectors have not been paid in several months, the ministry archives have not been maintained, various statistics are poorly kept, and the government lacks trained auditors. In turn, state agents who wish to undertake these practices have a clear interest in weakening the state's administrative capacities. The absence of transparency, public information, or economic data is often designed to protect abuses by state elites, and in turn serves to diminish the ability of state agents to enforce rational-legal norms. Leaders might in theory prefer a higher degree of state capacity, but in practice they choose not to invest in it.

A recent study of the education sector in Uganda is suggestive in this regard.[74] The authors conducted detailed field surveys in schools

72. These nonwage benefits are usually skewed toward the top of the civil service. Olowu gives the example of Tanzania, where benefits in kind amount to as much as 400 percent of the salary at the highest levels of the civil service, but only 35 percent at the lower levels. Bamidele Olowu, "Redesigning African Civil Service Reforms," *Journal of Modern African Studies* 37 (1999): 1–23, p. 6.
73. The World Bank, *World Development Report, 1997*, p. 95.
74. Emmanuel Ablo and Ritva Reinikka, "Do Budgets Really Matter? Evidence from Public Spending on Education and Health in Uganda," World Bank Policy Research Paper (Washington, DC: World Bank, undated).

throughout the country, initially to compensate for the dismal quality of the data available from the government. Indeed, the Ministry of Education lacked adequate data for such basic information as the number of teachers in the classroom, their salaries, or the total number of students enrolled. Whereas official numbers suggested stagnant enrollments in the first half of the 1990s, the authors' field data suggested increases of roughly 60 percent. Such an absence of facts about the sector appears to have coincided with systematic abuse at the district level. The authors found that between 1993 and 1995, on average 27 percent of capitation grants from the central government actually reached the schools for which they were intended, and that only 36 percent of the mandatory school fees were actually spent at the school level during the same period. District officials appear to have kept the major part of these mistargeted funds. Without much more precise information, the complicity of Ministry of Education officials in local corruption in Uganda cannot be ascertained and one hesitates to throw accusations around, particularly since the Ugandan government under Museveni has repeatedly affirmed education as one of its strongest priorities.[75] A wide array of factors, such as poor official statistics, contribute to state deficiencies but the combination of breakdowns in state capacity and governmental corruption is too systematic across the continent to be coincidental.

Over time, neopatrimonialism has a profoundly corrosive effect on technocratic competence. In most countries of the region, there are inadequate professional incentives for graduates to demonstrate technical competence within the bureaucracy. Ambitious young technocrats with the appropriate training are quickly dissuaded from taking policy initiatives that risk rocking the boat. They find there is little institutional demand for such ventures as improving the ministry database or rationalizing accounting procedures and that their efforts to do so generate indifference if not hostility. The technical skills they brought to their positions atrophy over time, or they find that they are more appreciated and much better remunerated in the private and donor sectors and tend to emigrate from the public service.

75. On the other hand, other accounts suggest the endemic nature of corruption in Uganda and are critical of government efforts to reduce it. See Rachel Flanary and David Watt, "The State of Corruption: A Case Study of Uganda," *Third World Quarterly* 20 (1999): 515–36. The authors cite (p. 523) a 1998 government survey on corruption, which found that 40 percent of all service users paid a bribe to service workers in order to get the service; and that 63 percent of respondents reported having paid the police a bribe.

In sum, by the early 1980s, the state administration was well on its long journey of decay. Technocratic pockets battled with politicians to assert rational decision making but more often than not found themselves on the short end of the stick. Some observers have retrospectively viewed the 1960s and 1970s as halcyon days for African administrations and blame their decline on the economic crisis and the "antistate" bias of structural adjustment. The next chapter of this book will show that the adjustment process has further undermined state institutions and capacity, but it must be emphasized that a number of political practices began undermining the administration soon after independence. Given the centralization and personalization of power in these regimes, the administration played only a small role in designing economic policies. One explanation for the often-remarked predilection of African administrations for highly hierarchical decision making and control-oriented policy regimes may well be their attempt to enhance their own limited power and prerogatives vis-à-vis a political system that sought to undermine them. Similarly, Hyden explains the predilection for detailed economic planning in the region in the 1960s and 1970s as resulting from the view that planning provided a bulwark for the technocrats against patrimonial practices.[76]

THE IDEOLOGICAL CONTEXT

The ideas embodied in the structural adjustment programs that came to dominate policy debates in Africa following the emergence of economic crisis can be considered as part of what might be called the *new liberal orthodoxy* (NLO). Other observers have described this process of policy convergence, labeling it either "the triumph of neoclassical economics,"[77] or the "Washington consensus,"[78] or, in the African context, the "adjustment with growth" consensus.[79] This is a body of economic ideas largely

76. Hyden, *No Shortcuts to Progress*, p. 64.
77. Thomas Biersteker, "The 'Triumph of Neoclassical Economics in the Developing World: Policy Convergence and Bases of Governance in the International Economic Order," in James Rosenau and Ernst-Otto Czempiel (eds.), *Governance without Government: Order and Change in World Politics* (New York: Cambridge University Press, 1992), pp. 102–131.
78. John Williamson, "Democracy and the 'Washington Consensus,'" *World Development* 21, no. 8 (1993): 1329–36.
79. John Ravenhill, "Adjustment with Growth: A Fragile Consensus," *Journal of Modern African Studies* 26 (1988): 179–210; see also Gerald K. Helleiner, "The IMF, the World Bank and Africa's Adjustment and External Debt Problems: An Unofficial View," *World Development* 20 (1992): 779–92, especially pp. 780–1.

manufactured in the universities, think tanks, and policy circles of the West, in particular in North America, and based on research and publications often financed by the Western aid agencies – in particular the international financial institutions (IFI), the IMF, and the World Bank.[80] It emerged during the late 1970s and 1980s, in the course of over a decade of policy debates, and in the context of the implementation of adjustment programs. The NLO should not, however, be viewed as a purely Western creation, imposed from the outside on Third World societies.[81] Non-Western countries and individuals have played an often central role in the acceptability of the new orthodoxy, while much of the opposition to the NLO was and has continued to be based in the West.

As Dani Rodrik has argued, "What is remarkable about current fashions in economic development policy (as applied to both developing and transitional economies) . . . is the extent of convergence that has developed on the broad outlines of what constitutes an appropriate economic strategy. . . . Faith in the desirability and efficacy of these policies unites the vast majority of professional economists in the developed world who are concerned with issues of development."[82]

Compared with the 1960s and 1970s, there came to be considerably greater agreement on some basic principles of sound development policy, even if significant differences remained. The exact contours of the NLO are subject to some debate. Williamson cites ten separate principles of macroeconomic policy, over which he suggests there was broad agreement in Latin America by the late 1980s:[83]

1. Fiscal discipline
2. Public expenditure (an emphasis on investment rather than consumption)

---

80. For an interesting assessment of the contribution of the World Bank to this set of ideas, see Nicholas Stern and Francisco Ferreira, "The World Bank as an 'Intellectual Actor,'" in Devesh Kapur, John P. Lewis, and Richard Webb (eds.), *The World Bank: Its First Half Century* (Washington: Brookings Institution Press, 1997), pp. 523–610.
81. Miles Kahler. "Orthodoxy and Its Alternatives: Explaining Approaches to Stabilization and Adjustment," in Joan Nelson (ed.), *Economic Crisis and Policy Choice: The Politics of Economic Adjustment in the Third World* (Princeton, NJ: Princeton University Press, 1990), pp. 33–62.
82. See his essay "Understanding Economic Policy Reform," *Journal of Economic Literature* 34 (1996): 9–41, p. 9. Rodrik argues that this consensus does not extend much beyond the world of professional economists.
83. Williamson, "Democracy and the 'Washington Consensus.'"

3. Tax reform (to broaden the tax base and cut marginal rates)
4. Financial liberalization
5. Exchange rate at competitive level
6. Trade liberalization
7. Foreign direct investment (barriers to it should be removed)
8. Privatization of state enterprises
9. Deregulation of all competitive markets
10. Secure property rights

Williamson argues that a very broad consensus exists for each of these ideas, even if reasonable experts might disagree on the margin of these principles. Many observers have viewed the list as too expansive.[84] Williamson probably exaggerates the degree of support for privatization, for instance. For purposes of the argument and in order not to get sidetracked into a long-winded discussion about development policy, I would synthesize from this general list three principles as the core of the NLO: fiscal discipline, outward orientation, and the basic reliance on markets.[85]

84. For example, the Washington Consensus has been criticized in this sense by Christopher Colclough and James Manor (eds.), *States or Markets? Neo-Liberalism and the Development Policy Debate* (Oxford, UK: Clarendon Press, 1991). A number of scholars pointed to the economic performance of the East Asian countries to criticize the small role granted to the state by Williamson. See, for instance, Robert Wade, *Governing the Market: Economic Theory and the Role of Government in East Asian Industrialization* (Princeton, NJ: Princeton University Press, 1990). A much larger literature has criticized the Washington consensus as too narrow, arguing that it should have included such issues as equity, gender, and the environment. See, for instance, Luis Carlos Bresser Pereira, Jose Maria Maravall, and Adam Przeworski, *Economic Reform in New Democracies: A Social Democratic Approach* (Cambridge, UK: Cambridge University Press, 1993); or Robin Broad and John Cavanagh, "The Death of the Washington Consensus?" *World Policy Journal* 16 (1999): 79–88. But these critiques misunderstand Williamson's objective, which was not to define the right development policy framework, but rather a minimum common denominator – the issues on which he believed there was broad agreement.
85. I do not include "secure property rights" in my list, although the notion that they should be legally secure and enforced in a routine manner has gained extremely wide acceptance under the impulse of the "governance" movement in recent years. In Africa, it is perhaps the most widely accepted of our four principles, even if (or perhaps because) it is an area in which Africa continues to make little progress. I omit it from this essay only because it focuses on more traditional economic concerns, and including governance would complicate matters. As the discussion in Chapter 2 made clear, there is much evidence that uncertain property rights continue to be a critical constraint on economic recovery in the region.

Fiscal discipline: This principle is the same as Williamson's first. It implies that nations broadly live within their means and do not resort to significant deficit spending beyond purely temporary measures in the context of a stabilization effort. No serious economic policy analyst believes that monetary expansion or borrowing abroad is a long-term solution for macroeconomic equilibrium.

Outward orientation: This notion combines principles 5 and 6 of Williamson. There can still be reasonable disagreement regarding the desirable speed of trade liberalization, the merits of infant industry-type arguments for temporary protection measures, or even the extent to which trade strategy should emphasize traditional as opposed to nontraditional exports. But today there is broad agreement in the policy community that African economies will benefit from a long-term reduction in protection and an increase in competitiveness to increase exports.

Reliance on markets: The principle combines numbers 4 and 9 of Williamson. It is not a call to laissez-faire. Rather, it is the principle that where markets work reasonably well, and when there is no prima facie evidence of market failure, government intervention should be limited. This leaves ample room for a governmental role for the provision of public goods or for markets where monopoly, externalities, or information asymmetries make governmental intervention desirable. Again, significant disagreements may develop over the exact implications of the principle, but it enjoys wide support.

The Africa of 1980 was largely hostile to the economic ideas embodied in the new liberal orthodoxy.[86] Rather than an outward orientation, policy elites were deeply wedded to the principles of import substitution industrialization, viewed as the best way to promote rapid domestic industrialization. Systematic state intervention in the economy through control over domestic prices, rationed credit, a large public enterprise system, and control over the agricultural marketing chain were all designed to provide the government with a control of the "commanding

---

86. Much of the following discussion is based on the excellent review of these issues in Michael Lofchie, "The New Political Economy of Africa," in David E. Apter and Carl G. Rosberg (eds.), *Political Development and the New Realism in Sub-Saharan Africa* (Charlottesville: University Press of Virginia, 1994), pp. 145–83; Tony Killick, *A Reaction Too Far: Economic Theory and the Role of the State in Developing Countries* (London: Overseas Development Institute, 1989); and John Waterbury, "The Long Gestation and Brief Triumph of Import-Substituting Industrialization," *World Development* 27 (1999): 323–41.

heights" of the economy, which it would steer to development thanks to the power of economic planning.

There were many reasons for the prevalence of *statist* economic ideas in the region. It should first be noted that African policy elites were not alone in these views, which probably constituted the dominant development paradigm in the 1950s and 1960s.[87] Indicative planning was widely espoused all over the developing world, as well as in countries like France. The Soviet Union was quite widely held up as an example of a country that had used central planning to engineer rapid structural transformation. Indeed, the planning ministries that sprouted up all over Africa were soon staffed and financed thanks to generous aid from the Western donors. There were early skeptics of the usefulness of planning, given African conditions,[88] while a few observers such as the Frenchman René Dumont was deeply critical of the first generation of plans in the region;[89] nonetheless, Nobel Laureate Gunnar Myrdal probably summed up a widespread consensus when he argued in 1968,

[That] large-scale intervention, coordinated in a plan, is needed to bring about economic development follows as an inference from the realization that these countries have long remained in a state of relative stagnation, while the Western world has for many generations developed rapidly. A strong, induced impetus is needed to end that stagnation and bring about economic progress, which apparently is not coming spontaneously, or at least fast enough.[90]

Import substituting industrialization was similarly widely supported in the West as an appropriate development strategy, as was the view that low-income countries would not likely be able to spearhead their growth through their traditional exports. As Chudson put it in 1961, "The rate of growth in the demand for their exports of primary commodities, even on fairly optimistic assumptions, is not likely to satisfy the need for expanded imports associated with desired rates of economic growth."[91]

87. Waterbury does a masterful job of analyzing the wide intellectual foundations for statist economic policies in this period in his essay "The Long Gestation and Brief Triumph."
88. For instance, Wolfgang Stolper, *Planning without Facts: Lessons in Resource Allocation from Nigeria Development* (Cambridge: Harvard University Press, 1966).
89. René Dumont, *False Start in Africa*, 2d ed. (New York: Praeger, 1969).
90. Myrdal, *An Asian Drama*, p. 715.
91. Walter Chudson, "Trends in African Exports and Capital Inflows," in Melville J. Herskovits and Mitchell Harwitz (eds.), *Economic Transition in Africa* (Evanston, IL: Northwestern University Press, 1964), pp. 337–56. Similar views are expressed in Benveniste and Moran, *Handbook of African Economic Development*, especially, pp. 106–30, p. 341.

This "export pessimism" was widely shared, including by many of the leading development thinkers in the West.[92]

Similarly, many mainstream economists believed the structuralist arguments according to which various cultural factors, economic rigidities, and technical and infrastructural deficiencies that are prevalent within low-income economies create bottlenecks, shortages, and distortions that limit the ability of private economic agents to respond appropriately to market incentives. These structuralist arguments justified high levels of state intervention in the economy. For instance, many Western experts supported the view that a low price elasticity of supply for most African farmers undermined the relevance of price incentives to increase production and put a premium on emphasizing state parastatals that would promote the dissemination of new technologies to the sector.

The rapid growth of public enterprises in the 1960s and 1970s was invariably justified as necessary given the weakness of the private sector. In Côte d'Ivoire, for instance, a succession of five-year plans described the need for public enterprises to serve as a "relay" for private sector investment, which, by itself, would not be adequately forthcoming.[93] In truth, throughout the region, most of the parastatals the donors have sought to privatize these last twenty years are organizations for which they financed the expansion in the two decades following independence, explicitly to spearhead the development process.

In Africa, the technocratic arguments of the structuralists overlapped nicely with the paternalism of the colonial administration, which viewed local populations if not with some contempt, at least with a healthy dose of condescension. The European-trained African technocrats and their donor supporters who inherited this administration at independence usually adopted similar attitudes, which confirmed their superiority and increased their power. As Scott has argued about the government's efforts to engage in a large scale village resettlement scheme in Tanzania, "the seeds of coercion had been sown, by a politicized, authoritarian bureaucracy and also by Nyerere's underlying conviction that the peasants did not know what was good for them."[94] The structuralist models depicted economic dualism, with the high-productivity "modern" or "Western"

92. Waterbury, "The Long Gestation and Brief Triumph."
93. See, for instance, Bernard Contamin and Yves-A Fauré, *La bataille des entreprises publiques en Côte d'Ivoire: l'histoire d'un ajustement interne* (Paris: Karthala, 1990).
94. James C. Scott, *Seeing like a State: How Certain Schemes to Improve the Human Condition have Failed* (New Haven, CT: Yale University Press, 1998), p. 231.

sector and the low-productivity "traditional," "indigenous" or even "backward" sector. So, in practical terms, modernization seemed to require a large role for the state.

A good example of these dynamics is provided by the Office du Niger in Mali.[95] A parastatal created in 1932 by the French colonial authorities to launch a large-scale irrigation project on the Niger River in what was then the French Sudan, it would turn into one of the largest colonial enterprises in west Africa, with 200 expatriates supervising 6,000 African workers, and would receive somewhere between $83 and $175 million in investments between 1928 and 1959. Its wildly ambitious objective was to irrigate one million hectares and spearhead an agricultural revolution in the country. Following independence, the Office du Niger would continue to benefit from governmental largesse as a parastatal. Between 1961 and 1966, for instance, it would receive 11 percent of total national public investment! It would be the primary vehicle for the government's misguided socialist experiments in agriculture in the late 1960s and 1970s that sought to turn peasants into employees of the office. Its staffing would mushroom, corruption grow, and losses accumulate. Major aid programs from China, France, the Netherlands, the United States, the European Union, and the World Bank would support the office, first to continue the colonial project, and from the late 1970s on, to rehabilitate, reform and eventually privatize what had turned into a fiscal albatross for the government. Original objectives of irrigating a million hectares for cotton and rice production proved completely unrealistic and fewer than 50,000 hectares were ever in production at any given time. By the mid-1990s, the World Bank was expressing satisfaction about the evolution of the parastatal, now partly privatized and manned by only 360 employees, but overseeing impressive growth in smallholder rice production. The Bank nonetheless conceded that the Office du Niger accounted "for a good share of the country's present indebtedness."[96]

Second, and related, the historical context helps explain the emergence of statist economic ideas. Socialist economic ideologies were likely to be irresistible to governments that emerged from the African nationalist movements, in the context of the Cold War. Moreover, economic nationalism was justified by the fear of neocolonialism and a keen sense of

95. This account has been pieced together from "Mali Success Story: The Office du Niger," unpublished manuscript, World Bank, June 1996. I thank Serge Michailof for having attracted my attention to the Office du Niger story.
96. Ibid, p. 26.

international vulnerability following independence. Given the legacy of colonial rule, Africans were absent from the narrow formal private sector that did exist, overwhelmingly in the hands of British and French or Lebanese and Indian businessmen and protected from African competition by colonial law and practice.[97] As a result, there were typically remarkably few links between the nationalist leaders and the private sector, which the former viewed with some hostility. The policies of nationalization and economic regulation during the 1960s were often motivated by the state's need to increase its control over the national economy: foreign companies with close links to the metropole and or European settler interests dominated the modern sector, while the traditional economy was in the hands of an "uncaptured" peasantry, which also largely escaped the state's limited extractive capacity.[98] This tendency was reinforced in day-to-day administration because, as suggested above, weak administrators viewed statist policies as a way to strengthen their own position vis-à-vis the politicians. For the technocrats, rational-legal authority and statism went hand in hand.[99]

Third, statist views were politically expedient. It is not clear that the leaders of the nationalist movements that took control of governments at independence had tailored their economic views to suit their political and material interests. Statist economic views were too much part of the anticolonial *zeitgeist* of the times to believe that these were not in some part disinterested. Nonetheless, once national movement leaders in power, these economic ideas were reinforced by their evident convergence with political exigencies. A large public sector afforded patronage possibilities that – as described above – buttressed political stability, while extensive government intervention in the economy created numerous possibilities for rent-seeking, even if it had quickly proven incapable of promoting rapid development. I return to the linkages between economic ideas and political interests later.

By the mid-1980s, the new liberal orthodoxy (NLO) had been generally accepted by a wide spectrum of opinion in policy circles outside of

97. This point is particularly emphasized by Paul Kennedy, *African Capitalism: The Struggle for Ascendency* (Cambridge, UK: Cambridge University Press, 1988).
98. The seminal work here is Goran Hyden, *Beyond Ujamaa in Tanzania: Underdevelopment and an Uncaptured Peasantry* (London: Heinemann, 1980).
99. Goran Hyden makes a similar argument in his book *No Shortcuts to Progress: African Development Management in Perspective* (Berkeley: University of California Press, 1983), pp. 63–7 and passim.

Africa. For example, few serious experts were still recommending that Brazil "delink" from the world economy, even if the precise role of the tradeables sector in its overall development strategy was still debated. Likewise, massive deficit spending was not viewed as a viable long-term option for low- or middle-income economies. There might, finally, be debates about the implementation of privatization programs, but few analysts still contested that states should divest themselves of commercial holdings in competitive markets. In Latin America and much of Asia, these basic principles had become part of the policy mainstream, and policy debates had moved on to other more narrow issues of "second generation" reform.

The majority of political elites within Africa remained profoundly ambivalent about the core principles of the NLO, however. As argued in Chapter 2, governments in Africa have officially professed their support of such principles by repeatedly committing themselves to implementing stabilization and adjustment programs with international financial institution (IFI) funding since 1979. On the other hand, the record of extremely uneven reform implementation that was reviewed in the last chapter suggests that real preferences have diverged from officially expressed ones.

Given their relations with the donors and the politics of conditionality, it has usually been impolitic for individual governments to voice their disapproval of the NLO too openly. The kind of opposition Nyerere voiced publicly in the early 1980s became more rare as governments officially committed themselves to IFI-funded adjustment programs. Only the occasional outburst, usually in front of a domestic audience, has suggested continuing ambivalence. Thus, Senegalese prime minister Habib Thiam told the national parliament in early 1991 that he would not follow the World Bank's advice to eliminate fertilizer subsidies because "it is not possible to develop agriculture without public subsidies. . . . it is such a serious problem, it should not be left to the experts."[100] At the time, it might be noted, the removal of subsidies was official policy as part of an adjustment loan with the World Bank. Recent studies of the relationship between aid and reform suggest a deep skepticism toward reform by leading governmental technocrats in the 1980s in Côte

100. Samba Ka and Nicolas van de Walle, "The Political Economy of Structural Adjustment in Senegal, 1980–1991," in Stephan Haggard and Steven B. Webb (eds.), *Voting for Reform: Economic Adjustment in New Democracies* (New York: Oxford University Press, 1994), pp. 290–359, p. 346.

d'Ivoire, and show support limited to a very narrow stratum of officials largely not shared by the bureaucracy in Kenya.[101]

The ambivalence regarding the NLO is more evident from the work of various international forums in which African governments express themselves with fewer inhibitions. Thus, the economic policy work of the OAU and the Economic Commission for Africa – most notably the 1980 *Lagos Plan of Action* and the 1989 *Alternative African Framework to Structural Adjustment Programs for Socio-Economic Recovery and Transformation* (AAF-SAP) – continues to express wide disagreement with new liberal orthodoxy policies, even if there has been evidence of limited convergence over time. Commenting on the AAF-SAP, Callaghy wrote that it was "a warmed-over version of the Lagos Plan of Action with vague and contradictory, largely statist, policy proposals that could not be implemented under the best of conditions, all of which are linked to renewed demands for substantially increased external resource flows and debt relief."[102]

Of the different components of the NLO, fiscal discipline seems to be the most widely accepted. The continuing wide disparity between revenues and expenditures in many countries is widely agreed to be undesirable. From the Lagos Plan, the AAF-SAP, and their various descendants to much of the independent African policy literature, there has come a recognition of the importance of "living within one's means." However, African governments have used various international forums to make calls for debt forgiveness and continuing increases in concessionary aid to finance ambitious development programs, diminishing the credibility of the professed new fiscal conservatism. One searches these official documents in vain for real agreement on the rest of the NLO agenda. The desirability of greater exports is asserted, but then disparaged as likely to be counterproductive because of "fallacy of composition" issues[103] or as

101. See the two case studies for the World Bank project "Aid and Reform in Africa." Elliott Berg, Patrick Guillaumont, Jacques Pegatienan, and Jacky Amprou, "Aid and Reform in the Côte d'Ivoire," unpublished paper, Washington, DC, December 1999; and F. S. O'Brien and T. C. I. Ryan, "Aid and Reform in Africa: Kenya Case Study," unpublished paper, Washington, DC, August 27, 1999.

102. Thomas Callaghy, "Africa and the World Economy: Caught between a Rock and a Hard Place," in John Harbeson and Donald Rothchild (eds.), *Africa in World Politics* (Boulder, CO: Westview Press, 1991), p. 55.

103. According to this argument, African efforts to increase their traditional exports will result in an actual decline in export prices because of excessive supply. Most economists agree that Africa supplies a large enough proportion of certain tropical crops like cocoa to be able to affect prices in this manner. However, the result of African passivity has been a loss of market share for these very commodities to more aggressive exporters such as Malaysia.

unlikely to be successful because of northern protectionism.[104] Economic liberalization or privatization is viewed as a donor-inspired project that is fueled by suspect ideological and political motives.

Of course, by itself, resistance from official Africa to the NLO might be imputed solely to nonideological factors, such as the desire to protect rent-seeking. It is harder to explain the hostility of a wide array of independent groups and intellectuals, who are otherwise harshly critical of their governments. In truth, negative views of the new liberal orthodoxy are widely held across a broad cross section of African intellectuals and civil society. Signs of partial policy convergence toward the NLO can be identified. Regional journalistic publications such as *l'Autre Afrique*, *West Africa*, or *Jeune Afrique*, as well as much academic literature demonstrate some evolution in the perception of Africa's economic crisis. External explanations of the economic crisis and the need for a "new international economic order" to improve the international terms of trade continue to be presented, but they are now accompanied by a critique of local government performance and specific domestic policies. Most African policy circles now admit that the performance and policies of governments partly explain the crisis of the 1980s, a change from the dominant view a decade ago that external factors were almost entirely to blame.

Admittedly, some African intellectuals and economists have bought into the new liberal orthodoxy. For instance, Koulibaly provoked much controversy in Francophone Africa by arguing that economic liberalization alone could lead African states such as his native Ivory Coast to rapid economic growth.[105] Nonetheless, the dominant view of the NLO consensus regarding adjustment continues to be negative. Noneconomists are particularly hostile to the NLO. In their analyses of Africa's economic crisis, prominent intellectuals too often seem to believe that to disparage a policy reform as "neoclassical" or "liberal" or "neoliberal" or "monetarist" is enough to condemn it out of hand, without necessitating further analysis.[106] Several premises, for the most

104. This, despite the compelling evidence that northern protection has not been a significant brake on African exports. See Alexander J. Yeats, Azita Amjadi, Ulrich Reincke, and Francis Ng, "Did External Barriers Cause the Marginalization of Sub-Saharan Africa in World Trade?" World Bank Policy Research Working Paper no. 1586. (Washington, DC: World Bank, March 1996).

105. Mamadou Koulibaly, *Le Libéralisme, Nouveau Départ pour l'Afrique Noire* (Paris: l'Harmattan, 1992).

106. Among others, see the following prominent works: Claude Ake, *Democracy and Development in Africa*; Axelle Kabou, *Et si l'Afrique refusait le développement?*

part unexamined, seem to underlie this condemnation. First, the NLO is assumed to imply increases in income inequalities and poverty. African intellectuals – even those otherwise quite critical of their governments – seem to take for granted that state intervention in the economy before the crisis served to redistribute income from the rich to the poor and that reform would thus necessarily have regressive implications. International financial institution economists have never fully accepted these arguments,[107] but the debate has changed in the 1990s, as the IFIs have devoted increased lending to the social sectors, at least in part to counter this criticism that their lending was increasing social inequality and poverty.[108] In any event, it is difficult to know the extent to which this charge against the NLO by independent intellectuals is accepted by policy elites. Although governments have often criticized the social cost of adjustment in international forums, concern about poverty and inequality do not seem to otherwise weigh much on the national policy agenda.

Second, the NLO is argued not to apply well to Africa, given African sociocultural realities. Thus, the trade-oriented success stories from Asia are believed not to have implications for African economies. For example, Etounga-Manguelle blames Africa's economic stagnation on African attitudes about economics, authority, and community rather than inappropriate economic policies, and he argues that Africa needs "a cultural structural adjustment" more than an economic one.[109] In her long essay, *Et si l'Afrique refusait le développement?* Kabou argues that "the sociological and especially psychological conditions for the success of free enterprise are not yet present in Africa, not by a long shot"

(Paris: l'Harmattan, 1991); Jean-Marc Ela, *Quand l'etat pénètre en brousse: les ripostes paysannes à la crise* (Paris: Karthala, 1992); Mahmoud Mamdani, "Uganda: Contradictions of the IMF Programme and Perspectives," *Development and Change*, 21 (1990): 427–67; Daniel Etounga-Manguelle, *L'Afrique a-t-elle besoin d'un programme d'ajustement culturel?* (Ivry-sur-Seine: Editions Nouvelles du Sud, 1990); and Adebayo Olukoshi, *The Politics of Structural Adjustment in Africa* (London: James Currey, 1992).

107. Howard White provides a good summary of the debate with numerous citations in his essay, "Review Article: Adjustment in Africa," *Development and Change* 27 (1996): 785–815. See also Florencia Castro-Leal et al., "Public Social Spending in Africa: Do the Poor Benefit?" in *World Bank Research Observer* 14 (1999): 49–72; and Lionel Demery and Lynn Squire, "Macroeconomic Adjustment and Poverty in Africa: An Emerging Picture" *World Bank Research Observer* 11 (1996): 39–59.

108. The increased lending for poverty alleviation has been a notable characteristic of the World Bank under the leadership of James Wolfensohn.

109. Etounga-Manguelle, *L'Afrique a-t-elle besoin d'un programme d'ajustement culturel?*

(p. 84).[110] In his last book, the late Claude Ake similarly rejected the NLO agenda for the sake of "a self-reliant, indigenous development process" based on decentralized community level initiatives that he viewed as more in tune with local needs and culture.[111]

Third, many African intellectuals consider liberalism a doctrine that serves the interests of international capital and will only enhance Africa's economic dependence on the West. Jean-Marc Ela's text *Quand l'etat pénètre en brousse: Les ripostes paysannes à la crise* is not unrepresentative of this view.[112] A generally insightful critique of past state intervention in agriculture, it calls for development based on the peasantry's dynamism and initiative, freed from technocratic state control, as a way of pulling African economies out of their current crisis. Other than its hostility toward cash crops and plantation agriculture, argued to worsen poverty and hunger (e.g., p. 131), the book's arguments, particularly its critique of large public sector plantations and excessive state taxation of farmers, seem fairly compatible with World Bank adjustment programs in countries like Cameroon or Côte d'Ivoire. Yet Ela goes out of his way repeatedly to castigate the IFIs and their "liberal" doctrines, which serve the interest of international capital's strategy "to subjugate all the vital sectors of African economies by blocking the emergence of local counterweights that might result from internal socioeconomic dynamics" (p. 10). Throughout, economic liberalization is viewed as little more than a plot to emasculate African states and promote the full takeover of African economies by large multinational corporations.

Among African professional economists, the picture is somewhat different, with a number of leading economists working clearly within the NLO. The development of the Nairobi-based African Economic Research Consortium (AERC) is one of several efforts that have promoted mainstream policy research tending to support the NLO.[113] Nonetheless, it remains striking how many of the most prominent African economists remain at best skeptical of NLO doctrines. The works of Samir Amin, Hakim Ben Hammouda, Thandika Mkandawire,

110. Kabou, *Et si l'Afrique refusait le développement?*
111. Ake, *Democracy and Development in Africa.*
112. Ela, *Quand l'etat pénètre en brousse.*
113. AERC research projects have resulted in a number of recent publications. See, for instance, Ademola Oyejide, Ibrahim Elbadawi, and Paul Collier, *Regional Integration and Trade Liberalization in Sub-Saharan Africa* (New York: St. Martin's Press, 1997); and Machiko Nissanke and Ernest Aryeetey, *Financial Integration and Development: Liberalization and Reform in Sub-Saharan Africa* (London: New York: Routledge, 1998).

or Moustapha Kassé all provide good examples of this skepticism.[114] Kassé, for example, views Senegal's economic crisis as resulting from its "mode of accumulation based on mining and agricultural export activities" (p. 192). He does suggest that "no country in the world can for ever live beyond its means" (p. 194), thus agreeing with the first element of the NLO, fiscal discipline. But the strategy he develops to overcome the crisis involves the growth of a demand-driven internal market spearheaded by extensive state planning, a technological revolution, contractual agreements between labor and management, all of this to be financed by a sharp increase in foreign aid (pp. 189–95).

CONCLUDING REMARKS

The combination of pervasive political clientelism, an ideological proclivity for state intervention in the economy, and low capacity are the three factors internal to the state that largely determined Africa's economic performance in the postcolonial era. They resulted in the excessive growth of the state apparatus, ill-advised sectoral policies, and unsustainable macro policies that largely brought about economic stagnation and eventually the economic crisis that has befuddled the region since 1980.

That is not the entire explanation for the crisis of course. Highly volatile commodity prices complicated economic policy making, particularly in the 1970s. The resulting wide swings in the trade balance and in state revenues taxed the managerial capacities of often relatively inexperienced governments. Furthermore, relying on optimistic commodity forecasts, governments had put in place wildly ambitious development programs that implied sustained rapid increases in public investments. The relatively low rate of return on these investments contributed further to the pressures on the balance of payments and to international indebtedness.

114. Recent works include Samir Amin, *L'empire du chaos: La nouvelle mondialisation capitaliste* (Paris: L'Harmattan, 1991); Hakim Ben Hammouda, *l'economie politique du post-ajustement* (Paris: Karthala, 1999); Thandika Mkandawire and Richard Soludo, *Our Continent, Our Future: African Perspectives on Structural Adjustment* (Trenton, NJ: Africa World Press, 1999); and Moustapha Kassé, *Crise economique et ajustement structurel* (Ivry-sur-Seine: Editions Nouvelles du Sud, 1990). I do not mean to lump these scholars together, and it should be noted that they represent a wide diversity of views, with some much closer to the NLO than others. But all dispute at least one of the three principles enunciated above and all have been sharp critics of the current adjustment programs.

The interaction between economic ideas, low capacity, and the politics of clientelism within the state also largely explain the reaction of African decision makers once the economic crisis fully emerged in the late 1970s. By then, certain patterns were well set. In most countries, the neopatrimonial element had fairly clearly come to dominate the rational-legal, and regime presidentialization had advanced considerably. State capacity had undergone a serious decline. The ideological enthusiasm for state-led import substitution industrialization policies had waned, but these policies remained popular for noneconomic reasons. The next chapters examine how state elites responded to these challenges.

4

State Responses to the Permanent Crisis

The first years of Tanzania's economic crisis in the 1980s were marked by the government's intense political and ideological opposition to the economic liberalization policies proposed by the multilateral donors.[1] President Julius Nyerere, the country's undisputed leader since independence and a long-standing advocate of "African socialism and self-reliance," quickly emerged as one of the most eloquent opponents of reform programs. He argued in a wide number of international forums that the effort demanded of his country represented an intolerable burden, with potentially devastating effects on political stability. Until his retirement from politics in 1985, Tanzania achieved virtually no progress on coming to grips with its devastating economic crisis. Balance of payments and fiscal deficits hovered in the double digits as a percentage of GDP, while real GDP per capita declined by some 20 percent between 1976 and 1983.

Nyerere was comforted in his position by the growing volume of aid the country received, which helped limit the impact of the crisis.[2] In fact, much of the large infusions of aid by bilateral donors, notably the Scandinavians, was explicitly motivated by ideological solidarity with Nyerere's stance against the IMF. As a result, the break with the IMF notwithstanding, Tanzania was a leading recipient of aid in the region. Indeed, the World Bank itself continued to provide substantial support, despite misgivings about the country's policy stance. From 1981

1. For the background to the crisis and the flavor of debates in this period, see James H. Weaver and Arne Anderson, "Stabilization and Development in the Tanzanian Economy in the 1970s," in William R. Cline and Sidney Weintraub (eds.), *Economic Stabilization in Developing Countries* (Washington, DC: The Brookings Institution), pp. 335–74.
2. Howard White, *Aid and Macroeconomic Performance* (New York: St. Martin's Press, 1998), pp. 195–221.

to 1986, the Bank officially insisted that the government come to agreement with the IMF as a prerequisite for a structural adjustment loan, but it continued to disburse an average of $83 million a year in project funding.[3]

Nyerere's retirement and the arrival of Ali Hassan Mwinyi in the presidency in November 1985 were widely viewed as likely to facilitate reform, given the latter's reputation as a technocrat and reformer. The resumption of IMF lending following a deal in 1986 and the government's agreement to devalue the shilling that year consolidated this reputation, and donor support increased accordingly. By the early 1990s, the country began to make its way onto IFI "good pupil" lists.[4] One World Bank study of the reform process was even subtitled "Resolute Action." However, divisions over policy within the government continued and the single party apparatus, the Chama Cha Mapinduzi (CCM) became known for its opposition to economic liberalization. Many of the policies the government agreed to carry out were opposed by key players within the state apparatus, including Nyerere himself, who continued to head the party for a number of years after retiring from office.

In recent years, reform implementation has been slow and uneven. By the mid-1990s, a series of devaluations had finally helped eliminate the parallel market for foreign exchange, and considerable internal and external liberalization had been achieved.[5] On the other hand, much of the beneficial effects of liberalization have continued to be undermined by corruption and the antiprivate sector attitudes prevailing in the state;[6]

3. The complex relations between Tanzania and the World Bank through the 1980s are described in the World Bank, *World Bank/Tanzania Relations, 1961–1987*, Report No. 8329, Operations Evaluation Department (Washington, DC: World Bank, January 16, 1990). For a discussion of this period, see pp. 41–8. The disbursement totals are provided in Table 8.1, p. 100.

4. Darius Mans, "Tanzania: Resolute Action," in Ishrat Husain and Rashid Faruqee (eds.), *Adjustment in Africa: Lessons from Country Case Studies* (Washington, DC: World Bank, 1994), pp. 352–426.

5. The reform experience in the 1990s is reviewed by Michael Gavin, "Saving and Investment in the Tanzanian Economic Reform," in Jo Ann Paulson, *African Economies in Transition. Volume 2: The Reform Experience* (New York: St. Martin's Press, 1999), pp. 120–78. See also Benno Ndulu, *Managing Tanzania's Economy in Transition to Sustained Development* (Nairobi, Kenya: ESRF, 1997); and Phil Raikes and Peter Gibbon, "Tanzania, 1986–1994," in Poul Engberg-Pedersen et al., *Limits of Adjustment in Africa: The Effects of Economic Liberalization, 1986–94* (Oxford: James Currey, 1996), pp. 215–308.

6. See the damning evidence in Michael F. Lofchie and Thomas Callaghy, *Diversity in the Tanzanian Business Community and Its Implications for Growth*, Report to the USAID Mission, Dar es Salaam, Tanzania, Contract #621-0176-C-00-5035-00, December 5, 1995.

fiscal deficits have remained unsustainably high, and the largely unprofitable parastatal sector has continued to weigh heavily on the economy, with more than 400 companies still in government hands.[7]

Why has policy reform not proceeded more quickly? The political instability that Nyerere predicted would erupt in response to reform never materialized. Economic decline and growing poverty has resulted in few organized protests, and the CCM has continued to dominate national politics. The country is characterized by relatively little ethno-regional tension, although persistent strains between Zanzibar and the mainland have increased in recent years. The political elite appears to have accepted the principle of an incremental democratization process, again despite the relative absence of popular protest.[8] Faster progress on economic reform would perhaps have spurred greater popular participation, but the last two decades offer little evidence that policy makers had much cause to worry about popular reactions to their policies.

Obstacles to reform implementation must be sought elsewhere. It is tempting to explain the government's resistance purely in terms of the attachment high-level officials have to the various rent-seeking and corrupt practices that exist as a by-product of the state's pervasive intervention in the economy. Clearly, by the early 1980s, various forms of illicit economic activity had become rampant at every level.[9] As the private economy went into recession and the fiscal crisis worsened, civil servants could take advantage of their positions as the administrators of a wide array of licenses, taxes, subsidies, quotas, and rationing mechanisms to derive extra income. The partial reform instituted since 1985, it should be noted, has not stemmed corruption, which appears to have continued to grow. In fact, in 1999, Transparency International classified the country as the seventh most corrupt country in the world out of sample of 99 countries. In Africa, only Cameroon and Nigeria were viewed as more corrupt.[10]

The case of Tanzania nonetheless also suggests that ideological factors have interacted with other factors to shape policy making during the last

---

7. "Tanzania 2000, a Survey," *The Financial Times*, July 24, 2000, pp. 1–5, provides a useful review of recent reform implementation.
8. Goran Hyden, "Top Down Democratization in Tanzania," *Journal of Democracy* 10 (1999): 142–55.
9. See Aili Mari Tripp, *Changing the Rules: The Politics of Liberalization and the Urban Informal Economy in Tanzania* (Berkeley: University of California Press, 1997), especially pp. 180–8.
10. From data taken from Transparency International, 1999, at their web site: *http://www.transparency.de/documents/cpi/index.html*.

twenty years and to slow down the progress in reform. Few observers have taken seriously the role of ideology in African policy making, preferring instead to see ideological pronouncement as little more than "a convenient rhetoric."[11] But Nyerere's opposition to reform was clearly largely ideological, and few have doubted his sincerity. Perhaps, many state agents defended the policies of the Arusha declaration long after they had proven disastrous for economic growth because of the rent-seeking they made possible, but some at least were as sincere as the charismatic Nyerere.

Finally, the Tanzanian case compels us to examine the cumulative impact of economic crisis on the capacity of states to bring about renewed growth. The last twenty years have not been kind to the state apparatus. The cumulative impact of the crisis has, for instance, included the collapse of the purchasing power of the civil service, which tumbled 94 percent in real terms between 1969 and 1985.[12] Never particularly effective, public administration has progressively deteriorated even further, and donors have increasingly taken over the management of key public tasks. Public infrastructure has also seriously deteriorated. Inter-city telephone service was at best haphazard in the mid-1990s, while the road network is probably worse today than in the 1970s, after years of underexpenditure on maintenance.[13] Once the pride of Nyerere, key social services, such as health and education, have slowly decayed. Today, the primary reason for declines in school enrollment appears to be the poor quality of educational services, including semiliterate teachers.[14] Not only do all of these factors complicate the renewal of growth today, even if the government adopted investor friendly macroeconomic and

11. The phrase belongs to Ravi Gulhati, who argues the only important motivation of leaders is "political survival." See his essay, "Who Makes Economic Policy in Africa and How?" *World Development* 18 (1990): 1147–61, pp. 1150–1. For an interesting early analysis taking seriously the role of ideology, albeit in a somewhat different approach from the one adopted here, see Crawford Young, *Ideology and Development in Africa* (New Haven, CT: Yale University Press, 1982).

12. Mike Stevens, "Public Expenditure and Civil Service Reform in Tanzania," in David L. Lindauer and Barbara Nunberg (eds.), *Rehabilitating Government: Pay and Employment Reforms in Africa* (Washington, DC: World Bank, 1994), pp. 62–81.

13. One World Bank report suggested that in the early 1990s less than half of the necessary maintenance expenditures for the road network were expended. See p. 24, Ian G. Heggie, *Management and Financing of Roads* (Washington, DC: World Bank, 1995).

14. Study cited by Raikes and Gibbon, "Tanzania: 1986–1994," p. 291.

sectoral policies. In addition, the government's very ability to design and carry out policies must be in doubt.

What explains the lack of greater progress on economic policy reform in countries like Tanzania? What has been the role of ideology? How has the government's ability to manage economic affairs evolved over time? Have aid resources aided or undermined the reform process? This chapter explains how state officials have responded to the crisis. It seeks to explain the patterns of partial and failed reform that were described in Chapter 2. I emphasize the interaction between ideology, the narrow material and political interests of state elites, and the declining level of state capacity. It is important to ask how the economic crisis and the policy reform process has affected these three underlying determinants of economic policy making. Clearly, economic crisis always represents a threat to the administrative, political, and ideological status quo. One would expect economic crisis to have a negative impact on the administration, while the wholesale failure of old economic policies would logically put pressure on dominant economic paradigms. Given the internal logic of regimes so reliant on control over the economy, the impact of policy reforms emphasizing liberalization must have been particularly strong.[15] Throughout, this chapter emphasizes the evolving nature of adjustment politics. I view these dynamics as unfolding over time, with new and changing issues emerging as a result of the failure to undertake reform and restore macroeconomic equilibrium in the previous period.

Chapter 1 argued that policy outcomes are also a function of the relationship with the international donors, but this complex issue deserves a full chapter of its own, so I will defer the discussion of the international context until Chapter 5. This neat separation of the domestic and international sphere is artificial but necessary for narrative purposes, to avoid loading this chapter with even more material than it already contains. Nonetheless, I stress at the outset that all three of these factors are worsened by the nature of the relationship with Western donors.

This chapter is divided into three sections following the introduction. The first section focuses on the political adjustments that state elites have made to the evolving crisis in order to preserve regime stability. Opposition to adjustment from the political elite has shifted over time, from

15. This point was well developed in Jeffrey Herbst, "The Structural Adjustment of Politics in Africa," *World Development* 18 (1990): 949–58. See also Alice Sindzingre, "Crédibilité des etats et nouvelles insécurités: l'economie politique des réformes en Afrique," unpublished manuscript, Paris, CNRS, December 1996.

out-and-out rejection to a strategy of manipulation and partial implementation that has sought to gain political advantage from the adjustment process. A second section examines the evolution of impact of the
economic crisis and of failed adjustment efforts on African attitudes to
the crisis. I show that the legacy of failure in the 1980s and 1990s has
been both cause and effect of opposition to policy reform, reducing its
perceived political, economic, and administrative viability. Finally, a last
section focuses on the political consequences of two decades of partial
reform.

THE ADJUSTMENT OF NEOPATRIMONIALISM

Fiscal austerity and donor calls for liberalization directly challenged the
central mechanisms of neopatrimonial rule: the dispensation of favors
and rents using access to state resources by state elites. As many
observers have noted, austerity results in fewer positions of patronage,
as well as smaller rents. The growth of public employment certainly
slowed down in the 1980s and particularly 1990s. There was a general
slowdown in government procurement, building and infrastructure contracts, and other forms of public sector expenditure that had long provided opportunities for corruption and influence peddling. It is important
to place this evolution in context, however. As shown in Chapter 2,
overall government consumption and development expenditures were
not declining, thanks to the rapid growth in foreign aid – at least until
the mid-1990s. This evolution of growing government austerity combined with rapidly growing aid resources displaced patrimonial dynamics to new arenas. As might be expected and will be discussed in the next
chapter, much clientelistic activity has moved to the aid sector over the
last two decades.

The second challenge to neopatrimonial rulers was posed by the donor
efforts to bring about economic liberalization and real institutional
reform. The elimination of government controls, subsidies, and licenses;
the simplification or decrease of taxes and tariffs; and the liberalization
of domestic prices all directly undermined key instruments of political
control. How have governments responded to this threat? The initial
reaction of political elites was to prevaricate and attempt to prevent real
reform, in the belief that it was more destabilizing than nonreform. This
was rational, not least because many political elites failed to realize the
gravity of the crisis. As the crisis was often triggered by a sudden drop
in commodity export prices, many thought that prices would rebound.

Indeed, the World Bank's own price commodity forecasts throughout this period were also consistently too optimistic.[16] Rather than accede to demands from the donors that undermined their hold on power, leaders accepted donor finance as a stop-gap measure until the situation improved itself.

By the mid-1980s, it was becoming clear that the conditions that had caused the crisis were not going away. Still, political elites resisted policy reforms. Chapter 2 showed little real progress on institutional reforms such as privatization before the 1990s. Until then, most governments were playing a complex game with the donors, seeking to extract a maximum of resources from them while giving up a minimum of actual reforms. Governments accepted the need for some basic macroeconomic stabilization policies, but they mostly refused to countenance real institutional reform and were only rarely willing to undertake the broad adjustment measures without which sustained stabilization was probably impossible. This resulted in the kind of partial implementation described in Chapter 2. Governments prevaricated. They pleaded for more time to study the issues, or they simply deceived the donors, promising measures they then failed to undertake or soon reversed. Collier notes that the government of Kenya agreed to undertake the same set of agricultural reforms four times during the 1980s and yet failed ever to sustain the reforms past the end of the donor support.[17] Throup and Hornsby's analysis of recent Kenyan politics shows that Moi was an extremely reluctant policy reformer throughout the 1980s because "any attempt to liberalize the economy would not only reduce the patronage available to the regime in terms of remunerative jobs and access to loans, but would also economically reward the Kikuyu areas, the bastion of the opposition."[18] The reasons the donors allowed governments like Moi's to avoid liberalization is examined in the next chapter. Here, the point to make is that the dominant initial reaction of most governments was to seek to preserve the status quo.

16. See Angus Deaton, "Commodity Prices and Growth in Africa," *Journal of Economic Perspectives* 13 (1999): 23–40.
17. Paul Collier, "The Failure of Conditionality," in Catherine Gwin and Joan M. Nelson (eds.), *Perspectives on Aid and Development*, Overseas Development Council Policy Essay Number 22 (Baltimore: Johns Hopkins University Press for the ODC, 1997), pp. 51–78, p. 60. Such cases are legion. For numerous examples and a masterful analysis see Tony Killick, *Aid and the Political Economy of Policy Change* (London: Routledge, 1998).
18. David W. Throup and Charles Hornsby, *Multi-Party Politics in Kenya: The Kenyatta & Moi States and the Triumph of the System in the 1992 Election* (Oxford, UK: James Currey Press, 1998), p. 597.

As it became clear that the crisis would not go away, in a second phase elite attitudes changed somewhat. Structural adjustment programs became more routinized and donor information on local economies somewhat better, making complete noncompliance harder. The government debt burden increased and the cost of breaks in donor funding more onerous. Perhaps most important, leaders began to understand the range of opportunity and threat posed by different elements of the crisis and adjustment agendas. A good deal of prevarication and obfuscation has continued to this day, but other strategies became more evident as well. In this second phase, which can be very roughly linked in time to the second decade of the crisis, top state leaders have sought to accommodate themselves to the permanent crisis in several ways. While the complete removal of state interference in the economy might have eliminated rent-seeking, leaders have understood that partial reform and the actual implementation process would provide them with new kinds of rents, as well as with discretion over the evolution of rents within the economy. They understood that the uncertainty and chaos of the reform process might cut into the overall size of rents, but these conditions would almost certainly increase rent-seeking, and they determined they would seek to increase their control over the latter. In other words, we have witnessed an *instrumentalization* of the reform process, in which donor pressures and the logic of reform are used by leaders to justify measures that are often not at all in the spirit of economic liberalization, but which serve to enhance political control. In sum, structural adjustment programs are increasingly being used to strengthen neopatrimonialism. Three trends worth discussing in particular are first, the attempts to recentralize power in order to more carefully manage the reform process; second, attempts to redesign rent-seeking networks to make them more compatible with the new fiscal and economic realities; and third, the state's withdrawal from development activities.

Reasserting Presidentialism

One response to economic austerity and donor pressures that has been evident throughout the region has been attempts to centralize power around the presidency. Understanding the challenge posed by the crisis and the need to maintain discretionary control over state resources, always one of the cornerstones of neopatrimonial power, state leaders have typically sought to reassert their primacy within the local political economy. This recentralization of power has been expressed in three broad ways. A first highly suggestive trend is very simply the growing importance of presidential administrations in the region. Exact numbers of employees are difficult to find, and shares of administrative budgets have often been dissimulated, but the size of buildings and compounds are suggestive and the few numbers available are eye popping. In Kenya, the office of the president grew from 18,213 employees in 1971, already an imposing number, to 43,230 in 1990.[19] This meant that one in six civil servants in Kenya worked for the presidency!

Second, state leaders have used this larger presidency to manage the reform process directly. The reform program has been taken away from regular ministerial channels and managed either directly from the presidency or from an ad hoc adjustment structure over which the presidency exerts considerable control. In Nigeria, the Babangida regime sought to strengthen the economic management discretion of the presidency in the second half of the 1980s by removing the Budget Department from the Ministry of Finance and Economic Development relocating it to the president's office. The Central Bank was also made directly responsible to the office, and a post of Secretary of the Federal Military Government was recreated in order to "increase presidential power over the ministries."[20] In Senegal, the government created an interministerial committee to manage the reform process. In Tanzania, the government resorted to several presidential commissions of inquiry to advance the process of reform. The Cameroonian government created the Ministry for the Stabilization of Public Finances to oversee the entire process of reform. In other countries, a special reform unit has been created within the presidency or state house. In Côte d'Ivoire, the presidency centralized all economic policy decision making by the late 1980s, relegating the ministries to a strict implementation role. [21]

19. World Bank, *Kenya: Re-Investing in Stabilization and Growth* (Washington, DC: World Bank, 1992), p. 51. Jennifer Widner provides a political explanation of this growth in her book, *The Rise of a Party State in Kenya: From Harambee! To Nyayo!* (Berkeley: University of California Press, 1992), especially pp. 130–1, 144–5.
20. Tom Forrest, *Politics and Economic Development in Nigeria* (Boulder, CO: Westview Press, 1993), pp. 108–9.
21. "Any decision of consequences, especially in the field of economic policy, is taken by the president himself" according to p. 126, Jacques Pégatiénan and Bakary Ouayogode, "The World Bank and Côte d'Ivoire," in Devesh Kapur, John P. Lewis, and Richard Webb (eds.), *The World Bank: Its First Half Century* (Washington, DC: The Brookings Institution Press, 1997), pp. 109–60. The authors argue that the donors encouraged this tendency by negotiating directly with the presidency and all but ignoring the ministries.

The creation of these new structures or the movement of decision making into the presidency does not tell us much about the commitment of government to the reform process; regardless of his ambitions regarding reform, the president would want to control what was likely to be a delicate political process. But these new structures also provided an extra cabinet position or two to dispense, mollified donors by giving the impression of government commitment to reform, and pulled the reform process out of the regular channels, over which the president and his closest associates would not have had as much control. In addition, by the late 1980s there was remarkably little technical capacity within the normal administration in most states, and there were advantages to creating a new structure that could then be endowed with greater capacity. Finally, these structures provided the president with a useful insulation against donor pressures. Presidents have not wanted to be in direct contact with donors over reform negotiations, which would implicate them directly in implementation problems. Instead, new cabinet-level positions have been created and close collaborators picked to head these new structures. These officials could be shuffled in and out depending on the needs posed by negotiations with the donors. In Cameroon, for instance, the ministry has had half a dozen ministers since 1987, and the minister's seniority within the cabinet has varied over time.

The third trend has been to reassert presidential control over key forms of rent-seeking. Reno has carefully documented the efforts by President Momoh in Sierra Leone to control key informal markets, notably the diamond trade in the early 1990s.[22] But the best example of this trend is probably the emergence of the Direction et Contrôle des Grands Travaux (DCGTX) in Côte d'Ivoire.[23] Initially created as a technical assistance unit in the Ministry of Public Works to oversee technical aspects of infrastructure projects, it was moved to the presidency in 1982 and emerged after 1987 as a veritable state within the state through which the presidency controlled every major construction project in the country. It was overwhelmingly staffed by expatriate French experts, on the basis of short-term contracts that could only enhance their loyalty to the president. The DCGTX controlled all the major public sector

22. William Reno, *Corruption and State Politics in Sierra Leone* (New York: Cambridge University Press, 1995), especially Chapter 7.
23. The following account is based in part on Michel Galy, "Les avatars de la DCGTX en Côte d'Ivoire," *Politique Africaine* 52 (1993): 135–9; pp. 120–2 and passim in Pégatiénan and Ouayogode, "The World Bank and Côte d'Ivoire."

contracts on behalf of the president, giving him enormous personal discretion with very little accountability over a large share of the state budget. By 1989, the DCGTX had become more than a giant procurement agency. That year, it started to play a central role in macroeconomic policy formulation and actually was delegated to negotiate on behalf of the government an adjustment loan with the Bank, in a process that excluded virtually all high-level ministerial Ivoirian officials.

Instrumentalization of the Reform Process

A second characteristic of this second phase of the permanent crisis has been the attempt by political leaders to derive political advantage from the reform process. The centralization of presidential power has often been engineered in the guise of economic liberalization or some other kind of reform. Leaders like Houphouët-Boigny viewed privatization as a way of recentralizing power, reasserting presidential control over clientelist networks, and weakening potential political contenders. In their interesting study, Contamin and Fauré show how the process of public enterprise reform during the 1980s reasserted presidential control over key elements of the state apparatus.[24] The World Bank, which had enthusiastically supported the process and had publicly argued that the government's privatization campaign demonstrated local ownership, were horrified to discover several years later that their funding for parastatal restructuring and privatization during the 1980s had actually helped result in a larger and less independent parastatal sector. Contamin and Fauré conclude that far from economic liberalization, the government's primary objective in this ten-year reform process was the "recentralization of ... patrimonial regulation" (p. 330) through the parastatal sector, although they recognize that part of that process helped reduce parastatal losses and improve their management. Updating the research in 1997, Contamin shows that a further privatization campaign in the 1990s has had much the same effect.[25] What is clear from these accounts is that the top leaders in Côte d'Ivoire are unwilling to call into question either the patrimonial nature of the political economy they have built

24. Bernard Contamin and Yves-A Fauré, *La bataille des entreprises publiques en Côte d'Ivoire: l'histoire d'un ajustement interne* (Paris: Karthala, 1990).
25. See Bernard Contamin, "Entreprises publiques et désengagement de l'Etat en Côte d'Ivoire," in Bernard Contamin and Harris Memel-Fotê (eds.), *Le modèle Ivoirien en question: crises, ajustements et recompositions* (Paris: Karthala, 1997), pp. 89–108.

since independence nor its fundamentally statist nature, even though they recognized the need to reintroduce greater discipline in the system. The structural adjustment process and financial support from the donors helped them undertake this fundamentally political task.

Côte d'Ivoire, a mature regime, used privatization to reassert presidential power in the context of crisis. In other countries, new regimes have similarly selected parts of the reform agenda to help consolidate presidential power. In Cameroon, Paul Biya used the reform process to strengthen the economic power of his Beti kinsmen at the expense of the better established commercial networks dominated by northerners and Bamileke businessmen. There is much evidence, for instance, that the privatization process was manipulated to favor certain groups at the expense of others.[26] This process was particularly clear in the late 1980s attempts to reform the rice import policies.[27] A price stabilization fund was established in agreement with the donors to protect the northern rice parastatal and which would have served to tax the Fulani traders who controlled the import market. The fund never raised significant revenues but appears to have served to weaken traditional importers for the benefit of Beti commercial networks close to the Ministry of Commerce and Industry.

In Kenya, Jennifer Widner describes efforts by Moi to reorganize the organizations in the export crop sector – essentially tea and coffee – not to liberalize but rather to weaken certain farmer groups; redirect the state effort to favor Kalenjin strongholds; turn what had been private cooperatives, like the Kenya Planters' Cooperative Union, into parastatals; and lessen the autonomy of existing parastatals like Kenya Tea Development Authority.[28] Throughout the time this was going on, the government was officially committed to liberalization and was receiving donor support to undertake it.

In some cases, new leaders' positive attitude toward reform has appeared because statist policies reward networks of influence and rent-seeking that are still linked to the previous regime and are thus not fully controllable by the new regime. Thus, Diouf in Senegal seems initially to have seen economic liberalization as well as political liberalization as a

26. For a discussion with examples, see Piet Konings, "La liquidation des Plantations Unilever et les conflits intra-élite dans le Cameroun Anglophone," *Politique Africaine* 35 (1989): 132–7.
27. I explored this issue at length in my essay "Rice Politics in Cameroon: State Capability, Commitment and Urban Bias," *Journal of Modern African Studies* 27 (1989): 579–600.
28. Widner, *The Rise of a Party State*, pp. 183–7.

way of weakening the barons left over from the Senghor era.[29] Analogous dynamics were clearly at work in the early days of Mwinyi's rule in Tanzania. Similarly, more recently, in Zambia, during the first five years or so of his rule, President Chiluba used both the privatization and breakup of INDECO, the big public holding company, and the liberalization of the agricultural sector to redirect rent-seeking networks away from the United National Independence Party (UNIP), the old single party.[30] Commitment to reform has weakened since then in Zambia for multiple reasons, but the growing patronage needs of the ruling Movement for Multiparty Democracy (MMD), now a virtual single party, helps explain the change in attitude. Having rid these organizations of the old UNIP networks, Chiluba has reasserted state control in various ways to build his own power base through them.

The State Withdrawal from Development

Many African states appeared to be withdrawing from development activities during the 1990s, focusing on sovereignty expenditures and allowing donors to increasingly take the lead in producing the public goods that are usually viewed as central to the state's developmental functions. In Chapter 2, I argued this was prima facie evidence of a state that did not worry too much about societal responses to austerity and policy change. Here, my focus is on the political motives for governments to undertake this withdrawal. A dual explanation is in order. On the one hand, governments are concentrating their increasingly limited resources on the key issue for them, maintaining the unity of the political class, the main beneficiaries of the sovereignty expenditure focus. As budget constraints have hardened, leaders have preferred to spend their money to keep their elite coalition together rather than invest in mundane activities like building schools or undertaking vaccine campaigns, particularly given the donor predilection for such thankless tasks.

On the other hand, this withdrawal has also provided advantageous opportunities for state elites. Once a development activity has been taken away from the state and effectively privatized,[31] state elites can turn

29. See Ka and van de Walle, "The Political Economy of Structural Adjustment in Senegal, 1980–1991," in Stephan Haggard and Steven B. Webb (eds.), *Voting for Reform: Economic Adjustment in New Democracies*. (New York: Oxford University Press, 1994), pp. 290–359.
30. On Zambia, see Lise Rakner, *Reforms as a Matter of Political Survival. Political and Economic Liberalisation in Zambia 1991–1996* (Ph.D. dissertation, University of Bergen, Norway, 1998).
31. I have been influenced in my thinking on these issues by the essay by Béatrice Hibou, "De la privatisation des économies à la privatisation des Etats," in Béa-

around and undertake it for a profit in a private capacity. Although top state elites did not engineer this privatization, they stop resisting it when they find how well they can accommodate themselves to the new realities. Throughout Africa, many NGOs have been created to undertake activities that used to be a state responsibility, often with donor support. Some observers have contrasted the NGO sector favorably with the public sector as an instrument of development.[32] But in many countries, the NGO sector seems in large part an emanation of the state elite. In Niger, for instance, the majority of NGOs appear to be operated by moonlighting civil servants and ex-ministers of cabinet.[33] In several cases, high-level officials left government to create NGOs in order to receive donor support that had once gone to the official's ministry. NGOs have largely escaped the critical scrutiny state structures have endured these last two decades, but their low levels of institutionalization, small size, and flexibility, as well as the absence of the kinds of mechanisms of accountability that still exist for many state institutions can be perceived as an advantage by unscrupulous staff. Indeed, the evidence suggests high levels of corruption in donor-funded NGOs that certainly rivals corruption within the state. In Niger, again, in 1998, one donor took to court nine of twelve NGOs it had worked with, charging them with misappropriation of funds.[34] Most donors appear to be willing to countenance abuses, however, which they often justify as due to low capacity and institutional immaturity. Ironically, their solution is institution-building efforts not unlike the ones they undertook for several decades in the central state.

African NGOs are overwhelmingly funded by outside donors. In a curious twist of this kind of privatization, however, we see members of the political elite receiving state support for the NGOs they create, in some cases to undertake activities previously undertaken by the state. In

trice Hibou (ed.), *La privatisation des Etats* (Paris: Karthala, 1999), pp. 11–70.

32. The literature on NGOs remains remarkably uncritical and almost entirely fails to place the NGO sector within local politics. The best works include Roger C. Riddell and Mark Robinson, *Non-Governmental Organizations and Rural Poverty Alleviation* (Oxford, UK: Clarendon Press, 1995); David Hulme and Michael Edwards (eds.), *NGOs, States and Donors: Too Close for Comfort?* (New York: St. Martin's Press, 1997); Marie-Christine Geuneau and Bernard J. Lecomte, *Sahel: Les paysans dans les marigots de l'aide* (Paris: l'Harmattan, 1998). A more critical stance is adopted in Susan Dicklitch, *The Elusive Promise of NGOs in Africa* (New York: St. Martin's Press, 1998).

33. This was true of every single one of the three dozen NGOs I interviewed in the summer of 1998 in Niamey. See my essay, "Moins d'Etat, Mieux d'Etat? The Politics of State Retrenchment in West Africa," unpublished Report for USAID/OECD Club du Sahel, December 16, 1998.

Guinea, the president's wife has created an NGO that assists in the distribution of school textbooks, financed by central state budgets. Other presidential spouses also have created NGOs. The president's wife in Burkina Faso, Chantal Campaoré, was actively fund raising in the French-African business and diplomatic community in early 2000 for her Suka Foundation, to undertake humanitarian activities.[35]

But the most curious example of this phenomenon is the Edouardo Dos Santos Foundation, named after the president of Angola.[36] Since 1996, the president has encouraged national and multinational corporations present in Angola to contribute to his foundation, which has the objective of promoting social and welfare objectives. It has undertaken a number of projects, from financing a center for abandoned children to organizing scientific and policy workshops in the capital. Distancing himself publicly from the decay of his own state administration, the president presents his foundation as more effective in promoting development. Increasingly, the foundation undertakes development tasks in collaboration with and apparently funded by the state, albeit without any public accountability. The foundation resembles part conventional development NGO, part traditional presidential political slush fund, and part presidential shakedown scheme, since foreign firms in the country (notably the oil companies) feel obliged to contribute significant funding on a regular basis. The foundation benefits the president materially, with numerous family members on the payroll and little transparency in its budget, but it also is designed to benefit him politically since it allows him to undertake carefully selected development tasks and deliver services to key constituencies in a manner the dilapidated central state may no longer be able to achieve.

THE VIABILITY OF REFORM

What is the relationship between the exigencies of neopatrimonialism and the persistence of economic ideas hostile to policy reform? Are these ideas merely epiphenomenal manifestations of the material interests of neopatrimonial elites, or can they be perceived as independent of them? I define economic ideas as shared beliefs about the advantages and

34. Confidential interview, Niamey, July 1998.
35. See *La Lettre du Continent*, May 11, 2000.
36. The following account is closely based on Christine Messiant, "La Fondation Edouardo Dos Santos; à propos de l'investissement de la société civil par le pouvoir Angolais," *Politique Africaine* 73 (1999): 82–102.

disadvantages of specific policy-relevant ways of organizing production and consumption of goods and services. A recent trend in the 1990s has sought to establish the autonomous power of ideas on the making of economic policy.[37] Much of this literature has responded to the assertions of a crude rational choice approach that would have ideas be little more than phony rationales for material interests. This is a useful corrective, but it provides little help in determining what it means exactly to say that economic ideas can be independent of interests. As Jacobsen has stated, the strongest case for the autonomous power of economic ideas – the argument that ideas stand and fall on their own intrinsic merit – "first must demonstrate that interests are interpenetrated by ideas but then ideas must be shown to exert influence untainted by the interests they have just been shown to interpenetrate."[38] This approach strikes me as unhelpful for the materials on which this book is focusing. The self-interest for African state elites of implementing statist economic policies is simply too obvious to deny. Nonetheless, to reduce policies to rent-seeking motivations alone strikes me as equally absurd. The statist economic policies described in this chapter held the support of groups that were hardly rent-seekers – including the donors and antigovernment intellectuals. Instead, it is most useful to examine the complex inter-relationships between material interests and economic ideas. We need to recognize that ideas about how economies work often provide the intellectual apparatus within which agents work out their material interests. Economic ideas are conditioned by the interpretation that individuals have of their own interests, but the institutions and organizations they help design in turn eventually condition those interests. In sum, feedback loops and path dependencies that are mediated by institutions can provide ideas with some limited autonomous power over material interests.

37. Important recent works in this literature include Judith Goldstein and Robert Keohone (eds.), *Ideas and Foreign Policy: Beliefs, Institutions and Political Change* (Ithaca, NY: Cornell University Press, 1993); Peter A. Hall. "Policy Paradigms, Social Learning and the State: The Case of Economic Policy Making in Britain," *Comparative Politics* 25 (1993): 275–96; Hall, Peter A. (ed.), *The Political Power of Economic Ideas* (Princeton, NJ: Princeton University Press, 1989); Kathryn Sikkink, *Ideas and Institutions: Developmentalism in Brazil and Argentina* (Ithaca, NY: Cornell University Press, 1991); John Kurt Jacobsen, "Much Ado about Ideas: The Cognitive Factor in Economic Policy," *World Politics* 47 (1995): 283–310; and Marc M. Blyth, "Any More Bright Ideas? The Ideational Turn of Comparative Political Economy," *Comparative Politics* 29 (1997): 229–50.
38. Jacobsen, "Much Ado about Ideas," p. 286.

Peter Hall has suggested that decision makers assess the merits of economic policy quite practically in terms of its ability to solve specific problems, and of its compatibility with existing structures.[39] Decision makers assess the "viability" of new policies on three levels: the political, but also the economic and the administrative. Looking at each in turn will prove very useful to our understanding the relationship between economic ideas and material interests. In the discussion that follows it is important to disaggregate state actors. In particular, I distinguish technocrats from politicians for analytical convenience, even though the line between them is a gray and fluid one. Indeed, it is important to ask what factors lead a technocrat, defined as someone who is not primarily a rent-seeker, to become a politician, defined as someone who is primarily a rent-seeker.

Political Viability

Political viability refers to the political appeal of the proposed policy changes. Will they appeal to dominant political players? Are the policies perceived as politically feasible? For many observers, the great political drawback of adjustment programs is that they are terribly unpopular with the population, and political leaders know this. When a Nyerere or Kaunda talks of the threat of urban riots, they are then alluding to this risk, although it is difficult to know how sincere they are when they express these fears, and the extent to which they are engaging in rhetoric in order to exact concessions from the donors. Clearly austerity is never popular, and insofar as the general population may conflate structural adjustment programs and the crisis they are trying to overcome, the former may be unpopular. But it is not clear at all from the little public opinion data available that Africans are completely hostile to the underlying principles of adjustment. Indeed, these data suggest a very different interpretation of the risks to political elites.

To be sure, African public opinion appears ambivalent about reform policies of liberalization, deregulation, and privatization. The handful of systematic attitudinal surveys available concur that there is at best limited and ambivalent support for the liberalization reforms and their objectives. Thus a 1995 survey conducted in the capital of Madagascar

39. See the introduction to his edited volume, *The Political Power of Economic Ideas* (Princeton, NJ: Princeton University Press, 1989). See also his useful essay "Policy Paradigms, Social Learning and the State: The Case of Economic Policy Making in Britain," *Comparative Politics* 25 (1993): 275–96.

reported that over 90 percent of the respondents blamed internal causes for the country's economic deterioration rather than international factors, apparently siding with the dominant donor explanation for the crisis.[40] An incredible 40 percent say they have paid a bribe to a government official in the previous year. Yet 90 percent support only minimal or no privatization at all, 73.2 percent believe that the state should play a leading entrepreneurial role in the economy, and only 10 percent support a minimalist state that would limit its economic role to one of arbiter.

Similarly ambivalent findings have emerged from attitudinal surveys in Ghana.[41] There, Bratton and his colleagues found that citizens appear to believe in the benefits of free market principles and individual entrepreneurship, with 70.2 percent agreeing with the statement that people should be free "to earn as much as they can, even if this leads to differences in income" (p. 24), and 72.4 percent agreeing that "it is better to have goods available in the market even if the prices are high" while only 27.6 percent felt that "it is better to have low prices, even if there are shortages of goods" (p. 28). On the other hand, nearly two-thirds of respondents (66.0%) believed the government to be the best provider of jobs; 72.5 percent agreed with the statement that "all civil servants should keep their jobs, even if paying their salaries is costly to the country," and 69.8 percent believed that "the government should retain ownership of its factories, businesses and farms" (p. 29). These opinions are particularly interesting, given Ghana's reputation as one of the most successful reformers, in which local "ownership" of the reform process has been achieved. Interestingly, this support for the government comes despite the view that government officials are corrupt: 76.2 percent of respondents believed that "most government officials and politicians are mainly concerned with enriching themselves" (p. 32). Indeed, opposition to the economic reform program appears to be as much related to the

---

40. Only 4 percent blamed the crisis on the exploitation of Madagascar by the rich countries, while 39.3 percent blamed the corruption of high-level government officials and 21.3 percent the monopoly over wealth by a small minority. See Table 3, Mireille Razafindrakoto and Francois Roubaud, "Ce qu'attendent les Tanaraniviens de la réforme de l'Etat et de l'économie," *Politique Africaine* 61 (1996): 54–72.
41. See Michigan State University, American University, and the Center for Democracy and Development, *Attitudes to Democracy and Markets in Ghana: A Report on a National Sample Survey Conducted in July 1999*, Report submitted to the U.S. Agency for International Development (USAID/Ghana Award no. 641-G-00-99-00294), September 30, 1999.

view that "people close to the government" had been the minority believed to benefit from the reform program, as to the notion that the program had imposed "too high costs" and should be ended, a view supported by almost two-thirds (62.5%) of all Ghanaians (p. 27).

These data are ambiguous and often contradictory. They do suggest that the unpopularity of adjustment programs has much to do with the perception that these programs have been implemented in such a way as to enrich elites, and does not necessarily reflect a deep-seated hostility to the principles of economic reform. In turn, this finding suggests a second way to approach the political viability of adjustment.

Complete implementation of reform undermines key political instruments of African states such as patronage and rent-seeking, on which political leaders have staked their political survival. As Herbst has argued, economic reform will require the "structural adjustment of politic" and the curtailment of the clientelism that is central to power in African politics.[42] In this argument, liberal economic policies are particularly problematic in Africa in political terms. African state leaders understand this and it shapes their attitudes toward adjustment, much more than the fear that populations will oppose policy reform with violence.

Leaders' notion of the political viability of reform has changed over time. Their initial reaction was almost entirely negative because they viewed rapid reform as incompatible with the methods of rule they had fashioned during several decades of rule. Over time, this changed: from the view that reform was not viable, leaders have understood they had no choice but to adapt their methods of rule to the evolving environment, with a seemingly permanent fiscal crisis, intense donor scrutiny, and so on. Over time and through experimentation, they found that their hold on power could withstand the partial implementation of adjustment programs. It remains true that political elites do not believe they can survive without recourse to a policy regime of systematic interference in the economy, but they have learned to adapt this interference, as I argue in the next section.

Economic Viability

Economic viability refers to the perception that a set of economic ideas will provide solutions to an economic problem. To what extent do

42. Herbst, "The Structural Adjustment of Politics in Africa."

Africans perceive reform policies can solve the economic crisis in Africa? The answer is generally very little. First, underlying much of the opposition to reform is a deep-seated pessimism about Africa's economic potential, which colors all policy decision, including the one to engage in rent-seeking activity. Decision makers often appear to doubt the capacity of African economies to compete effectively on the world market. This argument, it must be admitted, is speculative, but a number of interviews confirm a prevalent view that the African private sector is simply too retrograde to industrialize successfully, that cultural factors will continue to prevent the emergence of capitalist economies in the region, or that African governments will never find the discipline to achieve fiscal balance or stamp out corruption.[43] This pessimism is of course a far cry from the heady nationalism of the independence era, but it has fed on the legacy of failures since the 1960s, and in many respects it has turned into a self-fulfilling prophecy. Governments that have built political stability on predation on the private sector view it as weak and dependent. Officials see a private sector dominated by rent-seekers and they forget this results from their own policies for the last thirty years.

Given the ideological predisposition of most decision makers against stabilization and economic liberalization at the beginning of the crisis, a second explanation for the continuing opposition to reform must be found in the absence of policy learning in the region. A striking characteristic of economic policy debates in Africa is their weakness. As I shall argue in the next chapter, governments have largely implemented policies designed in Washington and European capitals by Western experts. The role of African decision makers has been largely passive, at least until the implementation stage. No viable heterodox alternative to the IMF/World Bank's orthodox reform plans has emerged, and few countries in Africa have made a serious attempt at a heterodox stabilization plan during the last decade.[44] As a result, "counterfactuals" or, in other words, the relative merits of different approaches have only rarely been tested and a dialectical process of comparison, confrontation, and mutual learning between orthodoxy and heterodoxy has not happened in Africa to the same extent as in Latin America or Asia. That process of learning in other parts of the world has resulted in the adoption of policies inspired by the new liberal orthodoxy (NLO) identified in the

43. This pessimism is one of the themes of the works by Etounga-Manguelle and Kabou cited Chapter 3.
44. I would argue that Tanzania in the early 1980s and Zambia in 1986–88 represent the only true heterodox experiments in Africa during the 1980s.

last chapter. In Africa, by comparison, there has been little policy learning.[45] Indeed, many technocrats may have grown hostile to reform policies precisely because the reform process seems to emasculate them to the benefit of foreign experts.

The power of the civil service relative to the weakness of outside inputs into economic decision making throughout Africa has also made policy reform less likely. In other contexts, the civil service has been found to be a poor vehicle for policy reform, and new ideas are more likely to emerge from outside.[46] Yet a number of factors have weakened outside influences on the civil service in the region. The authoritarianism of the states in the region preclude extensive public participation to policy debates. Until recently, only a handful of states could claim to have a free press, for example. Governments have left little public space in which policy debates could occur and have constrained the organizations that would both sponsor and advance the debate, such as the media, unions, business associations, research institutes, and universities. In addition, the weakness of universities and research centers has undermined policy learning. African social scientists have generally been discouraged from engaging in critical policy-relevant research by governments that view the university as a teaching center, if not a diploma mill, rather than as a center of research and dialogue. With a handful of exceptions, there are remarkably few links between the university and government, the former simply too weighed down by inadequate funding, an excessive number of students, and political interference to contribute to policy making. The traditional weakness of university and research institutions has been exacerbated by the economic crisis that has devastated budgets, leading to the expatriation of many of the region's best intellectuals who might have contributed to domestic policy debates. Thus, Oniang'o and Eicher note that the number of students at the University of Nairobi has grown by a factor of four in the last ten years, despite declining budgets. The total budget for the university's library was $50,000 in 1998. One result has been the loss of the best faculty: they note that the Agriculture College, with over a thousand students in the early 1990s, had only four faculty members with

45. See Mandika Mkandawire and Charles C. Soludo, *Our Continent, Our Future: African Perspectives on Structural Adjustment* (Trenton, NJ: World Press, 1999), for a similar argument.
46. See, for example, Peter Hall regarding the spread of Keynesian ideas in the industrialized countries: "Conclusion," in Peter A. Hall (ed.), *The Political Power of Economic Ideas* (Princeton, NJ: Princeton University Press, 1989), pp. 378–9.

Ph.D.s![47] All over the region, the emigration of top academics and intellectuals has reached distressing proportions. One recent World Bank report thus claims that 23,000 qualified academic staff are emigrating from Africa each year, and that some 10,000 Nigerian academics have emigrated to the United States alone.[48] The immediate consequence is the impoverishment of public debate about how to overcome the crisis.

Skepticism about the economics of the new liberal orthodoxy has been fueled by the failure of NLO-inspired programs in recent years. In Ghana, the unsatisfactory nature of early reform results apparently led Rawlings to increase his commitment to reform.[49] In most countries, however, partial and mostly unsuccessful implementation of the first generation of programs has served to erode commitment to reform. Many people blame the reform program for the general economic crisis and doubt the validity of reform policies. Partial implementation of a reform program is thus doubly negative; the program is almost sure to fail, requiring further sacrifices, yet the people's patience and tolerance for austerity is also eroded. Moreover, the absence of a clear adjustment success story across the continent increases the sense that these policies will not provide economic solutions. African elites see that even reformist Ghana has not attracted significant new capital or investment, and the limited progress that country has made is not nearly attractive enough to convince them to adopt the same risky policies.

Political leaders derive a second lesson from the uneven record of the last decade: that the economic costs of nonimplementation of adjustment are minimal and that nonreform is sustainable. In 1980, at the outset of adjustment programs in countries like Côte d'Ivoire or Senegal, it was possible for leaders to believe that nonimplementation would have dramatically negative results for the economy and state. International capital would dry up, the state would go bankrupt, social systems would fall

---

47. See their essay, "Universities and Agricultural Development in Africa: Insights from Kenya," paper presented to the Conference titled "Transforming the Agricultural Research System in Kenya: Lessons for Africa," Bellagio Study and Conference Center, Bellagio, Italy, October 19, 1998.

48. Robert Blair and Josephine Jordan, *Staff Loss and Retention at Selected African Universities: A Synthesis Report*, AFTHR Technical Note no. 18, Technical Department, Africa Region (Washington, DC: The World Bank, 1994). These guesstimates do seem extremely high. For a particularly eloquent and instructive statement of the pressures facing African academics, see Ambroise Kom, "Intellectuels Africain et enjeux de la démocratie: Misère, repression et exil," *Politique Africaine* 51 (1993): 61–8.

49. See Donald Rothchild (ed.), *Ghana: The Political Economy of Recovery* (Boulder, CO: Lynne Rienner, 1991), especially the essay by Nugent.

apart, and so on. Now two decades later, state elites view nonimplementation with more confidence. They understand that conditionality has turned out to be largely toothless; aid continues to flow and debts to be rescheduled. The fiscal crisis has continued to worsen but the state has adapted, and sociopolitical stability seems less threatened by the status quo than by reform.

Unlike Latin American leaders who have at one time or another seriously believed in the possibility of a heterodox program of stabilization and adjustment, in Africa, no coherent alternative to IFI-inspired adjustment has emerged that politicians can rally around. NLO policies are the "only game in town," but when leaders compute the relative cost/benefit ratios of serious reform and the current muddling through, they increasingly opt for the latter.

Administrative Viability

Administrative viability refers to the sense that the state apparatus is capable of implementing the new set of policies. In other words, is structural adjustment compatible with the abilities and prejudices of the administration? The dominant understanding of this issue in the literature has come under the rubric of the "orthodox paradox," according to which the central conundrum of economic liberalization is that it demands that state agents undertake actions that will weaken the state.[50] The paradox is viewed as particularly salient if interventionist states have emerged over time at least in part to increase the discretionary power of state agents pursuing rent-seeking and clientelist political strategies. Why, in a word, would state agents in such states support policy reforms?

Grindle has made an interesting claim about the impact of economic crisis and reform attempts on administrative capacity that is relevant here.[51] She distinguishes between several types of government capacity: she distinguishes *administrative* capacity, or the ability to carry out routine administrative functions, from *institutional* capacity, defined as the ability to set basic economic and political rules and norms, and from *technical* capacity, defined as the ability to establish and manage macro-

50. Miles Kahler, "Orthodoxy and Its Alternatives: Explaining Approaches to Stabilization and Adjustment," in Joan Nelson (ed.), *Economic Crisis and Policy Choice: The Politics of Economic Adjustment in the Third World* (Princeton, NJ: Princeton University Press, 1990), pp. 33–62.
51. Merilee S. Grindle, *Challenging the State: Crisis and Innovation in Latin America and Africa* (New York: Cambridge University Press, 1996), pp. 31–45.

economic policy. She agrees that most kinds of state capacity have declined in most areas as the result of the economic crisis, but she argues that technical capacity has improved as the result of governmental and donor investments in various instruments to improve macroeconomic management. She points to the teams of well-financed technocrats that now exist in many governments to negotiate with the donors and help devise macroeconomic policy. Distinguishing this technical capacity is a useful contribution, though I am less sanguine about its extent. Most of these macroeconomic teams are reliant on donor support and technical assistance. Without salary supplements provided by the donors, the most competent technicians soon leave the government, lured by higher salaries and better working conditions in the private and aid sectors.[52] More seriously, there is little evidence to suggest that these teams have much impact on the rest of the government, or that they have played much of a role on transferring their technical capacity to the rest of the state apparatus. In Zambia, in the early 1990s, the IFI-supported team in the Ministry of Finance was derisively referred to as the "Harvard boys" within the rest of the administration, because the technical assistance was provided by the Harvard Institute of International Development. Their special privileges appeared to be widely resented, and they were perceived as belonging to the donors rather than to the government.[53] Indeed, the striking characteristic of these expensive donor efforts to create technical capacity on behalf of their adjustment programs is how little local support for the adjustment program they have engendered.

Civil servants' attitudes toward economic reform are often difficult to assess because very little data exist that allow us to measure them with any objective precision. It is important not to see state structures as monolithic, but to recognize that African state administrations are made up of individuals with a wide variety of backgrounds, training, and values. In particular, it is useful to distinguish low-level state personnel from high-level state managers. Low-level staff feel threatened by adjustment; they read in the newspapers that the IMF wants reductions in the civil service of some 30 percent, or that it wants to take away their housing allowance. They understand intuitively that devaluation would hurt their purchasing power.

52. For examples from Kenya, see John Cohen, "Foreign Advisors and Capacity Building: The Case of Kenya," *Public Administration and Development* 12 (1992): 493–510.
53. Interviews, Lusaka, June 1994.

High-level staff are not similarly threatened by reform; many probably recognize the need to cut government expenditures, and they know they would be unlikely to be included among the 30 percent. Some take considerable pride in their professional credentials and training, and they willingly distinguish themselves from the great mass of undertrained and unproductive civil servants whom they realize the state could do without. As one young technocrat in the Cameroon Ministry of Finance told me in 1993, "fewer than 10 percent of the staff in the ministry do all the work anyway."[54] Many officials benefit materially from their role in implementing the current set of policies, but it would be abusive to identify senior civil servants too completely with the political elite that constitutes the primary beneficiary of rent-seeking. Middle-level state managers who are isolated from the public and not directly linked to the granting of licenses, say, do not necessarily have much of a link to rent-seeking activities. In any event, as senior administrators, they also long for a more ordered and rule-driven bureaucratic process. It is not unreasonable to suggest that they believe they would, on the whole, benefit from a smaller, more effective state that had a well-defined set of functions and the means to carry them out.

If this speculation is correct, why haven't the senior ranks of the civil service stood up more forcefully on behalf of reform? First, by training and socialization, many of these senior officials are ambivalent about reform. They often believe deeply in key elements of the old policies. In Côte d'Ivoire, Elliott Berg and his colleagues make clear that through much of the adjustment era, the senior decision-makers have simply not accepted the IFI's prescription for the country.[55] Trained for the most part within a highly statist tradition in France, they accepted the need for narrowly defined stabilization but were extremely skeptical of reforms like privatization or price liberalization that would lessen the state's ability to lead the development process.

Their attitudes are not always purely ideological, of course. In many cases, attitudes are ultimately linked to the neopatrimonial and nondemocratic nature of African states, particularly as they have evolved over the last two decades of economic crisis. Individual career choices within the state apparatus are affected by perceptions of how the economy functions and how it could function. The decision of middle-level bureau-

54. Interviews, Yaounde, June 1993.
55. Elliott Berg, Patrick Guillaumont, Jacques Pegatienan, and Jacky Amprou, "Aid and Reform in the Côte d'Ivoire," unpublished paper for the World Bank project "Aid and Reform in Africa," Washington, December 1999.

crats to invest in technocratic skills instead of, say, political connections, is shaped by perceptions about the relative power of rational-legal and patrimonial tendencies within the administration and the other factors that will influence the returns from these investments. As the crisis has evolved and the formal administration has weakened in favor of ad hoc adjustment structures dominated by the donors and the presidency, the perception has grown that reform promises are not credible and that investing in their success is not a winning proposition. As Cohen has written about Kenya, "In a perverse way, the apathy, irrationality and incompetence that characterizes many of Kenya's public servants is a direct result of their seeking to survive in a fragmented bureaucracy that has been cowed by Moi and his faithful supporters, fragmented by very competitive tribal and regional cliques and affected by increasing tolerance of public servants reaping personal benefits while balancing these competing pressures."[56]

As suggested above, neopatrimonialism weakens the technocratic element within the state. As the crisis has lasted, the latter has atrophied. Pessimism about the political viability of policy reform shapes the attitudes of senior technocrats within the state administration, who might otherwise support the IFI agenda. One of the reasons that bureaucrats have not fought for policy reform is, ironically enough, that they do not believe their neopatrimonial overlords will respect the more liberal policies that are put in place. The bureaucracy's commitment to economic liberalization is invariably weakened by the perception that the most senior political leaders benefit directly from the current policy mix and are not likely to give it up. This pessimism has increased over time, as successive attempts at reform have been undermined by the rent-seeking behavior. For example, many government officials oppose privatization in practice if not in theory because they believe the process will inevitably be manipulated by politicians for personal gain.[57]

THE CONSEQUENCES OF PARTIAL REFORM

The manipulation of the reform process for political ends can result in some significant progress on reform. Critics have complained about the tendency of key elements of reform implementation, such as

56. John M. Cohen, "Importance of Public Service Reform: The Case of Kenya," *Journal of Modern African Studies* 31 (1993): 449–76, pp. 466–7 and passim.
57. This was a recurring theme in interviews with senior civil servants in Zambia, in June 1994.

privatization transactions, to result in windfall profits for certain politically favored groups, who gain ownership via nontransparent processes. Such cases can be viewed as unfortunate, and they probably serve to delegitimate privatization in the long run, but insofar as privatization is viewed as a good in itself, its immediate beneficiaries might be viewed as a necessary political cost of the reform, without which it might not have happened. In some cases, neopatrimonial management of the reform process has resulted in this kind of progress. In Côte d'Ivoire, for instance, Contamin and Fauré make clear their view that the recentralization of neopatrimonial networks has allowed greater control over government expenditure and thus progress on sustainable macroeconomic stabilization. In Zambia, whatever the defects of the privatization process, it is clear that the fiscal burden posed by subsidies to parastatals is a thing of the past, one reason for improvements in the fiscal situation.[58] One can object to the distributional implications of the privatization process in these cases or decry the ethical lapses of these regimes, but one nonetheless should recognize that real privatization occurred. The right policy question in such cases is whether the new private owners will receive the same kinds of costly discretionary benefits and subsidies enjoyed by the old public enterprise, which made privatization desirable in the first place. The cynical view is that the boundaries between the private and public are so blurred that in these countries the transfer of assets to the private sector may not make much of a difference insofar as the owner is a member of the political class.[59] That cynical view will indeed be the realistic view in many cases. We witness cases in which newly privatized firms get no-bid contracts with the state, benefit from key exemptions, or continue to access subsidized credit.

Nonetheless, it must be recognized that some real progress on reforms such as privatization has been made. Even the most patrimonial of states have realized the advantages of reining in rent-seeking and insulating parts of the economy from it. As I have argued throughout this book, in these hybrid regimes, it is possible that a genuine reform impulse wins out within the state apparatus. Moreover, there are private advantages to pushing through the reform process. Privatized firms usually do not

58. See Lise Rakner, Nicolas van de Walle, and Dominic Mulaisho, "Aid and Reform in Zambia: A Country Case Study," paper for the World Bank Project on Aid and Reform in Africa, Available on the website (*http://www.worldbank.org/ research/aid/africa/papers.html*).

59. A good example of such a view point is Béatrice Hibou, "De la privatisation des économies."

require such large subsidies to operate, for instance, because their new owners reject the social obligations of their predecessors: they slim down their staffs, they give up on nonprofitable activities. Thus, they will act differently from the public company.

What then are the long-term consequences of the dynamics described in this chapter? Is the real albeit limited amount of reform enough to sustain economic progress? I argue that the process of partial reform weakens state capacity further and thereby strengthens neopatrimonial tendencies within the state. In the long run, this makes real reform less likely and in a minority of cases can lead to substantial state decay. I distinguish several scenarios for the future evolution of these dynamics, with state collapse and the descent into warlordism as one outcome for the weakest states.

Liberalization and Rent-Seeking

A new wave of scholarship on policy reform is emerging and it tends to be more skeptical about the claims made on behalf of policy reform; it has used careful fieldwork to focus on the unintended consequences of reform and its side effects. A number of observers have focused on rent-seeking and corruption in Africa during this period of partial reform. Lewis and Stein thus note that financial sector liberalization in Nigeria resulted in a dramatic increase in corrupt practices within the banking sector.[60] Similarly, Hibou has shown that trade liberalization reforms in French west Africa have typically increased customs fraud and rent-seeking to benefit from tariff exemptions.[61] In his examination of state decay in Sierra Leone, William Reno argues that adjustment-sponsored liberalization policies strengthened the political elite's control of parallel markets and undermined the ability of the state to control them.[62] Similar claims are made by observers of reform processes outside of Africa.[63]

60. Peter Lewis and Howard Stein, "Shifting Fortunes: The Political Economy of Financial Liberalization in Nigeria," *World Development* 25 (1997): 5–22.
61. Béatrice Hibou, *l'Afrique est-elle protectioniste?* (Paris: Karthala, 1996).
62. Reno, *Corruption and State Politics in Sierra Leone.*
63. Luigi Manzetti and Charles Blake, "Market Reforms and Corruption in Latin America," *Review of International Political Economy* 3 (1996): 671–82; Richard Snyder, "Politics after Neoliberalism: Regulation in Mexico," *World Politics* 51 (1999): 173–204; Joel Hellman, "Winners Take All: The Politics of Partial Reform in Postcommunist Transitions," *World Politics* 50 (1998): 203–34; Gordon White, "Corruption and Market Reform in China," *IDS Bulletin* 27 (1996). White's essay is part of a special issue of the IDS bulletin on these issues and contains several other interesting case studies.

Many of these observers proceed from the observations that economic liberalization reform programs have resulted in an increase in rent-seeking to the theoretical claim that rent-seeking is a paradoxical result of liberalization. Thus, writing about Mexico, Richard Snyder argues that "by vacating institutionalized policy domains, neo liberal policy shocks give political incumbents opportunities to expand their authority and their support bases by reregulating sectors of the economy."[64]

This is initially a puzzling claim. Rent-seeking results from imperfectly competitive markets that are regulated by the state. Supporters of reform have often argued that liberalization would decimate rent-seeking, since, in a reasonably competitive market following liberalization, rents would be driven down to inconsequence by the dynamics of supply and demand.[65] So, how can even partial reform increase rent-seeking?

One possible answer focuses on political culture and attitudes. For instance, Gordon White argues that in China economic liberalization has led to a dramatic increase in corruption, because of the attitudinal changes it has brought about. The weakening of the state and the widespread dissemination of neoliberal ideology made corruption more socially acceptable and the state less able to prevent it. This type of claim has been extended to Mozambique, by Harrison, who argues that liberalization and the "uncertainty" created by reform has changed the values of officials and increased their propensity toward corruption.[66] I am skeptical that such claims can be generalized in Africa, however. While the claim that personal attitudes about corruption becoming more lenient is essentially untestable, my own subjective sense is that African public attitudes are and have always been ambivalent and divided, quick to condemn the allegations of corruption by others, but much more lenient toward the corrupt practices of kith and kin. More likely than resulting from attitudinal shifts is the fact that corrupt practices are much more likely to be publicized today than twenty years ago thanks to political liberalization and the growth of independent media. As Naim has argued relative to Latin America, the "corruption eruption" may be more of a matter of perception than a reality; the fact that we hear so much about corruption may actually be a good sign, proof that it has become less

64. Snyder, "Politics after Neoliberalism," p. 174.
65. See for example, Deepak Lal, "The Political Economy of Economic Liberalization," *The World Bank Economic Review* 1 (1987): 273–300.
66. Graham Harrison, "Corruption as Boundary Politics," *Third World Quarterly* 20 (1999): 153–67.

acceptable.[67] As long as it is considered newsworthy, moreover, corruption has not become routine and accepted. Thus, it is hard to accept the argument of an attitudinal shift.

A second, more promising claim is that liberalization unleashes economic forces that promote corruption and clientelism. If rent-seeking is impossible in fully competitive markets, logically, liberalization could result in increased rent-seeking only if, first, it was incomplete and did not fully close the gap between a good's border price and its regulated price. Virtually by definition, liberalization reduces the overall size of rents, but it does not necessarily reduce the amount of rent-seeking. The process of liberalization might plausibly lead to heightened rent-seeking insofar as the fight for a slice of a diminishing pie would be intense. Moreover, reform is an inherently uncertain time: actors are not sure how much longer they can benefit from rents and are more likely to fight for those that appear accessible. In addition, as documented in Chapter 2, liberalization reforms are often phony and do not cut into rents as much as official pronouncements would suggest. Officially, a price has been deregulated and is now set by market forces, but in practice, state intervention of some form continues to generate some kind of rent.

Second, liberalization programs can result in increases in corruption, if liberalization in one market creates new opportunities for rent-seeking in another, which remains regulated. Thus, Hellman describes rapid trade liberalization in Eastern Europe coexisting with the continuation of input subsidies, so that firms with access to, for instance, cheap regulated oil can sell it at a handsome profit on international markets.[68] Another example of partial reform presents us with a somewhat different dynamic relating to profiteering around privatization transactions; this is the case when a privatized firm retains many of the advantages accruing to the old public firm: various subsidies, exemptions, or a legally protected monopoly. Again, it is important to point out since this is often misunderstood, the rent-seeking results from the incomplete application of the reform rather than from the logic of the reform itself.

These scholars are right, nonetheless, to point out that the reform process, as it has been carried out around Africa for two decades, has often been manipulated to generate new opportunities for rent-seeking

---

67. Moises Naim, "The Corruption Eruption," *Brown Journal of World Affairs* 2 (1995): 245–61.
68. Hellman, "The Politics of Partial Reform," p. 219.

in a manner that undermines rather than enhances economic efficiency. Elites have taken advantage of the uncertainty of reform to promote their interests, and the decline of state capacity and of the power of the technocratic element has facilitated the growth of corruption.

The Decline of Capacity

The perpetuation of austerity for an extended period of time and the manner with which the adjustment process has been managed serves to weaken bureaucratic rationality and reinforce the patrimonial tendencies of these regimes. Again, this varies across countries and time. In all countries, a noticeable decline in state capacity has set in. But the stronger the state initially and the more professional its administration, the better it has probably been able to resist. John Cohen has written convincingly of the decline of the Kenyan administration, suggesting that the loss of capacity and politicization within the senior levels of the civil service was a primary constraint on economic reform in Kenya in the 1990s.[69] Nonetheless, the Kenyan state retains more professionalism and implementation capacity than is the case, say, for the weaker states in west Africa. The latter never had much capacity and the twenty-year economic crisis has seriously weakened the state. When scholars talk of state decay in Africa and the risk of complete collapse, they have such states in mind, not the state in Kenya, in Côte d'Ivoire, or in the other more institutionalized ones.

Nonetheless, the style of management of the reform process I have described weakens the state everywhere. First, the resources available to the state apparatus have simply been inadequate. Two decades of woefully small operations and maintenance budgets have cumulatively cut deeply into the ability to implement policy. Second, permanent large fiscal deficits have brought about a constant recourse to crisis management, which has weakened the rational management of public resources. A third factor has been the disempowerment of the central state bureaucracy to the benefit of the presidency or to ad hoc structures dominated by the president, the donors (see next chapter), and the NGOs. For all these reasons, the state's ability to undertake a reasonable reform effort has almost certainly weakened over time.

One type of capacity that has clearly suffered is extractive capacity, or the state's ability to collect tax revenues from its population. Increas-

69. Cohen, "Public Service Reform," p. 472.

ing revenues efficiently probably holds the key to overcoming the current crisis in a way that does not undermine long-term development. To be sure, tax effort in Africa has traditionally been low, with about half of the countries in the region with state revenues of under 20 percent of GDP, compared to an average of over 40 percent for the rich industrialized countries.[70] But rather than increase that capacity to overcome the crisis, countries have been unable to increase tax revenues, one of the signal failures of adjustment. An examination of certain areas such as taxes on traded goods suggests what is going on: Hibou catalogues the variety of mechanisms that governments in Francophone Africa have increasingly allowed to cut into their revenues, from officially granted exemptions on tariffs and various fees and licenses, to underinvoicing and other kinds of fraud. Hibou reports that revenue not collected was estimated to amount to 35 percent of total tariff revenues in Côte d'Ivoire in the early 1990s, 83.5 percent in Burkina Faso, and a stunning 117 percent in Cameroon.[71] A 1999 report by Benin's own Ministry of Finance estimated that only a tenth of all taxpayers regularly paid their taxes, and that revenue losses due to corruption amounted to 25 percent of total revenues.[72] The Malawian government, for its part, estimates that "almost a third of government revenue is stolen annually by civil servants."[73] All over the region, it is clear, corruption undermines state efforts to raise the level of government revenues.

The point to make here is the path dependency of the dynamics described. Over time, the underinvestment in state capacity by state elites has strengthened the relative power of neopatrimonial interests within the state; these prevent extraction thereby weakening the state apparatus further. As a result, over time, the ability of rational-legal elements within the state to control events and force accountability on the political class atrophies further. The sum result after two decades of this

---

70. African data is provided in Janet G. Stotsky and Asegedech Wolde Mariam, "Tax Effort in Sub Saharan Africa," *International Monetary Fund Working Paper*, WP/97/107. (Washington, DC: IMF, September 1997); similar data on the industrialized countries is provided by Vito Tanzi and Ludger Schuknecht, "The Growth of Government and the Reform of the State in Industrial Countries," *International Monetary Fund Working Paper*, WP/95/130 (Washington, DC: IMF, December 1995).
71. Béatrice Hibou, *l'Afrique est-elle protectioniste?* (Paris: Karthala, 1996), pp. 183–4.
72. "L'économie Béninoise mise à rude épreuve par la corruption," *Marchés Tropicaux et Méditerranéens* (April 16, 1999): 801.
73. "Accounting Musty – DPP: One-Third Government Money Stolen Annually," in *The Nation* (Malawi), April 27, 2000, p. 1.

downward cycle is that the prospects for reform are far worse than they were at the onset of the crisis. Even leaders who want to undertake reform find that the state has been hollowed out – it is unable to implement even the most basic policies and has been taken over by rent-seeking and corrupt practices.

A Decline into Warlordism?

Some astute observers have surveyed this situation and predict widespread state collapse, as the inevitable next phase.[74] Central authority will not be sustained and politics will increasingly be dominated by warlords who control a part of the territory and survive off the manipulation of international rents or some high-value commodity like diamonds or oil.[75] Cases like Sierra Leone, Somalia, or Zaire/Congo clearly provide support for these pessimistic scenarios. But how generalizable are these national experiences? Pessimists argue that a significantly large number of states in Africa decayed into civil war in the 1990s, implying that there is something about either the end of the Cold War or the impact of economic crisis that has been devastating for state structures. Since their arguments are not dissimilar to many of the views expressed in these pages, it is important to be clear about the specificity of this book's argument. First, it is not at all clear that state collapses have dramatically increased in recent years. Some conflict-ridden countries have been nonviable as unitary states since independence. Thus, Angola, Sudan, or Chad have never really known peace. For every collapse that appears due to the withdrawal of the superpowers, Liberia being perhaps the paradigmatic case, there are cases like Ethiopia or Mozambique where the end of the Cold War appears to have had a salutary effect on state building. Nor is the recessionary impact of economic crisis and adjustment a cause of many of these conflicts. The conflict is often over resources, which in fact have attenuated the impact of recession. Several states that had previously collapsed, like Uganda or Chad, appear

74. See Leonardo Villalon and Phillip Huxtable (eds.), *The African State at a Critical Juncture: Between Disintegration and Reconfiguration* (Boulder, CO: Lynne Rienner, 1998); and I. William Zartman (ed.), *Collapsed States: The Disintegration and Restoration of Legitimate Authority* (Boulder, CO: Lynne Rienner, 1995).

75. The leading exponent of such a view is William Reno, *Warlord Politics and African States* (Boulder, CO: Lynne Rienner, 1998).

to have reemerged as centralized states, albeit fragile ones. In sum, African states may be somewhat more vulnerable to collapse, but most are proving resilient. The adaptation of neopatrimonial practices I have described has protected most regimes, even if they appear increasingly dilapidated.

Reno is correct to explain state collapse in countries like Sierra Leone as the result not of societal pressures on weak states but rather as the breakdown of state leaders' ability to accommodate elite factions and arbitrate the access to state resources. In terms of the arguments of this book, President Momoh failed in his political management of the adjustment process. The fundamental difference between the chaos in Sierra Leone and, say, the civil war in Nigeria in the late 1960s is that the former was preceded by a virtual collapse of the state apparatus whereas the latter was about the legitimate sovereignty of a still-viable state.

It is important, nonetheless, to be clear that state collapse is not a choice of state elites, as Reno and others sometimes imply.[76] The Sierra Leone "model" does not describe a situation in which state leaders have willingly pursued a deliberate strategy to destroy the state and turn themselves into warlords. The descent to state collapse is the mostly unintentional result of increasingly desperate leaders who have progressively sawed off the state branch on which they based their neopatrimonial rule. To be sure, political disorder and state collapse is instrumentalized by elites, but this does not mean that state leaders willingly allow the state to collapse because they believe they can benefit from it. Instead, state elites continue to derive short-term advantage from every circumstance, no matter how chaotic, even as their failure to navigate the contradictions of neopatrimonial rule leads the state astray. Having too long undermined state capacity for political reasons, at some point the bureaucracy no longer performs at all, order breaks down, and leaders find it increasingly hard to manage the interelite accommodation processes that are at the core of political stability.

Reno and others have alerted us to the various sources of profit that continue to exist in the middle of civil wars and warlord states. Thus, Sierra Leonese diamonds continue to enrich some as do drug and gun running. The most shocking such example is perhaps the unseemly

---

76. The argument that state leaders derive an advantage from the destruction of the central state is a feature of works such as Daloz and Chabal, *Africa Works*; or of Jean François Bayart, Stephen Ellis, and Béatrice Hibou, *La crimilisation de l'etat en Afrique* (Paris: Editions Complexe, 1997).

struggle over famine relief in countries like Somalia or Sudan.[77] These activities provide revenues that probably help start and then sustain civil wars in countries like Angola or Sierra Leone.[78] At the same time, the profits to be derived from these activities should not be exaggerated and are not comparable to the much larger profits to be derived from rent-seeking in stable economies.

Two decades of economic crisis and the decline of central state capacity have increased the vulnerability of African states to breakdown. But state collapse is far from the inevitable consequence, judging from the variety of national experiences in Africa this last decade. At the other extreme from the small number of regimes that collapsed as a result of the multiple crises they had to face in the 1980s and 1990s are states like Ghana and Uganda, in which strong leaders have sought to reconstitute stable political economies. Both Rawlings and Museveni are less sincere economic reformers than the donors like to believe. Progress on reform has actually been uneven, with fiscal deficits running at 8.3 and 10.2 percent of GDP on average during the 1990s in Uganda and Ghana, respectively.[79] There is enough evidence from both countries of corruption and rent-seeking close to the presidency to suggest that these men are not that dissimilar to other African leaders. It is more likely that both leaders have been motivated by the ambition to rebuild a viable and relatively stable economic order over which they could preside. To reemphasize a point made above: neopatrimonialism free-rides on well-functioning market institutions. In Sierra Leone, excessive free-riding destroyed the public good, and all that is left now are relatively small sources of rent-seeking in a war-torn economy. In Ghana or Uganda, both states that had essentially collapsed by the late 1970s, these institutions have been recreated by relatively strong and able leaders. Particularly in Ghana, the central state's ability to regulate the economy, defend property rights, and maintain order has been reestablished. Nonetheless, the evidence suggests that the logic of the system remains one of pervasive political clientelism.[80] Progress on economic reform is undeniable,

---

77. Alex de Waal, *Famine Crimes* (Bloomington: Indiana University Press, 1997).
78. A recent collection of articles examining this process is Mats Bernal and David Malone (eds.), *Greed and Grievance: Economic Agendas in Civil Wars* (Boulder, CO: Lynne Rienner, 2000).
79. *African Development Indicators*, p. 190. This compares with an average of 5.9 percent for the Africa region.
80. On contemporary Ghana, in addition to materials already cited, see Alice Sindzingre, "Politiques Economiques, Instabilités et Secteur Privé," in Comi Tovlabor (ed.), *Ressources Politiques et legitimité an ghana* (Paris: Kasthala, in press); E.

but the state continues to protect key areas of discretion, which continue to generate important rents for state elites. In both countries, the question remains whether the current leaders have empowered state technocrats enough to sustain the current trends once they have left office.

Most regimes are somewhere between a Sierra Leone-like collapse and the reconstituted states of Uganda or Ghana. Most have found ways to persevere, using the resources and new opportunities presented by the reform process to maintain power. I have shown that in many countries, there is a retreat from the paradigmatic use of state power to effectuate economic development. That does not mean, however, that these regimes are somehow less stable. Some regimes have succumbed to pressures and have not managed this transition. But for others, sovereignty expenditures they have managed to protect from the adjustment process allows them to continue to use state resources to fashion elite accommodation. Populations have progressively come to expect less and less from the state and have rarely protested this retreat from developmental obligations.

How stable is this evolution? Two outstanding issues remain to be investigated, which will provide clues as to the long-term stability of the dynamics I have explored in this chapter. One is the role of the international context, and in particular the Western donors in, first, building up the political economy described here and, second, in shaping events. That is the topic for Chapter 5. Another is the prospects for fundamental political change through democratization. The early 1990s witnessed the most serious domestic threat to the status quo in the region in a wave of democratization that affected most countries. Would the arrival of regular multiparty politics and basic political rights change the dynamics of postcolonial Africa and the prospects for change? That will be the issue of Chapter 6.

Gyimah-Boadi (ed.), *Ghana under PNDC Rule* (Dakar: CODESRIA, 1993); and Richard Jeffries, "The Ghanaian Elections of 1996: Towards the Consolidation of Democracy?" *African Affairs* 97 (1998): 189–209. On Uganda under Museveni, see Holger Bernt Hansen and Michael Twaddle (eds.), *Developing Uganda* (Athens: Ohio University Press, 1998); and Nelson Kasfir, "No Party Democracy in Uganda," *Journal of Democracy* 9 (1998): 49–54.

5

The Crisis and Foreign Aid

In events a couple of weeks apart in the fall of 1999, the Western donors announced that Cameroon was slated to be among the first nations to receive significant debt relief in the context of the revised highly indebted poor countries (HIPC) initiative;[1] and Transparency International (TI) announced that Cameroon had for the second year in a row received the dubious distinction of ranking as the most corrupt nation in the world in the annual TI Corruptions Perceptions Index.[2] The discourse surrounding the first event was emblematic of the world community's concern for poverty alleviation and economic renewal in Africa. The discourse surrounding the latter event was deeply cynical about governance in places like Cameroon, even if imperfections in TI's methods were duly noted. But the two events appeared to take place in two distinct and unconnected worlds. Governmental corruption in Cameroon was little remarked on in the HIPC announcements, while the news stories about the country's ranking made no mention that its government was due to receive several hundred million dollars from the world community in extra financial support.

This disconnect would be only mildly ironic in isolation. But, indeed, a key feature of Africa's twenty-year crisis has been the critical role played by the financial support of Western donors for governments in

1. The enhanced highly indebted poor countries (HIPC) debt initiative was confirmed at a meeting in Paris in December 1999. See M2 Press Wire, "Donors Pledge 3.7 Billion Dollars for Growth and Poverty Reduction in Africa," December 13, 1999; "Creditors Making Major Changes in Debt Relief to Poor Countries," *Africa Recovery* 13 (1999): 1; and Kevin Morrison, "Understanding Debt Relief," Overseas Development Council Issue Brief (Washington, DC: Overseas Development Council, August 1999).
2. Timothy O'Brien, "Here's One List Nobody Wants to Make," *New York Times, Sunday Week in Review*, October 31, 1999, p. 5.

188

the region. The domestic dynamics I have described in the three previous chapters occurred in the context of a massive flow of resources from governments in the West to governments in Africa. As the region's international economic marginalization has increased, with its share of international trade, foreign direct investment, and global economic activity all shrinking to negligible proportions, it has come to receive historically unprecedented amounts of foreign aid. By the early 1990s, Africa's relationship with the international economy was almost entirely mediated by public aid flows.

Over the last three decades, several hundred billion dollars have been transferred from the developed countries to sub-Saharan Africa. This flow of resources has taken place in a very distinctive context, with the evolution of an array of national and international institutions to manage the flows and the web of relationships that they have given rise to, between donor and recipient, among the donors, and within recipient countries. This institutional context of aid has profoundly conditioned both its political and economic impact on the region. In this chapter, I analyze the web of institutions that have structured the aid relationship in Africa, going back to the end of colonialism, but with a special focus on its evolution as the African crisis has worsened over the last two decades. These institutions have formed an evolving international regime, with a set of norms, principles, and procedures that have been designed to defend certain economic and ideological interests and to promote international stability. In economic terms, I argue that the aid regime has actually slowed down the process of policy reform and has helped sustain the old policies. In political terms, it has served to protect and sustain weak governments in the region and has actually exacerbated the neopatrimonial tendencies in decision making that were described in the last chapter.

On its own terms, the aid regime in Africa has been a success. It oversaw a steady and at times rapid increase in the transfer of public resources to Africa from the late 1950s to the early 1990s. It ensured a relatively peaceful transfer of power to independent governments at the end of colonialism and oversaw their entrance into the international community of states. Virtually all developmental activities in the region have received support from foreign aid. From the delivery of health services to the construction of roads and the introduction of high-yield maize varieties, aid has often played a preponderant role in efforts to improve the welfare of African populations. Following the emergence of a major economic crisis in Africa in the late 1970s, it can similarly be credited with managing Africa's burgeoning debt-servicing obligations so that all but two African states did not default on their debts, remaining members in good standing of the international community.

In recent years, however, aid has come under fire from all sides. It is widely criticized for having failed in its stated objective of promoting economic development and it is increasingly viewed as having engendered a dangerous dependency in the recipient nations of the African region. Some critics of the current situation seek to make a sharp distinction between the last two decades in which the donor community has conditioned its aid on fostering economic policy reform, and the earlier period of the 1960s and 1970s, in which unconditional project assistance is said to have dominated, and the relationship between donor and recipient is argued to have been based on mutual respect and reciprocity. In this view, the structural adjustment era of the 1980s and 1990s has been the antithesis of the postcolonial aid regime: punitive, where the aid regime had been generous and altruistic; neoliberal instead of social-democratic; and based on an asymmetric power relationship rather than a partnership. In fact, this rhetoric is extremely deceiving. The adjustment regime, or the set of procedures and norms that have governed donor-African relations during the last two decades, should be understood as based on very much the same internal logic as the previous postcolonial regime, and indeed constituted an attempt to rescue and extend that regime in the face of massive debt and economic crisis.

This chapter is divided into six sections. Section two examines what I call the *postcolonial aid regime*, to describe the set of institutions that was put into place to manage aid to Africa in the immediate period after the independence period. Section three analyzes the impact of the aid regime on decision making in the region. Section four then describes the evolution of this regime toward the *adjustment regime* of the 1980s and 1990s, which has grappled with Africa's burgeoning economic crisis and rising debt-servicing obligations. I examine this regime, its norms and procedures, and its political implications, before assessing the contradictions that have helped undermine the stability of the regime in recent years. The regime that was put in place progressively through the 1980s was in many respects based on a completely different public discourse from the previous aid regime. At least in part, it was based on the ambition to bring about meaningful reform. However, many of the procedures and norms of aid today are deeply entrenched and have long been institutionalized, often for several decades. Far from being a break with this regime, the advent of structural adjustment lending has amounted to an attempt to sustain the regime, as the donors have not enforced its reformist objectives. Section five analyzes the achievements of the adjustment regime in the 1990s. The regime made possible an enormous increase in both aid flows to the region and in the region's debt. Further, aid has undermined administrative capacity and rationality, even as it protected the African state from suffering the consequences of its own policy mistakes and corruption. A final section concludes the argument by examining whether a postadjustment regime is likely to emerge.

THE EMERGENCE OF THE POSTCOLONIAL AID REGIME

To appreciate the current role of foreign aid in the African political economy, it is important to adopt a historical perspective and understand the progressive development of contemporary aid institutions. The origins of the current international aid system can be traced to several more or less simultaneous initiatives following the end of World War II and the beginning of the Cold War. In January 1949, U.S. President Harry Truman announced his Point 4 program of technical assistance to developing countries. In the same month, a gathering of the Commonwealth countries met in Colombo, the capital of what was then Ceylon (now Sri Lanka). The meeting launched the "Colombo Plan," which called for cooperation between rich and poor nations within the Commonwealth. Two months later the United Nations created the Expanded Programme of Technical Assistance (EPTA), the forerunner of the United Nations Development Program. Following these initiatives, aid flows to developing countries grew rapidly and nearly constantly for the next three decades to the early 1990s. Total aid volume was just under U.S.$6 billion in 1960, U.S.$8 billion in 1970, and U.S.$33.5 billion in 1980.

African nations were not initially important beneficiaries of these flows, largely because they remained under colonial domination. Thus, Liberia and Ethiopia were typically the only two African countries to receive assistance for much of the 1950s. After decolonization, Africa's share of total official development assistance (ODA) resources rose progressively. The international community felt an unusually strong responsibility for promoting African development, as the continent was widely viewed as having been particularly ill-treated by colonialism and in most need of external assistance. Thus, accounting for some 12 percent of the world's population, it received roughly a fifth of total offical development assistance (ODA) from the early 1960s until the early 1980s.

A system of international assistance to developing countries soon took shape, in which several key procedural norms emerged progressively to shape the emergence of an aid regime. A regime can be defined as

sets of implicit or explicit principles, norms, rules and decision-making procedures around which actor expectations converge in a given area of international relations. Principles are beliefs of fact, causation and rectitude. Norms are standards of behavior defined in terms of rights and obligations. Rules are specific prescriptions and proscriptions for actions. Decision-making procedures are prevailing practices for making and implementing collective choices.[3]

The primary purpose of international regimes is to promote mutually beneficial cooperation among sovereign units with the ultimate objective of promoting international stability. When thinking about aid to Africa, it is useful to conceive of it in holistic fashion and link together what first appear as disparate phenomena. Regime analysis can do that by showing the links between organizational behavior at the micro level, ideational debates among policy makers, and broad foreign policy decision making at the national level.

Of course, not all national behavior can be explained by the regime; various specific national circumstances also influenced key decisions, and I do not mean to suggest that aid has had a uniform impact throughout the region. Countries like Mauritius and Botswana, for instance, appear to have escaped many of the aid patterns observed in other countries in the region, and it will be important to learn from these exceptions. In every country, at least some aid escaped the dynamics described here. Nonetheless, my analysis will suggest the extent to which the evolution of aid over time resulted from a series of policy and institutional choices by the donor governments, aid bureaucracies, and recipient governments. The choices were not inevitable, and other policies and other institutional designs might have prevailed, but they did not. These choices, inevitably, reflected the interests, values, perceptions and misperceptions, and power relations of the main actors. Outcomes also reflect classic collective action dynamics in which the donors, acting quite

---

3. Stephen D. Krasner (ed.), *International Regimes* (Ithaca, NY: Cornell University Press, 1983), p. 2. A critique of regime theory is provided in Susan Strange, "Cave! Hic Dragones: A Critique of Regime Analysis," in Stephen D. Krasner (ed.), *International Regimes* (Ithaca, NY: Cornell University Press, 1983), pp. 355–68. See also Stephan Haggard and Beth A. Simmons, "Theories of International Regimes," *International Organization* 41 (1987): 491–517. A previous and rather different attempt to use regime theory to look at American foreign aid is Robert E. Wood, *From Marshall Plan to Debt Crisis: Foreign Aid and Development Choices in the World Economy* (Berkeley: University of California Press, 1986).

logically individually, have produced together an aid system with unintended consequences.

The Planning Paradigm

First, aid was conceptualized in the context of a specific understanding of the development process. The development economics of the period viewed the poor countries as trapped in a low-income equilibrium and unable to generate adequate investment by themselves to promote capital formation and rapid growth.[4] An influx of capital from the outside was needed to provide the spurt of growth that would make economic "takeoff" possible.[5] Public aid was necessary given imperfections in international private capital markets. This justification for aid was integrated into what might be referred to as a *planning paradigm*. The apparent success of socialist planning in the Soviet Union had in part spurred an interest in planning in the West, notably in the French Fourth Republic, which established a ministry of planning in 1945; and it led directly to the implementation of development planning in India following independence.[6] The elaboration and implementation of a three- to five-year economic plan was soon widely viewed as highly desirable for rapid development.[7] It helped make explicit and rational the needs, choices, and trade-offs a developing nation had to face. Governments could target a desirable rate of economic growth and establish explicitly the capital needed to achieve it; given various assumptions about the available private sector investment and government revenue possibilities, the five-year plan could identify the capital "gap" that aid resources would fill. And the actual five-year plan, with its technocratic prose and impressive confidence about its precise estimates of economic parameters, had the advantage of dividing the tasks of development into discrete projects the

4. An excellent intellectual history of aid is provided in Anne O. Krueger, Constantine Michalopoulos, and Vernon W. Ruttan (eds.), *Aid and Development* (Baltimore: Johns Hopkins University Press, 1989), Chapters 2–3.
5. In an interesting recent paper, William Easterly argues convincingly that this notion of aid filling a "financing gap" continues to this day to have a powerful intellectual impact on the development community's thinking about aid. See his essay, "The Ghost of Financing Gap: How the Harrod-Domar Growth Model Still Haunts Development Economics," World Bank Policy Research Working Paper 1807 (Washington, DC: World Bank, August 1997).
6. Albert Waterston, *Development Planning: Lessons of Experience* (Baltimore: Johns Hopkins University Press, 1965), pp. 28–44.
7. For example, W. A. Lewis, *Development Planning: The Essentials of Economic Policy* (New York: Harper & Row, 1966).

donor agencies could finance. Indeed, the planning paradigm had an enormous impact on the aid regime. By the mid-1970s, virtually every country in Africa officially structured its development effort through a planning process, which provided a semblance of rationality to the aid process, despite the inadequate governmental capacities to make it work and the tendency of the donors to seek to escape its constraints, because it provided an official coordinating framework for all development activity.

An integral component of the planning paradigm was the idea that aid was temporary. With economic growth, the gaps would be filled and the necessity of aid would disappear, as the government would take on project expenses, as planned. Officially, aid projects were meant to train the staff who would eventually replace the foreign experts and create or strengthen the services that would one day be housed in capable central ministries. In sum, institution building was a central objective of the paradigm.

Bilateral Dominance

Another norm was the Western donors' preference for bilateral over multilateral organizations to disburse their aid. This was not inevitable. Aid giving could have been viewed as inherently an international activity, particularly for the smaller countries of western Europe that did not have global foreign policy objectives. Moreover, from the inception of the aid system, the desirability of channeling aid through a small number of multilateral agencies was widely and regularly proclaimed. The greater effectiveness of multilateral agencies, less likely to be preyed on by non-developmental concerns, was similarly asserted. In addition, the same sentiments of international solidarity and cooperation that constituted an early and powerful motivation for aid had lain behind the creation of the United Nations system,[8] and much of the early impetus for aid came out of the work of the U.N., particularly the Economic and Social Council (ECOSOC). Through the 1960s, the U.N. exerted considerable intellectual leadership on aid issues, playing a key programmatic role notably through the unquestioned leadership of its specialized agencies on sectoral issues such as agriculture, health, and population. The 1970s, the era of the new international economic order did witness a spurt of growth of U.N. assistance. Nonetheless, the U.N. agencies never

8. David Lumsdaine, *Moral Vision in International Politics: The Foreign Aid Regime* (Princeton, NJ: Princeton University Press, 1993).

accounted for as much as a tenth of total aid flows, and this declined sharply in the 1980s, so that by the early 1990s, the entire U.N. system collectively provided only about 6 percent of total ODA.

The decline of the U.N. role in aid was at least in part due to the power of commercial, foreign policy, and bureaucratic lobbies within the donor countries. Indeed, the 1980s would witness the ascendency of other international organizations, most notably the World Bank and the European Development Fund of the European Community, both organizations clearly controlled by the donor countries. Overall, the share of multilateral aid in total ODA actually increased from some 7 percent in 1960 to 30 percent in 1994, even as the U.N. system's role declined.

In any event, after some initial hesitation, virtually every member state of the OECD established some form of assistance program, albeit often in embryonic fashion and with ad hoc procedures, as agency institutionalization proceeded more progressively. In Sweden, the first aid activities were financed as early as 1953, but the Swedish International Development Authority (SIDA) was not created until 1965.[9] In Britain, the Department of Technical Co-operation was created in 1961, giving way to the Ministry of Overseas Development Assistance in 1964. In then West Germany, the Ministry for Economic Co-operation was established in 1961. Ten bilateral donors could be identified among the OECD countries in the year 1960; by 1970, some seventeen OECD donors were identified, and by 1980, in addition to these core Western donors, two dozen or so donors could be identified, notably from the Eastern Bloc and China, and the Middle East (OPEC countries but also Israel). By then, as well, an array of multilateral and regional institutions had been created.[10] In all, one report from the early 1980s suggested that eighty-two multilateral and bilateral donors offered significant amounts of development assistance to the region.[11]

9. The early years of Swedish aid are reviewed in Sixten Heppling, "The Very First Years," in Pierre Fruhling (ed.), *Swedish Development Aid in Perspective* (Stockholm: Alkmqvist and Wiksell International, 1986), pp. 13–26.
10. In addition to the original specialized U.N. agencies, such as the Food and Agriculture Organization (FAO), UNESCO, World Health Organization (WHO), and International Labor Organization (ILO), all of which came to provide limited aid programs, one might mention the creation of such organizations as the World Food Program (created in 1963), the United Nations Industrial Development Organization (1967), and the regional banks (the African Development Bank and the Asian Development Bank, both created in 1966, to complement the Inter-American Development Bank, created several years earlier).
11. Elliot J. Berg, *Rethinking Technical Co-operation* (New York: United Nations Development Program, 1993), p. 132.

An Intergovernmental System

The aid system that emerged was essentially intergovernmental, with rich country governments providing resources to poor country governments. The early literature on aid is remarkably silent regarding the third sector; northern NGOs had simply not yet entered the picture, while directing aid at civic organizations in developing countries was widely viewed as an abuse of prevailing norms of national sovereignty. Again, it should be emphasized this evolution was not inevitable, even if it was perhaps predictable. The governments of recently decolonized nations loudly and successfully demanded a complete monopoly over aid resources, and on the whole the donors acceded to it, recognizing the need to strengthen weak governance structures and integrate the new nations into the international community.[12] In effect if not in theory, donors aided governments, not their populations.

In some international forums, less developed country (LDC) governments engaged in the rhetoric of entitlement, suggesting that substantial and regular aid inflows were their right. This never was an unambiguous norm of the regime, as the developed countries steadfastly refused to recognize such a right on either legal or moral grounds.[13] Nonetheless, in practice, the system worked as if aid had become an entitlement, since aid appeared to be forthcoming regardless of government actions, and since donor governments committed themselves to either increasing aid resources for the foreseeable future, or at the very least to maintaining them at their current levels.[14] Although it is often argued that aid was a weapon in the Cold War, the West only rarely punished countries that expressed an ideological preference for the Eastern Bloc. Socialist Guinea received roughly the same amount of aid per capita as pro-West Côte d'Ivoire.[15] Further, donors did not choose to punish governments

WTF?

---

12. Robert H. Jackson and Carl G. Rosberg. "Why Africa's Weak States Persist: The Empirical and the Juridical in Statehood," *World Politics* 35 (1982): 1–24.

13. For instance, Robert Tucker, *The Inequality of Nations* (New York: Basic Books, 1977).

14. This was notably the case for all the donor countries that regularly reaffirmed their commitment to attain or maintain the U.N.'s targeted aid level of 0.7 percent of GNP, initially agreed to in the first United Nations Conference on Trade and Development (UNCTAD) meeting in 1968, and then regularly reaffirmed by most developed countries throughout the 1980s.

15. According to the DAC statistics, Guinea received an average of $15 in ODA per capita, while Côte d'Ivoire received $17 from 1975 to 1984.

for their misguided political and economic mishaps. Benin, with half a dozen military coups in its first decade of independence, received the same regular increases in aid volume as did stable and civilian Gambia nearby. "Success story" Cameroon, with a growth rate of 8.5 percent from 1975 to 1984, got an average of U.S.$22 in ODA per capita, while "basket case" Madagascar, with a 0.3 percent annual growth rate during the same period, received U.S.$17.

Donor Control over Allocation Decisions

The final norm of the postcolonial regime is related to this last point: donors retained the final say over all allocation decisions. This too was ~~not~~ inevitable. The same governments that pushed for making aid an entitlement also sought to increase recipient government control over the expenditure of funds. Regardless of the rhetoric of the period about partnership, donors retained final decision-making power. This is reflected in both the preference for project aid over program aid and in the presence of conditionality to govern program aid. Taken to its logical conclusion, the planning paradigm would have required donor countries to contribute program aid to the overall plan rather than to finance discrete project activities within it. But this was not possible, as domestic pressures on aid agencies to prove that their assistance was effective led donors to favor project-type assistance and the tangible benefits projects provide. Commercial pressures led in the same direction, notably through the practice of aid tying. Throughout the 1960s and 1970s, project aid constituted two-thirds of all aid to Africa. Donors similarly controlled the various kinds of program aid, through strict disbursements schedules and the exercise of prior conditions. Although the scope and scale of conditionality rose in the 1980s,[16] the donors had always imposed conditions on their program aid.

To a certain extent, of course, financial fungibility made this donor control illusory. The additional resources provided by aid allowed governments to undertake projects and policies they might not have been able to afford otherwise. The point is that the norm of apparent donor control over allocation decisions was an important element of the system. For example, there can be little doubt that it facilitated domestic support for steady increases in aid through this period.

16. Paul Mosley et al., *Aid and Power: The World Bank and Policy Based Lending in the 1980s* (London: Routledge, 1991).

What were the consequences of these norms on the system of aid to Africa that emerged? On the donor side, several patterns were soon set. First, overall aid allocation to Africa was largely random. A large literature exists on the motivations behind *individual* donor allocation decisions.[17] This literature points to a combination of commercial, humanitarian, foreign policy, and ideological motivations as influencing individual donor allocations, which varied across countries and time. As aid became institutionalized in the 1960 and 1970s, distinct aid management systems emerged in each of the donor countries, with different aid politics. In some countries, foreign policy considerations dominated allocation decisions; in others, commercial or humanitarian motives proved more important. There were national programmatic and organizational differences. Some bilateral aid agencies were more autonomous than others, for instance, and better able to resist pressures from foreign policy or commercial constituencies. The analytical capabilities of bilateral and multilateral agencies varied considerably, as did their implementation capacities and the extent to which they relied on external private firms for the implementation of projects. Finally, the number of governmental agencies that undertook aid activities also varied across donor countries. These differences have been well analyzed elsewhere and need not concern us.[18]

More interesting for my purposes is the impact of the overall system of aid, incorporating these several dozen individual donors acting with

17. See, for example, Roger Riddell, *Foreign Aid Reconsidered* (London: ODI, 1987); Alberto Alesina and David Dollar, "Who Gives Foreign Aid to Whom and Why?" National Bureau of Economic Research Paper, no. 6612, 1998; Peter J. Schraeder, Steven W. Hook, and Bruce Taylor, "Clarifying the Foreign Aid Puzzle: A Comparison of American, Japanese, French and Swedish Aid Flows." *World Politics* 50 (1998): 294–323; and Lumsdaine, *Moral Vision*.

18. For example, American aid is well analyzed in Judith Tendler, *Inside Foreign Aid* (Baltimore: Johns Hopkins University Press, 1975); Michael Clough, *Free at Last? U.S. Policy toward Africa and the End of the Cold War* (New York: Council on Foreign Relations); and Dennis A. Rondinelli, *Development Administration and U.S. Foreign Aid Policy* (Boulder, CO: Lynne Rienner, 1987). On French aid, see Jacques Adda and Marie-Claude Smouts, *La France face au sud: le miroir brisé* (Paris: Karthala, 1989); Teresa Hayter, *French Aid* (London: ODI, 1966); and Serge Michailof, *La France et l'Afrique: vade-mecum pour un nouveau voyage* (Paris: Karthala, 1993). Comparative Studies are provided in George Cunningham, *The Management of Aid Agencies* (London: Overseas Development Institute, 1974); Olav Stokke (ed.), *Western Middle Powers and Global Poverty* (Uppsala: Scandinavian Institute of African Studies, 1989); and Carol Lancaster, *Aid to Africa: So Much to Do, So Little Done* (Chicago, IL: Chicago University Press, 1999).

[handwritten marginal note: gave certain firms their aid to behind motivations where certain]

minimal coordination. In what might be called the *aid allocation paradox*, the different motivations influencing the different donors at any one time resulted in aid flows being randomly distributed across the continent. One donor's foreign policy motives might benefit one set of countries, but other donors, with different concerns, would focus their attention on a different set of countries. For instance, the strong humanitarian motives of one donor to focus aid on needy countries did not in fact result in a clear need-based allocation of overall aid. American largesse toward Cold War "ally" Liberia or Zaire did not result in those nations receiving more aid than other African nations, simply because other donors did not follow the lead of the United States. Similarly, many donors appeared to shy away from former French colonies, at least in part because France's aid was so heavily concentrated there.

As a result, Cunningham's verdict twenty-five years ago that the overall allocation of aid across recipient countries had "no rational basis" seems justified for this entire period.[19] Certainly, through the mid-1990s, overall flows responded neither to the economic performance of recipients nor to their level of need.[20] The only clear bias in aid allocation related to the size of the recipient country. Throughout this period, small countries received a disproportionately large volume of aid. As the donors expanded the breadth of their programs across Africa, they opened field offices and developed country programs even in the continent's smallest countries. The minimum volume of aid that appears to have justified a field presence was typically quite large relative to what were exceedingly small economies. Thus, there is a strikingly strong negative correlation between the size of a country, everything else being equal, and the amount of aid per capita it received. Nigeria, the biggest country on the continent, received roughly U.S.$1 of aid per capita during the period 1975–84, while tiny Cape Verde and Djibouti, for example, received U.S.$144 and 212 a year, respectively, during this same period. This bias probably followed in part from the intergovernmental logic of the system, in which all developing country governments were entitled to an aid program, in the same way each got a seat in the U.N. General Assembly.

One result of this logic was that aid was quite widely distributed across LDC countries. Indeed, a striking trend over this period was the

19. Cunningham, *The Management of Aid Agencies*, p. 5.
20. The former is documented and argued convincingly in Craig Burnside and David Dollar, "Aid, Policies and Growth," World Bank Policy Research Working Paper Number 1777, 1997. For an analysis of need-based aid, see Howard White, "How Much Aid Is Used for Poverty Reduction?" *IDS Bulletin* 27 (1996): 83–99.

progressive deconcentration of donor programs. Invariably, donors had started with aid programs that focused on a small number of recipient countries. Over time, however, new recipients were invariably added and the number of field offices expanded. (A similar process was leading the different donors to diversify the sectoral composition of their aid effort.) Thus, as Lumsdaine notes, in 1960–61 half the donors gave 40 percent or more of their aid to only two recipients; by 1980–81, fifteen out of eighteen Development Assistance Committee (DAC) donors gave their top five recipients less than 40 percent of their total aid.[21] By the latter date, each donor typically had an aid program of varied, multisectoral programs in three dozen countries.

A second important result of the aid regime was the rapid proliferation of aid agencies present in Africa. This institutional proliferation virtually ensured the problems of aid coordination that have bedeviled aid since then.[22] With several dozen donors engaged in literally hundreds of development activities, aid represents a tremendous managerial burden to governments. Donors regularly invoked the need for coordination among themselves, to deal with this increasingly unwieldy system, but to little effect.[23] Right at the dawn of the regime, in 1961, the Development Assistance Committee was created by the member states of the Organization for Economic Cooperation and Development (OECD) to track the efforts of these agencies and seek to improve their coordination.[24] But it has never enjoyed more than an advisory function and has had little impact on the day-to-day administration of aid programs in the field. Some relatively superficial mechanisms were established to promote coordination at the country level. The member states delegated the United Nations Development Program (UNDP) field offices with the task of overall country aid coordination, a mandate it was poorly equipped to implement and which has been more or less forgotten by the donors.[25] The UNDP was instrumental in organizing donor

21. Lumsdaine, *Moral Vision*, pp. 256–8.
22. This is a primary theme of Nicolas van de Walle and Timothy Johnston, *Improving Aid to Africa* (Baltimore: Johns Hopkins University Press, for the Overseas Development Council, 1996).
23. Dale Whittington and Craig Calhoun, "Who Really Wants Donor Coordination?" *Development Policy Review* 6 (1991): 295–309.
24. Development Assistance Committee, *Development Cooperation* (Paris: OECD, 1962), pp. 9–10.
25. Maurice Williams, *AID Coordination and NATCAP Evaluation: UNDP's Role in Aid Effectiveness* (New York: United Nations Development Program, January 1995); see also Elliot Berg, *Rethinking Technical Co-operation* (New York: United Nations Development Program, 1993).

roundtable meetings, one of several formal and informal forums that came into being during the 1980s for donor representatives at the recipient country level. These were no doubt useful for disseminating information among donors and government, but there is little evidence they have resulted in more effective coordination of actual programming.

THE IMPACT OF AID ON DECISION MAKING

As this system of aid institutionalized itself, it also began to shape the nature of decision making in the region. Officially, every government linked aid to a formal economic planning and budgeting process. Soon after independence, every country had an ongoing three- to five-year economic planning process, reinforced by donor-funded technical assistance, which linked to an annual government budget. Officially, donors invoked the plan to justify their own activities and allowed it to set much of the policy agenda. A government presented for donor funding the different projects it had identified as high priority in its plan. The plan provided a framework in which multiple, seemingly independent projects could be coordinated and redundancies avoided. Within a decade, most foreign assistance was, on face, provided in the context of the government's planning process. Indicative planning allowed for a public debate about governmental choices and the opportunity costs of the priorities it made explicit. It also had the advantage of providing a rational framework for the aid that was coming to governments from a bewildering number of sources.

Donor disenchantment with government planning was nonetheless almost immediate.[26] Most plans were based on improbably optimistic assumptions, were often unrealistic about governmental capabilities, and were full of bad, poorly thought-out projects. The planning process often suffered from inadequate national statistics,[27] poorly trained staff, and unduly ambitious objectives. Even well-designed plans required enormous discipline and cohesion from governments that too often had neither. Inconsistent sectoral pricing policies and an uncertain macroeconomic policy context often undermined project performance, even before the middle 1970s signaled the emergence of major disequilibria. Finally, five years is a long time, and all too often plans were made

26. René Dumont, *False Start in Africa* (New York: Praeger, 1966), especially pp. 99–101.
27. See Wolfgang F. Stolper, *Planning without Facts: Lessons in Resource Allocation from Nigeria's Development* (Cambridge, MA: Harvard University Press, 1966).

irrelevant by unpredictable events like droughts or international trade shocks.

Beyond its own weaknesses, indicative planning was soon viewed by donors as unduly constraining, given various political and bureaucratic pressures they faced. Thus, donors soon began to undermine a rational planning process by imposing their own accounting, procurement, auditing, and evaluation timetables and procedures on their projects, even though the imposition of multiple procedures weighed heavily on local managerial capacities and undermined the primacy of local administrative structures. Commercial pressures asserted themselves on donors in the form of aid tying – the favoring of national domestic suppliers and personnel in all project procurement. Aid tying has been shown to substantially lower the real value of aid and to add substantial managerial costs to recipients; yet, by the mid-1970s, 60 percent of all aid was fully or partly tied.[28] There is an anecdote that because of aid tying the Egyptian government's rural development services had to repair over a dozen different types of water pumps that each donor had insisted on purchasing for its project. This story may be apocryphal, but it is suggestive of the disruption caused by aid tying on local planning structures.

Second, criticism emerged in the 1960s that aid agencies lacked a strategic vision of recipient country problems and that aid programs tended to be a haphazard collection of individual projects, undermining their effectiveness and impact. Soon, most agencies moved to some kind of country programming exercise, in which aid activities were all linked to a set of overarching objectives, related in turn to an assessment of the national economy. The fashion for country programs has since waxed and waned; by the 1970s, most agencies had heeded the advice that they needed to be more sensitive to local needs and priorities. Country programs were refashioned to involve greater consultation with government in the design of aid activities. The language of "partnership" entered the aid lexicon, as various consultative bodies were created to facilitate communication between donor agency and government representatives.

Both of these innovations had the advantage of facilitating multiyear programming and making annual variation in aid flows more predictable to recipient governments. They tended to legitimate the notion of aid as an entitlement. But the bilateral procedures and timetables they put in place were invariably not coordinated with the government's planning

28. Catrinus Jepma, *The Tying of Aid* (Paris: OECD, 1991).

process, or for that matter, with the similar exercises being put in place by other donors. Over time, the inevitable result was a weakening in the authority of the government's procedures, increasingly only one of multiple development-planning frameworks in the country.[29]

Third, the pressure from domestic critics to maximize short-term effectiveness also led donor agencies to seek alternatives to the central government. To satisfy their own bureaucratic exigencies and to escape the growing corruption and ineffectiveness of local government structures, donors progressively established parallel systems of procurement and recruitment for expending project funds. They devised their own separate auditing and evaluation mechanisms and ceased trying to upgrade those of government. Most significantly, they located their aid activities in separate institutions created specially for that purpose, financing the emergence all over Africa of stand-alone project structures.[30] In Tanzania, for instance, donors were implementing no fewer than fifteen stand-alone projects in the health sector in the early 1990s, each with its own procurement, auditing, and evaluation procedures.[31] Similarly, Berg gives the example of forty-four distinct projects in Malawi's agricultural sector alone.[32] Guinea's primary education subsector was receiving support in the mid-1990s from international organizations like UNESCO, the United Nations International Children's Emergency Fund (UNICEF), the World Bank, the African Development Bank, the European Union, and the Francophone organization, the Agence de Coopération Culturelle et Technique (ACCT). The subsector was also receiving project assistance from bilateral donors such as the United States, France, Japan, and Canada, and from volunteer organizations like the Peace Corps.[33] Far from being able to coordinate all these activities, a ministry probably could not even set basic sector policy parameters in such an environment.

29. An excellent discussion of these dynamics in the context of west Africa is provided in Jean-David Naudet, *Vingt ans d'aide au Sahel* (Paris: OECD, 1999).
30. Even when the project was formally within the ministerial structure, it was likely to be self-contained, with its own budget and staffing.
31. Mboya Bagachwa et al., *A Study of Danish Aid Effectiveness in Tanzania* (Dar es Salaam: Economic Research Bureau and the Social and Economic Research Foundation, 1996).
32. Elliot J. Berg, *Rethinking Technical Co-operation* (New York: United Nations Development Program, 1993), p. 132.
33. Kathryn Anderson-Levitt and Ntal-I'Mbirwa Alimasi, "Are Pedagogical Ideals Embraced or Imposed?" in Margaret Sutton and Bradley Levinson (eds.), *Theory, Method and Experience in the Study of Educational Policy Formation and Appropriation* (Westport, CT: Ablex Publishing, in press).

In addition to posing a substantial burden on already weak local managerial systems, these stand-alone project structures had a nefarious impact on the state's developmental role. In the short run, they had the advantage of being less bureaucratic, less corrupt, and more responsive to donor needs; in the long run, they tended to substitute themselves for government agencies. Even if their original mandate had been circumscribed, the institutional decay around them propelled their role expansion. Moreover, better funded and more flexible than the ministries, they drained the central government of qualified staff and undermined institution building in the central ministries. Wilson thus describes a World Bank project in Kenya that hired away Kenyan civil servants to man one of its projects.[34] The project offered salaries of between $3,000 and $6,000 a month, compared to a total compensation package of roughly $250 for a senior economist in the civil service. This kind of pay differential is probably fairly common throughout the region and explains the substantial loss of senior decision makers from so many African government bureaucracies.[35]

It is conceivable that disciplined and capable recipient governments with a clear development strategy would have been able to extract developmental effectiveness out of this aid system. On the other hand, these governments would probably not have needed aid. In fact, various sociopolitical factors encouraged the dysfunctional elements of the aid regime, which soon increased. Despite the technocratic language that had surrounded the institutionalization of development assistance, aid often encouraged patrimonial tendencies and undermined attempts to create a rational-legal public administration. As African economies worsened in the 1970s, these negative side effects of aid began to be exacerbated.

True, most African governments officially sought to create effective aid oversight institutions to manage the increasingly complex system and integrate it into formal national decision-making systems. By the late 1970s, virtually every country in Africa had a formal process of project selection, monitoring, and evaluation. But rare were the governments that managed to cope with the managerial burden posed by external assistance and actually use the formal process effectively. In Senegal, for example, one study in the mid-1990s suggested that fewer than half of all projects

---

34. L. S. Wilson, "Kenyanization and African Capacity Shuffling," *Public Administration and Development* 13 (1993): 489–99.
35. See the discussion in Berg, *Rethinking Technical Co-operation*, pp. 209–14.

were receiving any kind of formal evaluation by the Ministry of Planning, and that the overwhelming majority of projects were conceived within the donor agencies with little or no attention to the local planning context.[36] Similarly, in Tanzania, an elaborate system existed whereby sectoral ministries were supposed to identify and present aid project proposals (along with all other proposals) to the Ministry of Finance and the Planning Commission, in line with budgeting and planning guidelines established by those two bodies. The latter, in turn were to assemble an interministerial technical committee to review all proposals, and forward them to the cabinet, which then presented a comprehensive budget to the sovereign parliament. In practice, a study of aid in Tanzania suggests this system never really worked and entirely broke down in the 1980s. The reasons were that first, cash-starved ministries rarely waited for the cumbersome formal process to play itself out, instead seeking quick direct agreements with donors; and second, donors presented their own projects to the sectoral ministries, already identified and evaluated, even to including tied procurement and personnel decisions.[37]

These two examples are typical, and it should be noted that these breakdowns in the system had no impact on the flow of aid to these two countries, which routinely stood out as among the most aided countries in the region. Given these norms, governments had few if any incentives to invest in more effective aid management systems, since doing so would not affect the volume of aid they received. In fact, government attempts to better manage aid would have probably slowed down the flow, given the limited absorption capacity of the administration. By the mid-1970s, most governments were passive in their relationships with donors. Few governments regularly took the initiative to design project proposals. Most regular project monitoring and virtually all evaluation were conducted by and for the donor agencies, with little or no governmental participation.

A few governments escaped this pattern, suggesting that it was not unavoidable. Botswana, in particular, stands out as an exception well worth describing.[38] Thanks in part to a remarkably strong Ministry of

---

36. Ibrahima Gaye, Mouhamadou Sy, Malick Sow, Demba Faye, and Moctar Mbodj, *Etude sur l'efficacité de l'aide en Afrique: cas du Canada au Sénégal*, unpublished report, Ecole Nationale d'Economie Appliquée, Dakar, 1995.
37. Bagachwa et al., *A Study of Danish Aid Effectiveness*, pp. 43–48.
38. The following account is informed by Gervase Maipose, Gloria M. Somolekae, and Timothy A. Johnston, *Aid Effectiveness in Botswana* (Washington, DC: Overseas Development Council, February 28, 1996); Kyvik Nordas Hidlegunn, Gilbert Sekgoma, and Gloria Somolekae, *Managing Good Fortune: Macro-*

Finance and Development, the government was able to institute and enforce a disciplined system in which all aid was carefully integrated into the indicative planning process. Since independence, the Ministry of Finance and Development has seconded a number of its planning and finance officers to each of the line ministries to help ensure the quality of sectoral projects and to promote coordination of the government's development activities. By law, a development project must be in the national plan before the government will incur expenditures for it; or a parliamentary resolution must be passed, making explicit the "supplementary estimates" for the sums required for the projects. As a result, all aid activities become integrated into the planning and budgeting process, which enhances the prospects for project sustainability and local ownership. The result has been relatively effective foreign aid, which has contributed to a record of sustained economic growth that is unrivaled in the region.

Many other countries had similar formal aid management structures on paper. It is thus important to ask why Botswana was relatively unique in ensuring the ability of these structures to promote reasonably effective aid and economic development. Several factors appear important. First, Botswana has possessed effective leadership and a relatively stable and legitimate government genuinely committed to promoting economic development. By virtually all accounts, Botswana has one of Africa's least corrupt and most developmental governments, which has consistently managed to reinvest a large proportion of profits from the diamond industry to secure long-term development.[39] Second, the country has maintained reasonable macro and sectoral policies, which have also promoted growth; and third, it has avoided major balance of payments and fiscal deficit crises.[40] This stability and prosperity has fed on itself and has helped Botswana to escape the capital flight, exodus of

economic Management and the Role of Aid in Botswana, evaluation report 6.98, prepared for the Norwegian Ministry of Foreign Affairs (Bergen: Chr. Michelsen Institute, 1998); and Stephen Lister (ed.), *Aid, Donors and Development Management* (Windhoek, Namibia: Nepru Publications, 1991).
39. On the underlying political and economic explanations for this Botswana exceptionalism, see Stephen John Stedman (ed.), *Botswana: The Political Economy of Democratic Development* (Boulder, CO: Lynne Rienner, 1993); Charles Harvey, "Botswana: Is the Miracle Over?" *Journal of African Economies* 1 (1992): 335–68.
40. Harvey, "Botswana: Is the Miracle Over?"; and Stephen R. Lewis, "Policy Making and Economic Performance: Botswana in Comparative Perspective," in Stephen John Stedman (ed.), *Botswana: The Political Economy of Democratic Development* (Boulder, CO: Lynne Rienner, 1993).

skilled staff from the public sector, and skepticism of foreign investors that has plagued other economies in the region. Interestingly, the
need to integrate all development activities into the national planning
process has jarred some donors, not used to this level of government
ownership.[41]

In much of the rest of the continent, governments proved unable to
manage the rising flow of aid resources, and various negative side effects
began to assert themselves. Paradoxically, though it was overwhelmingly
directed at the state, aid usually weakened the state's developmental
capacities, even as it encouraged public sector growth and consumption.
The norm that aid be primarily directed entirely at the public sector had
profound implications for the type of development it sponsored. Whatever donor rhetoric and intentions, the evidence suggests that aid served
to expand the size of the public sector and fueled government consumption.[42] As is well described elsewhere,[43] the policies governments
adopted in the 1960s and 1970s tended to favor consumption over
investment, imports over exports, and urban interests over rural interests. Governments may well have favored such policies anyway, but aid
helped both to lead governments in that direction and then to sustain
these policies, long after they had proven themselves ill-advised.

Without overall coordination or the integration of aid activities into an
overall strategy, much aid became little more than a large number
of independent projects. These were usually aimed at addressing some
pressing developmental problem but often proceeded haphazardly,
without the benefit of any concerted government policy. As Olivier de
Sardan puts it, "Each project acts as a sovereign and autonomous institution, impervious to other projects or to the local administration."[44]
Donors captured the different parts of the state to which they directed projects, with little attention to the long-term budgetary implications of their
interventions or to the project's sustainability after the end of external

41. Maipose et al., *Aid Effectiveness in Botswana*.
42. Peter Boone, *The Impact of Aid on Savings and Growth*, unpublished paper,
London School of Economics, 1994.
43. For example, Robert H. Bates, *Markets and States in Tropical Africa: The Political Basis of Agricultural Policies* (Berkeley: University of California Press,
1981).
44. Jean Pierre Olivier de Sardan, "L'espace public introuvable: chefs et projets dans
les villages Nigeriens," *Revue Tiers Monde* 40 (1999): 139–67, p. 151; a similar
point, made in the context of health projects in Uganda can be found in Sam
Agatre Okuonzi and Joanna Macrae, "Whose Policy Is it Anyway? International
and National Influences on Health Policy Development in Uganda," *Health
Policy and Planning* 10 (1995): 122–32.

support.[45] Governments' discipline waned as ministries and various project units now sought privileged relations with specific donors, agreeing to spending obligations the government was in no position to respect and allowing donors to set ministerial policy by default. In agriculture, for instance, it was not unusual by the late 1970s to have half a dozen different public structures each funded by a different donor and each offering farmers extension services, with little attention to coordinating their technical advice or linking it back to the ministry's own extension service.

Not included in the design or monitoring of projects, government officials came to view donor resources as a series of free excludable benefits to be appropriated: the project vehicle, the cash for operating expenses, the "sitting fees" to attend meetings, and so on. Inevitably, these benefits often came to be managed by governments following a nondevelopmental logic. Some economists have recently posited a "voracity effect" according to which aid increases corruption by increasing the resources that various local actors can fight over.[46] At fault, however, was less aid in general than a large flow of aid resources provided through *projects* to a weak administration with little absorptive capacity, in an environment of growing scarcity. Project jobs, fellowships, housing, cars, and various types of procurement were often doled out on the basis of family, ethnicity, and or political affiliation rather than merit. As the fiscal crisis worsened, project benefits were among the only goodies to distribute, and the access to project resources became a more important motivation for seeking out donor support than the ostensible development objective of the projects.[47]

Even before the economic crisis brought about an acceleration of the decline of central government, aid had instituted the principle that much if not most development activity would take place outside of normal governmental channels. The proliferation of independent project structures

---

45. A recent examination of the sustainability issue is Julie Catterson and Claes Lindahl, *The Sustainability Enigma: Aid Dependency and the Phasing Out of Projects. The Case of Swedish Aid to Tanzania*, a study of the Expert Group on Development Issues (London: Almqvist and Wiksell, 1999).

46. See Philip Lane and Aaron Tornell, "The Voracity Effect," *American Economic Review* 89 (1999): 22–46; and Alberto Alesina and Beatrice Weder, "Do Corrupt Governments Receive Less Aid?" National Bureau of Economic Research Working Paper 7108, Cambridge, MA, May 1999.

47. This was true not only in the capital, but also in the countryside with local officials, as Jean Pierre Olivier de Sardan makes clear in his fascinating case study of cantonal chiefs in Niger, "L'espace public introuvable." He describes chiefs seeking to control project resources purely to control the material benefits these will procure for him and his followers.

had a particularly pernicious effect on government policy making. These structures imposed high coordination costs if the state was to effectively oversee a public development effort. They increased the amount of core development activities that were effectively "off budget," and thus they were more difficult for finance and planning ministries to monitor and coordinate. They short-circuited the political and managerial processes by which governments think through trade-offs, establish policy priorities, and are held accountable by the citizenry. Sustaining project activities after the end of donor support became more problematic because the project's long-term budgetary burden had never been anticipated.

[handwritten margin note: aid projects undermining state sovereignty.]

During this same period, the economic policies pursued by most governments were also having negative consequences for aid, as economic agents did not respond to improvements in infrastructure or the introduction of new technologies with investments that would not in any event have been profitable. In the regime of economic controls and rationing that emerged, the scope of government was expanded well beyond its realistic capacities, resulting in systematic bottlenecks, scarcities, and fiscal crisis. This further undermined attempts to integrate all development policy making within an indicative planning framework: corruption and rent-seeking increased, short-term crisis management began to prevail, and the donors increased their tendency to give up on the central state and seek ad hoc managerial solutions to project implementation issues. As the economic crisis persisted, many of these problems worsened. The infrastructural and institutional capacities that had been built up in the earlier period decayed. Recurrent expenditure budgets were cut back to levels that barely allowed key services to function and severely curtailed most maintenance activities. The exodus of qualified staff from the state accelerated.

[handwritten margin note: shit hits the fan]

In a recent book, Peter Uvin has sought to establish a causal link between various donor practices in Rwanda and the advent of genocidal violence there in 1994.[48] His book shows convincingly that donors in that country were complacent about all the obvious signs that the Hutu regime hard-liners were preparing a genocide, and then failed to respond adequately to the beginning of violence. He goes further, however, and also blames the aid system for contributing to a climate of "structural violence" in which growing inequality, social exclusion, and

[handwritten margin note: post-colonial]

---

48. Peter Uvin, *Aiding Violence: The Development Enterprise in Rwanda* (West Hartford, CT: Kumarian Press, 1998).

prejudice and hatred fed the frustrations and enmity that exploded in 1994. Even if one accepts the concept of "structural violence," what is the evidence that the aid regime I have described advanced the kinds of dramatic social inequities that Uvin has in mind? Constructing a counterfactual reality to the postcolonial Africa described here is no easy task. Aid was clearly integral to the process of modernization in the region, which has mobilized ethnic identities, sometime to murderous levels and it is awkward to imagine what Africa would look like without three decades of aid. In the end, it is difficult nonetheless to argue that Africa would have been a kinder, gentler place without aid. To be sure, aid reinforced the biases and prejudices of the governments it assisted and provided extra resources to elites linked to the state, thus contributing to social stratification. The aid establishment was complacent about existing inequalities. Uvin argues effectively that in Rwanda, donors were often obtuse about the realities of Hutu–Tutsi polarization. However, at the same time, the aid system introduced a developmental discourse on basic needs, equality, and human rights that was profoundly at odds with the kinds of prejudice Uvin describes, even if actual aid practices did not always live up to the universalist ambitions of its own rhetoric. Aid is responsible for many of the social services that do occur in the region; it may not have been as progressive in its impact on social inequalities as it could have been, but to believe that patterns of public expenditures would be more progressive in the absence of the donors is difficult. The contention of this book about the negative effects of aid is thus quite distinct from arguments like Uvin's. My argument is more narrowly that aid had an often detrimental impact on the public institutions charged with development and that it reinforced neopatrimonial tendencies within the state.

THE EMERGENCE OF THE ADJUSTMENT REGIME

Two somewhat contradictory impulses combined to motivate the emergence of a modified aid regime in the 1980s, what can be called the *adjustment regime*. The first was the immediate need to respond to Africa's emerging economic crisis, with the ultimate objective of promoting stability in the region. Perhaps the critical immediate motivation for the development of the adjustment regime was the rise of debt following the commodity booms of the mid-1970s and the recognition by the international community of an international crisis following the

Mexican default in August 1982 – even if by then African countries like Zaire or Ghana had already been in the international emergency room for several years. For most states in the region, what had been recurring balance of payments and fiscal crises exploded into full-fledged crises *GLOBALIZATION economic* thanks to the international economic volatility of the second half of *interdependence* the 1970s. A combination of Cold War, neocolonial, and humanitarian considerations led the West to put a high premium on stability in the region and respond to these appeals. The regimes in early Francophone casualties like Côte d'Ivoire and Senegal found it easy to mobilize French support, while Kenya, Zambia, or Zaire received a sympathetic ear from the United States, particularly after the Soviet invasion of Afghanistan.

Humanitarian impulses, notably following the tragic Ethiopian famine of the early 1980s, strengthened the resolve in the West and added to the legitimacy of assisting African governments with increases in aid. The fear that political decay would spread through the region also weighed on the donors, with collapsed states in countries like Chad or Uganda, civil war in Mozambique and Angola. Donors repeatedly justified their generous support of Mobutu in Zaire, for example, as a choice of "Mobutu or chaos."[49]

The international financial institutions had their own motives for an international cooperative effort to help Africa. The IMF had underestimated the seriousness of the crisis and had lent unwisely to the continent. By the early 1980s, it found itself dangerously overexposed there.[50] Without a major influx of new capital into the continent, several countries, it was feared, would default on their debt obligations, and cause a big crisis for the Fund.

The second impulse was one of reform, based on a critique of the aid system as it had evolved over the previous twenty years. By the late

---

49. Michael G. Schatzberg, *Mobutu or Chaos? The United States and Zaire, 1960–1990* (New York: University Press of America, 1991). As recently as 1987, a World Bank report was lauding Zaire's commitment to structural adjustment and the promotion of foreign investment and calling for a "major effort" at increasing aid to the country. See Leonce Ndikumana and James K. Boyce, "Congo's Odious Debt: External Borrowing and Capital Flight in Zaire," *Development and Change* 29 (1998): 195–217, p. 210.

50. Devesh Kapur, "The Weakness of Strength: The Challenge of Sub-Saharan Africa," in Devesh Kapur, John P. Lewis, and Richard Webb (eds.), *The World Bank: Its First Half Century* (Washington: Brookings Institution Press, 1997).

1970s, the postcolonial aid regime had clearly reached an impasse, even in the absence of the burgeoning crisis. An incredible array of organizations, agreements, programs, and procedures had been put into place. To say that every public institution in the continent had received some kind of donor support is perhaps no exaggeration. Yet, the results seemed meager. Africa's record of poverty alleviation and economic growth was clearly inferior to those of other regions of the developing world. Institution building was lagging relative to what had been achieved in other countries. Aid evaluations suggested that the internal rate of return to development projects was lower in sub-Saharan Africa (SSA) than in any other region.[51] Plenty of evidence indicated that much aid was not working, and the sense that reform was necessary grew throughout the donor community. The World Bank, for its part, had come to be frustrated by its lack of success at promoting development in Africa through traditional project lending.[52] A series of internal reports had placed the blame on the policy environment in recipient countries and the Bank was looking for new lending instruments with which to influence policy. Moreover, at the height of its MacNamara presidency hubris, the Bank was looking for new missions to justify continued expansion.

But the blame for the disappointing results was soon placed on the Africans themselves rather than on the aid system itself. Indeed, the main evaluation of aid of this period, the Cassen Report, provided a substantially upbeat overall assessment of donor performance.[53] The 1981 World Bank's Berg Report perhaps best symbolized the consensus that did emerge about the causes of the unfolding crisis.[54] Relatively uncritical of donor behavior, it focused its criticism on African governments and the policies they had pursued as the explanation for the crisis.

The Berg Report advocated a package of major policy reforms as the solution to the crisis, which eventually would be called structural adjustment. It argued that beyond short-term stabilization, African economies needed more efficient allocation mechanisms to increase their long-term trend growth rates. Note that when Africa's economic crisis began, many observers blamed worsening conditions entirely on exogenous conditions.

I concur

---

51. For a review, see Robert Cassen et al., *Does Aid Work? Report to an Intergovernmental Task Force* (Oxford, UK: Oxford University Press, 1986).
52. Kapur, "The Weakness of Strength."
53. Cassen, *Does Aid Work?*
54. The World Bank, *Accelerated Development in Sub Saharan Africa* (Washington, DC: World Bank, 1981).

The Berg Report's contention that domestic policies had played a key role in precipitating the crisis was initially a controversial and much criticized position.[55] By the mid-1980s, however, there was a broad consensus that some kind of domestic policy reform was necessary to get Africa back on track;[56] disagreement focused on the nature and parameters of reform. Oddly enough, the report also called for the doubling of aid flows to the region over the next decade to help leverage this effort at policy reform, suggesting a relatively benign view of the aid process.

In sum, the twin initial purposes of the adjustment regime were to manage Africa's economic crisis, with the ultimate objective of promoting stability in the region, while simultaneously pushing through fundamental reform. These two purposes, it should be clear, were largely contradictory. For the donors, large resource flows to Africa were designed both to leverage policy reform from governments and to protect them during a period of rapid change. Adjustment to new international realities was inescapable; financial support would prod governments in the right direction in a more orderly manner that protected political stability. Adjustment is often characterized as profoundly destabilizing for governments, but in the logic of its architects the substantial flow of resources to governments would allow them to adjust to the new international realities. On the other hand, for African governments, donor support lessened the imperative to undertake reform. Without donor support, market pressures would have become overwhelming and the current policies could not have been sustained. With it, however, governments could much better resist attacks on the status quo. There is now much evidence to suggest that macroeconomic policy reform was probably delayed by the massive flows of aid in the 1980s.[57] From the outset,

---

55. For a flavor of the disputes around the Berg Report, see John Sender and Sheila Smith, *What's Right with the Berg Report and What's Left of Its Critics?* (Sussex, UK: IDS, 1984); see also Trevor Parfitt, "Lies, Damned Lies and Statistics: The World Bank/ECA Structural Adjustment Controversy," *Review of African Political Economy* 47 (1990): 128–41.

56. This intellectual history is admirably analyzed in John Ravenhill, "A Second Decade of Adjustment: Greater Complexity, Greater Uncertainty," in Thomas Callaghy and John Ravenhill (eds.), *Hemmed In: Responses to Africa's Economic Decline* (New York: Columbia University Press, 1993), pp. 18–53; and his earlier essay, "Adjustment with Growth: A Fragile Consensus," *The Journal of Modern African Studies* 26 (1988): 179–210.

57. See, in particular, SASDA, *The Macroeconomics of Aid*, Report no. 7, Ministry of Foreign Affairs, Sweden, 1994; and Howard White, *Aid and Macroeconomic Performance: Theory, Empirical Evidence, and Four Country Cases* (London: Macmillan, 1998).

then, the regime was characterized by a contradictory set of objectives to promote change and order at the same time. One of the two had to give.

Procedures of the Adjustment Regime

Initially in an ad hoc manner and then increasingly institutionalized, a set of *procedures* emerged to manage African's persistent crisis. The immediate concern was the day-to-day management of Africa's burgeoning debt. The United Nations system organized several conferences to sound the alarm. The World Bank established the Special Facility for Africa (SFA) in 1984 to mobilize funds more quickly for the region, allowing it to sidestep delays in the negotiations over replenishment of International Development Association (IDA) VIII. In 1987, the SFA gave way to the Special Program of Assistance to Africa (SPA), designed to provide quick disbursing loans to highly indebted low-income countries in the region.[58] The Paris Club of bilateral holders of African public debt was delegated to manage Africa's bilateral public debt in an increasingly routinized manner.[59]

A fundamental principle of the new adjustment regime concerned the role of *conditionality*. In exchange for financial support, African governments agreed to a set of reform measures. More specifically, it might be added, conditionality was ex ante. That is, governments received financial support before undertaking policy reform. The World Bank identified a core menu of measures of market liberalization, deregulation, and privatization that have continued to dominate its adjustment programs, even if a host of other measures, from civil service reform to judicial reform, has also featured in adjustment programs. Conditionality had always been a feature of aid, but the 1980s witnessed an "explosive growth" in the explicitness and detail of the conditions donors attached to their aid.[60] This was particularly true for the set of new lending instruments that were devised to channel quick-disbursing funds

[margin note: Contingent aid]

58. Operations Evaluation Department, *The Special Program of Assistance for Africa: An Independent Evaluation* (Washington, DC: World Bank, 1997).
59. On the Paris Club, see Matthew Martin, *The Crumbling Facade of African Debt Negotiations* (New York: St. Martin's Press, 1991), especially Chapter 3; see also Matthew Martin, *Official Bilateral Debt: New Directions for Action*, EURODAD Policy Paper (Brussels: EURODAD, 1994).
60. The phrase comes from p. 5 of Tony Killick, *Aid and the Political Economy of Policy Change* (London: ODI, 1998). See also Kapur, "The Weakness of Strength."

to Africa to meet the pressing needs for finance, notably stand-by agreements, Extended Fund Facility (EFF) loans, Structural Adjustment Facility loans (SAFs), Enhanced Structural Adjustment Facility loans (ESAFs), Structural Adjustment Loans (SALs), and Sectoral Adjustment Loans (SECALS), all devised by the IFIs to increase the total flow of resources to Africa and enhance the speed with which they could be mobilized. The World Bank's first structural adjustment loan in Africa was extended to Senegal in 1979. By 1989, more than half the countries in Africa were in the middle of Bank-funded structural adjustment programs, and in all, some thirty-six countries in the region had signed a total of forty-nine adjustment program loans plus an additional forty-one sectoral adjustment program loans with the Bank.[61]

Each of these instruments in turn put in place or strengthened modalities that expressed in explicit fashion the agreement with recipient governments on the policy reforms to be adopted: the letter of intent, the policy framework paper or the public investment program, to mention only those of the IFIs.[62] These procedures were designed to enforce the conditionality the donors viewed as the backbone of the adjustment process. Over time, as conditionality proved to be imperfect, donor management of the reform process became more intensive and increasingly invasive of government decision making. Loans were distributed in tranches, with an explicit schedule of actions to be undertaken by the government before the disbursement of each tranche. Governments were regularly threatened with nondisbursement to encourage them to implement the loan agreements.[63] Large IFI missions descended on the government at regular intervals to monitor implementation and prepare the policy documents the government was supposed to provide the donors but almost invariably failed to. Donors insisted on having independent audits undertaken of parastatals and expenditure reviews of ministries, openly doubting the accuracy of the government's own financial accounts. *Pre Nup!*

61. Eva Jesperson, "External Shocks, Adjustment Policies and Economic and Social Performance," in Giovanni Andrea Cornia, Rolph van der Hoeven, and Thandika Mkandawire (eds.), *Africa's Recovery in the 1990s: From Stagnation and Adjustment to Human Development* (New York: St. Martin's Press, 1993), p. 12.
62. These are well described in Chapter 1 of Killick, *Aid and the Political Economy*.
63. A 1994 World Bank letter to the Chadian prime minister stipulated that it would give the government "a delay of two months to undertake the financial reform program. Otherwise, it would suspend all activities in the country." Letter cited in Robert Buijtenhuijs, *Transition et elections au Tchad, 1993–1997* (Paris: Karthala, 1999), p. 77.

Donor–government relations were structured by the regular meetings of the Consultative Group and Paris Club designed to gain promises of policy reform from African governments and help them respect their debt-servicing obligations. When it became clear that debt-servicing obligations would not be met on a regular basis, various debt-relief facilities were also developed (Toronto and Naples terms, the Fifth Dimension, etc.).[64] Regular rescheduling exercises became a feature of the system. Thus, between 1980 and 1986, twenty-five countries in the region rescheduled their debts with the Paris Club some 105 times,[65] suggesting that for many countries debt rescheduling became an almost annual ritual.

THE IMPACT OF THE ADJUSTMENT REGIME

Regime Outputs

The adjustment regime can be credited with several outputs. First, as described at length in Chapter 2, it has achieved some partial reform. Second, the adjustment regime has been considerably more successful in its objective of maintaining relative political stability – certainly until the emergence of popular protest and political reform in 1989 and arguably since then as well. Although "IMF bread riots" were predicted by many observers, in fact there was little initial increase in spontaneous protest against the region's authoritarian governments. The combination of partial reform, continued economic stagnation, and the dramatic weakening of state capacity did not enhance the legitimacy of Africa's strong men, but neither did it directly undermine them. It is difficult to establish a counterfactual in this area, but providing these governments with sizable amounts of discretionary resources has surely allowed them to cope better with the political consequences of their disastrous economic record. In that sense, adjustment programs have been a resounding success, given how many of the old leaders have managed to weather economic crisis and the shock of democratization. Thus, since 1980, the average African state leader has managed to remain in power an average of 11.6 years.[66]

64. These different modalities are well described in the World Bank's successive *World Debt Tables* publications, particularly the editions of 1992/93 and 1996.
65. Operations Evaluation Department, *The Special Program*, p. 24.
66. These averages do not include adjustment for the leaders who are rightly censored by virtue of the fact that they were in power at the end of 1998. The numbers are adapted from the data appendix of Henry S. Bienen and Nicolas van de Walle, *Of Time and Power: Leadership Duration in the Modern World* (Stanford, CA: Stanford University Press, 1991).

Remarkably, seven of the leaders in power at the beginning of that year were still in power at the end of 1998.[67] Although the democratization wave of the early 1980s would result in a leadership turnover in eleven cases, in most other cases, leaders managed to survive the limited democratization they put in place under domestic and international pressure.[68] This longevity in power by so many corrupt and incompetent regimes despite an absolutely disastrous economic record must stand out as the truly most remarkable characteristics of Africa's recent political history.

Surely, the record would have been quite different in the absence of the massive increase in aid to the region in the 1980s and 1990s, the third direct output of the adjustment regime. At independence, total aid flows to Africa had constituted under 2 percent of GDP, levels comparable to developing countries in other regions. As late as 1983–84, it constituted only 5 percent of GDP. Yet by 1994, aid totaled 11 percent of sub-Saharan African GDP, compared with an average of 1 percent for all other low-income developing countries. The rise of program lending fueled much of this increase, going from less than a tenth of all aid during the 1970s to more than a quarter.[69] Increased aid was a fundamental component of the adjustment regime; this was clear from the outset. The need to at least double aid volume was perhaps the only thing on which the "Berg Report" and the Organization of African Unity's Lagos Plan of Action could agree. It was a focal point of every major conference on Africa during the 1970s and 1980s and was one of the motivations for establishing the Special Program on Africa and the Global Coalition for Africa.[70]

Recent aid patterns are described in Table 5.1. Although overall aid totals to the region declined by an estimated 24 percent in real terms between 1990 and 1996, most of the decline is accounted for by four countries (Kenya, Somalia, Sudan, and Zaire), which collectively saw their aid decline by $2.3 billion during the 1990s.[71] Aid totals did

---

67. They were Dos Santos (Angola), Masire (Botswana), Gouled (Djibouti), Nguema (Equatorial Guinea), Bongo (Gabon), Moi (Kenya), Eyadema (Togo), and Mugabe (Zimbabwe).
68. Similarly, according to Bruce Baker, twenty of the thirty-nine rulers who had not tolerated opposition parties before 1990 were still in power at the end of 1997. See his essay. "The Class of 1990: How Have the Autocratic Leaders of Sub-Saharan Africa Fared under Democratization?" *Third World Quarterly* 19 (1998): 115–27.
69. van de Walle and Johnston, *Improving Aid to Africa.*
70. John Ravenhill, "Adjustment with Growth."
71. Stephen A. O'Connell and Charles C. Soludo, "Aid Intensity in Africa," paper presented to the AERC/ODC conference entitled "Managing the Transition from Aid Dependence in Sub-Saharan Africa," Nairobi, May 21–22, 1998.

Table 5.1. Official Development Assistance (ODA) to Africa, 1997

	ODA 1996 (Mil.$)	ODA 1997 (Mil.$)	ODA per capita ($)	ODA/GNP (%)	Real Annual % Change, 1987–97 (%)
Angola	544	436	49.0	13.2	
Benin	293	225	52.0	13.5	
Botswana	81	125	54.7	1.7	0.3
Burkina	418	370	39.2	16.5	
Burundi	204	119	31.8	18.2	
Cameroon	413	501	30.2	4.9	6.5
Cape Verde	120	110	307.7	28.6	
Central African Republic	167	92	50.0	17.9	
Chad	305	225	46.1	19.0	
Comoros	40	28	80.0	18.7	
Congo-K	167	168	3.7	3.2	−15.4
Congo-B	430	268	158.7	23.0	3.5
Côte d'Ivoire	968	444	67.5	9.9	3.4
Djibouti	97	87	156.5	‥	
Equatorial Guinea	31	24	75.6	13.6	
Eritrea	157	123	42.4	20.6	
Ethiopia	849	637	14.6	14.2	−2.7
Gabon	127	40	112.4	2.6	
Gambia	38	40	33.0	9.7	
Ghana	654	493	37.3	10.5	−1.1
Guinea	296	382	43.8	7.8	
Guinea-Bissau	180	125	165.1	71.4	
Kenya	606	457	22.1	6.7	−4.7
Lesotho	107	93	53.0	8.4	
Liberia	207	95	73.7	‥	

Madagascar	364	838	26.6	9.5	6.8
Malawi	501	350	50.0	22.9	-0.6
Mali	505	455	50.5	19.4	-0.4
Mauritania	274	250	117.6	26.4	
Mauritius	20	42	17.7	0.5	
Mozambique	923	963	51.2	43.2	1.0
Namibia	189	166	119.6	5.7	
Niger	259	341	27.7	13.2	-3.2
Nigeria	192	202	1.7	0.4	7.9
Rwanda	674	592	100.1	48.8	6.1
Sao Tome	47	33	335.7	117.5	
Senegal	582	427	68.2	12.4	-6.9
Seychelle	19	15	237.5	3.7	
Sierra Leone	196	130	42.3	21.3	
Somalia	91	104	9.3	..	-18.1
S.Africa	361	497	9.6	0.3	
Sudan	230	187	8.4	..	-16.9
Swaziland	31	27	33.3	2.3	
Tanzania	894	963	29.3	13.7	-1.9
Togo	166	124	39.2	13.2	
Uganda	684	840	34.7	11.3	7.6
Zambia	614	618	66.7	19.3	0.8
Zimbabwe	374	327	33.2	4.5	-1.6
Sub-Saharan Africa total	16,749	15,065	28.1	5.6	-1.1
Sub-Saharan Africa, excluding Republic of South Africa, Nigeria	16,196	14,366	12.3	4.9	..

Source: Calculated from Development Assistance Committee, *1999 Development Co-operation Report* (Paris: Organization for Economic Co-operation and Development, 1999), p. A65.

not decline for most countries in the region during this time, however, even if they no longer attained the rapid and steady increases of the 1980s.

The 1990s witnessed the emergence of what some observers have called an *aid dependency syndrome.*[72] By then, most African governments had come to be extremely reliant on aid resources. In 1990–95, aid represented the equivalent of over 50 percent of African government revenues and 71 percent of their public investments. In many countries in the region, virtually the entire nonrecurrent component of the budget as well as large parts of the recurrent budget were financed by the donors. At the macro level, public finances were highly dependent on donor support, as well as the annual rituals of the Paris Club, Consultative Group meetings, IMF consultation missions, and tranche disbursement schedules. Quite aside from the flow of aid, the physical presence of donors provided significant resources to the local economy. Kenya, a country that has managed to attract a significant U.N. presence as a regional agency "hub," was estimated by the *Financial Times* to have received more foreign exchange from the U.N.'s presence than from horticulture, tourism, coffee, and petroleum products. The presence of some twenty-three U.N. offices in Nairobi brought in an estimated $350 million a year in the late 1990s, including, for instance some $130 million in salaries to the 1,291 national and 922 international staff engaged by those agencies![73]

Not all countries were as attractive to donors as Kenya, but most African countries were overrun with donors and their activities at the sectoral level. It was not unusual for forty-odd bilateral and multilateral donors plus twice that many Western NGOs to be implementing over a thousand distinct aid activities, and essentially dominating if not taking over key governmental functions.[74] Entire ministries were being marginalized from their own areas of responsibility, with sectoral policy increasingly designed in aid missions and donor capitals and implemented "off budget" by self-standing project units outside central

72. Project 2015, *Aid Dependency: Causes, Symptoms and Remedies* (Stockholm, Sweden: SIDA, 1996); Deborah Bräutigam, *Aid Dependence and Governance*, unpublished paper, American University, 1999; and Robert Lensink and Howard White, *Aid Dependence: Issues and Indicators*, a study of the Expert Group on Development Issues (Stockholm: Almqvist & Wiksell International, 1999).

73. "UN Presence Keeps Kenyan Economy Afloat," *Financial Times* (London), January 15, 2000, p. 5.

74. van de Walle and Johnston, *Improving Aid to Africa*.

Table 5.2. *The Evolution of External Debt, 1980–1994*

	Total External[i]		As % of Exports		As % of GNP		Debt Service Ratio[ii]	
	1980	1997	1980	1995	1980	1997	1980	1997
Sub-Saharan Africa	84.0	198.2	90.9	241.7	30.6	66.3	9.7	13.7
Côte d'Ivoire	7.4	15.6	208.3	418.6	76.9	165.3	39.4	27.4
Ghana	1.4	6.0	115.8	366.5	31.6	88.6	13.2	29.5
Kenya	3.4	6.5	168.6	248.2	48.1	64.7	21.6	21.5
Mali	0.7	2.9	227.2	467.1	45.4	119.2	5.1	10.5
Nigeria	8.9	28.5	32.1	274.5	10.1	75.6	4.1	7.8
Tanzania	2.6	7.2	349.7	585.2	48.3	97.2	21.5	12.9
Zambia	3.3	6.8	200.7	528.7	90.7	184.6	25.3	19.9
Latin America and the Caribbean	258.7	702.8	206.0	212.0	36.2	33.9	36.9	35.6
South Asia	38.1	161.3	161.1	218.7	17.4	25.7	11.6	20.5

[i] In billions of current US dollars.
[ii] Debt service as a percentage of exports of goods and services.
Sources: Calculated from World Bank, *World Development Report,* various years (Washington, DC: World Bank); and the World Bank, *World Development Indicators, 1998* (Washington, DC: World Bank, 1998).

government, which has lost much of its sense of accountability and responsibility.

Fourth, the adjustment regime produced an equally massive increase in international debt. With the exception of the oil exporters, private Western bankers had not expressed much interest in lending to African countries. When the debt crisis broke out in Latin America in 1982, debt levels in Africa tended to be lower relative to the size of the economy and a much greater proportion of this amount was public debt.[75] As shown in Table 5.2, Ghana, the star pupil of the IFIs during the 1980s, saw its external debt more than double relative to its economy. Overall, sub-Saharan Africa's debt more than tripled between 1980 and the late 1990s, even after taking into account various debt forgiveness schemes.

75. Carol Lancaster and John Williamson, *African Debt and Financing* (Washington, DC: Institute for International Economics, May 1986).

Was this increase incidental to the way the adjustment regime functioned? On the contrary, it was an inevitable and predictable product of the regime. The cornerstone of the regime was constantly increasing resource flows to Africa; these flows allowed the World Bank and IMF to maintain the myth that their loans would one day be repaid, thus protecting their credit rating as well as, more generally, their reputation for infallibility.[76] Western governments, moreover, sought to maintain allied African governments in power. Thus, Kapur describes France's regular interceding with the Bank on behalf of west African client states like Côte d'Ivoire or Cameroon.[77] Regular infusions of new capital helped finance the almost annual debt rescheduling exercises while at the same time lessening considerably any incentive African governments had to undertake the stabilization and adjustment measures that might have reinvigorated their economies. During 1990–1995, the average African government is estimated to have paid only 57 percent of the debt service due in any given year; the remaining was either rescheduled (17 percent), canceled entirely (11.4 percent), or added onto service arrears (14.2 percent).[78]

At the same time, as is clear from Table 5.2, the annual burden of servicing this debt has not grown nearly as fast from 1980 to 1997, and annual servicing requirements are lower in Africa than in other regions as a result of the various adjustments made by the donors to lessen servicing burdens. First, the 1990s has witnessed increasing debt forgiveness, which has slowed down the growth of overall debt. Virtually all the major bilateral donors have forgiven some part of their old loans to low-income Africa countries. In January 1994, France announced it would assist the devaluation of the CFA franc with a major debt initiative for the fourteen countries of the Zone, in which it forgave all arrears and half of the future maturities on official development assistance debt, amounting to about $3 billion.[79] In all, between 1988 and 1995, over $13 billion of bilateral debt were forgiven.[80]

Second, the various lending instruments that were mobilized on behalf of Africa have become increasingly concessional. Until the highly

76. Killick, *Aid and the Political Economy*, pp. 133–51.
77. Devesh Kapur, "The Weakness of Strength."
78. O'Connell and Soludo, "Aid Intensity in Africa," Table 9; note that the debt-servicing performance was almost certainly worse in the 1980s.
79. See World Bank, *The World Debt Tables, 1996* (Washington, DC: World Bank, 1996), p. 32.
80. Ibid., p. 219.

indebted poor countries (HIPC) initiative in 1999, the IFIs had not undertaken any formal debt forgiveness, but they had used various other techniques that lowered annual servicing requirements, by increasing grace periods and lowering the effective interest rates.[81] The World Bank rescheduled much old International Bank for Reconstruction and Development (IBRD) lending with IDA financing for this purpose, as did the IMF with the highly concessional ESAF loans.

By one estimate, these various donor initiatives amounted to between $16 and $46 billion in debt relief between 1988 and 1998 for Africa's thirty low-income economies alone.[82] The effects of these different developments are clear from Table 5.2, which shows that servicing ratios increased by much less than the stock of debt, albeit with a high degree of variation across debtors. It might be noted that this strategy has also proven advantageous to the international financial institutions, since their exposure in the region has been greatly reduced over time and they have become less vulnerable to defaults.

Critics of the system are undoubtedly correct to argue that the current system of debt management is piecemeal and chaotic, imposing extremely high transaction costs.[83] But it must be understood that the underlying problem continues to be the need to finance the large and systematic fiscal and balance of payments deficits that most African governments are still running twenty years after the beginning of their debt crisis.

Norms and Myths of the Regime

The adjustment regime has generated several peculiar *norms* and *myths*, which in many respects suggested a great deal of continuity with the earlier postcolonial aid regime. The first norm has been that little actual progress on policy reform has to be achieved to remain a member in good standing of the regime. Throughout the 1980s, there was a

81. World Bank, *Reducing the Debt Burden of Poor Countries: A Framework for Action* (Washington, DC: World Bank, 1994).
82. Christina Daseking and Robert Powell, "From Toronto Terms to the HIPC Initiative: A Brief History of Debt Relief for Low Income Countries," International Monetary Fund Working Paper WP/99/142 (Washington, DC: International Monetary Fund, October 1999).
83. In addition to references already cited, see Ibrahim Elbadawi, "Consolidating Macroeconomic Stabilization and Restoring Growth in Africa," in Benno Ndulu and Nicolas van de Walle (eds.), *Agenda for Africa's Economic Renewal* (Washington, DC: Overseas Development Council, 1996).

tremendous disjuncture between the reality and the rhetoric of progress on adjustment. Meetings between the government and its creditors, U.N. summits, and the annual meetings of the IFIs were replete with communiques and announcements "commending" African governments for the "hard work" they had demonstrated. Governments complained about the austerity that was demanded of them and complained of the sociopolitical difficulties involved with implementing reform programs. The impression was given that adjustment was a kind of favor that governments were extending to the West, at tremendous cost.

This rhetoric has facilitated the steady increases in aid and lessened the pressure to achieve real progress on reform. The humanitarian impulse that has been one of the pillars of the regime has kept the donors on the defensive regarding the hardships they were "imposing" on governments. As a result, donors have found it hard to withdraw aid from governments for failing to implement promised measures. This was not inevitable. The IFIs could have sanctioned failure to abide by the imposed conditionality with much greater harshness than they chose to do. In fact, failure to implement promised reforms has not affected a government's ability to access further infusions of capital. Indeed, as long as governments do not formally default on their debt-service obligations or openly contest the regime, they do not need to fully service their debt or implement many of the policy reforms they have promised.

Even in countries in which Bank–government relations have been quite rocky and tranche disbursement have been delayed because of nonimplementation of loan conditions, differences have been papered over in public and programs have not been formally terminated.[84] Belying the image of adversarial relations and conditionality overkill, Bank staff have been extremely accommodating to government procrastination and prevarication on program implementation. Remember Collier's example – that Kenya has agreed to some of the same conditions in each of four successive Bank policy reform loans over a period during which Kenya was almost invariably labeled "a good pupil" by the IFIs: this could be repeated for all too many other countries in the region.[85]

---

84. See Killick, *Aid and the Political Economy*, pp. 133–51, for numerous examples.
85. Paul Collier, "The Failure of Conditionality," in Catherine Gwin and Joan M. Nelson (eds.), *Perspectives on Aid and Development*, Overseas Development Council Policy Essay Number 22 (Baltimore: Johns Hopkins University Press for the ODC, 1997), pp. 51–78.

Senegal, for instance, has managed to reschedule its debt-service obligations more than a dozen times since 1981.[86] Indeed, Senegal, did not receive any less donor support during this period than say Ghana or Burkina Faso despite achieving much less actual policy adjustment. It has benefited from relatively generous debt forgiveness on several occasions, most notably from France in 1989 on the occasion of the Francophone world summit held in Dakar, and again in 1994 during the devaluation episode. Despite the harsh rhetoric of conditionality, level of support and policy performance have simply not been any more linked during the 1980s and 1990s than they had been in the 1960s. Thus, the seven countries that benefited first from the Paris Club Naples terms for debt stock reduction in 1994–95 were Uganda, Cameroon, Chad, Guinea, Mauritania, Senegal, and Togo, none of which (except for Uganda) had any kind of track record as economic reformers. None, it might also be added, had undergone a change of regime during the democratization of the early 1990s.

Throughout the 1990s, the IFIs argued that they were becoming increasingly selective in their lending and would reward good performing countries with greater aid.[87] Stung by studies suggesting that not only had aid often rewarded bad policies, but that in fact there may even have been a positive correlation between corruption levels and aid flows in the 1980–1995 period, the donors vowed to toughen their stance.[88] In 1997, the IMF withdrew from Kenya to protest government corruption, for example. Several other recipient governments saw aid tranches delayed and loans withdrawn because of the emergence of corruption scandals. This public rhetoric almost certainly exaggerates the degree of real change, however. In 2000, the IMF was renegotiating a lending program with Kenya despite little evidence that the Moi government had changed its modus vivendi.[89] The reasons for this inability of the donors to lend more selectively are complex and have been well described

86. Samba Ka and Nicolas van de Walle, "The Political Economy of Structural Adjustment in Senegal, 1980–1991," in Stephan Haggard and Steven B. Webb (eds.), *Voting for Reform: Economic Adjustment in New Democracies* (New York: Oxford University Press, 1994).
87. This new attitude was showcased in the World Bank, *Assessing Aid: What Works, What Doesn't and Why* (New York: Oxford University Press for the World Bank, 1998).
88. Burnside and Dollar, "Aid, Policies and Growth," argue the former, while Alesina and Weder, answer the title of their essay, "Do Corrupt Governments Receive Less Aid?" with a tentative no, on the contrary.
89. "Dancing in Kenya to the Donors' Tune," *The Economist* (August 5, 2000), p. 43.

elsewhere;[90] the primary reasons appear to be extremely strong internal pressures to lend, and poor mechanisms of accountability for failed programs.

Donor dominance over the adjustment process has thus been largely a myth despite donors' control over debt negotiations and increasing attempts to micromanage the policy reform process. African governments have needed donor support, given their inability to attract private capital and their continuing deficits; on the margin, they had to humor the donors, but the unwillingness of the latter to enforce conditionality ensured that governments could use the extra resources they received to avoid policy reform and further their own agendas.

A second norm of the regime was the absence of popular participation in the process. The adjustment regime was profoundly antidemocratic. The donors tended to view adjustment as a technical exercise, in which politicians needed to be disempowered in favor of "technocrats," who alone would understand the need to promote greater economic rationality. Failures in implementation were invariably blamed on politics, just as temporary advances in implementation were credited to the all-too-brief influence of individual technocrats. This simple distinction between technocrats and politicians turns out to be largely spurious. No matter how credentialed with fancy advanced degrees, ministers of finance had reached their position either because they were savvy political operators or because, though they were powerless and without a political base, the politicians had found it useful to appoint them. In the latter case, they were typically part of a "good-cop-bad-cop" routine, in which the president used them temporarily to maintain good relations with the donors and, too often, help rationalize nonimplementation of the reform program.[91]

The donors' focus on individual technocrats led them to forget that their programs would fail without the support of the political class. The technocrats they supported in fact could rarely sustain the necessary alliances, without which reform implementation could not be carried through. Further, the donors' aversion to politics led them to make public relations mistakes. They encouraged a closed style of decision making, judged to be more propitious for policy reform, and did not reward governments that practiced a more participatory style of politics. They did not explain the process of reform to the press or the opposition, did not

90. Mosley et al., *Aid and Power*, and Killick, *Aid and the Political Economy*, provide the two most complete discussions of these issues.
91. This point is well made in Killick, *Aid and the Political Economy*, p. 117.

release loan documents or the background studies that had prepared them, allowed the government to bad-mouth agreements it had signed weeks before, and were remarkably complacent about government corruption involving public funds, even when it clearly undermined implementation of their own programs. Authoritarian governments, for their part, found this bias for a closed style of decision making quite amenable. They had no interest in opening their books to their legislature, let alone to a real opposition or free press. External support from the IFIs made them less vulnerable to the absence of domestic legitimacy.

The Impact on Decision Making

Individual technocrats in some cases parlayed this intermediary role into real influence. The long-time minister of finance in Ghana, Kwesi Botchwey, is perhaps the best example.[92] A small number of officials in Ghana's Ministry of Finance and Central Bank have been able to achieve a degree of notoriety from their central role in negotiations with the donors, even if, as I have just argued, their power is largely illusory. Nonetheless, this should not obscure the fact that the combination of sustained economic crisis and micromanagement of the reform process by the donors has systematically undermined the technocratic basis of decision making.

The perpetuation of the African state's fiscal crisis in the 1990s has resulted in the further deterioration of basic administrative capacity, given the buildup of years of woefully inadequate expenditures on salaries and physical plant. Governments progressively moved to full-time short-term crisis management and had even less time for regular aid management or overall planning. The aid regime had problematized the issue of institution building, even if it had not managed to promote it on a regular basis, and had often condoned practices that undermined it. It had promoted a class of able local managers. The striking thing about the first decade of adjustment was the extent to which the long-term needs of institution building in sub-Saharan Africa were forgotten, both by the donors and by governments themselves. The decay of the civil service was allowed to accelerate, national statistics collection systems

92. His key role in setting policy in the 1980s is well documented, notably in Thomas Callaghy's fine case study, "Lost between State and Market: The Politics of Economic Adjustment in Ghana, Zambia, and Nigeria," in Joan Nelson (ed.), *Economic Crisis and Policy Choice: The Politics of Economic Adjustment in the Third World* (Princeton, NJ: Princeton University Press, 1990).

deteriorated and were all but gutted in some countries, and little or no attention was paid to the dismal quality of the judicial system, although again it varied in quality across the countries of the region.

Even much nonadjustment aid has been reoriented to fit the new context of economic crisis, particularly in the 1990s. Many of the parastatals that had been created with donor support in the 1960s and 1970s received project aid for their "rehabilitation" in the 1980s, which all too often has segued into their liquidation or privatization in the 1990s. Similarly, many sector- or institution-specific projects are designed to support the general logic of the reform process. Various social sector projects are designed explicitly to alleviate the growing incidence of poverty. Given the evolving impact of the economic crisis on these countries, the function of aid has undergone significant changes. One impact of the chronic fiscal crisis has been the decline of the investment budget and development expenditures in general. Increasingly, aid has substituted itself for core development tasks: thanks to aid, roads continue to be built, children vaccinated, condoms distributed, teachers trained. In the environment of the 1990s, the traditional trade-off in aid between maximizing the impact on short-term welfare and long-term institution building has grown significantly more problematic for donors. In a context of increasingly deficient public institutions and economic austerity, the short-term needs are pressing and aid may in many instances improve people's immediate welfare, not an achievement to sneeze at; but donor interventions are increasingly purely stop-gap measures, unlikely to be sustained or replicated by the government. They have also allowed if not speeded up the withdrawal of governments from their developmental obligations, as I documented in Chapters 2 and 4. Aid has always been based on a model of "graduation", according to which it is designed to end and be replaced by a locally provided service or good.[93] By the second decade of crisis and structural adjustment, this model has broken down in much of the region, as donors have been forced to recognize that basic public goods will not be provided without external support for the foreseeable future. Aid is increasingly substituting itself for the government.

A key feature of the adjustment regime has been the final decline of national economic planning and budgeting in most African countries.

---

93. Thus, by the early 1990s, after two decades of sustained economic growth, many donors began to withdraw their aid from Botswana; see Maipose et al., *Aid Effectiveness in Botswana*.

Whatever government attention and much of the resources that had once been devoted to the plan are now committed to the World Bank inspired Public Investment Program (PIP) and Public Expenditure Review (PER) processes, which started to be put in place during the 1980s to improve government planning and protect key public sector investments from fiscal austerity. These processes are dominated by World Bank staff and are typically undertaken with some kind of ad hoc structure, a special ministry of stabilization, or a section of the presidency, rather than integrated into the government's already existing structures.[94] Meanwhile, the planning commission or ministry of planning continues to exist but is largely ignored by the donors and no longer plays a significant public policy role. While originating from commendable public policy goals, these processes are largely external to the government and driven by donor concerns. They tend to reduce the accountability and transparency of key national economic decision making and, in fact, export them to Washington and other Western capitals. They also tend to supplant the country's own decision-making mechanisms, reducing them to irrelevance. Thus, the national budget that was presented on behalf of the Tanzania government to the Paris Club in February 1995 recorded a surplus for recurrent expenditures, while the national budget presented by the government to the parliament and voted upon that same year included a deficit.[95] Similarly, Buijtenhuijs describes the national budgetary process in Chad being delayed for several months in 1996 simply because the Ministry of Finance had to wait for an IMF mission to come to the country and presumably approve or even set budgetary choices.[96]

The inevitable result of this evolution has been the reinforcement of nondevelopmental tendencies within local policy decision making, along the lines described in Chapter 3. As state capacity has waned and the fiscal squeeze increased, neopatrimonial tendencies have asserted themselves with growing rent-seeking and indiscipline on the part of political elites. The responsibility of the aid system in this evolution, while only partial, is clear – even if, as I wish to emphasize, aid is also responsible for a large proportion of the development work that does take place and does improve the welfare of target populations. But aid's complicity in the current institutional devastation can clearly be linked to its role in

94. Elliot Berg, "Aid and Public Sector Reform," prepared for the University of Copenhagen Conference on Aid, October 9–10, 1998.
95. van de Walle and Johnston, *Improving Aid to Africa*, p. 93.
96. Buijtenhuijs, *Transition et elections au Tchad*, pp. 76–7.

sustaining weak governments in power while at the same time emasculating their developmental institutions.

CONCLUDING REMARKS: THE BREAKDOWN OF THE ADJUSTMENT REGIME?

Several interrelated factors began to undermine the adjustment regime in the mid-1990s. First, the objectives ascribed to the adjustment regime by its primary actors changed over time and put increasing pressure on the regime. In particular, with the end of the Cold War, the premium put on political stability in Africa has declined. Whereas supporting incompetent dictators like Mobutu or Doe with generous infusions of international finance had seemed necessary if regrettable during the 1980s, today donors can act on their consciences and drop them. The end of the Cold War did not have the same impact for all donors, but it played a key role in changing attitudes toward aid in donors such as the United States.

Second, Africa's wave of democratization after 1989, in part abetted by the end of the Cold War, in turn has also put pressure on the regime. It provides another dimension by which to evaluate the governments in the region and makes it harder for the West to support the more corrupt and authoritarian governments there. Moreover, the wave of democratization facilitated the emergence of local NGOs, which in alliance with Western NGOs lobbied Western governments strenuously for the greater accountability and transparency of the international financial institutions.

Third, and most important, the size of the resource flow to Africa could not continue to increase forever. After almost three decades of steady increases, aid levels to Africa peaked in 1992–93 and have been stagnating since then. As argued above, ever-increasing resource flows were a cornerstone of the regime, the element that gave it its short-term stability. In the long run, successful adjustment would have resulted in progressively lower resource requirements; had adjustment worked, African economies would have increased their exports to world markets, attracted private investment, and renewed with economic growth. Over time, they would have come out of the aid emergency room, started to meet servicing obligations, and eventually even *graduated* from aid. In the absence of any such successes, these resource increases could not be sustained indefinitely. The World Bank and IMF have continued to ask for substantial resource increases from their paymasters throughout the 1990s, but these requests have fallen on increasingly deaf ears. In any event, the IFIs' exposure in the region has also waned, thanks to creative management of their portfolio on the continent. In particular, the IMF is no longer as vulnerable to the threat of default. This has allowed the IFIs greater freedom in their programs in the region, including the possibility of being more selective in their lending and enforcing conditionality somewhat more strenuously than in the past.

Fourth, the legitimacy of the regime has come under increasing criticism, both in the donor countries and within Africa itself. In the West, aid has come under increasing fire. The absence of any clear success story to point to in Africa after two decades of adjustment has finally made the public impatient, even in countries like those of Scandinavia where there has long been a strong consensus on behalf of aid.[97] When the adjustment regime started, the general assumption had been that public resource flows were an essential prerequisite for development – in other words, inadequate levels of foreign private investment made official development assistance necessary. It was even argued that public capital flows facilitated private investment. The explosion of private capital transfers to all regions of the world except Africa during the 1990s has contributed to a change in donor attitudes. Increasingly, the objective of donor-led adjustment has come be viewed as the reintegration of Africa into the world economy, so it too can access private capital. Many mainstream analysts have increasingly come to the conclusion that Africa's large aid flows may be serving as a signal to private investors to stay away from the continent.[98]

Within Africa, adjustment has also come to be widely viewed as a failure. In common parlance, indeed, structural adjustment has become synonymous with the region's economic crisis. The press and public often blame it for all negative trends in economic conditions. Economic stagnation, the rise of poverty, the breakdown of public services, or the declining purchasing power of civil service salaries have all been blamed on adjustment in both academic and journalistic accounts. Blaming adjustment makes superficial sense in that it has dominated discussions about economic policy making for a long time now, and during this time, economic conditions have at best not improved and, far more often, dramatically worsened.

97. See my essay, "Aid's Crisis of Legitimacy: Current Proposals and Future Prospects," *African Affairs* 98 (1999): 337–53.
98. For example, Collier, "The Failure of Conditionality."

Specialists understand that this approach to policy reform confuses the crisis and the efforts to address it. They know that things might be considerably worse without the implementation of reform measures and/or the resources brought to countries that signed up for adjustment loans; by increasing the net resource flow to these countries, adjustment has probably provided a macroeconomic shot in the arm to economies that were starved of private capital flows. But the specialists have been drowned out of the public debate, for at least two reasons: first, structural adjustment has dominated African public discourse about economic policy making for so long that it is easy to forget the counterfactual. After two decades of official commitment to adjustment, it is easy to assume that economic reform measures have been fully implemented.

In addition, the donors and governments have been guilty of over-selling programs. The World Bank in particular has consistently released excessively optimistic forecasts for countries in adjustment. As suggested by the World Bank's so-called Wapenhans Report, the pressures to move money have led operational Bank staff to gloss over national implementation difficulties, while the Bank's front office has on regular intervals released reports on the region of the "light at the end of tunnel" variety, presumably to defend itself from external criticism.[99] For their part, African governments have had quite different incentives to exaggerate the impact of adjustment; it allows them to deflect popular criticism onto external agents like the Bank for the never-ending economic crisis. Unpopular retrenchment measures that would in any event be inevitable without substantial increases in state revenues can be blamed on external conditionality.

The adjustment regime can be viewed as a failure in the sense that it has lost this public relations battle. Economic reform is never easy to undertake as it entails absolute and relative costs to large segments of the population, particularly in the short run. One of the ironies of the present situation is that adjustment has become highly unpopular even where little actual reform has taken place. Generating adequate support for policy reform in the future will be all the harder, a result for which governments and donors have only themselves to blame.

99. The World Bank, Portfolio Management Task Force, *Effective Implementation: Key to Development Impact* (Washington, DC: World Bank, 1992), commonly named for its lead author, Willi Wappenhans.

Despite the clear decline of adjustment, in what direction the aid regime is likely to evolve is far from clear. I have argued that the adjustment regime was in large part an attempt to sustain the norms and procedures of the postcolonial aid regime. By the mid-1990s, aid was facing its most severe crisis, and the pressures for change were greater than ever before. Aid agencies were beginning to experiment with new approaches, while a number of more or less radical proposals were making the rounds in and out of Africa, including renewed attention to debt relief.[100] There appears to be a growing appreciation for the need for greater attention to institution building, notably following the World Bank's 1997 World Development Report, which focused on the role of the state in development. The donor community has responded to criticism by claiming to have moved toward a new approach, which emphasizes local ownership and governance issues.[101] It is still too early to tell whether this new terminology reflects real changes.

More fundamentally, can the donors and African governments build a system of aid that directly promotes the emergence of developmental states devoted to bringing about rapid economic growth and poverty alleviation? In the West, the reality is that there is no clear constituency for more effective aid. Donor agencies themselves have proven impervious to previous reform attempts, as bureaucratic exigencies have repeatedly emerged as more determinant than the need for greater developmental effectiveness.[102] For its part, the general public has a superficial view of aid, whether generally for it, as in western Europe, or generally opposed to it, as in the United States. In either case, the public is unlikely to press effectively for such relatively technical issues as capacity building or donor coordination. On the other hand, the community that benefits directly from the current aid system may be sincerely devoted to the cause of African development but cannot be considered an agent for change in the context of the issues of this chapter. This is notably the case for much of the NGO community. Long-time advocates of a larger aid flow to the region and at times ferocious critics of the bilateral and multilateral aid programs, the NGOs nonetheless have a

---

100. They are summarized in van de Walle, "Aid's Crisis of Legitimacy."
101. John. H. Johnson and Sulaiman S. Wasty, "Borrower Ownership of Adjustment Programs and the Political Economy of Reform," World Bank Discussion Paper No. 199, (Washington, DC: World Bank, 1993).
102. This point was brilliantly argued over twenty years ago by Judith Tendler in *Inside Aid*.

traditional view of aid processes, including a belief in small independent projects and a visceral distrust of the central state.[103] Moreover, their emergence as significant donors in the last ten years has directly contributed to the problem of donor proliferation discussed earlier.

It appears therefore that the impulse for reform must come from Africa itself. Africans would of course be the main beneficiaries of a more productive aid system and thus have the greatest incentive to push for change, even if the current era of aid fatigue and fiscal stringency in the West is unfortunately an inauspicious time to make demands on the donor agencies. The wave of democratization that rolled through Africa in the early 1990s represents the greatest potential window for significant political change in the region since independence. Could democratization result in political dynamics better able to make good use of aid and promote economic growth? The impact of democratization and the potential for change is the topic to which I turn in the next chapter.

103. For a good discussion of these issues, see David Hulme and Michael Edwards (eds.), *NGOs, States and Donors: Too Close for Comfort?* (New York: St. Martin's Press, 1997). See also Alan Fowler, "The Role of NGOs in Changing State-Society Relations: Perspectives from Eastern and Southern Africa," *Development Policy Review* 9 (1991): 53–84.

6

Democratization and the Prospects for Change

The spread of the "third wave" of democratization to Africa in the early 1990s represented the most significant political change in the continent since the independence period three decades before. Throughout the continent, significant political liberalization resulted in the emergence of a free press, opposition parties, independent unions and a multitude of civic organizations autonomous from the state. In twenty-nine, out of forty-seven states in the region, the first multiparty elections in over a generation were convened between 1990 and 1994.[1] In a smaller set of countries, elections were fully free and fair and resulted in the defeat and exit from power of the erstwhile authoritarian head of state. By the end of the decade, only a small minority of states were not officially multiparty electoral democracies, even if the practice of democratic politics was often far from exemplary.

Has the new, more open, political climate undermined economic reform in Africa? Has there been a negative (or positive) correlation between economic and political reform in the 1990s? What has been the impact of democratization on the patterns described in earlier chapters? It is important to understand the impact of democratization on African economies because it can provide real insights into the dynamics of change in Africa's political economy.

At the beginning of the 1990s, the dominant point of view among observers of the African scene appeared one of optimism about the

1. Africa's wave of democratization is explored in Michael Bratton and Nicolas van de Walle, *Democratic Experiments in Africa* (New York: Cambridge University Press, 1997). In addition to these states, of course, Botswana, Gambia, Mauritius, and Zimbabwe have conducted regular multiparty elections since their independence, and Senegal since 1979. Gambian democracy suffered a considerable setback, however, when a military coup took power in 1994.

region's politics, but pessimism about its economic prospects. Rather curiously, today that assessment seems reversed. During the period 1994–1997, as documented earlier, Africa witnessed its best economic results in over a decade. The IFIs have suddenly become cautiously optimistic about the region, relieved to be able to argue that their policy package is finally bearing fruit. The usually cautious *Economist* went so far as to declare that "Sub-Saharan Africa is in better shape than it has been for a generation," pointing out that its overall growth rate was 4.4 percent in 1996, "faster than for two decades."[2]

On the other hand, the recent ethnic violence that put an end to the democratic regime in Burundi, factional street fighting in the Congo's capital in 1993 and then again throughout 1997, and highly flawed second multiparty elections in Mali, Zambia, and Madagascar have led many observers to belittle the degree of political liberalization actually achieved in the past and the prospects for democratic consolidation.[3] The countries that are increasingly viewed as stable and evolving in the right direction are regimes like Museveni's in Uganda, or Rawlings's in Ghana, neither of which can really qualify as consolidating democracies.

So how can the relationship between democratization and economic policy making be characterized?[4] When the wave of democratization reached Africa in the early 1990s, most academic observers were pessimistic about the ability of African countries to combine successfully the "dual transitions" of economic and political reform. The most common view was that "all good things" did not go together and that one reform

2. "Emerging Africa," *The Economist* (June 14, 1997), p. 16. As this book was being revised, Africa once again made the cover of the British news weekly, this time under the title, "The Hopeless Continent" (May 13, 2000), suggesting a marked change in attitude!

3. Célestin Monga, "Eight Problems with African Politics," *Journal of Democracy* 8 (1997): 156–70; Marina Ottaway, "African Democratization and the Leninist Option," *Journal of Modern African Studies* 35 (1997): 1–15. But for a more upbeat assessment, see Larry Diamond, *Prospects for Democratic Development in Africa*, Essays in Public Policy, Hoover Institution (Stanford, CA: Stanford University, 1997). See also the discussion in John Wiseman, "The Continuing Case for Demo-Optimism in Africa," *Democratization* 6 (1999): 128–55.

4. A long and distinguished academic tradition studies the long-term relationship between democracy and growth, a slightly different set of issues from those addressed here, and one marked by a far more sanguine view of the relationship. Good surveys are provided in Adam Przeworski and Fernando Limongi, "Political Regimes and Economic Growth," in *Journal of Economic Perspectives* 7 (1993): 51–69; and Larry Diamond, "Economic Development and Democracy Reconsidered," *American Behavioral Scientist* 35 (1992): 450–99.

process would undermine the other.[5] This pessimism appeared to be based, first, on the common assumption that democratization would increase societal pressures on governmental decision making. In this view, Africanists were echoing the view that democratization in other regions of the world resulted in a sharp increase in political participation. As Haggard and Kaufman summed up the view, "New democratic governments face exceptionally strong distributive pressures, both from groups reentering the political arena after long periods of repression and from established interests demanding reassurance."[6] Observers were particularly worried about the impact of more open government on policy reform in Africa, where both processes were viewed as highly vulnerable to reversal.

Second, and related, by redistributing power from the executive to the more participatory legislative branch of government, democratization was believed to weaken the autonomy of the executive to design and implement policy, which also undermined the prospects for macroeconomic stabilization.[7] In a trenchant essay, Jeffries argued that democratic politics would further weaken the already tottering African state and

5. Henry S. Bienen and Jeffrey Herbst, "The Relationship between Political and Economic Reform in Africa," *Comparative Politics* 29 (1996): 23–42; Thomas Callaghy, "Civil Society, Democracy and Economic Change in Africa: A Dissenting Opinion about Resurgent Societies," in John W. Harbeson, Donald Rothchild, and Naomi Chazan (eds.), *Civil Society and the State in Africa* (Boulder, CO: Lynne Rienner, 1994), pp. 231–54; Peter Gibbon, Yusuf Bangura, and Arve Ofstad (eds.), *Authoritarianism and Democracy and Adjustment* (Uddevalla, Sweden: Nordiska Afrikainstitutet, 1992); Jennifer A. Widner (ed.), *Economic Change and Political Liberalization in Sub-Saharan Africa* (Baltimore: Johns Hopkins University Press, 1994); and Richard Jeffries, "The State, Structural Adjustment and Good Governance in Africa," *Journal of Commonwealth and Comparative Politics* 31 (1993): 20–35. Less pessimistic accounts are provided in John Healey and Mark Robinson, *Democracy, Governance and Economic Policy: Sub-Saharan Africa in Comparative Perspective* (London: Overseas Development Institute, 1992); and Peter Lewis, "Economic Reform and Political Transition in Africa: The Quest for a Politics of Development," *World Politics* 49 (1997): 92–129.
6. Stephan Haggard and Robert R. Kaufman, *The Political Economy of Democratic Transitions* (Princeton, NJ: Princeton University Press, 1995), p. 152. See also Marc Lindenberg and Shantayanan Devarajan, "Prescribing Strong Medicine: Revisiting the Myths about Structural Adjustment, Democracy and Economic Performance in Developing Countries," *Comparative Politics* 25 (1993): 169–83.
7. For instance, Haggard and Kaufman, *The Political Economy of Democratic Transitions*; a good discussion of these issues can be found in Joel S. Hellman, "Winners Take All: The Politics of Partial Reform in Postcommunist Transitions," *World Politics* 50 (1998): 203–34.

"exacerbate . . . problems of corruption, wastefulness and short sighted economic policy formulation."[8] Jeffries concluded his analysis by criticizing as naive donors such as the World Bank that believed democratization would improve the prospects for structural adjustment programs. Instead, he concluded, donors should first promote "the development of more efficient and capable government bureaucracies" (p. 34).

These assumptions suggested that the wave of democratization that hit Africa in the early 1990s represented a sharp historical discontinuity in the mode of governance throughout the continent and its relationship with the outside world. Today, with the benefit of a couple of years of hindsight, it is possible to make a first tentative assessment of the economic consequences of democratization in Africa and to examine these assumptions more carefully. In fact, as our data will reveal, there appears to be little significant difference between the democracies and the non-democracies in sub-Saharan Africa (SSA) in terms of their economic performance over the last couple of years, in a context of modest economic improvement for the region as a whole. The more interesting issue is what this tells us about economic decision making in Africa and the evolving nature of continental political economy. In the context of the themes of this book, the democratization wave that swept the region constituted the most fundamental political change since independence and, therefore, it held out the possibility that different patterns of economic decision making would emerge. How would the corrupt and largely incompetent modes of governance described in these pages be affected by the move to multiparty electoral politics? Examining the impact of democratization thus allows us to problematize the issue of change within the contemporary African political scene and distinguish the more permanent structures within African politics from the merely epiphenomenal.

The analysis starts in the next section with a review of the salient dimensions of political reform in Africa in the early 1990s. I review some of the underlying reasons for the wave of democratization that occurred in the region, and then argue that the extent of political reform was significant in most of the countries in the region, even if it usually fell well short of liberal democracy. A third section attempts a rigorous analysis of the impact of democratization by making both longitudinal and cross-sectional comparisons of economic performance. The chapter then turns its attention to explaining why democratization appears to have so little

8. Jeffries, "The State, Structural Adjustment," p. 20.

effect on economic performance. I show that political reform in the 1990s did little to upset the major institutions of African politics, at least in the short term.

AFRICA'S DEMOCRATIZATION WAVE, 1989–1995

This chapter's first task is to characterize with some precision the degree of actual political change in Africa in the early 1990s. I start by briefly examining the underlying causes of democratization and then assess the political change that occurred.

The Causes of Democratization

Democratization is always a complex process involving the interaction of agency and structural factors, domestic and international ones, and economic and noneconomic ones. The wave of democratization that struck Africa in the early 1990s was no exception. Rather than attempt a comprehensive analysis,[9] I wish here to link the events of the early 1990s to the neopatrimonial politics described in Chapters 3 and 4.

A brief stylized account of democratization in Africa can be formulated in the following manner: by the late 1980s, many regimes in Africa were undergoing a legitimacy crisis brought about their dismal economic performance and worsening economic conditions. Restive populations were increasingly willing to contest central state power, notably through the fledgling civic associations that had begun to emerge during the 1980s in response to state decline. The first phase of the democratization wave that hit Africa in the early 1990s consisted of political protests against incumbent governments. Often not specifically political when they began, these protests quickly escalated into demands for regime change, often as a result of clumsy government responses to the protesters. African politics had long been punctuated by more or less spontaneous protest, but now governments found it harder to repress or

9. The interested reader is referred Bratton and van de Walle, *Democratic Experiments*. Among the recent major works from different perspectives, see Richard Joseph (ed.), *State, Conflict and Democracy in Africa* (Boulder, CO: Lynne Rienner, 1999); John A. Wiseman (ed.), *Democracy and Political Change in Sub-Saharan Africa* (New York: Routledge, 1995); Jean Pascal Daloz and Patrick Quantin (eds.), *Transitions democratiques Africaines* (Paris: Karthala, 1997); and Julius O. Ihonvbere and John Mukum Mbaku (eds.), *Multiparty Democracy and Political Change: Constraints to Democratization in Africa* (London: Ashgate, 1998).

accommodate the protesters. On the one hand, with the end of the Cold War, the donors were increasing their emphasis on human rights and were less tolerant of government repression. On the other hand, the economic crisis and strong fiscal pressure on states made it harder to coopt or placate dissent with access to state resources. Perhaps more important, the economic crisis was putting pressure on the state elite accommodation processes that had long served to maintain political stability. With fewer resources at their disposal and an increasingly decrepit state apparatus that was difficult to control or command, leaders found it harder to sustain critical clientelist networks, with the result that the old political aristocracy was more likely to fractionalize. A growing number of old-style politicians were withholding their support from governments that had excluded them from power and its perquisites. Although the political protests that spurred on the democratization movement were typically initiated by students, civil servants, and an array of civic associations, it is this class of excluded politicians that typically emerged during the transition to take control of new governments following national conferences and multiparty elections. Far from being political novices, they were often long-standing members of the state elite, with long careers in past cabinets, but who had had a falling out with the head of state and had been consigned to the political wilderness at some point in the 1980s.[10] Thus, in the Central African Republic, the first democratically elected president, Ange Patassé, had been prime minister under Bokassa, as had Trovoada in São Tomé and Lissouba in Congo. Most of the new heads of state that emerged in the 1990s had at the very least previous cabinet experience. Even so-called outsiders often had extensive links with the authoritarian state. For example, in Zambia, Fred Chiluba, a long-time unionist did not have cabinet experience, but much of the rest of the Movement for Multiparty Democracy (MMD) leadership did.[11]

In sum, and this is the first salient point regarding political reform in Africa in the 1990s, democratization resulted at least in part from a crisis in the postcolonial neopatrimonial order described in Chapter 3. Democratization often proceeded furthest in the weakest states – for example, in Benin or the Central African Republic, in which this state crisis was most pronounced. On the other hand, in many of the more developed

10. On this point, see the perceptive essay by Patrick Quantin, "Les élites politiques face aux transitions démocratiques," in *l'Afrique politique, 1995: le meilleur, le pire et l'incertain* (Paris: Karthala, 1995), pp. 277–85
11. Ibid., p. 282.

states – in Kenya, say, or Côte d'Ivoire – the process of centralization of power described in Chapter 3 allowed state leaders to survive the initial set of street protests and adjust to new political realities, although they often had to concede some political reforms to the democratic forces.

The second point concerns the role of the donors. Given the importance of aid to most African economies and to the functioning of the state, one might expect that donors played a key role in shaping the democratization episodes of the early 1990s. Yet, the evidence does not support the argument that donor pressures for political reform had a significant impact on the emergence of political protests. Protests were not correlated either with the degree of dependence on aid, the level of international debt, or with the imposition of political conditionality by the donors.[12] Interestingly, however, the emergence of protest was positively correlated with the number of adjustment and stabilization loans signed with the international financial institutions in the 1980s.[13] The more loans a country had agreed to with the Washington institutions, the more likely there was to be political protest at the end of the decade. Since there is no correlation between the number of loans signed and the amount of policy reform actually implemented, this variable cannot be viewed as a proxy for policy reform or the hardship endured by the population due to structural adjustment. Bratton and van de Walle found no statistical evidence to link the rise of political protest to such indicators of economic reform as changes in the size of the fiscal deficit or of inflation.[14] Instead, based on the discussion in the last chapter, the most plausible interpretation is that a high number of loans weakened central states by disrupting central decision making, creating the impression that key decisions were made by foreign bureaucrats and thus undermining the little legitimacy they still possessed.

As democratization moved from protest to an intense struggle over basic political rules and debate over the nature of the regime to emerge, the role of the donors changed. It is clear that incumbents with greater access to economic resources were more likely to negotiate more effectively with surging democratic forces. Here the willingness of donors to support incumbents often played a key if unwitting role. In both Benin and Zambia, the IFI decision to withdraw support from incumbents in the middle of the political transition may well have sealed their

---

12. See Bratton and van de Walle, *Democratic Experiments in Africa*, pp. 135–6.
13. Ibid., pp. 132–3, 151.   14. Ibid.

fates.[15] On the other hand, generous French support to Biya in Cameroon and to Houphouët-Boigny in Côte d'Ivoire probably played a key role in the survival of those regimes.[16] In Cameroon, the decision by the IMF and French government to extend new adjustment credits to the country in 1991, right at a critical period of the transition, was enormously helpful to Biya, allowing him, for example, to keep salary arrears down to manageable levels. Though much more critical of the regime and eventually to close its aid mission in Yaounde in 1993, even the United States had forgiven U.S.$73.4 million of debt as late as 1990.[17] Similarly, the decline of aid to Kenya, which can be linked to the growing political conditionality from the Western donors, occurred only after 1993, after the democratization movement had crested. From 1988 to 1993, the period during which the regime was under the most internal threat, Kenya averaged well over a billion dollars in annual aid.[18]

The Rise of Illiberal Democracies

The political change in the region from the late 1980s to the mid-1990s was profound and unprecedented. Overall, in nominal terms, the Freedom House indices for political rights and civil liberties improved by an average of 1.00 and 1.28 between 1988 and 1994, and 1988 and 1992, respectively.[19] Part of this process of political reform was a wide-

15. The Benin story is well told in Chris Allen, "Restructuring an Authoritarian State: Democratic Renewal in Benin," *Review of African Political Economy* 54 (1992): 43–58; and Richard Westebbe, "Structural Adjustment, Rent Seeking and Political Liberalization in Benin," in Jennifer Widner (ed.), *Economic Change and Political Liberalization in Sub-Saharan Africa* (Baltimore: Johns Hopkins University Press, 1994), pp. 80–100. On Zambia, see Lise Rakner, *Reforms as a Matter of Political Survival. Political and Economic Liberalisation in Zambia 1991–1996* (Ph.D. dissertation, University of Bergen, Norway, 1998).
16. For an examination of French political conditionality, see Richard Banégas and Patrick Quantin, "Orientations et limites de l'aide Francaise au développement démocratique," *Revue Canadienne d'Etudes du Développement*, Special Issue (1996): 113–33.
17. See my essay, "The Politics of Non-Reform in Cameroon," in Thomas Callaghy and John Ravenhill (eds.), *Hemmed In: Responses to Africa's Economic Decline* (New York: Columbia University Press, 1993), pp. 357–97, p. 383.
18. World Bank, *African Development Indicators*, p. 297. Thus, Kenya averaged $1.1 billion between 1988 and 1993, and $640 million between 1994 and 1997, in constant 1995 U.S. dollars. Note that there have been further decreases since then.
19. See Bratton and van de Walle, *Democratic Experiments*, p. 287. This is on a scale of 1 to 7 for both indicators.

spread movement toward multiparty electoral politics. By the second half of the 1990s, multiparty politics with more or less regular elections had become the norm in Africa. Only nine African countries had held competitive, multiparty elections in the period 1985–1989. Between 1990 and 1998, in comparison, some seventy legislative elections involving at least two parties were convened in forty-two of the region's forty-eight countries. All but two of these elections resulted in legislatures with more than a single party. In addition, there were over sixty presidential elections with more than one candidate during this time. Only seven states in the region (Eritrea, Rwanda, Sudan, Somalia, Swaziland, Uganda, Congo/Zaire) did not convene multiparty elections. Moreover, a process of institutionalizing regular elections appears to have begun: by the end of 1998, twenty-six countries had convened second elections, usually on schedule – that is, at the end of the constitutionally fixed term of office-holders elected during the first elections. This routinization of elections contrasts sharply with previous periods, in which competitively elected legislatures more often than not were displaced by military coups before they finished their term.

Thus, multiparty systems have emerged all over the continent. Much less clear, however, is the extent to which these countries are progressing toward democratic consolidation, by which democratic norms and values are institutionalized and routinized by the political system. Instead, the exercise of democratic politics is often highly imperfect in these countries. Several prominent observers have recently suggested that many of Africa's new democracies may be described as increasingly "illiberal."[20] Regular, competitive multiparty elections are held, thereby qualifying the country as an "electoral" democracy, but the day-to-day practices of the state are marked by abuses. Political freedoms and civil rights may be formally recognized but they are imperfectly observed in practice, particularly between electoral exercises when they are more likely to be flouted. Human rights abuses are not uncommon, even if the worst abuses are rarer than in the authoritarian past. A nominally free press is harassed in myriad ways, and the government retains a radio monopoly. Certain groups, notably key members of the executive branch and the military, may, in effect, be above the law. The judiciary is officially independent, but it is poorly trained, overworked, and easily compromised.

20. See Fareed Zakaria, "The Rise of Illiberal Democracy," *Foreign Affairs* 76 (1997): 22–43; and Larry Diamond, "Is the Third Wave Over?" *Journal of Democracy* 7 (1996): 20–37.

The combination of chronic "illiberalism" with regular, competitive multiparty elections lends itself to considerable cynicism about the latter. Some observers have described as the "fallacy of electoralism" the notion that these elections constitute meaningful political exercises in giving citizens real choices over the distribution of power and resources.[21] In a thoughtful essay, Richard Joseph has call these systems "virtual democracies," in which largely meaningless elections are put on strictly for the sake of international "presentability."[22]

The illiberal and virtual democracy theses advance two propositions that can be carefully examined. First, just how democratic are these regimes? Table 6.1 demonstrates the divergent paths which Africa's multiparty regimes have taken. African countries that conducted at least one multiparty election in the 1990s may be distinguished according to whether Freedom House categorizes them as "free," "partly free," and "not free."[23] Clearly, knowing a system is multiparty says very little about the degree of freedom allowed in the regime.

The combination of competitive elections and a relatively poor level of political and civil rights is striking and seems to reinforce the thesis of illiberal democracy. By this definition, thirty of Africa's multiparty systems are illiberal. Indeed, the twelve multiparty systems in the "not free" category may be more accurately termed "pseudodemocracies,"[24] so egregious is their gap between democratic ideals and current practice. Hence, while most countries of Africa are having multiparty elections, there is a wide range in the actual practices surrounding these elections. Africa offers a striking contrast with the world's older, multiparty systems in the West, which are all classified by Freedom House as "free." Nonetheless, Table 6.1 also suggests that Africa exhibits a wide range of democratic performances and that perhaps as many as a quarter of these regimes are in the process of consolidating-democratic practices. Moreover, overall, even Africa's pseudodemoc-

---

21. Terry Lynn Karl, "Dilemmas of Democratization in Latin America," *Comparative Politics* 22 (1990): 1–20.

22. Richard Joseph, "Africa, 1990–1997: From *Abertura* to Closure," *Journal of Democracy* 9 (1998): 3–17.

23. Freedom House rates all countries of the world on a seven-point scale for both political rights and civil liberties (1 representing the most free and 7 the least free), and then combines the two scores to produce an index. Freedom House then attributes a "free" rating to countries with average ratings of 1–3, "partly free" to those between 3 and 5.5, and "not free" to those averaging between 5.5 and 7 (Freedom House, 1998).

24. The term is from Diamond, "Is the Third Wave Over?"

Table 6.1. *Status of African Multiparty Systems (1998) and Legislative Elections, 1990–1998*

Free	Partly Free	Not Free
Benin (2)	Burkina Faso (2)	Cameroon (2)
Botswana* (1)	*Central African Republic* (2)	Chad (1)
Cape Verde (2)	Comoros (3)	*Congo (B)* (2)
Malawi (1)	Ethiopia (2)	Côte d'Ivoire (2)
Mali (2)	Gabon (2)	Djibouti (2)
Mauritius* (2)	Ghana (2)	Equatorial Guinea (1)
Namibia (2)	Guinea-Bissau (1)	Gambia* (2)
São Tomé (3)	*Lesotho* (2)	Guinea (1)
South Africa (1)	Liberia (1)	Kenya (2)
	Madagascar (2)	Mauritania (2)
	Mozambique (1)	*Niger* (3)
	Nigeria (1)	Togo (1)
	Senegal* (2)	
	Seychelles (2)	
	Sierra Leone (1)	
	Tanzania (1)	
	Zambia (2)	
	Zimbabwe (2)	
Number: 9	18	12
Number of Elections, 1990–1998: 16	31	21

Notes: Countries shown in bold and italics: the incumbent was ousted as part of transition to multiparty rule. Countries with *: multiparty system was in existence for an extensive period of time before 1989. All regimes that are not multiparty are excluded from this analysis. Burundi (Not Free, 1 election in 1993) and Angola (Not Free, 1 election in 1992) were excluded because of the resumption of civil war and end of multiparty rule in those countries. Congo-Kinshasa (Not Free), Eritrea (Partly Free), Rwanda (Not Free), Somalia (Not Free), Sudan (Not Free), Swaziland (Not Free), Uganda (Partly Free) are not included because of the absence of multiparty elections.

Source: Freedom House, 1998/99 Indices, taken from the Freedom House Website: http://freedomhouse.org/PDF_docs/research/ratings.pdf

racies typically did undergo some degree of political liberalization in the early 1990s.

Second, are the gains of Africa's democratic transitions being eroded? Rather than undergoing the consolidation of democratic practices, according to these skeptics, Africa is heading back to the days of uncompetitive elections, banned opposition, and a shackled press. In fact, however, the evidence tends to suggest otherwise. Examining Freedom

House's annual indices for political rights and civil liberties from the period of initial democratization (1989–1994) to the present (1998–1999) does not suggest a net worsening of the quality of governance in the region since the peak of the democratization wave. Between 1993 and 1998, political rights actually improved in twelve countries, stayed the same in twenty, and worsened in fifteen. The "third wave" may be over in Africa[25] but there is no reason to believe that all the recent gains are being eroded. Rather, the region's countries are engaged on a variety of distinct paths, only some of which include a marked decline in the quality of democracy.

Although much of Africa has multiparty systems, those in which the incumbents were actually ousted are far fewer. Table 6.1 identifies the countries in which incumbents were actually ousted as a result of the democratic transition and its founding election, as well as the countries in which regular multiparty elections anteceded the 1990s. This information paints a somewhat more nuanced picture of the continent's situation, for it shows quite clearly that the majority of the "illiberal" democracies are countries in which the transition to multiparty rule proved to be seriously flawed. Most never really had a transition, and the turn to multiparty competition amounted to little more than an erstwhile authoritarian ruler donning the garb of democracy and tolerating regular elections as a successful strategy of holding onto power. Convening regular elections brings with it a modicum of international respectability and the resulting foreign aid, and it does not threaten these leaders. These seem to confirm the "presentability" thesis. The countries in which the democratic transition included the ouster of the incumbent, on the other hand, have on the whole performed better. Only two – Niger and Congo – of the thirteen are in the "not free" category, both as a result of military coups that overturned most of the gains of the transition. The other eleven countries that transited have seemingly been able to maintain most of the democratic gains made during the democratic transition.

The predominance of countries in the "not free" and "partly free" categories gives the impression that things have gotten worse and that the democratic transitions of the early 1990s have been betrayed. In fact, a majority of the countries that underwent real transitions have sustained the progress made, while even the most illiberal multiparty systems are most likely freer today than they were before the democratization wave.

25. Ibid.

THE ECONOMIC IMPACT OF DEMOCRATIZATION

This section reviews the actual economic record of African states following democratization at the beginning of the 1990s. As stated earlier, African economies enjoyed a substantial improvement in growth rates in the 1990s. Thus, overall, Africa's economic output rose every year between 1994 and 1997, with average growth rates over 5 percent in both 1996 and 1997, respectively, and an estimated average growth rate of 3.4 percent for 1998.[26] This is a short time period, but given the widespread prediction that democratization would result in a worse economic performance, the obvious question to ask is whether political reform in the early 1990s can claim credit for this improved performance.

Comparing Economic Performance

To examine the impact of democratization on economic performance, I create the following subcategories of countries. First, five countries – Botswana, Gambia, Senegal, Mauritius, and Zimbabwe – were already multiparty democracies in 1989. These states were far from perfect democracies. The incumbent has never lost an election in Zimbabwe, for example, while Diouf's defeat in 1999 was the first such defeat in Senegal. Except arguably for Mauritius, all of these governments have demonstrated authoritarian tendencies on multiple occasions. But all of these states have had significantly greater pluralism than the remaining states in the region over an extended period, with at least two decades of relatively stable multiparty electoral politics. I thus create a category called "old democracies" for these states.

Of the remaining forty-three countries in the sample, only Sudan and Liberia did not undergo significant political reform in the early 1990s. Of these, I exclude eleven in which past civil war and/or current political strife would have precluded normal economic policy making. By this criterion, Liberia, Sudan, Angola, Chad, Ethiopia, Eritrea, Rwanda, Sierra Leone, Somalia, Mozambique, and Zaire are excluded.[27] Several

26. Calculated from the World Bank, *African Development Indicators*, Table 2–18.
27. Note that in previous work (Bratton and van de Walle, *Democratic Experiments*), I defined Mozambique as having undertaken a complete political transition. Nonetheless, the consequences of a decade-long civil war of tragic destructiveness continues to powerfully condition economic performance in the country. Chad was excluded for similar reasons. For its part, Liberia may or may not have successfully ended its civil war and begun a transition to democratic governance with the elections conducted in July 1997.

of these states achieved good economic performance in the 1990s, but this is clearly far more related to the return of peace than it is to regime characteristics. Thus, Mozambique has enjoyed the highest growth rate in the region in the 1990s, but it remains considerably poorer than it was before its devastating civil war. Following a similar logic, I exclude Burundi, a country whose democratic transition was too quickly reversed by a military coup in October 1993 and plunged into civil strife to allow a meaningful before and after comparison.

This leaves thirty-one countries in the sample. Of these, twenty-nine countries in sub-Saharan Africa convened *founding* elections between November 11, 1989, and December 31, 1994. The first date is that of the Namibian elections and constitutes a handy starting point for this wave of democratization in Africa. The latter date is somewhat more arbitrary, but conveniently allows us at least two points of economic data following the transition and covers all of the free and fair elections in which an incumbent was ousted. These were founding elections in the sense that the office of the head of government was openly contested following a period during which multiparty political competition had been denied. For many countries, this was the first election in over a decade, and for most the first multiparty election since the immediate postindependence period. Of these thirty-one states, Namibia and South Africa are excluded because the presence of an economic boycott before their transition makes a "before and after" comparison misleading, while Djibouti is excluded because of the absence of adequate data. This leaves twenty-eight states for which an analysis of the impact of democratization can be realized.

I undertake two types of comparisons. First, the performance of the new democratic regimes is compared with those of countries that did not engage in a full transition. Of the twenty-nine countries, thirteen could claim to have passed a relatively stringent test of democratization: a transition election had been widely viewed as "free and fair," typically by international observers, and the loser had publicly accepted the results.[28] Such a minimal, procedural definition of democracy helps to distinguish these states from the others in the data set, in which the degree of polit-

28. See Bratton and van de Walle, *Democratic Experiments*, Chapter 3, for a complete justification of this classification. The countries in each category are listed at the bottom of Table 2. Note that in all of these countries, except for Guinea-Bissau and Seychelles, the incumbent was also ousted during the founding election. The latter two cases are included because of the widespread agreement by domestic and international observers that their founding elections had been free and fair.

ical liberalization had fallen short of a complete transition to democracy in some way, despite the convening of elections. Comparing the economic performance of these two sets of countries should generate some insight into the economic impact of democratization.

As I have already suggested, it is unfortunately difficult to distinguish all the cases as clearly as one would like. Most of the nondemocratic states can legitimately claim significant political liberalization during this period. Typically, they held multiparty elections in which an incumbent ruler more or less stage managed multiparty elections that he could not lose and has since then tolerated some degree of opposition, again so long as it is not threatening. The more egregious pseudodemocracies are easy to exclude from the "new democracies" category. For instance, no one claims Cameroon and Togo to be democracies, given the obvious abuses of executive power and the continuing limitations on basic civic and political rights, and despite some real liberalization during the early 1990s. However, the Rawlings government in Ghana, say, can claim to have won two reasonably free and fair elections in 1992 and 1996. Despite the government's occasional crackdowns and attempts at intimidation, a free press and opposition parties do exist.[29]

On the other hand, Zambia's democratic reputation has been tarnished by evidence of the government's continuing authoritarian proclivities and various abuses of its power.[30] The point is that honest observers can differ about which states belong in which category. Rather than rely entirely on judgments some will find questionable, the comparison between "new democracies" and "nondemocracies" is complemented with a second kind of comparison, across time. Regardless of the exact nature of the regime, it can be argued that all of these regimes have been significantly liberalized, with the onset of elections since 1989 to have had an impact on economic decision making. I thus compare the economic performance of all the twenty-nine states of sub-Saharan Africa that are in my sample before and after 1991 to attempt to determine the economic impact of this new political climate.

29. E. Gyimah-Boadi, "Ghana's Encouraging Elections: The Challenges Ahead," *Journal of Democracy* 8 (1997): 78–91; and Terrence Lyons. "Ghana's Encouraging Elections: A Major Step Forward," *Journal of Democracy* 8 (1997): 65–77.
30. Caroline Baylies and Morris Szeftel, "The 1996 Zambian Elections: Still Awaiting Democratic Consolidation," *Review of African Political Economy* 71 (1997): 113–28; and Michael Bratton and Daniel Posner, "A First Look at Second Elections in Africa, with Illustration from Zambia," in Richard Joseph (ed.), *State, Conflict and Democracy in Africa* (Boulder, CO: Lynne Rienner, 1999), pp. 377–408.

Finally, I create a smaller category of "liberal democracies," which includes the nine states that Freedom House categorized as liberal in 1998: Benin, Botswana, Cape Verde, Malawi, Mali, Mauritius, Namibia, São Tomé, and South Africa. This category include seven states in which incumbents were ousted in elections in the 1990s and brings back into the analysis states I otherwise excluded from the analysis (for example, South Africa). The before and after comparison makes no sense for this category, but their performance in the 1990s can be usefully compared with the other categories.

Comparing the Samples

I first look at the economic performance of African economies. The two indicators used are real GDP growth and inflation, two standard measures of economic performance. The economic record for 1986–1988, the three last years before the onset of democratization on the continent, is compared with the equivalent record for the first three years after the founding election of the emerging democracy.[31] When data were not available for 1998, the data reported cover the last available year, almost invariably 1997.

The results are provided in Table 6.2, for the four categories of regimes. The table provides estimates comparing the slightly longer periods 1986–1991 and 1991–1995, and 1995–1998 to lessen the impact of single-year data points. Since these are overall growth rates that do not take into account population growth, typically well above 2 percent annually, our estimates suggest that all three categories are barely growing at all in per capita terms. Interestingly, these numbers suggest that the current official optimism about the region appears to be based largely on the growth record in the war-torn countries I have excluded from my analysis. In countries not previously undermined by civil war, the mid-1990s does not appear to have brought on substantially better economic performance.

Otherwise, no single pattern emerges from these estimates. The numbers suggest that the old democracies and nondemocracies have both slightly outperformed the new democracies, both before and after the transition period, and the partly overlapping category of liberal democracies has performed slightly above the regional average. Unfortunately, this differential is too small to be significant in analytical or statistical terms, given

31. If no founding election could be identified, I used the period of data for 1993–1995, since the modal year for founding elections was 1992.

Table 6.2. *Economic Performance before and after Transition Elections*

	1986–91	1991–95*	1995–98	Period around Transition	
				1986–88	3 Years After
New Democracies					
Annual GDP growth[i]	2.5	2.3	4.1	2.3	3.1
Average inflation rate	22.4	29.0	21.2	19.3	31.0
Average terms of trade[ii]	120.5	103.0	99.0	129.6	100.6
Nondemocracies					
Annual GDP growth[i]	3.1	2.8	6.5	3.2	3.8
Average inflation rate	19.8	16.5	11.6	24.4	18.3
Average terms of trade[ii]	113.8	101.2	99.4	118.1	100.8
Old Democracies					
Annual GDP growth[i]	5.6	2.7	4.5	6.4	2.8
Average inflation rate	10.5	11.9	9.4	11.1	12.1
Average terms of trade[ii]	108.7	102.1	100.8	111.1	100.4
Liberal Democracies					
Annual GDP growth[i]	3.4	4.5			3.6
Average inflation rate	17.0	18.3			18.8
Average terms of trade[ii]	102.7	98.6			104.6

Notes
[i] in Constant U.S. dollars.
[ii] 1995 = 100.
New democracies include Benin, Cape Verde, Central African Republic, Congo, Guinea-Bissau, Lesotho, Madagascar, Malawi, Mali, Niger, São Tomé, Seychelles, Zambia; *Nondemocracies* include Burkina Faso, Cameroon, Comoros, Côte d'Ivoire, Equatorial Guinea, Gabon, Ghana, Guinea, Kenya, Mauritania, Nigeria, Swaziland, Tanzania, Togo, and Uganda; *Old democracies* include Botswana, Gambia, Mauritius, Senegal, Zimbabwe; *Liberal democracies* include Benin, Botswana, Cape Verde, Malawi, Mali, Mauritius, Namibia, São Tomé, and South Africa.
Source: Calculated from World Bank, *African Development Indicators* (Washington, DC: World Bank, 2000); not all of the estimates are based on the same number of data points, as coverage varies by indicator.

the high degree of variance within each category of states and the large number of countries that were removed from the data set before these averages were calculated. From this small number of observations, it is not possible to say either that there were significant differences in growth performance before and after the transition period, or that the sample of new democracies performed better or worse than the nondemocracies. The liberal democracies may well have demonstrated a superior record, but more data points are needed before such a conclusion can be confirmed.

Much the same conclusion emerges from a comparison of inflation rates, also reported in Table 6.2, although several factors clearly unrelated to regime condition the results. The new democracies averaged a 19.3 percent annual increase in the consumer price index increase for the three years before transitions began (1986–88) and a 31 percent increase for the three years following their founding election; the set of comparable nondemocracies achieved rates of 24.4 percent and 18.3 percent for the same two periods. The jump in inflation rates in the new democracies is entirely due to the effect of the January 1994 devaluation of the CFA franc in the ex-French colonies, which spurred a sharp rise in inflation in 1994–95. Given the unwillingness to devalue and give up fixed parity with the French franc, during the early 1990s these countries embarked on tough internal deflation programs. As a result, they had extremely low inflation, which averaged only 5.1 percent for the three years preceding their transitions, for the countries for which data exist. In comparison, the non-CFA countries in the sample of comparable states averaged 26.2 percent. France and the countries of the Zone finally agreed to a devaluation in January 1994 and as a result, inflation shot up in many countries of the Zone, to an average of 16.3 percent for the three years after transitions. Note that this was still less than the mean level of inflation in the rest of Africa, where it averaged 23.8 percent. In the subcategory of CFA country democracies, countries go from an average of 3.7 percent to 19.9 percent during this same period. In sum, increases within the Zone have much more to do with the 1994 devaluation and its aftermath than with political dynamics.

The particularities of the Franc Zone almost certainly have also had an impact on these growth data. Overvaluation of the currency and attempts to force depreciation and avoid devaluation progressively dampened economic dynamism across the zone after 1988. This effort was particularly noticeable in the richer countries along west Africa's coast (Côte d'Ivoire, Senegal, Cameroon, Benin), where overvaluation was the highest. Its negative impact on growth rates cut across political regimes, as did the salutary effect of the devaluation in January 1994. Thus, throughout the Zone, 1994 and 1995 saw a sharp increase of agricultural export-led growth.[32] One can be skeptical that this growth will be sustained, but the point is that its effects are confounding for the

32. Jacques Alibert, "Un bilan de la dévaluation du franc CFA," *Afrique Contemporaine* 179 (1996): 16–26; and Jean A. P. Clément, Johannes Mueller, Stephane Cosse, and Jean le Dem, *Aftermath of the CFA Franc Devaluation*, Occasional Paper 138, International Monetary Fund (Washington, DC: IMF, May 1996).

analysis. Given problems of reliability and comparability,[33] the only safe interpretation of these data is that they provide no evidence that increases in political competition and participation in the 1990s can be associated with lower economic growth or inflation.

Finally, Table 6.2 also reports on the evolution of the external terms of trade during this period. The data suggest a significantly greater average deterioration in the terms of trade for the new democracies since the late 1980s. This places the economic performance of the new democracies in a more favorable light, even if the quality of the data again urge cautious conclusions. For example, during the first three years following its transition, Zambia's terms of trade underwent a 40 percent decline, as copper prices tumbled.[34]

In one sense, at least, these findings are surprising. Because the actual process of regime transition is highly disruptive, one would expect worse economic performance, ceteris paribus, from the countries having undergone significant political reform, notably with incumbents losing power.[35] First, real transitions generate considerable uncertainty and presumably discourage investors, either the local kind who seek to protect their capital by exporting it or the foreign kind, which defers investments until the political picture clears up. Second, incumbent governments in the process of losing power are unlikely to be cautious stewards of the macroeconomy. Instead, they are likely to resort to desperate splurges of public expenditure to remain in power, or, once all appears lost, to asset stripping. Both can exert a cost on the economy with which the incoming government will be saddled. Finally, during the transition period itself, there is likely to be an interregnum of some length during which no government is effectively in power. Again, it is easy to imagine such a situation resulting in suboptimal management of the economy.

Why do the data presented not clearly identify an economic cost to the actual transition? It may be that transition effects are swamped by the exogenous factors just identified, such as the CFA devaluation and

---

33. On the abysmal quality of African data, see Alexander J. Yeats, "On the Accuracy of Africa Observations: Do Sub-Saharan Trade Statistics Mean Anything?" *World Bank Economic Review* 4 (1990): 135–56. The inflation data are particularly problematic as they typically concern only prices in the capital city and are often based on outdated consumption patterns.

34. In addition, severe drought throughout southern Africa in 1992–93 also hit the economy hard. See Lise Rakner, *Reforms as a Matter of Political Survival.*

35. I have examined the economic costs of Africa's democratic transitions at greater length in my essay, "Economic Reform in a Democratizing Africa," *Comparative Politics* 32 (1999): 21–42.

weather variability. Or it may reflect the superficial nature of democratization, which was not viewed by investors as substantially changing the economic environment in the country.

COMPARING GOVERNMENT PERFORMANCE

Economic growth and inflation are outcome variables and are influenced by a lot of factors other than the actions of governments. The analysis of the last section suggests that various exogenous factors have weighed heavily on the region's economies. In addition, it may be that there is a lag of several years before policy reform yields dividends in terms of improved performance. To best judge the economic impact of democratization on Africa in the 1990s, it is thus appropriate also to examine the actual policies pursued by governments. One standard measure of government policy performance is the size of the fiscal deficit, as it is widely accepted that large deficits precipitated the crisis and must be reduced for sustained growth to reemerge. Table 6.3 compares the evolution of the size of fiscal deficits before and after the transition period. The data include estimates of the deficit both with and without the contribution of grants, most of which consists of external resource flows. The quality and cross-national comparability of these data are questionable.[36] They do suggest that democratization has had little impact on the size of the fiscal deficit.

Interestingly, these data appear to show substantially higher average levels of deficits among the new democracies both before and after the transitions, as well as for the category of liberal democracies in the 1990s. These differentials turn out not to be statistically significant, however, given large variations within each group of states. Analysis reveals that the observed difference is largely due to the presence of several highly aid-dependent small states in the sample – in particular, the extraordinarily high deficits in São Tomé, Cape Verde, and Guinea-

36. Thus, the main data set used (World Bank, *African Development Indicators, 1997* [Washington, DC: World Bank, 1997] does not report data for the period for four of the countries in the data set (Equatorial Guinea, Lesotho, Swaziland, and Congo/Zaire). Most annoyingly, there are wide and unexplained divergences between this data set and others that were consulted. They even vary widely across different publications of the World Bank. Thus, compare the estimates provided in Table 3, with those reported in Lawrence Bouton, Christine Jones, and Miguel Kiguel, *Macroeconomic Reform and Growth in Africa*, World Bank Policy Research Working Paper, no. 1394 (Washington, DC: World Bank, December 1994); or in the World Bank, *Adjustment in Africa*.

Table 6.3. *Economic Policy Performance before and after Transition Elections*
(as a percentage of GDP)

	1986–91 (Average)	1991–95 (Average)	1995–98	Period around Transition	
				1986–88	3 Years After
Fiscal Balance (excluding grants)					
New democracies	−13.7	−16.3	−14.0	−13.7	−14.9
Nondemocracies	−9.0	−8.5	−4.3	−9.9	−8.7
Old democracies	−2.3	−2.9	−4.41	−2.7	−3.9
Liberal democracies		−13.4	−12.9		−12.7
Fiscal Balance (including grants)					
New democracies	−6.6	−8.9	−7.2	−5.4	−8.2
Nondemocracies	−4.5	−4.5	−4.0	−5.3	−4.6
Old democracies	−1.1	−1.1	−2.6	−1.9	−4.6
Liberal democracies		−7.9	−7.2		−7.0
Government Consumption					
New democracies	19.0	18.8	17.1	19.8	18.0
Nondemocracies	16.6	15.6	13.0	16.8	15.5
Old democracies	16.4	16.5	15.3	17.1	16.5
Liberal democracies		22.2	21.4		22.3
Investment					
New democracies	14.4	15.6	12.3	12.7	14.7
Nondemocracies	8.4	7.5	6.0	7.8	6.3
Old democracies	5.8	6.2	7.6	5.7	6.3
Liberal democracies		13.5	13.5		12.3

Note: Negative values for fiscal balance implies a net deficit.
For countries included in each regime category, see Table 6.2.
Grants refers to Capital grants provided to the government, which consist in large part of foreign aid.
Source: Calculated from World Bank, *African Development Indicators, 2000* (Washington, DC: World Bank, 2000), various tables.

Bissau, in each case averaging between a third and half of GDP during this period, and entirely sustained by foreign aid. I discuss the political impact of aid in a later section. The important point to retain from this analysis is that the data emphasize the continuing importance of international public flows to sustain what have remained extremely imbalanced fiscal systems.

Table 6.3 also reports data on the share of government consumption in GDP, and the share of GDP devoted to investment – two other standard measures of governmental policy performance. Since a standard objective of reform programs has been the slimming down of the state and the reorientation of expenditures toward investment, it is a good measure of the reform progress made. Again, there is little evidence of a distinct break between the time periods around the transition. The share of both government consumption and of investment in GDP appears systematically higher in the new democracies, but once again, this differential is not significant and largely disappears when São Tomé, Cape Verde, and Guinea-Bissau are excluded from the data set.[37]

The evidence presented so far suggests that the democratization of African politics in the early 1990s has not had the kind of dramatic effect on economic performance and government policy making predicted by many observers in the early 1990s. If there is any trend in the data it is toward economic improvement, although it is faint so far and does not appear solely related to regime type. Other, largely exogenous factors, such as the evolution in the terms of trade and the French imposed devaluation of the CFA franc appear to have exerted a more powerful influence on economic conditions. The remainder of this chapter will interpret this continuity.

THE POLITICAL IMPACT OF DEMOCRATIZATION

In sum, the significant political liberalization that occurred in the 1990s has not so far had a significant impact on economic performance. The most one can say is that the new democracies may be in the process of outperforming the nondemocracies, but that it remains much too early to reach definite conclusions about the impact of political reform. To understand this situation, I examine the assumptions that typically undergird the view that democratization would negatively affect economic reform and performance. I then emphasize the institutional continuities that appear to have prevailed across the changes in regime.

A Participatory Explosion?

The prediction that democratization was going to introduce to Africa a participatory explosion, in which populist and interest group pressures

---

37. It should be noted in this context that World Bank cross-national studies of African economies often exclude states with a GNP inferior to U.S.$1 million, arguing that aid flows to these states prevent meaningful policy comparisons. See, for example, World Bank, *Adjustment in Africa*.

would compel governments to increase their expenditures to maintain popularity, has proven to be fanciful. There has always been something of a *protest cycle* in African countries, in which leaders responded to periodic protests and political crises by resorting to patronage and subsidies benefiting key constituents.[38] But the macroeconomic significance of these practices was due less to the power of interest groups than to the fragile legitimacy of leaders and the weak mobilizational capacities of their single parties. In the 1990s, there have been several episodes of governments seeking to retain waning electoral support by temporarily opening the public purse, but these cases do not validate the political business cycle theories of Western democracies, in which macroeconomic stability is threatened when government responds to a mobilized electorate right before an election.[39] The more egregious cases have been in the liberalized autocracies like Ghana (the election in 1992) or Kenya (1992) rather than in the second elections for the new democracies like Zambia (1996), Benin (1995), or Mali (1997). It might also be noted that the early data regarding second and third elections in Africa following democratization have been characterized by declining participation rates, relative to the earlier founding elections.[40] Table 6.4 shows that the proportion of registered voters bothering to vote has declined to below two-thirds. Given low levels of voter registration, it has not been unusual for less than a third of the adult population to bother voting in subsequent elections.

As I have argued throughout this book, African political systems have been characterized by their relatively low levels of political participation. It was fanciful to expect democratization to change this state of affairs quickly. Compared to the more mature democracies of the West, civil society has long been poorly organized and nonrepresentative. True, the political salience of associational life varies across countries in the region, and its variation will increase over time; nonetheless, nongovernmental actors that could channel and mobilize participation following the political liberalization of the early 1990s were typically only recently formed, with shaky finances and small memberships. Their

38. See, for instance, John A. Wiseman, "Urban Riots in West Africa, 1977–1985," *Journal of Modern African Studies* 24 (1986): 509–18.
39. For instance, William Nordhaus, "The Political Business Cycle," *Review of Economic Studies* 42 (1975): 169–90; and Michael S. Lewis-Beck, *Economics and Elections: The Major Western Democracies* (Ann Arbor: University of Michigan Press, 1990), pp. 137–52.
40. For a discussion, see Michael Bratton, "Second Elections in Africa," *Journal of Democracy* 9 (1998): 51–66.

Table 6.4. *First and Second Legislative Elections in Africa, 1989–1998*

	First Election (n = 41)	Second Election (n = 26)
Number of parties competing	13.1	12.2
Number of parties winning seats	6.3	7.6
Number of effective parties	2.85	2.4
Share of seats to biggest party	63.1	69.7
Turnout (% of registered voters)	63.9	61.3

Source: Data assembled and calculated by author.

clout remains often undermined by their fragmentation, notably along ethnoregional lines.[41]

A lively written press has emerged, but its circulation levels and outside surveys suggest it reaches no more than a small proportion of the urban population. Overwhelmingly, radio remains the medium by which Africans receive their news and it typically remains safely in government hands. For instance, a survey of rural southern Cameroon in 1994 estimated that 0.2 percent of rural households read newspapers on a regular basis, while 44 percent listened to the radio.[42] Accounts of the 1999 presidential election in Senegal emphasized the key role that newly legalized private radio stations had played in publicizing the message of the opposition and in monitoring polling stations on election day, sharply raising the cost to the government of any attempt to tamper with the results.[43] But the privatization of the air waves remains limited to a minority of states in the region, as most governments have proven unwilling to let go of their monopoly over this strategic means of communication.

41. Thomas Callaghy, "Civil Society, Democracy and Economic Change in Africa: A Dissenting Opinion about Resurgent Societies," in John W. Harbeson, Donald Rothchild, and Naomi Chazan (eds.), *Civil Society and the State in Africa* (Boulder, CO: Lynne Rienner, 1994), pp. 231–254; René Lemarchand, "Uncivil States and Civil Societies: How Illusion Became Reality," *Journal of Modern African Studies* 30 (1992): 177–91; Célestin Monga, "Civil Society and Democratization in Francophone Africa," *Journal of Modern African Studies* 33 (1995): 359–81; and Peter Lewis, "Political Transition and the Dilemmas of Civil Society in Africa," *Journal of International Affairs* 93 (1992): 323–40.
42. Georges Courade and Véronique Alary, "Les planteurs Camerounais ont-ils été réévalués," *Politique Africaine* 54 (1994): 74–87, p. 80.
43. For instance, "Les ondes de la transparence: avec peu de moyens, les radios privées freinent les velléités de fraude," *Libération* (February 28, 2000): 6.

Similarly, a small active opposition may conduct well-publicized protests in the parliament or outside the presidential palace, but it typically cannot rely on the support of large segments the population, particularly outside the capital, and it does not mobilize large crowds with any regularity. For the most part, the increase in participation compared to the ancien régime has been no more than modest.

The claim is sometimes made that the democratic forces that took power in the early 1990s represented a new social coalition. The emergence of such a coalition, representing different economic interests, might have had programmatic policy implications. As I argued above, however, the language of social coalitions is in fact highly misleading for Africa, because interest groups and professional associations are poorly organized and comparatively weak there, and because the structure of national economies has tended to lessen the salience of class identities and cleavages.[44] In some countries, nonetheless, it is true that private business had actively supported the democratization movement, and appeared ready to influence the emergent democratic governments. They had become fed up with autocratic governments whose brand of desultory management, misguided policies, and corruption created a climate in which it was difficult for business to remain profitable. Business funding was critical to the success of the democracy movement in many countries.[45] As a result, businessmen exerted considerable influence in the first cabinets following democratization in countries like Madagascar, Benin, and Zambia.

This led directly to progress on institutional reform issues of importance to private business, in particular, privatization, notably of public utilities, whose inefficiencies had long hampered business competitiveness. This influence must not be exaggerated: business rarely spoke with one voice, particularly in areas like trade reform on which it was divided. Rent-seeking motivations did not disappear with democratization, which sometimes resulted in little more than the eviction of one set of crony businessmen in favor of another. Governments could moreover placate business with favors, while seeking policy inspiration from other parts of the alliance that had brought them to power.

Interestingly, the move to multiparty politics did have the effect of changing the process of elite accommodation within the state elite, and

44. For a review and references, see John Healey and Mark Robinson, *Democracy, Governance and Economic Policy: Sub-Saharan Africa in Comparative Perspective* (London: Overseas Development Institute, 1992).
45. Bratton and van de Walle, *Democratic Experiments in Africa*, pp. 167–8.

this may, in time, have important political consequences. During the 1970s and 1980s, leaders sought to build broad elite coalitions, involving all the country's ethnoregional groups. Political alliances were broad, even if they were shallow, notably in social terms. Indeed, the inclusiveness of these coalitions was one of their legitimating properties.[46] Democratization has created a new dynamic, in the context of advanced economic austerity. Now that state leaders can seek legitimacy from the ballot box, they are more likely to seek to build minimally winning coalitions that provide an electoral majority but make no claim to inclusiveness. In the region's more democratic countries, characterized by more or less free and fair elections, this dynamic is promoted by the overwhelmingly ethnoregional nature of political parties and voting.[47] Whereas the old single party had usually sought nationwide support, the new government party in countries like Zambia, Malawi, or Benin may prove content with the construction of a multiethnic coalition that will gain somewhere between half and two-thirds of the votes. In pseudo-democracies like the ones prevailing in Cameroon, Kenya, or Côte d'Ivoire, this dynamic is emerging even more clearly. The composition of the cabinet and official pronouncements suggest that Paul Biya no longer seeks Bamileke support,[48] for example; in Côte d'Ivoire, the Bedie regime's antinorthern rhetoric was striking in its stridency before the December 1999 coup toppled him,[49] while the Moi regime has made

46. On this point, see the excellent discussion in Jean-François Bayart, *L'etat en Afrique: la politique du ventre* (Paris: Fayard, 1987), especially pp. 193–226; and Donald Rothchild and Michael Foley, "African States and the Politics of Inclusive Coalitions," in Donald Rothchild and Naomi Chazan (eds.), *The Precarious Balance: State and Society in Africa* (Boulder, CO: Westview Press, 1988), pp. 149–71.
47. See Nicolas van de Walle and Kimberly Butler, "Political Parties and Party Systems in Africa's Illiberal Democracies," *Cambridge Review of International Affairs 13* (1999): 14–28. The case of Zambia is admirably explored in Daniel Posner, "Ethnicity and Ethnic Politics in Zambia" (unpublished chapter of Ph.D. dissertation, Harvard University, 1999).
48. Recent ethnic politics in Cameroon are well covered in Luc Sindjoun, *La politique d'affection en Afrique Noire: société de parenté, "société d'état" et libéralization politique au Cameroun*, Occasional Paper Series, African Association of Political Science, no. 2 (1998); and Hélène-Laure Menthong, "Vote et communautarisme au Cameroun: "un vote de coeur, de sang et de raison," *Politique Africaine 69* (1998): 40–52. See also Francis Nyamnjoh, "Cameroon: A Country United by Ethnic Ambition and Difference," in *African Affairs 98* (1999), 101–18.
49. Personal communication, Barbara Lewis. These issues are also discussed from a slightly different perspective by Richard C. Crook in his essay. "Winning Coalitions and Ethno-Regional Politics: The Failure of the Opposition in the 1990 and

fewer efforts to court Kikuyu voters as the 1990s progressed.[50] These are dangerous strategies: there are inherent costs in excluding such key parts of the electorate, which may in the long run undermine national stability. At the same time, for politicians operating on a short time horizon, they are tempting solutions to the need to maintain patronage-based political machines in an environment of growing resource scarcities.

A Weakened Executive?

The second assumption was that democratization would result in the weakening of executive authority and this worsened the prospects for sound economic policies. During the transition, pro-democracy forces in a number of African countries had indeed voiced their ambition to weaken the institutional power of the presidency in order to reduce the abuses of power that had characterized the ancien régime. As a result of these transition debates, checks on executive power were instituted in a number of countries.

In Madagascar, Congo, the Central African Republic (CAR), Benin, and Niger, the executive did not secure a clear legislative majority and the national legislature used this new power to significantly check presidential action. The result of weak government parties lacking a clear majority following the transition was the near paralysis of legislative politics.[51] In none of these countries did the same party lead a legislative majority by the end of 1998, except in the CAR, where a much weakened Patassé barely survived thanks to French support and despite repeated military mutinies. Military interventions ended the democracy in Congo and Niger, while opposition parties won nominal control of parliaments following second elections in Madagascar and Benin, albeit with no more impressive a majority.

1995 Elections in Côte d'Ivoire," *African Affairs* 96 (1997): 215–42. Crook argues that ethnic issues were first manipulated by the opposition during the 1990s elections, only to be then adopted by the majority in 1995. Since then, the government's antinorthern stance has emerged much more clearly. See "Fishermen Feel, Xenophobia in 'Pure Ivoirian' Pride," *New York Times*, August 8, 1999, p. 3, and "Turbulences en Côte d'Ivoire," *Le Monde*, October 8, 1999, p. 32, for more recent informations on these ethnic issues.

50. The ethnic dimensions to the 1997 elections are well described in Joel D. Barkan and Njuguna Ng'ethe, "Kenya Tries Again," *Journal of Democracy* 9 (1998): 32–49.

51. At the same time, in other work, I have shown that the weaker the largest party, the more likely the democratic gains from the transition are to be preserved in the 1990s. See van de Walle and Butler, "Political Parties and Party Systems."

In the endless parliamentary squabbling that occurred in these countries following the transition, sustaining progress on economic reform proved very difficult. In Benin, for instance, President Soglo and the parliamentary opposition sparred for most of 1992–1994 over the extent of presidential prerogatives. Lacking a solid majority in the legislature, Soglo had difficulties even passing his budget in 1994, when the legislature rejected his proposals for civil service salary and student stipend increases and proposed substantially higher ones that the government protested would have undermined its adjustment program.[52] The deadlock was eventually overcome through the intervention of the supreme court, but not before paralyzing reform for many months and leaving the government's capacity to undertake policy reform compromised. But was this evidence of political participation playing itself out in the more open climate of multiparty politics? Magnusson's careful account suggests instead that it was factional infighting within a fairly narrow political class in the midst of growing popular alienation. He points out, moreover, that civil service and student organizations were actually weakened by the fall of the single party; the new democratic order had brought about the multiplication of weak and competing unions and student organizations and the end of corporatist arrangements between privileged single-peak organizations and the government.[53]

In most countries, the movement to multiparty politics has been characterized by the relatively quick emergence of a dominant party system, following the first and or second multiparty election. Indeed, as shown in Table 6.4, the average share of legislative seats going to the winning party was strikingly high in first elections (63.1%) and then even higher in second elections (69.7%). The party that thus emerges may owe its dominance to ethnic reasons or to superior leadership, or just as often to its ability to manipulate electoral rules, and to the advantages of incumbency. It wins a strong majority of seats in parliament and then systematically uses the advantages of incumbency to strengthen its position. As Van Cranenburgh has argued with respect to Tanzania, "the superior organizational, material and symbolic resources of the govern-

52. See the illuminating analysis by Bruce Magnusson, "Benin: Legitimating Democracy: New Institutions and the Historical Problem of Economic Crisis," *l'Afrique politique 1996, démocratisation: arrêts sur images* (Paris: Karthala, 1996), pp. 33–54.
53. Ibid. See also the interesting work by Richard Banégas, "Marchandisation du vote, citoyenneté et consolidation démocratique au Bénin," *Politique Africaine* 69 (1998): 75–88.

ing party" are likely to result in the emergence of a dominant party system.[54] Just as important in the democracies in which a new majority emerged in the 1990s, the new government party thrives and gets stronger electorally, despite the inevitable fractionalization of the democratic alliance that spearheaded the transition. Thus, the MMD in Zambia retained its solid legislative majority following the 1996 elections, despite the progressive defection to the opposition of most of its original members.[55] These dynamics largely explain why so few incumbents have lost free and fair elections following the transition, with only presidents in Benin and Madagascar suffering electoral defeats.

Hence, far from a weakened executive, with a small number of exceptions, the continuation of executive dominance of the political system following the introduction of electoral politics remains patent. It is indeed striking and puzzling that not a single democratizing state chose to move to a parliamentary form of government that enshrined parliamentary dominance over the executive. It is hard to avoid the sentiment that an opportunity was lost in many of these transitions to undermine the neopatrimonial tendency toward presidentialism and introduce parliamentary control of government, which is inherently less prone to individual abuses of power. This is particularly true in some of the smaller countries in the region, like Mali, Benin, or Malawi, which seemed well suited to parliamentary government. The fact that many of these countries did engage in constitutional engineering during their transitions, in some cases undergoing substantial changes in electoral rules, only makes the failure for a single one to adopt some form of parliamentary system more puzzling.[56] Surely, it speaks at least in part to the continuing attraction to African politicians of the neopatrimonial model of presidentialism.

This executive dominance is enhanced by the state apparatus. Whatever new formal mechanisms of accountability and transparency have

54. Oda Van Cranenburgh, "Tanzania's 1995 Multi-Party Elections: The Emerging Party System," *Party Politics* 2 (1996): 535–47, p. 545.
55. Caroline Baylies and Morris Szeftel, "The 1996 Zambian Elections: Still Awaiting Democratic Consolidation," *Review of African Political Economy* 71 (1997): 113–128.
56. Such constitutional engineering was usually designed to manage minority and ethnic divisions. See Andrew Reynolds, *Electoral Systems and Democratization in Southern Africa* (New York: Oxford University Press, 1999); Timothy D. Sisk, and Andrew Reynolds (eds.), *Elections and Conflict Management in Africa* (Washington, DC: United States Institute of Peace, 1998); and Harvey Glickman, (ed.), *Ethnic Conflict and Democratization in Africa* (Atlanta, GA: African Studies Association Press, 1995).

been adopted by the new regime are likely to be overshadowed by a state apparatus that democratization has not purged of its long-standing authoritarian tendencies. Administrations have too long been used to functioning with few external constraints to change quickly. Parliaments often lack the technical expertise and administrative savvy to exercise whatever new powers of control they have gained over executive decision making. Judiciaries, suffering from legacies of inadequate resources and political interference, also need time to assert their prerogatives. As Kwasi Prempeh notes, the African judiciary have often continued to implement a "jurisprudence of executive supremacy" instead of a new "jurisprudence of constitutionalism," even in countries in which constitutional reform gives it considerable independence.[57]

Institutional Continuities

In sum, the evidence suggests that democratization has not altered long-standing political patterns in African politics. In time, democratization may profoundly change these patterns, but by itself, the onset of multiparty electoral politics left unchanged many of the defining characteristics of African politics, notably presidential dominance and low participation. Much the same could be said about other features of these neopatrimonial rule. Whatever the initial intentions of the new regimes, they were susceptible to the same pull and push factors that have long favored neopatrimonial practices in the region. On the one hand, the transition did little to change the enduring weakness of vertical and horizontal accountability mechanisms facing executives. On the other hand, clientelism and rent-seeking have continued to be attractive to poorly integrated political systems, with weak interest aggregation institutions, ethnic divisions, and underperforming economies.

One highly imperfect but suggestive measure of this continuity is the size of the cabinet of ministers, which I already examined in Chapter 2. Comparing the size of cabinets over time and across regime type may be instructive regarding the persistence of antidevelopmental neopatrimonial practices. It might be argued that democratic regimes would result in bigger cabinets as they would face pressures to be inclusive. On the other hand, it might be argued that their cabinets would be smaller, given a reaction against the neopatrimonial tendencies of their predecessors.

57. H. Kwasi Prempeh, "A New Jurisprudence for Africa," *Journal of Democracy* 10 (1999): 135–49.

I collected data on cabinets at two points of time: July/August 1988 and August/September 1996. New democracies had cabinets averaging 19.5 and 20.6 members, respectively, while nondemocracies averaged 26.4 and 24.8 members for the two periods. The two biggest cabinets were in authoritarian states: Gabon, with forty-seven members at the earlier date, and Cameroon's cabinet in 1996, which included forty-two members.

The stability in cabinet sizes over time is striking, as if most countries had a fixed cabinet size through a political tradition respected by successive regimes. Ethnic diversity in a country probably increases cabinet size, as the government seeks to preserve national unity by including elites from all salient ethnoregional communities. Interestingly, this dynamic has not increased with the return of elections. Only in Madagascar and Malawi, both countries with serious ethnoregional divisions, have cabinets sharply increased in size over this period, from twenty-two and eleven to thirty-four and thirty, respectively. Overall, the practice of bloated cabinets, following long-standing national neopatrimonial traditions, has remained remarkably stable through the transition period.

Where there have been political discontinuities around the transition, they have favored improved policy making, at least in the initial days of the new government. A major theme of the fight against the old ruler had typically been the need to lessen corruption, mismanagement, and the politicization of decision making. This was to some degree self-serving: the democratic alliance was in part composed of men and women left out of the presidential patronage system. At the same time, clean government was one theme that could unite the often disparate democratic coalitions. Intellectuals, church leaders, and human rights activists could agree with the out-of-power politicos on the need to stamp out corruption, if nothing else. Thus, in countries like Benin, Mali, Madagascar, or Zambia, the first set of economic appointments emphasized apolitical technocrats, in part to reassure the donors and in part to lead this fight for good government. In most cases, however, these technocrats have seen their influence wane over time. The best example of this phenomenon may be Zambia.[58] The first MMD cabinet in 1991

58. The following account is largely derived from Lise Rakner, Nicolas van de Walle, and Dominic Mulaisho, "Aid and Reform in Zambia: A Country Case Study," Chr. Michelsen Institute, Bergen, Norway, unpublished paper for the Aid and Reform in Africa Project, World Bank, September 1999; and Dennis Chiwele and Nicolas van de Walle, "Democratization and Economic Reform in Zambia."

included prominent human rights activists, such as the first minister of justice, Roger Chongwe. It included several apolitical good government advocates such as the first minister of agriculture, Guy Scott, a white farmer with no previous political experience. Dipak Patel, a south Asian businessmen who represented the private sector community as minister of industry, was known to be a critic of the corrupt and inefficient parastatal sector.

By the end of 1994, all of these men had left government. The Zambian cabinet was soon dominated by older politicians who had once played a prominent role in the Second Republic under Kaunda, and who often had a well-deserved reputation for corruption. Once the voice of good government rhetoric of the most uncompromising variety, Chiluba put together a patronage machine to rival Kaunda's. By 1994, for instance, he had named forty-three MMD members of parliament (MPs) as deputy ministers (albeit without cabinet status), in addition to the twenty-three ministers of government and the handful of MPs in official parliamentary functions. The perquisites that came with this nomination were in sharp contrast to the net salary of roughly 150 dollars a month earned by regular backbenchers and would presumably be an instrument of presidential control of parliament.

Finally, policy continuity was more likely because few of the democratic governments reached power with a mandate to implement a specific set of economic policies. The literature has sometimes wrongly portrayed the democratic movements as motivated largely by opposition to structural adjustment.[59] Indeed, the dynamics that propelled the transition process forward often had little to do with economic policy issues. Transition politics was more typically concerned as much with such issues as how to reign in executive abuses of power, ensuring ethnoregional balance and, particularly toward the end of the transition process, constitutional debates. Although many of the initial protests that had begun the process of democratization expressed the economic grievances of groups like the civil service and students and a general anger about corruption and mismanagement, economic policy choices rarely featured prominently in national conferences or in the elections that marked the end of the transition. Instead, the democratic forces typically came to

Zambia Democratic Governance Project Monitoring and Evaluations Studies, report prepared for the U.S. Agency for International Development, Lusaka, Zambia, September 1994.

59. See Gibbon et al., *Authoritarianism, Democracy and Adjustment*, for a discussion.

power with a vague promise to improve living conditions by ridding the country of the dictator and his cronies.

Once in power, harsh budgetary realities and persuasive IFI experts as well as their own permanent secretaries convinced most governments against drastic changes in policy. Ideational continuities were reinforced by the fact that the political personnel who came to power with the new democratic governments were typically very similar to the outgoing political personnel. Not only did the government invariably retain virtually all the ministerial permanent secretaries of the previous regime, but much of the cabinet also had previous ministerial experience in the ancien régime.

Moreover, the dismal state of the civil service throughout the continent promoted continuity. In the transition countries of Eastern Europe, the new democratic governments that emerge have at their disposal a reasonably professional and effective civil service to carry out a set of new policies. This was much less likely in the regimes in sub-Saharan Africa, where three decades of economic crisis had devastated the professionalism, resources, and infrastructure of the state apparatus, sapping its capacity and morale. In many countries, the state barely functions and is capable of only the simplest administrative tasks. A significant reorientation of policy may not be possible in the short to medium term. The main constraints on state action continue to be self-induced, in other words, rather than imposed by external participatory pressures or institutional counterweights to executive dominance.

The Aid Regime

The final factor favoring continuity has been the relationship with the donors. It is useful to dismiss the claim that the fledgling democracies have been sustained thanks to extraordinarily generous external financial support. The pressure to democratize exerted by the Western donors and then their support for the ensuing democratic experiments led some to claim that they represented the main motor behind democratization.[60] These observers could point to countries like Zambia, in which the donors did reward the Chiluba government with an almost doubling of aid in the couple of years following the 1991 founding election. However,

60. For instance, Samuel Decalo, "The Process, Prospects and Constraints of Democratization in Africa," *African Affairs* 91 (1992): 7–35; and Richard Jeffries, "The State, Structural Adjustment and Good Governance in Africa," *Journal of Commonwealth and Comparative Politics* 31 (1993): 20–35.

the overall numbers on foreign aid tell a different story, with no real difference between the two sets of countries. According to the data of the OECD Development Assistance Committee, there is virtually no difference between the evolution in aid levels between the new democracies and nondemocracies. The new democracies received more aid per capita than did the nondemocracies, both before and after the transition, but this is largely an artifact of the "small country bias" of aid, resulting in very high totals going to such microstates as Cape Verde and the Seychelles. Comparing the average level of aid during the period 1990–1995 with the average for the period 1985–1990 yields an average increase of 37 percent in ODA for the nondemocracies and 33 percent for the new democracies. On the other hand, comparing the shorter periods of 1992–95 and 1988–1991 yields an average increase of 6 percent for the new democracies and a decline of 3 percent for the nondemocracies, which suggests a minor advantage to the democracies.[61]

The United States appears to be the only major donor systematically seeking to reward political liberalization in Africa,[62] and it is no longer an important enough donor to shape the overall resource flows to the region. Other bilateral donors generally did not resort to political criteria for their allocation of aid with any consistency or persistence. In fact, France, the biggest bilateral donor to the region, clearly favored authoritarian regimes like Cameroon, Côte d'Ivoire, and Togo with sharp increases in aid in the early 1990s, seemingly intent on helping vulnerable leaders there survive the democratization wave.[63]

Despite much support for the general principle of democratization, changes in aid volumes during the 1990s appear to have much more to do with the increasing willingness of the leading donors to selectively reward countries that follow their economic policy prescriptions. Thus, World Bank support to democratic Zambia sharply increased after 1991, but so did its support of authoritarian but pro-policy reform regimes in

---

61. Calculated from Table 12-5, World Bank, *African Development Indicators, 1997.*
62. The promotion of democracy was elevated to a central objective of all USAID programs by the Clinton administration. For a discussion, see Todd J. Moss, "US Policy and Democratization in Africa: The Limits of Universal Liberalism," *Journal of Modern African Studies* 33 (1995): 189–209.
63. This leads Célestin Monga to argue that the donors have a prodictatorship bias in their aid. Only for France, however, do the data clearly bear him out. See his essay, "Eight Problems with African Politics," The French case is well discussed in Banégas and Quantin, "Orientations et limites de l'aide Francaise," and Tony Chafer, "French African Policy: Towards Change," *African Affairs* 91 (1992): 37–51.

Uganda and Ghana. The year 1994 similarly witnessed substantial increase in aid volumes to many Franc Zone countries, as the IFIs (along with France) sought to ensure the success of the devaluation.

Despite donor rhetoric about the importance of democracy, it appears that the quality of the multiparty electoral politics that has emerged in the 1990s has not much mattered to the donors as long as governments play the "presentability" game. Some donors have sanctioned the particularly egregious manipulation of elections, notably in Togo, where the United States, Germany and the European Union have all suspended aid at some point in the 1990s, in response to government repression of the democracy movement.[64] Still, aid to Togo averaged some 13 percent of GDP from 1990 to 1995, slightly above the region's overall average of 12.7 percent during this period (excluding South Africa and Nigeria), and not much different from the 14 percent it had averaged from 1985 to 1989. In comparison, the liberal democracy and fairly comparable economy, Benin, received 14.9 percent of GDP in aid. As with the aggregate numbers, the cases of Togo and Benin thus suggest perhaps a small premium for the new democracies, but hardly a revolutionary change from past patterns.

Not only have the rewards for democratization been small, in addition, the donors have not responded to democratization with any changes in aid delivery modalities. The features described in the last chapter remain in place. In sum, the donor–government relationship changes little following a transition. After a brief honeymoon, and despite perhaps a short spurt of larger aid volumes, the donors go back to their curious brand of toothless conditionality and micromanagement, while governments go back to a combination of passive resistance and accommodation to donor pressures in a context of endemic fiscal crisis.

CONCLUDING REMARKS

My analysis has pointed to a great degree of continuity in African political economy. Both domestic and international institutions and the interests they rest on and sustain can change only slowly. The wave of democratization that hit Africa in the early 1990s represents a watershed set of events, which will continue to impact African politics for years to come. In the long run, neopatrimonial politics and democracy are almost

---

64. See Kodjo Koffi, "Togo: les deux ruptures de la coopération," *Afrique Contemporaine* 189 (1999): 63–76.

certainly not compatible, insofar as the latter introduces institutions of horizontal and vertical accountability on the executive. So, it is not inconceivable that the imperfect democratization of the 1990s will in time represent the beginning of much more fundamental change. As I have emphasized, however, by itself the introduction of multiparty electoral politics does not create democracy overnight, at least in its "liberal" variety.

In some respects, the assessment made in this chapter may prove premature. The analysis was well worthwhile, however, because so many observers argued that democratization would have an immediate and significant impact. But the patterns that have emerged in the first few years following the transition and which this chapter tracked, may not be sustained in time. If it is true that these regimes are hybrid ones, in which rational-legal and patrimonial tendencies coexist, then the recent political reform represents a small defeat for the latter. All over Africa, the long struggle to consolidate liberal democracy will continue.

7

Conclusion

The optimism that greeted African independence in 1960 seems incongruous today. Then, few Western observers doubted that Africa would develop rapidly, and many made favorable comparisons between the prospects of African countries like Ghana and those of Asian countries like Korea, which in 1956 enjoyed roughly the same economic level.[1] Most Western observers believed that African countries would build rapid industrialization through revenues provided by handsome prices for the primary commodities of the region. Anticipating a continuation of the Korean War commodities boom, few observers anticipated the volatility and downward trend that primary commodities would undergo in the 1960s and especially 1970s. More crucially, they did not view manpower constraints as particularly onerous and tended to be impressed with leaders like Nkrumah or Nyerere, who were generally believed to be capable of great things. In retrospect, the capacity of foreign aid to promote economic growth and build effective public institutions was greatly overestimated.

At the end of what is a fairly pessimistic account of Africa's contemporary political economy, it may be useful to remember how wrong these earlier outside observers have proved to be. I hope that this account, too, has missed a key trend or a critical new development, which will in time prove my pessimism to be unwarranted.

Certainly, Africa has changed dramatically over the last forty years. A number of long-term trends have the potential to change the political

1. The optimism of the period is well analyzed in David Fieldhouse, "Decolonization, Development and Dependence: A Survey of Changing Attitudes," in Prosser Guiford and William Roger Louis (eds.), *The Transfer of Power in Africa: Decolonization, 1940–1960* (New Haven, CT: Yale University Press, 1982), pp. 483–514.

dynamics in the region. First, while the region's public institutions have deteriorated and atrophied, the number of skilled African professionals has never been greater, although they too often live in exile or are not made use of by those in power. Perhaps that will change. I want to believe that the wave of democratization of the early 1990s described in the last chapter constituted the first and sometimes timid steps of a transformation that will reverse the last several decades of brain drain from the region. It is easy to be cynical about the admittedly imperfect process of democratization in most countries in the region. Yet, the Africa of today offers great new possibilities for developmental governance that did not exist twenty years ago, largely as a result of these imperfect political openings. As Sklar has reminded us, democracy progresses in fits and starts, and even small islands of democratic practice within an authoritarian system can pave the way for real change in time.[2] Along the same lines, improvements in one country put pressure on neighboring countries to change as well. Recent undeniable improvements, such as the introduction of multiparty politics, the rise of the NGO sector, and the emergence of an independent press during the 1990s may in time lead to real changes in how politics is practiced in the region.

Democratization is not the only potential change agent. Other structural changes are taking place. The Africa of the independence period was an overwhelmingly rural place, with a sea of illiterate peasants and an exceedingly small urban elite. Today, after a half century of rapid urbanization, Africa boasts several of the world's largest cities. Although we describe African societies as largely rural, the truth is that well over a third of all Africans live in towns, and in parts of the continent, as many as half do. Charles Tilly has taught us that the growth of cities has been critically important to the historical development of both capitalism and the modern state.[3] In other regions of the world, the political rise of the middle classes and of civil society is associated with the growth of urban centers. Cities provide the economies of scale that nurture a capitalist class, which eventually acquires a political project. Perhaps the emergence of cities like Lagos or Abidjan holds the same promise. Aili Tripp has described the struggles of informal market entrepreneurs in Dar es Salaam to assert their rights and protect their businesses from

2. Richard Sklar, "Toward a Theory of Developmental Democracy," in Adrian Leftwich (ed.), *Democracy and Development* (Cambridge, UK: Polity Press, 1996), pp. 25–45.
3. Charles Tilly, *Coercion, Capital and European States, A.D. 990–1992* (Cambridge, MA: Blackwell, 1992).

grasping state officials, in a process that is almost certainly repeating itself in other major African cities.[4] Over time, these struggles may generate an indigenous capitalist class that will be able to negotiate a genuine development project with the state. The growth of these mega cities is not always pretty, but it may in time alter many of the political and economic dynamics that toady appear permanent.

Finally, perhaps neopatrimonialism holds within itself the prospects for change. One of the themes of this book has been that the political exigencies of neopatrimonial regimes are incompatible with economic growth. In at least some cases, however, the interest of political elites may shift in the direction of favoring policies that promote capitalist accumulation. *Jeune Afrique* recently suggested that the barons of the Biya regime in Cameroon were becoming less tolerant of corruption now that their own fortunes were well established.[5] The prospects for a sudden end of state corruption in Cameroon seem poor, given how systematically it is entrenched, but this anecdote does remind us that in time, some rent-seeking politicians will become real businessmen and lend their support for the stable property rights, effective legal system, and decent roads that are needed to protect their investments. Much of the capital lost in the massive capital flight from Africa in these last three decades might actually be reinvested in the region if the macroeconomic environment were to become decent, and then perhaps the family fortunes made by the state's manipulating intervention in the economy will be reinvested in productive private enterprises. The point is that African political systems are relatively young, and the internal dynamics that resulted in massive corruption may evolve toward less dysfunctional systems.

A SUMMARY OF THE ARGUMENT

The analysis of the policy reform process in Africa between 1979 and 1999 revealed several broad trends. First, from out-and-out rejection of policies they opposed on political and ideological grounds, African leaders have evolved toward a more sophisticated management of the reform process, which allows for some significant progress without threatening their hold on power. Thus, there has been undeniable

---

4. Aili Mari Tripp, *Changing the Rules: The Politics of Liberalization and the Urban Informal Economy in Tanzania* (Berekely: University of California Press, 1997).
5. "Cameroun: Mains propres à Yaoundé," *Jeune Afrique* (November 23–29, 1999): 29.

progress on key elements of the stabilization component of reform, including exchange rate policy reform and more recently fiscal adjustment. The progress on the institutional reform measures that constitute structural adjustment has been much more uneven. The discussion of reform implementation in Chapter 2 shows clearly that reform measures have been partially undertaken, reversed, diverted, compensated for, and manipulated so that they do not threaten leaders' control over discretionary state resources. Thus, overall government consumption does not appear to have declined significantly over two decades of reform and, once aid resources to states are included, the total amount of resources controlled by governments has probably risen by several percentage points of GDP in the last twenty years.

The patterns of partial implementation of policy reform in the 1980s and 1990s have to be understood in the context of African rulers attempting to protect and adapt their mechanisms of rule to the increasingly stringent fiscal situation and the exigencies of the international donors. The pervasive clientelism in Africa should not be confused with what I termed "populism" in other regions of the world such as Latin America. Unlike the latter, clientelism in Africa does not result in state structures with low autonomy from social forces. It cannot be considered a mechanism for substantial redistribution of resources. Instead, a narrow, relatively autonomous political class uses state clientelism to forge intra-elite accommodation, across ethnolinguistic, regional, or other cleavages. Clientelism does suffuse society down to the village level, but its primary beneficiaries are limited to the higher reaches of the political elite. In sum, the economic policy status quo is not protected by well-organized societal interests that effectively prevent governments from carrying out reforms they know to be necessary and desirable. Clearly, there are plenty of examples across the region of unions, professional organizations, or business associations lobbying the government to some effect. Not all states have been equally autonomous. Nonetheless, my argument is that the key obstacle to growth-oriented economic policies is much more likely to have been the small number of senior state decision makers who have found it difficult to reconcile reform with their understanding of their own material interests.

This book has shown that the patterns of policy outcomes are compatible with a "state-centered" approach to the politics of reform. African governments have usually favored their own state structures within the observed patterns of public expenditure and they have responded to the economic crisis by protecting the state from cuts more than protecting key societal constituencies. Within the broad category of government consumption, states have sought to protect elites more than the lower rungs of the state apparatus.

Second, the flow of international aid to the region has greatly conditioned the process of reform. Donors have on the one hand directed the process in an increasingly intrusive manner. The discourse and ideology of economic liberalization was clearly donor driven, with remarkably little local support. In the field, the donors are an increasingly obtrusive presence. On the other hand, the donors' conditionality has proven mostly ineffectual and the large and historically unprecedented flow of resources to the region has clearly reduced the urgency of reform, probably strengthening the status quo. In fact, Chapter 5 showed that aid practices have on balance served to strengthen neopatrimonial tendencies in these countries. Conditionality may have tightened in the late 1990s, as the decline in overall aid flows and growing donor disillusion with the reform record may be resulting in a tougher attitude.

Third, to manage and survive this period of austerity and uncertainty, African presidents have sought to recentralize power. Chapter 4 showed that the reform process has been both a motive for and the mechanism by which African leaders have intensified the presidential tendencies of their regimes. Even as economic liberalization aimed to decentralize economic decision making, leaders have sought to recentralize the levers of economic power. This strategy has often been compatible with stabilization policies, but not, usually, with the broader institutional agenda of adjustment. The recentralization of power has not proven equally successful everywhere in the region. Some leaders have not been capable of managing the combined burdens of economic austerity, partial reform and political liberalization. In countries like Sierra Leone and Congo, the result has been the exacerbation of factional struggles over state resources, leading to the collapse of the central state.

Fourth, the period under study has witnessed a further and perhaps inevitable deterioration of state capacity. Maintenance and operations budgets have been woefully inadequate. Governments and donors have allowed the purchasing power of state officials to undergo a steady decline. In addition, the institutionalization of crisis management over a twenty-year period has dis-empowered central administrations for the benefit of donor experts and ad hoc domestic decision-making structures. The decline of state capacity has invigorated patrimonial tendencies throughout the region, with a noted increase in corruption and rent-seeking and a weakening of mechanisms of accountability and transparency that serve to limit such abuses.

Fifth, and a logical consequence of the previous trends, the reform process has motivated a progressive withdrawal of governments from key developmental functions they had espoused in an earlier era. All over Africa, the withdrawal from social services is patent, particularly outside the capital. In the poorest countries of the region, donors and NGOs have increasingly replaced governments, which now provide a minor proportion of these services. Even in the richest countries, the state's ability and willingness to service rural constituencies has atrophied. Paradoxically, many of the states in the region are both more centralized and bigger, and yet they appear to do less development work than they did before adjustment.

Sixth, finally, the wave of democratization that swept through the region in the early 1990s does not appear so far to have had much of an impact on these patterns. The widely predicted explosion in political participation did not take place, and the nature of decision making has remained much the same in the new democracies. There are reasons to believe that in the long term, democratization may well improve economic management by increasing the accountability and transparency of governments. Nonetheless, the introduction of regular multiparty elections by itself will not immediately change what remain neopatrimonial states with low capacity and unchecked executive power.

These patterns are remarkably robust across Africa. To be sure, reform has progressed more in some countries than in others. There is significant intraregional variation in resource endowments, historical legacies, and degree of state institutionalization. This book has argued that neopatrimonial regimes are hybrid regimes, and the exact mixture of rational-legal and patrimonial authority varies across regimes. Where there is more of the rational-legal type, the prospects for sustained reform are probably better. Where patrimonial authority dominates, even the most basic stabilization efforts are difficult to sustain. I have tried to emphasize these differences. But at the end of this exercise, the relative uniformity of results across the continent can only be considered striking. Fairly institutionalized states like Kenya and Côte d'Ivoire do not appear to have made significantly more progress on getting their economies on track than have very poor and highly personalized regimes in, say, Guinea or Togo.

Uganda and Ghana are often held up as the two most assiduous reformers in the region. Yet, despite a large flow of aid, the success they have achieved has been recent (clear only in the second decade of reform) and appears (particularly for Uganda) highly dependent on the commitment of a single leader, who will soon leave office. Across a wide set of policy indicators, moreover, these two "success stories" do not appear that different from the African median. For instance, their average fiscal deficits in the 1990s are actually well above average for the region. They both have enjoyed above-average records of economic growth in the 1990s, that would look much more impressive if performance in the 1970s had not been so bleak. In fact, real gross national product (GNP) per capita in Ghana was still 16 percent lower in 1998 than in 1970. Similar numbers are not available for Uganda, but it is noteworthy that after an annual GDP growth rate of 7.1 percent during the 1990s, Uganda still had a GNP per capita of U.S.$332 (constant 1995 terms), slightly under the African average of $338. Finally, both countries clearly exhibit several of the regional trends described in this work, notably the increase in rent-seeking and corruption.

Table 7.1 provides data that can illustrate this point. It divides GNP per capita for 1998 by the same statistic (in constant 1995 terms) for 1970. Thus, a high number suggests rapid growth while a number less than 1 indicates negative growth. Incredibly, the data report an average across the region of negative growth: the average country had a GNP in 1998 that was 91 percent of its size almost thirty years before. On the one hand, the table shows meaningful economic performance differences. Zambians saw their income cut almost in half during this period, for instance, while the average Burkinabe was 40 percent richer in 1998 than she had been in 1970. At the same time, once extraordinary circumstances are taken into account, it is remarkable how little variation there is. The top of the table includes several countries (Congo, Sierra Leone, Chad, Rwanda) with repeated episodes of civil war and chronic instability. The bottom of the table includes island countries (Mauritius, Seychelles) that have always been much richer than their neighbors on the continent and have a very different sociological makeup, notably with large non-African populations and distinct colonial histories. Many of the better performers (Congo, Gabon, Cameroon) owe their limited success to the discovery of oil during the period. Swaziland and Lesotho's growth records appear solid, but their role as labor preserves for the Republic of South Africa makes their achievement ambiguous. In the end, the only African country to have escaped the patterns described in this book enough to have sustained consistently rapid growth is Botswana. With a GDP more than six times higher in 1998 than in 1970,

Table 7.1. *GNP per Capita Ratios, 1998/1970*

Congo/Zaire	0.32
Sierra Leone	0.48
Niger	0.55
Madagascar	0.59
Zambia	0.59
Central African Republic	0.74
Guinea-Bissau	0.75
Mauritania	0.80
Ghana	0.84
Chad	0.85
Rwanda	0.85
Togo	0.86
Average, sub-Saharan Africa	0.91
Senegal	0.93
Mali	1.06
Benin	1.08
Côte d'Ivoire	0.89
Nigeria	0.96
South Africa	0.96
Burundi	0.89
Gambia	1.09
Cameroon	1.27
Malawi	1.32
Sudan	1.36
Zimbabwe	1.10
Burkina Faso	1.40
Kenya	1.48
Gabon	1.37
Congo, Republic of	1.50
Swaziland	1.80
Lesotho	2.51
Seychelles	2.53
Mauritius	3.36
Botswana	6.44

Notes: The number reports GNP per capita in constant 1995 terms for 1998 divided by GNP per capita for 1970.

Source: World Bank, *African Development Indicators, 2000* (Washington, DC: World Bank, 2000). Missing values reflect the absence of data, usually for 1970.

it is the only country that can claim to have engineered a structural transformation during this period.

Thus, there is an African model of economic policy making that is robust. Nonetheless, an obvious extension of the research presented in this book would be to attempt to explain in a more regorous manner the intra-African variations that we do observe. It would be interesting to examine the impact of an array of institutional, sociological, and historical variables on policy reform performance. Is the course of policy reform affected by the exact degree of centralization of power, for instance, or by the strength of civil society? Are there major differences in the degree of state legitimacy or of state capacity, and do these explain differences in economic performance? Interesting new research by Pierre Englebert strongly suggests that there are meaningful cross-national differences on these types of variables, and that they do explain the ability of states to provide policies that promote economic development.[6] To advance this kind of research on the issues of economic policy reform treated in this book will require the development of adequate quantitative indicators of policy reform, as well as better measures of potential independent variables. The poverty of the quantitative data in such areas as fiscal or trade policy is striking, while precise data on institutional reform, such as the precise status of agricultural marketing, simply do not exist in comparable form for more than a handful of countries at a time. The data used in the public policy debates on reform is often quite inadequate and does not withstand scrutiny. Too often, for example, data on officially set prices or tariffs are utilized uncritically, though the evidence is that they may have little bearing on reality in the market place.

COMPARATIVE IMPLICATIONS

This book has argued that Africa presents us with a distinct politics of reform, because of the weakness of interest groups, on the one hand, and the patrimonial nature of state authority, on the other hand. That does not mean that the findings here do not have implications that extend beyond the region of Africa. On the contrary, there are at least two themes in this book that have implications for the literature on other regions of the world.

6. Pierre Englebert, *State Legitimacy and Development in Africa* (Boulder, CO: Lynne Rienner, 2000).

First, this book has argued that the literature on economic policy making is too focused on societal actors and needs to pay greater attention to the state and to the interests, economic ideas, and capacity to be found within the state apparatus. I have shown the merits of such an approach in Africa, but I suspect that a similar approach could pay dividends in other regions of the world as well. The general conditions that justify this approach in Africa exist in other regions as well, in countries where interest groups are extremely weak and where mechanisms of vertical and horizontal accountability for the executive branch of government are poorly developed. Even in the much more industrialized states of Latin America and Eastern Europe where interest group pressures on decision makers are more obvious, the literature may often overestimate how constraining those pressures are and underestimate the impact of factors within the state decision-making elite.[7]

On the one hand, there are of course neopatrimonial tendencies in regimes outside of suh-Saharan Africa, even where the degree of bureaucratic institutionalization is far more entrenched. In Latin America and in much of Asia, clientelism and the political manipulation of state resources shape policy outcomes. The connection between privilege or wealth and political power is also significantly more intimate than it is in the mature capitalist democracies of the OECD, even if there is more room for autonomous capitalist accumulation than in the fully patrimonial regimes of Africa. Reports following the fall of Benazir Bhutto in Pakistan revealed the systematic abuse of power for personal gain that characterized that regime.[8] Similarly, the Suharto clan reportedly controlled as much as a third of the Indonesian economy and sought to thwart policy reform measures in the wake of the financial crisis of 1997 because these threatened the profitability of key components of the family empire.[9] The unwillingness to expose the substantial family business interests to the vagaries of international competition was also a hallmark of the Hassan II regime in Morocco.[10]

---

7. For a similar critique of the literature, see Barbara Geddes, "The Politics of Economic Liberalization," *Latin American Research Review* 30 (1995): 195–206.
8. "House of Graft: Tracing the Bhutto Millions – A Special Report," *New York Times*. January 9, 1998, p. 1.
9. Dwight Y. King, "Corruption in Indonesia: A Curable Cancer?" *Journal of International Affairs* 63 (2000): 603–25.
10. These are reported in Jeffrey A. Coupe, "Monarchs and Markets: Economic Reform in the Kingdom of Morocco" (Unpublished Ph.D. dissertation, Michigan State University, 2000).

Most accounts of this kind of political corruption are journalistic. The public policy literature has rarely seriously addressed the impact of political corruption on policy making. Academic studies of the politics of economic reform have typically treated issues of clientelism and patronage as symptomatic of weak states attempting to buy support from key societal actors.[11] While characteristic of the political economy literature on adjustment, this weakness is of course not true of all literature on politics in, say, Latin America. Hagopian has carefully chronicled the role of traditional informal mechanisms in Brazilian politics.[12] Her focus has been to explain the impact of these informal mechanisms on the consolidation of democracy in that country, but her analysis could easily be transferred to the analysis of economic policy making, notably at the state level, where these dynamics appear most salient.

For the most part, the academic literature on adjustment in Latin America has paid too little attention to the ways in which social elites have navigated the reform era with their privileges intact.[13] This literature instead tells an often ideologically loaded story of "neoliberal technocrats" making an assault on the state under IFI pressure, against the interests if not active opposition of the enormous majority of the population. Because it almost invariably argues that the turn to neo-liberal policies was decisive and complete, and because it is ideologically ambivalent about economic liberalization and deregulation, much of this literature is compelled to argue that the 1980s and 1990s have witnessed a sharp rise in social inequality and undermined the welfare achievements of earlier regimes. Indeed, however, the striking thing about Latin America before the debt crisis was precisely the extraordinarily high levels of social inequality that prevailed in the region, the result of the very unequal distribution of assets maintained by oligarchic regimes. State intervention in the economy during the 1970s no doubt included social spending that reduced poverty on the margins, but it was almost certainly less progressive than is now commonly implied,[14] and surely its dominant impact was to protect and help reproduce existing patterns of

11. This is particularly striking in Robert H. Bates and Anne O. Krueger, *Political and Economic Interactions in Economic Policy Reform* (Oxford, UK: Basil Blackwell, 1993), because it includes several African cases in its sample.
12. Frances Hagopian, *Traditional Politics and Regime Change in Brazil* (New York: Cambridge University Press, 1996).
13. An exception is provided by Kurt Weyland, *Democracy without Equity: Failures of Reform in Brazil* (Pittsburgh, PA: University of Pittsburgh Press, 1996).
14. For instance, Marcelo Selowski, *Who Benefits from Government Expenditures? The Case of Colombia* (New York: Oxford University Press, 1979).

asset ownership. Scholars have paid inadequate attention to the persistence of this old inequality through the adjustment era, rather than the creation of new forms of inequality due to changes in public spending. Economists have made us aware that asset distribution has a much stronger impact on inequality than do government social spending and sectoral policies. Contrary to a prevalent view of the academic literature on reform in Latin America, the best longitudinal data on inequality in Latin America do not suggest systematic increasing inequality during the period of reform, but rather a mixture of dynamics across countries, and no evidence of increasing inequality in a majority of cases.[15]

On the other hand, even in states where the patrimonial tendencies are not strong, the findings of this book suggest a need to focus on the ability of state elites to maintain key interests through periods of reform. Studies from other regions suggest interesting parallels and comparisons with the African materials. Regarding the ex-socialist states in Europe and Asia, a number of analysts have emphasized the continuing power of the socialist *nomenklatura* in shaping policy reform outcomes, even after the collapse of the old order.[16] Shirk has analyzed the course of reform in the 1980s in China as heavily conditioned by the dynamics of interelite jockeying for power following the death of Mao.[17] Despite using an often different terminology, these works share with this book the general conclusion that policy outcomes reflect the interests of relatively autonomous state decision makers. This is not to say that key societal interests never weigh on the policy process, just that focusing on internal dynamics within the state may often hold the key to understanding outcomes.

Similarly, the African cases suggest the importance of not conflating interests and interest groups. Social power cannot be assumed from economic power; observers must identify the financial, ideological, and in particular organizational mechanisms through which it is asserted. Without organization, social actors usually lack the means to influence policy, while even the weakest states have instruments at their disposal to repress or coopt the emergence of organizations. A literature mostly

---

15. Klaus Deininger and Lynn Squire, "A New Data Set for Measuring Income Inequality," *World Bank Economic Review* 10 (1996): 565–92.
16. Joel Helman, "Winners Take All: The Politics of Partial Reform in Postcommunist Transitions," *World Politics* 50 (1998): 203–34.
17. Susan Shirk, *The Political Logic of Economic Reform in China* (Berkeley: University of California Press, 1993).

devoted to Latin America has emerged in the 1990s that devotes enormous attention to the bases of political support for reformist governments. It has advanced as a major puzzle the observation that governments overseeing "neoliberal" economic reforms have been able to maintain political support,[18] and it has problematized the construction of new social alliances as key to the success of economic growth-producing policies.[19] Governments will be successful in this view if and only if they are able to mobilize social groups powerful enough to maintain them in power and also to support pro-growth economic policies. The discretion of state actors lies entirely in their ability to form and hold this coalition together. The evidence assembled in this book suggests that in the absence of well-organized interest groups, states can survive in power for long periods of time with only limited popular support. Indeed, in at least some cases, the formation of a broad social coalition is not the precondition of successful economic policies but rather their consequence, and governments retain considerable discretion in coalition building.

I have posited that state elites in Africa have used access to state resources for individual enrichment. A state bourgeoisie is in the process of being constituted thanks to state intervention in the economy. Such a claim may not travel well to other regions, and it is important to identify the precise interests that drive the actions of the state elite. These may be much more complex than simply individual enrichment, given the much more substantial process of state formation countries in Asia or Latin America have undergone. I suspect that institutional and bureaucratic interests weigh much more heavily than they do in Africa, where I have shown that much of the behavior of state elites actually weakens state institution building. Perhaps, as Roeder has shown for the Soviet Union, a combination of internal bureaucratic struggles and the

18. See, for instance, Bruce M. Wilson, "Leftist Parties, Neoliberal Policies, and Reelection Strategies," *Comparative Political Studies* 32 (1999): 752–79; Barbara Geddes, "The Politics of Economic Liberalization," *Latin American Research Review* 30 (1995): 195–234; and Kenneth Roberts, "Neoliberalism and the Transformation of Populism in Latin America: The Peruvian Case," *World Politics* 48 (1995): 82–116.

19. See, for instance, Hector Schamis, "Distributional Coalitions and the Politics of Economic Reform in Latin America," *World Politics* 51 (1999): 236–268; Katrina Burgess, "Loyalty Dilemmas and Market Reform: Party-Union Alliances under Stress in Mexico, Spain and Venezuela," *World Politics* 52 (1999):105–34; and Richard Snyder, "After Neoliberalism: The Politics of Reregulation in Mexico," *World Politics* 51 (1999): 173–204.

ambition to strengthen state autonomy motivates behavior rather than personal enrichment.[20] But the evidence from Africa that does travel well is the lesson that even the weakest state apparatuses are capable of pursuing their interests.

Similarly, we need to pay special attention to the attitudes of decision makers about economic policies, not because their ideas about economic matters are generated in a purely autonomous manner, but because their views on the viability of reform and its economic, political, and administrative plausibility shape their willingness to take personal risks and investments on its behalf. The new liberal orthodoxy defined in Chapter 1 is quite deep in certain circles, but it simply does not extend broadly to countries involved in messy reform processes where technocrats have limited information, face many pressures, and worry about their own futures.

One is hard pressed to find an African equivalent to President Cardoso of Brazil, a policy intellectual of great visibility, who underwent a significant policy conversion, from favoring an inward policy orientation and widespread public ownership to promoting export orientation and privatization in office during the 1990s. Explanations of Brazil's economic policy program that do not take the economic policy metamorphosis of individuals like Cardoso seriously will at the very least be incomplete. How emblematic is Cardoso of a more general trend in Latin America? I cannot be sure, but the ideological conversion of the PRI in Mexico and the Peronists in Argentina under Menem is equally striking. One of the few African equivalents is the African National Congress (ANC) in South Africa, which espoused Marxist economic doctrine in opposition but has ruled the country in a far more liberal manner than did their Nationalist Party predecessors.[21]

In sum, the analysis in this book is part of an emerging literature on the role of state interests and specific interactions between state actors and specific societal groups during economic reform processes. Establishing the centrality of state actors to decision making outcomes helps to explain the manner in which specific state interests are protected during reform. The preponderant role of the donors and the principal–agent issues they introduce to reform dynamics are probably fairly

20. Philip G. Roeder, *Red Sunset* (Princeton, NJ: Princeton University Press, 1993).
21. On South Africa, see Steven Friedman, "Democracy and the Building of Post-Apartheid South Africa," paper presented to the Gulbenkian Foundation Workshop on Democracy and Development in Africa," Lisbon, Portugal, June 23–24, 2000.

unique to Africa; but elsewhere as well, state agents use the uncertainty and fluidity of reform periods to advance an agenda that may have little to do with the official objectives of reform. In other regions of the world also, we see state elites implementing partial reform in such a way as to protect certain interests. Elsewhere as well, economic liberalization ambitions have proven no match for the needs of sociopolitical regulation.

This leads to a second and related theme of this book, which resonates with an emerging literature. This is the survival and even extension of rent-seeking activities during periods of economic liberalization. Chapter 1 cited a number of works that have argued, as I have here for Africa, that in Latin America, China, and Eastern Europe, phases of liberalization have actually resulted in a dramatic expansion of rent-seeking and corruption. This is what might be called the "partial reform syndrome,"[22] and it is one of the emerging issues of contemporary comparative political economy.

The evidence suggests several interesting avenues for new research. First, the literature has been insufficiently precise on the reasons for this alleged increase in corruption. The evidence on levels of corruption and rent-seeking before and after reform is typically sparse and anecdotal, and it is hard to know with certainty that they have increased, despite the scandalous, largely journalistic, accounts to that effect. There is a need for more systematic empirical data on the actual levels across different countries. A number of new cross-national data sets are emerging on *perceptions* that corruption exists,[23] but the relationship between perception and reality may not be consistent across time and space, so that the value of these data sets for comparative work remains to be determined.

The literature also tends to conflate rents and rent-seeking. Neoclassical economic work has focused particularly on methods to measure the size of rents that are created by government intervention.[24] There is much

22. The term is Joel Hellman's from his essay, "Winners Take All: The Politics of Partial Reform in Postcommunist Transitions." See Chapter 1 for citations to other relevant work.
23. Half a dozen of these data sets are described in Alberto Alesina and Beatrice Weder, "Do Corrupt Governments Receive Less Aid?" National Bureau of Economic Research Working Paper 7108, Cambridge, MA, May 1999.
24. The locus classicus is Anne Krueger, "The Political Economy of the Rent-Seeking Society," *American Economic Review* (1974): 291–303; and Jagdish Bhagwati, "Directly Unproductive Profit-Seeking (DUP) Activities," *Journal of Political Economy* 90 (1982): 988–1002.

less guidance on how to measure the rent-seeking activity that takes place around rents. As I argued in Chapter 4, rent-seeking can actually increase even as the size of rents declines.

Clearly, reform periods are characterized by uncertainty and fluidity, both of which probably encourage rent-seeking. Control mechanisms that work reasonably well when policy regimes are fixed are probably less effective at preventing corruption in the sometimes chaotic atmosphere of crisis management. I am less persuaded by arguments suggesting that economic liberalization leads to attitudinal changes that result in greater corruption. There is a need to test such hypotheses more rigorously, perhaps with systematic recourse to public opinion surveys.

I am also skeptical about the full extent of reform in these situations of heightened corruption. Often, the literature assumes reform has been carried out because there are official claims to that effect. In fact, the African evidence suggests that much less reform is often accomplished than is claimed. If you take a snapshot of the reform process at any given time, ongoing programs, donor loans, and government rhetoric all suggest rapid movement. However, taking a longer term perspective allows one to realize how little progress is actually being achieved. I do not think this is unique to programs of economic liberalization, as is sometimes claimed, but believe it is typical of all reform programs that seek to effectuate a very real shift of economic power away from certain groups close to power and to the benefit of others. Liberalization does face special constraints, however, because it is groups within the state apparatus who are the losers and they have special resources with which to resist change.

The real insight of this literature, largely confirmed by the African materials examined here, is that it is extremely hard to eliminate rent-seeking behavior simply by changing policy regimes. Even with minor discretion over reform implementation, state agents find ways to restore some of the lost rents, or create new ones. The policy community was probably naive to think that economic liberalization would easily eliminate this kind of behavior. In fact, it now appears clear that even when they are fully implemented, many liberalization processes will leave a good deal of state regulation and intervention in place. Unless the economic reform process is accompanied by political changes that increase the checks on executive abuses of influence, rent-seeking activities will prove extremely resilient and the objectives of economic policy reform will be subverted.

Index

(continued from page iii)

Anna L. Harvey, *Votes without Leverage: Women in American Electoral Politics, 1920–1970*

Murray Horn, *The Political Economy of Public Administration: Institutional Choice in the Public Sector*

John D. Huber, *Rationalizing Parliament: Legislative Institutions and Party Politics in France*

Jack Knight, *Institutions and Social Conflict*

Michael Laver and Kenneth Shepsle, eds., *Making and Breaking Governments*

Michael Laver and Kenneth Shepsle, eds., *Cabinet Ministers and Parliamentary Government*

Margaret Levi, *Consent, Dissent, and Patriotism*

Brian Levy and Pablo T. Spiller, eds., *Regulations, Institutions, and Commitment*

Leif Lewin, *Ideology and Strategy: A Century of Swedish Politics* (English Edition)

Gary Libecap, *Contracting for Property Rights*

John Londregan, *Legislative Institutions and Ideology in Chile*

Arthur Lupia and Mathew D. McCubbins, *The Democratic Dilemma: Can Citizens Learn What They Really Need to Know?*

C. Mantzavinos, *Individuals, Institutions, and Markets*

Mathew D. McCubbins and Terry Sullivan, eds., *Congress: Structure and Policy*

Gary J. Miller, *Managerial Dilemmas: The Political Economy of Hierarchy*

Douglass C. North, *Institutions, Institutional Change, and Economic Performance*

Elinor Ostrom, *Governing the Commons: The Evolution of Institutions for Collective Action*

J. Mark Ramseyer, *Odd Markets in Japanese History*

J. Mark Ramseyer and Frances Rosenbluth, *The Politics of Oligarchy: Institutional Choice in Imperial Japan*

Jean-Laurent Rosenthal, *The Fruits of Revolution: Property Rights, Litigation, and French Agriculture*

Charles Stewart III, *Budget Reform Politics: The Design of the Appropriations Process in the House of Representatives, 1865–1921*

George Tsebelis and Jeannette Money, *Bicameralism*

John Waterbury, *Exposed to Innumerable Delusions: Public Enterprise and State Power in Egypt, India, Mexico, and Turkey*

David L. Weimer, eds., *The Political Economy of Property Rights*